THE WOUNDED
RESEARCHER

SPRING JOURNAL BOOKS
STUDIES IN ARCHETYPAL PSYCHOLOGY SERIES

Series Editor
GREG MOGENSON

OTHER TITLES IN THE SERIES

THE NEUROSIS OF PSYCHOLOGY: PRIMARY PAPERS TOWARDS
A CRITICAL PSYCHOLOGY
COLLECTED ENGLISH PAPERS, VOL. 1
Wolfgang Giegerich

TECHNOLOGY AND THE SOUL: FROM THE NUCLEAR BOMB
TO THE WORLD WIDE WEB
COLLECTED ENGLISH PAPERS, VOL. 2
Wolfgang Giegerich

DIALECTICS & ANALYTICAL PSYCHOLOGY:
THE EL CAPITAN CANYON SEMINAR
Wolfgang Giegerich, David L. Miller, Greg Mogenson

RAIDS ON THE UNTHINKABLE:
FREUDIAN *AND* JUNGIAN PSYCHOANALYSES
Paul Kugler

NORTHERN GNOSIS: THOR, BALDR, AND THE VOLSUNGS IN THE
THOUGHT OF FREUD AND JUNG
Greg Mogenson

THE ESSENTIALS OF STYLE: A HANDBOOK FOR SEEING AND BEING SEEN
Benjamin Sells

THE SUNKEN QUEST, THE WASTED FISHER, THE PREGNANT FISH:
POSTMODERN REFLECTIONS ON DEPTH PSYCHOLOGY
Ronald Schenk

FIRE IN THE STONE: THE ALCHEMY OF DESIRE
Stanton Marlan, ed.

THE WOUNDED RESEARCHER

Research with Soul in Mind

ROBERT D. ROMANYSHYN

Spring Journal Books
New Orleans, Louisiana

Published by
Spring Journal, Inc.;
627 Ursulines Street #7
New Orleans, Louisiana 70116
Tel.: (504) 524-5117
Fax: (504) 558-0088
Website: www.springjournalandbooks.com

Cover design by
Northern Cartographic
4050 Williston Road
South Burlington, VT 05403

Cover art:
Creación de las aves [*Creation of the Birds*] (1958)
by Remedios Varo
© 2005 Artists Rights Society (ARS), New York/VEGAP, Madrid

Printed in Canada
Text printed on acidfree paper

Library of Congress Cataloging-in-Publication Data Pending

Dedication

To my grandmother,
Natalie Marosh,
whom I never knew but who, unbeknownst to me,
has been the guardian of my life's vocation.

To her husband, my grandfather,
Stephen Romanyshyn,
whom I met in an-other time and an-other place
where our destinies crossed:
I re-member!

To the other ancestors
whom I have come to know on this journey.

And to the figure of the dream,
the street poet who has led me to that threshold
at the edge of the house of academia,
where my story and the stories of my ancestors
have their sense of an ending.

I dedicate this book to all of you
and leave it at
that place.

Grateful acknowlegment is made to the respective publishers for permission to reprint the following previously published materials:

Excerpts from *The Thought of the Heart and the Soul of the World* by James Hillman, published by Spring Publications, Inc., copyright © 1992 by James Hillman. Reprinted by permission of the publisher.

Excerpts from *Jung as a Writer* by Susan Rowland, published by Routledge, copyright © 2005. Reprinted by permission of Taylor & Francis Group, LLC.

Excerpts from *The Soul in Grief: Love, Death and Transformation* by Robert Romanyshyn, published by North Atlantic Books, copyright © 1999 by Robert D. Romanyshyn. Reprinted by permission of North Atlantic Books/Frog, Ltd.

"Orpheus. Eurydice. Hermes." translated by Stephen Mitchell, copyright©1982 by Stephen Mitchell, from THE SELECTED POETRY OF RAINER MARIA RILKE by Rainer Maria Rilke, translated by Stephen Mitchell. Used by permission of Random House, Inc.

Excerpts from DUINO ELEGIES by Rainer Maria Rilke, translated by J. B. Leishman/Stephen Spender. Copyright 1939 by W. W. Norton & Company, Inc., renewed © 1967 by Stephen Spender and J. B. Leishman. Used by permission of W. W. Norton & Company, Inc.

Excerpts from *Greeting the Angels: An Imaginal View of the Mourning Process*, by Greg Mogenson, copyright©1992. Reprinted by permission of Baywood Publishing Company, Inc.

Excerpts from *Sonnets to Orpheus*, M. D. Herter, Translator, copyright © 1962. Used by permission of W. W. Norton & Company, Inc.

Excerpts from *Truth and Method*, Hans Georg-Gadamer, copyright © 1975, Seabury Press, N.Y. Used by permission of The Continuum International Publishing Group.

Excerpts from COMPLETE POEMS: 1904-1962 by E. E. Cummings, edited by George J. Firmage, copyright © 1926, 1954, 1991 by the Trustees for the E. E. Cummings Trust. Copyright © 1985 by George James Firmage. Used by permission of Liveright Publishing Company.

Excerpts from *The Way and Its Power*, translated by Arthur Waley, published 1934, Houghton-Mifflin. Used by permission of Grove/Atlantic, Inc.

"The Way In," from *Selected Poems of Rainer Maria Rilke*, a translation from the German and commentary by Robert Bly, copyright © 1981 by Robert Bly. Reprinted by permission of HarperCollins Publishers.

"The Motive for Metaphor" and "Thirteen Ways of Looking at Blackbird," copyright © 1923 and renewed 1951 by Wallace Stevens, from THE COLLECTED POEMS OF WALLACE STEVENS by Wallace Stevens, copyright © 1954 by Wallace Stevens and renewed 1982 by Holly Stevens. Used by permission of Alfred A. Knopf, a division of Random House, Inc.

Excerpts from "East Coker" in FOUR QUARTETS, copyright © 1940 by T.S. Eliot and renewed 1968 by Esme Valerie Eliot, reprinted by permission of Harcourt, Inc.

Excerpts from "Little Gidding" in FOUR QUARTETS, copyright © 1942 by T.S. Eliot and renewed 1970 by Esme Valerie Eliot, reprinted by permission of Harcourt, Inc.

Excerpt from A BOOK OF LUMINOUS THINGS, AN INTERNATIONAL ANTHOLOGY OF POETRY, compilation copyright © 1966 by Czeslaw Milosz, reprinted by permission of Harcourt, Inc.

Contents

Acknowledgments

There are many people to whom I owe a debt of gratitude for their support and assistance during the long labor of this book. First, I must thank my wife, Veronica, who models a life devoted to the life of soul. She has been a continuing inspiration, and without her loving presence I am certain this book would not have been born. Over the years, she has been steadfast in her belief in the work, and her keen insights into many of the issues have brought an added breadth and depth to the text. In addition, she has been an invaluable colleague in the work of teaching this material to our students at Pacifica Graduate Institute.

Second, I need to express my sincere thanks to the graduate students at Pacifica who took the time to reply to my letter requesting their reflections on their experience of using the imaginal approach to research, its vocational and transference processes, and the alchemical hermeneutic method. Their work has given flesh to the ideas presented in this volume. And so, I name each of them here (in alphabetical order by last name) with my deepest appreciation: Jackie Bennett, George Callan, Conrad Gratz, Debbie Greenwood, Mary Harrell, James Hunt, Paul Jones, Erik Killinger, Carly Knapp, Dennis Langhans, Ellen MacFarland, Judith Orodenker, Kerry Ragain, John Rowe, Julie Sgarzi, Jo Todd, Kay Tomlinson, and Johanna Treichler.

Third, a special thanks goes to Jo Todd who worked with diligence, devotion, and care in formatting footnotes and checking sources. Her unfailing sense of good humor was indispensable in this tedious process, and her generous comments about the text sustained me in those moments of doubt that invariably accompany the work.

Fourth, I want to thank Charles Zeltzer for being such a wise shepherd of the soul. This work began again with a dream and the dream led me into analysis and the analysis led me back to the work. Charles helped me to see more clearly what this work wanted from me.

Finally, the work of thinking and writing always needs a sheltering place and Pacifica Graduate Institute offered that place. This work began in a conversation with Steve Aizenstat more than fifteen years ago, and it has been his genius to create that space where thinking is in service to soul. Thank you for that gift. I must also thank, in this connection, my dear friend Charles Asher, whose devotion to the work of soul never forgets the human dimension with all its attendant weaknesses. Charles brought me to Pacifica, and over the years it has been his quiet dignity and strength of conviction that has companioned me along the way. He is a good man to have on the journey of work and life. Also, for their generosity in providing a sheltering place, I must thank my good friends Siobhan and David Collins, who lent me their home in Governor's Bay outside Christchurch, New Zealand during my sabbatical. It was in their garden that this final draft was inspired, conceived, and brought forth.

Robert Romanyshyn
2007

Preface

The *Wounded Researcher* begins with the issue of how one writes down the soul in writing up one's research. This issue is the theme of the Introduction, in which a poetics of the research process is proposed. Such a poetics focuses on the "gap" between soul and the words we use to say it. In Part One, this issue of the gap is explored in three chapters, which form the theoretical core of an imaginal approach to research. Chapter 1 examines the issue of the gap within the difference between soul and the complex of psychology, and in Chapter 2 I propose that the Orpheus-Eurydice myth is the archetypal background for an imaginal approach to research, since Orpheus is the poet of the gap. I describe six moments of this myth in relation to an approach to research that would keep soul in mind. In Chapter 3 I offer a detailed description of the imaginal approach.

Part Two focuses on the research process. The question here is how, within the imaginal approach, the researcher differentiates what he or she brings to and wants from the work from the soul of the work, from what the work asks of the researcher. In Chapter 4 I explore this question in terms of research as vocation, and I illustrate this vocational aspect of research with soul in mind, using numerous examples from my graduate students. Research with soul in mind is re-search, a process of re-turning to and re-membering what has already made its claim upon the researcher through his or her complex relations to the topic. Research as re-search is a searching again for what one has already felt as a call, perhaps long ago and now only dimly re-called, and although the play on the word in this fashion is not quite etymologically sound, its written appearance and its sound when spoken lend themselves to this form of play. Re-search with soul in mind, re-search that proceeds in depth and from the depths, is about finding what has been lost, forgotten, neglected, marginalized, or otherwise left behind.

In order to secure the work on its own terms rather than having it be an unconscious confession of one's complexes, a process, which makes the unconscious ties of the researcher to the work more conscious, is needed. This process is described in Chapter 5 in terms of transference dialogues between the researcher and the "others" in the work, the "strangers" for whom the work is being done, the ancestors who wait as the weight of unfinished business in the soul of the work. I describe four levels of these transference or psychological dialogues and show in detail how they are based upon Jung's notion of active imagination. In Chapter 6 I give copious examples from my graduate students who have used this process in their dissertations.

Part Three focuses on method. While the process of transference dialogues can be used with any method and within any approach to research, over time a specific method has organically evolved out of the imaginal approach and its process. This method is called alchemical hermeneutics, and in Chapters 7, 8, and 9, I show how this method belongs to and transforms traditional notions of hermeneutics. Chapter 7 recovers the soul of method, and in Chapter 8 I present an overview of traditional hermeneutics and describe seven ways in which alchemical hermeneutics differs from traditional hermeneutics. In Chapter 9 I propose a hermeneutics of deep subjectivity, that is, a hermeneutics that makes a systematic place for the unconscious in the "Hermes" art of interpretation, and I show how traditional hermeneutics, when it does make a place for the unconscious, focuses on Freud and neglects Jung's understanding of the unconscious. In Chapter 10 I begin to introduce a Jungian view of the unconscious into the arts of Hermes, and I offer a phenomenological description of the practice of alchemical hermeneutics. In Chapter 11, I describe how Jung's understanding of the unconscious leads to an alchemical hermeneutic method that makes a place for dreams, symptoms, synchronicities, and the Jungian functions of feeling and intuition. I illustrate each of these areas with examples from my graduate students.

Part Four closes this work with a consideration of two implications of an approach to re-search that keeps soul in mind. In Chapter 12 I return to the issue of the Introduction to take up the question again of how one writes down the soul in writing up one's work, and in response I offer four suggestions for how to write in a way that is responsive to the depths of soul in one's work. In Chapter 13 I suggest that an approach to research that attempts to make the complex unconscious presence of the researcher in the work more conscious is necessary for a truly objective science and is the foundation of an ethical epistemology.

Falling into the Work

> ... *faciles descensus Averno:*
> *noctes atque dies patet atri ianua Ditis;*
> *sed revocare gradum superasque evadere ad auras,*
> *hoc opus, hic labor est.*

> ... easy is the descent to Avernus:
> night and day the door of gloomy Dis stands open;
> but to recall one's steps and pass out to the upper air,
> this is the task, this is the toil.[1]

Towards a Poetics of the Research Process

Twentieth century Oedipal man has forgotten his mythical forbears and is haunted by what he has failed to mourn.[1]

—Greg Mogenson

I am writing this introduction, the fifth one in the last few months, while sitting in a green valley in Governor's Bay just outside Christchurch, New Zealand, and now again, as before, I feel how the words fail to say what I have been trying to say in this work about research, which has haunted me these past fifteen years. How do I write down the soul of this work in writing up my thoughts about research that keeps soul in mind? I think of the poet T. S. Eliot here, who in one of his *Four Quartets,* "East Coker," speaks of being in the middle way and,

> Trying to learn to use words, and every attempt
> Is a wholly new start, and a different kind of failure
> Because one has only learnt to get the better of words
> For the thing one no longer has to say, or the way in which
> One is no longer disposed to say it.[2]

How long I have been in the middle of this work and am I no longer inclined towards it! Yes, in a way that is true. But there is also an obligation, an internal imperative that is more about the work than it is about me. There is a vocation in this work that requires a response. And so I ask again, as before, what am I trying to get hold of here? What am I trying to give shape to that so resists and has resisted all my efforts to bring form to? A few lines down in the same poem, Eliot speaks, I believe, to this imperative.

> There is only the fight to recover what has been lost
> And found and lost again and again.[3]

I am looking for something in this work on research that keeps soul in mind that is held in the word itself. Research with soul in mind is *re*-search, a searching *again*, for something that has already made its claim upon us, something we have already known, however dimly, but have forgotten. In Chapter 4 I take up this issue of how a researcher is claimed by a work through his or her complexes, and indeed if there is one theme that runs throughout this work, it is that in re-search with soul in mind the topic chooses the researcher as much as, and perhaps even more than, he or she chooses it. In addition, in this complex relation between the researcher and the topic, there lingers the weight of history that waits to be spoken. At moments, then, we have the work in our grasp, and the sense of it, even to the point, at times, of feeling as if it belongs to us. But then we lose sight of it before we have it firmly, and lose it again, because being claimed by the work puts us as researchers in service to the unfinished business in the soul of the work, in service to those for whom the work is being done. The struggle to recover what has been lost and found again is the struggle in the gap between what is said and what wants and needs to be spoken.

Another poet, John Keats, knew this difference between what one says and what wants to be spoken. In "Ode to a Nightingale," he is drawn into a reverie by the sweet sounds of the bird, and in his musings he knows that his words cannot compare to the music of the bird's song. Even in his death, the poet knows of the nightingale,

> Still wouldst thou sing, and I have ears in vain—
> To thy high requiem become a sod.[4]

The song of the nightingale is timeless. It is eternal, while his, the poet's, song is made for death. It is transient, and there is in this ode a deep sense of mourning that attaches itself to his knowing. This mood of mourning is another theme that threads itself throughout this work and that belongs to complex re-search that would keep soul in mind.

Research as re-search is a vocation, and the call of this work is as elusive as the morning song of the birds that fills this valley. Here I am content to listen to those songs, especially the song of the bellbird, and to let go of this work. Compared to those songs, these words seem always so feeble. Is that it? Listening to their songs, I know that I am in this moment less than the high requiem of those songs, and yet I am aware that I am at least for this moment more than I have been. The mourning that attaches itself to our knowing has a sweetly bitter quality that comes from yearning for something that, while never attained, is always with us.

Green! I used the word earlier to describe where I am—but it is a lie. This valley is not green. Green is only a word that declares the blindness at the heart of my vision and the poverty of my words. Green! A word that is an insult to the richness that surrounds me, a word that I give to, that I impose upon, this effulgent landscape. That word, compared to the greenness of the valley that seduces my vision, forces me to look again and return with regard to this moment that is the vocation of my vision. In this moment I wish I were a painter—but I am not, and besides, even the painter has to struggle with the gap between what he paints and what asks to be painted. Cézanne painted Mont Ste.-Victoire sixty times, trying to capture how it would change and become a different mountain with changes in light and in the seasons, trying to capture just one moment of the world's being. And the poet again, this time Wallace Stevens, has told us that there are thirteen ways—at least—of looking at a blackbird. In each stanza of the poem, he tells us what the blackbird is, and in each stanza implies that it is not that. I read his poem aloud and I wonder about how many ways there are of saying green and, in the context of this book, how many ways we have constructed to speak of soul.

What matters in this valley reverie at the start of this book on research is the difference between the fullness of an experience and the failure of language to say it, and the sweetly bitter sense of this knowledge. The poet again bears witness to this sorrow. In his poem "Study of Two Pears," Wallace Stevens enumerates, in the first five four-line stanzas, the chief perceptual qualities of the pears. The descriptions are very exact, almost scientific in their precision. He describes their forms and shapes and colors. But at the end of the poem, in the last two lines of the sixth stanza, Stevens says, "The pears are not seen / As the observer wills."[5] Not as the observer wills or speaks, the two pears slip the net of the poet's description!

But so what? What does this have to do with the theme of this book? Why drag in these two lines from a poet in a book that is concerned with the question of how one might do re-search that keeps soul in mind? Because, again, of the gap! In the gap between the saying and what slips away there is a sense of sadness, a feeling of mourning, and it is the quality of this feeling of mourning in our knowing that I am trying to give shape to in this work. To write down the soul, then, is to attend to its "greening," to its motion and its movement, to its elusive quality, which resists our efforts to enunciate it. In the gap there is always a remainder that asks not to be forgotten. The shadow of the unsaid haunts our saying, like the greening of the world does when we say "green" and remain aware of the difference. The difference lingers with its own terrible and relentless insistence, which, like an outgoing tide, sucks our words back into the fullness of being. To write down soul, then, is to attend to the mourning in our knowing for what our words leave behind.

I do not mean to suggest, however, that there is no excitement or joy in the act of coming to know what we do not know. The mood of mourning is not personal. It is not about the researcher's experience of some specific loss. Rather, this mourning resides in one's awareness of the gap between language and experience, and in this respect it is a phenomenological description of the mood of this difference. For psychology the mood of mourning resides in one's awareness of the difference between the words one uses to speak of soul and the reality of soul, and this too is meant as a phenomenological description. I will speak to this issue of soul and the language of psychology in some detail in Chapter 1, but for the moment I want to add just one other point with regard to the mood of mourning in re-search that would keep soul in mind. In addition to the mood of mourning residing in the gap between language and experience, mourning also characterizes the imaginal approach to research, which is the theme of Chapter 3. In this approach there is a fundamental shift from the point of view of the ego to that of soul in research. In this shift, as we will see throughout this work, the ego has to let go of the work, has to surrender a work made in time to the timeless realm of soul. The ego as author of the work has to "die" to the work to become the agent in service to those for whom the work is being done.

To remember not to forget soul in the way we think and speak of it is the challenge. But how do I do that? How do I keep soul alive in my thinking about it, just as I have to keep the greening of the world alive in the way that I speak about green? If the work of soul is against forgetting, then the challenge is to make sure that my ways of thinking about soul do not forget soul. The challenge is how do I speak about a way of doing re-search that keeps soul in mind that does keep soul in mind in its speaking.

I cannot write poetry, not only because I am no poet, but also because that is not the issue. In an unpublished book of poems and psychological reflections called "Dark Light," which interestingly enough has these past fifteen years shadowed this book on research like some invisible twin, I have considered how the psychologist might best be described as a "failed poet." In one of the many introductions I have written for that work, whose main purpose was and is to find a way of speaking about those transient epiphanies of soul that mark our daily round, those moments that in their appearance open a vision and in their parting leave a trail of sorrow, moments that awaken soul through beauty and Eros, I said, "The psychology I have practiced as therapist, teacher, and writer for the last thirty years is finally a psychology that has no name."[6] Now, as I look back on that statement, I wonder if we can be so in love with soul that our psychologies always begin to feel like so many failures to speak of this love. Even now, as I re-write this Introduction in the study of my home, I know that the green that fills my field of vision outside my window is the color of soul, one way in which soul manifests itself through the things of the world, to which I am always, even in the best moments, but a witness.

> It was a late Sunday afternoon, warm, the sun poised past the middle of the sky, as if it had not yet made up its mind to surrender to the night. The color of the light had a texture to it. I felt strangely at peace in its warm embrace. How long I had been sitting on a bench within this field of soft light, I could not say. It might have been minutes or hours. It could have been days or even an eternity. I was myself, there on that bench, and I was also this light, spread out across the green fields of grass and trees. More than a year since my wife had died, this moment came as a welcome surprise. From a place deep within my soul, I felt something budding within me, as if a shoot of the vegetable

world was breaking through the hard crust around my heart, struggling alongside the brute, dumb power of nature's life to leave the darkness of the earth and be warmed by the sun.

The green field of grass spread out in front of me began to undulate. Waves of pure greenness were pouring out of the bushes and trees, vibrating in some kind of wild ecstatic dance of freedom. It was as if greenness itself had escaped its forms in blade and leaf, in stalk and stem. No longer bound by form, color was shamelessly revealing itself in riotous, even erotic, abandonment. Green! A deep, rich, fresh, moist, wet, dripping green! A blue-green, yellow-green, green-green! A green so green that only the sky could be more blue. Pure color, yes! but with a pungent smell of the vegetable body. A heavy, cool, damp odor penetrating the cold corners of the dark interior jungle of life, green was displaying itself as the swelling force of the vegetable body. Green: a tumescent, throbbing pulsation; a rhythm, a tempo, a pace, a speed, a quivering, a small shudder of the body of creation. A frequency, a vibration, a radiance of the world's consciousness, perhaps even the first vibration of life. Something in me wondered if color is itself a kind of consciousness, and if consciousness, my own consciousness in this moment, is only another, different frequency of color. Green, yellow, blue, red, purple, orange: variations in the harmonies of a consciousness spread throughout all creation, enfolding mind in nature.

Freed of form, color was dancing with the light. The field of green before me was dissolving into an expanse of shimmering diamonds, crystals of radiant light catching the sun then releasing it. The field of green was alive, and I knew, without knowing how I knew it, that color was life.

Green was penetrating me with its life, with its throbbing vitality. Held in its grip, I felt my soul, perhaps for the first time since my wife had died, turn toward life, like the vegetable world turns toward the sun. This green life pulsating through me was a tropism, a primitive hunger asserting itself, an elemental force even deeper than the instinctual, a vegetable vitality even older than the vitality of the animal.[7]

This passage is from the book I wrote on the grieving process, and I include it here because it attempts to describe the kind of transient moment that can be neither willed nor repeated when we are awakened to the soul of an occasion, when an experience is deepened, re-figured, and reflected through the things of the world. An ordinary field on an ordinary Sunday afternoon becomes a field of reverie in which one who is grieving is called into wakefulness.

I had that experience, or better, it had me, and yet there was at that moment, and there remains even now in memory, the felt sense of that gap between the full, rich ripeness of that occasion of awakening and the words to describe it. Soul is not inside us. It is on the contrary our circumstance and vocation. It surrounds us, and we are called into the world, as we are called into our work, through this kind of epiphany. But how do we give voice to such moments, and how do we re-search those moments in our work when the soul of the work shines through the idea, the theory, the fact, and the data collected? How do we re-search these moments in order to keep soul in mind? Is reverie a legitimate dimension of a re-search process that would keep soul in mind?

These questions are the ones that have informed "Dark Light" and haunt, and have haunted, this book on re-search that would keep soul in mind. In the Introduction to "Dark Light" I wondered if there is an answer to these questions, and I still do. In that context I wrote:

> Perhaps what I have been doing is not psychology at all, because it has no dogma, no creed, no precise method. But if it is psychology, then it is and has been for me more of a style or a disposition, a way of being present in and to the world in a psychological way, no-thing as substantive then as a noun, but something adjectival, a qualifier to ways of living, loving, and working with soul in mind. If it has been and is a psychology, then it has been more of a continuing quest and longing to give form to a vague and hardly remembered sense of connection to things that perhaps I once had, ... and a continuing effort, which at many times has felt like an act of desperation, to be a witness for those simple and ordinary occasions that are always passing away with hardly any notice so that they are not forever lost, to preserve within the ordinary the miracle that might be overlooked. If any of this has been psychology, then it has been for me a way of being on a journey: psychologist as failed poet.[8]

But who is the psychologist as "failed poet," and what does this image say of the researcher? This book is an ongoing response to these questions, but for the moment I would offer that the psychologist/researcher as "failed poet" is one who stands in that gap between the fullness of experience and the "failure" of language to command it, one who is able to bear the tension between knowing and not knowing. The psychologist/researcher as "failed poet" is one who acknowledges the gap between the conscious and the unconscious and who within that space attends the cultivation of the symbol, whose epiphany Jung described as a transcendent function.[9] Or, to say this in another way, the psychologist/researcher as "failed poet" is one who stays in the gap between soul and the complex of psychology. He or she is one who knows that the language of psychology is a complex about the soul, which is the theme of Chapter 1.

In this gap, psychology does not have a name, or, to be more precise, its names are not to be identified with the matter of soul. In the gap between the conscious and the unconscious, the psychologist/ researcher as "failed poet" tries to speak in a way that forgets psychology for the sake of not forgetting to be psychological. He or she remains aware that his or her language is for the sake of qualifying events, that psychological language is in service to loosening the thing named from the grip of a meaning that has become too coagulated so that the soul can display its multiple unfoldings. From green to greening, something like that, is called for, a way of saying that does not monumentalize the occasion, pin it down with facts, exhaust it with explanations, or imprison it with ideas. The two pears of Wallace Stevens, which escape what the observer wills and says, are not the sum of their named qualities. They are the rhythm of those qualities, their radiance, the ways in which those qualities are connections with other things, as Stevens says in the two final lines of the last stanza: "The shadows of the pears / Are blobs on the green cloth."[10] These are the only lines in the six stanzas where the pears are pairing up with other things, where their qualities—their shape and color, size and texture—are qualified, where their qualities are not indexes of the pears themselves but are possibilities of relation with other things: the shape, size, color, and texture of a pear are shadows on a green cloth!

What is the shadow of our psychologies? How are our psychologies psychological? What qualifies them beyond their own names? What I am trying to avoid here is a psychology that builds a monument to soul. The journey now is at this place called The Wounded Researcher, and here is the dilemma. This is a book for the academy, and yet, speaking too academically always seems to defeat its purpose. The issue is the style of discourse that this work demands, its voice, which in the end is the question not only of who is writing this book, but also for whom is it being written. What is its voice beyond the one that I might wish it to have?

In this book, and particularly in Chapter 2, I will make the case that it is the Orphic voice that guides re-search with soul in mind, that the fantasy and myth behind re-search with soul in mind are the archetypal figures of Orpheus and Eurydice. Orpheus is, among other things, the poet of the gap, the poet of the border realms. He is, for Rilke, the one who comes and goes and the one to whom no monument should be raised, the one, in fact, for whom the only fitting tribute is the rose, which in its blooming is already beginning to fade. Orpheus is also, by his birthright, the poet of memory and mourning, the one who holds these two actions together, the one who teaches us that remembering is an act of mourning and that mourning is a creative work of re-membering. Throughout this book I will show how the themes of love, loss, mourning, descent, dismemberment, and anamnesis (or un-forgetting), among others, accurately depict the Orphic moment of the re-search process that would keep soul in mind. Orpheus and Eurydice are the faces of this process. They are the personifications of re-search that would keep soul in mind.

The effort, the challenge, and the difficulty that has haunted this work from the beginning, and has made every new start a different kind of failure, has been to find its proper voice. The only thing that I do know with any measure of confidence is that re-search that keeps soul in mind must attend to the feeling of mourning for what is left behind in our saying and knowing. Whatever is said must not lose touch with this feeling quality in our knowing.

Under the spell of Orpheus, I would suggest, the proper voice of re-search that would keep soul in mind is a poetics of the research process. A poetics of research, as opposed to an empirics of research, seeks to offer a plausible insight into the work by staying near it, by inhabiting the work as one might take up dwelling in a house, not, however, as a fixed or permanent resident, but as a sojourner, that is, as one who comes and goes, one who knows, then, that the "homes" that we build for soul from our ideas are temporary shelters, which, although only for the moment, are, for the moment, enough. A poetics of research invites the researcher to become the work through the powers of reverie and imagination and then to let go of it. It invites a researcher to hold onto the work by letting go of it. In Chapter 12 I will describe what I call a metaphoric sensibility as the kind of consciousness that one needs for a poetics of the research process. A metaphoric sensibility is necessary for a psychology that has no name, or better, for a psychology whose name would not forget that there are at least as many ways of looking at soul as there are ways of looking at a blackbird. If we are not as versed in this practice as the poets are, then at least as "failed poets," we might come close to the recognition that what we say in our psychologies about soul are and are not what soul is, and that we have an ethical responsibility to remain aware of this difference, as well as an ethical responsibility to acknowledge our participation in the bodies of knowledge we create. In Chapter 13 I will consider how a poetics of research steeped in a metaphoric sensibility can lead to the development of an ethical way of knowing and being.

Poetics is a term that belongs to the writings of Gaston Bachelard, and in one of his works he describes his poetics as a style of anima reading, which he contrasts with animus reading. Of this difference he writes:

> I am not the same man when I am reading a book of ideas where the animus is obliged to be vigilant, quite ready to criticize, quite ready to retort, as when I am reading a poet's book where images must be received in a sort of transcendental acceptance of gifts. Ah! to return the absolute gift which is a poet's image, our anima would have to be able to write a hymn of thanksgiving.[11]

A poetics of the research process, then, is a way of welcoming and hosting within our work the images of the soul, a way of attending to more than just the ideas or facts, and it requires a different style, a different way of being present. A poetics of research makes neither research into poetry nor researcher into poet. Rather, it deepens research and makes it richer by attending to the images in the ideas, the fantasies in the facts, the dreams in the reasons, the myths in the meanings, the archetypes in the arguments, and the complexes in the concepts. Doing so, re-search with soul in mind does become something akin to a hymn of thanksgiving in which the hymn in the work is an elegy in praise of re-finding what has been lost, or acknowledging what has been ignored or neglected. It is a way of inviting the "strangers" in the work across the threshold of the temporary dwelling that the researcher as "failed poet" has built in order to give a place for the unfinished business of the soul of the work to tell its dreams and visions of the work. In Chapter 5 I will describe the ritual space of transference that exists between a researcher and his or her topic as just such a temporary dwelling, where the researcher and his or her topic can sojourn for a while, and in Chapter 11 I will discuss the place of dreams, feelings, synchronicities, and other expressions of soul in the context of a method that is particularly attuned to a poetics of a re-search process that keeps soul in mind.

A poetics of the research process attends to the work of knowing as a journey of return. Doing re-search with soul in mind, one comes to know what one has already known without knowing it. I think here of the Earth as seen from space, that blue-green jewel floating in all that empty darkness, an unexpected image that has been one of the fruits of our technology. We stand upon the earth throughout our lives, but through our scientific research we have come to understand it. More often than not, however, we have little regard for how it under-stands us and has under-stood us as the home that stands-under our dreams and our visions. But that image of Earth, made from years of research, houses the human soul, and from the vantage point of outer space, we realize that our sojourn here is a journey of departure and return, that all that effort of research has about it an archetypal sense of knowing as remembering, and of this remembering as a homecoming, which on a smaller scale was the impetus for those reveries in the green garden of Governor's Bay. I once knew the greening of the world, and perhaps, even, I once was "green." But we forget until we are called again and re-membered, and then we know it again, or, perhaps, as the poet again says, know it really for the first time.

> We shall not cease from exploration
> And the end of all our exploring
> Will be to arrive where we started
> And know the place for the first time.[12]

A poetics of the research process is an archaeology of that process, an anamnesis of the soul's ways of knowing, in which knowing is a backward glance, a way of moving forward with regard for what has fallen in the gap, for what has been left behind, *dis*regarded, neglected, or otherwise forgotten. Knowing as return is about re-membering, where the work of memory is the work of mourning. As such, research is re-search, a searching again for what was once known and is making a claim upon us to re-turn with re-gard for the sake of re-membering.

To approach research in this fashion is to return to the beginnings of depth psychology. At the origins of depth psychology, we are taught that all finding is a re-finding, that the "object" found is the "object" lost. "Losing an object is the psyche's way of finding it," the Jungian analyst Greg Mogenson says.[13] Mourning, then, is not just the experience we have after loss. On the contrary, mourning is natural to soul. It is the way of soul, the soul's way of knowing and being, the activity of soul that challenges the ego-mind to hold onto what it possesses by letting go of it. In a poetics of the research process, the ego is not the center of the work. The work is not in the researcher any more than a dream is within a dreamer. On the contrary, the researcher is within the work. This shift describes an imaginal approach for the poetics of the research process. In this imaginal approach, the researcher has to "die" to the work so that the work can speak through him or her, so that the weight and wait of history that is the unfinished business in the soul of the work that claims a researcher through his or her complexes might come through.

In his remarkable book, *Symbolic Loss*, Peter Homans gathers ten essays that situate our inability to mourn as a central problem of our time.[14] He argues that our cultural monuments become problematic when the monument takes the place of the experience and relieves us of the work of mourning and remembering. This cultural inability to mourn is tantamount to the loss of soul on a collective level, and our psychologies, as I am arguing in this book, are part of this monumental problem. The language of psychology is the language of the rational mind making monuments out of its allusions to soul, thereby transforming them into illusions. Our psychological traditions, including depth psychology, forget that their ways of speaking about the life of soul conceal soul as much as they reveal it. Soul eludes the illusions of psychology. It escapes psychology's attempts to monumentalize it by pinning it down with its theories, measurements, facts, and procedures, like the greening of the world eludes our attempts to call it green, or the two pears of Wallace Stevens slip the net of what the poet wills or says.

Our psychologies are complex cultural-historical monuments, erected in the gap between soul and word, raised over the abyss we have made between mind and matter, and as such they have become problematic, relieving us of the work of re-membering the soul's abysmal existence and thus also giving us the task of mourning what we have forgotten. Re-search with soul in mind is an attempt to address this loss of soul in our ways of knowing. But as the epigram in the front of this book from the Roman poet Virgil indicates, the descent into the depths of soul is easy. Finding our way back, however, is the art and is the work.

Soul in the abyss! We live, the philosopher Martin Heidegger tells us, "[i]n the age of the world's night, [when] the abyss of the world must be experienced and endured."[15] It is at the lip of the void that the researcher as "failed poet" sets up his or her camp, and at this edge, what he or she might hear echoed from that place is the soul's grief. For the psychologist/researcher as "failed poet," and for a poetics of the research process, words matter, even though they fail. "The abyss— *bathus*—is about depth and the word is kin to grief—*penthos*—and to passion and suffering—*pathos*. Within this constellation, where words are like the stars of the soul, the abyss is the depth to which we are led by the suffering of grief over loss."[16]

As "failed poet" the researcher who would stay at the edge of the void to keep soul in mind suffers the passion of the work and endures the grief of his or her failure to say what wants and needs to be spoken. Thus, giving voice to the soul of one's work begins with allowing oneself to be addressed from that void, which depth psychology calls the unconscious. In addition, the work of saying what asks to be spoken in one's work is never complete. We begin and we fall short and we begin again. But as Eliot says in the same poem quoted at the beginning of this Introduction,

> There is only the fight to recover what has been lost
> And found and lost again: and now under conditions
> That seem unpropitious. But perhaps neither gain nor loss.
> For us, there is only the trying. The rest is not our business.[17]

The Wounded Researcher is not just a book about research in the traditional and usual sense. Rather, it is a book about how research is this re-searching activity of soul, its way of searching again for what has been lost, a finding that is a re-finding, as it is in therapy with soul in mind. Thus, psychological re-search with soul in mind is a form of therapy, just as therapy is a form of re-search. Or better still, both are a form of "e-ducation," a way of being drawn out of oneself into soul, into the soul of one's work and/or the soul of one's life.

A bit earlier in this Introduction, I quoted some lines from T. S. Eliot to the effect that we usually have the words for those things we are no longer disposed to say, and in this Introduction I have raised the issue of how one writes down the soul of one's work when one is writing it up. In this regard, I have a confession to make: I have been drawn into this work without being fully aware of what I am doing, and perhaps this is why the work continues to resist all my willful efforts to give it the form and shape that I design. "I" have been and "I" am the work that is being done. In working on this book, I am being worked on, and at times even being "worked over." Thus, the content of this book is also its process. *The Wounded Researcher* is a direct expression of what it proposes: a work chooses one as much as one chooses it and there is always that felt gap between what one says and what haunts one as wanting to be said.

So now, in a way, I have come full circle from the beginning in that "green" garden. Who is writing this work? This question is not merely rhetorical. Indeed, it is the central question that lies at the heart of re-search that is done with soul in mind. If I am less the author of this work and more its agent, who, standing at the edge of the work, is addressed by it, then the image of myself as the writer of this book is truly to be de-centered.

The cover of this book personifies this issue of who is writing a work when it is being written with soul in mind. It offers an image in reply to the question of who one is when he or she writes down the ways of soul. The image in the painting by Remedios Varo, entitled "Creation of the Birds," is utterly strange, perhaps even a bit alien. It seems to rise from the abyss, like a dream does. Indeed, for a long time I struggled with this image as I searched among many others looking for the image of the work. I resisted it, as one sometimes resists an image from a dream that seems utterly alien to the ego-mind, or as one is put off by those images from alchemy that seem wholly foreign to waking life. But, like dream images or those of alchemy, this one would not let go. It haunted me because it de-centers so well the usual expectation that the person who writes the words, who does the work, is identical with the characters or figures of soul who inform it, who give it its shape and tone, and who sing its song.

The image also depicts the scene of writing when one would attend to the soul of the work. The pen-like object in the figure's hand is connected to the strings of a violin, which is centered on the figure's heart, and the page is illuminated through a prism of sorts, which gathers the light of the stars and moon. The image seems to suggest that the scene of writing down the soul is one of surrender of mind to a heart in harmony with the *lumen naturae*, the light or spirit of nature. Writing down the soul seems to be a matter of the researcher's heart being in tune with the spirit and nature of the work. To be in this kind of attunement, one has to be in a certain mood. Look at the figure sitting at the table. He or she appears to be in a state of reverie, as if open to the deeper wisdom that flows from the rhythm of a heart attuned to nature. Is there not a rhythm like this to our writing when there is a resonance between the heart of the researcher and the nature of the work, a resonance so harmonious that it would be in such a moment hard to say who is writing and who is being written, a moment that enfolds us in a kind of ritual space, and which we often recognize when we violate that rhythm and become too willful in the work? Maybe we do become something alien to ourselves when we allow, or at least do not resist, that surrender. But maybe it is this descent from mind to heart that allows the voice of the soul in one's work to speak.

Of course, I am not claiming here that the image in the painting on the cover is the writer of this book. I would not attach my name to "his"—or is it "her"?—image. The image is closer to a *via negativa*, in which it functions to displace me from claiming possession of this work, which first claimed me. I do not have it any more than I have my dreams. They have me, and the process of doing re-search with soul in mind is the arduous task of differentiating what I bring to the work from what it brings to me. And so now, at this ending, I make note of one other feature in the painting. Three birds are present, two near the table and one near the window. Are they symbols of the sources of inspiration that come to us in those odd moments of creation and which seem like gifts so utterly unexpected? If so, then as with all forms of inspiration, we have to have ears to hear it. Perhaps, then, the bellbird singing in the "green" garden does matter, for its song has inspired this Introduction. Perhaps its song on those now-faraway mornings/ mournings was a part of this re-search, calling me beyond myself in those moments of reverie, inviting me under the spell of its lilt to imagine the voice of the work, drawing me out of myself, like some lover, to imagine the face of its longing and desire.

PART I

Theory

CHAPTER ONE

Soul and the Complex of Psychology

If we could reoriginate psychology … a way might open toward a meta-psychology that is a cosmology ….[1]

—James Hillman

Language is an intervention into psychology, not a neutral medium for it.[2]

Psychology is the web of all discourses.[3]

—Susan Rowland

INTRODUCTION

In his essay "On the Nature of the Psyche," Carl Jung makes the provocative statement that "[p]sychology is doomed to cancel itself out as a science and therein precisely it reaches its scientific goal."[4] Is the statement provocative because it suggests that psychology has been and is a questionable enterprise? Does the attainment of its scientific goal mean the end of psychology? If so, then what lies beyond psychology when it reaches its scientific goal? My intention in this chapter is to show how the notion of the psychoid archetype that Jung presents in this essay leads to a science of soul, which on the one hand takes psychology beyond itself and on the other forces a radical shift in psychology's attitude toward its own language. In the final section of this chapter, entitled "An Afterword," I will return to these two possibilities to suggest that they are not as incompatible as they might seem.

Jung himself confesses that the psychoid archetype does take psychology beyond itself. Concerning the reformulation of the archetype that he presents in this essay he says that in the end he discovered that he was enmeshed in "a net of reflections which extend far beyond natural science and ramify into the fields of philosophy, theology, comparative religion, and the humane sciences in general." These transgressions, he adds, caused him "no little worry."[5] What worries Jung here? Is he worried that these ramifications dissolve psychology? When psychology dissolves itself does it, for example, return to its roots in philosophy?

I do not think that this is the path that Jung is imagining, because he was always quite clear that his psychology had an empirical base and was not a metaphysics. Yet there are times when Jung sounds like a philosopher of old, like those philosophers of the ancient world who practiced philosophy as the love of wisdom. For example, in his essay "Psychotherapy and a Philosophy of Life," he says, "I can hardly draw a veil over the fact that we psychotherapists ought really to be philosophers or philosophic doctors—or rather that we already are so, though we are unwilling to admit it because of the glaring contrast between our work and what passes for philosophy in the universities."[6] Perhaps, then, it is not that psychology becomes philosophy but that the psychologist as a philosophic doctor has to draw upon the wisdom of philosophy and be conversant with its ways of knowing and styles of being.

So much of Jung's psychology is also concerned with religion. His book *Answer to Job* still stands, I believe, as one of the key texts of the 20th century.[7] Would a science of soul that takes psychology beyond itself become a religion? Notwithstanding this possibility for Jungian psychology to become another church or creed, which Richard Noll suggests is the case in his book *The Aryan Christ: The Secret Life of Carl Jung*, I would argue that for Jung the question of religion is definitively removed from the contexts of dogma and creed.[8] As his book on Job indicates, religion is about the responsibility we have as humans to become aware of the part we play in bringing to greater awareness the God-image in the psyche. This responsibility seems especially important today, when the powers of technology not only threaten to destroy us, but also imperil large portions of the earth. Of course, we cannot deny the many dangers that go with religion, as witnessed by the rise of fundamentalism, which, as Karen Armstrong shows in her book, *The Battle For God,* is the other side of technological modernity.[9] Nevertheless, as Lionel Corbett indicates, there is a religious function to the psyche, and Edward Edinger documents the necessity for a new God image.[10] Perhaps, then, a science of soul would be less about religion and more about the recovery of a religious sensibility in a world that has lost touch with the sacred.

Another ramification in Jung's thought that seems to lead psychology beyond itself is his forays into the symbolism of alchemy and astrology. With respect to the latter, Richard Tarnas in his new book, *Cosmos and Psyche,* shows in a comprehensive and remarkable fashion the connection between the movement of the planets and the archetypal patterns of the soul.[11] But again, as with philosophy and religion, a science of soul that would take psychology beyond itself does not become either astrology or alchemy. Both are ways of knowing and being present to the psyche and each becomes a *habitus* for a psychology that would keep soul in mind. Each becomes a way of remembering that psyche is indeed a part of nature and is not apart from it.

Of course, still another foray in Jung's psychology that one could say leads psychology beyond itself has been the thread of mythology. The depth psychologies of Freud and Jung have always reached into mythology, and James Hillman has emphasized throughout his work that myth-making is soul-making. Against the backdrop of myths, psychological events—from individual pathologizing to psychology's theory-making—are de-literalized. So Hillman deconstructs psychotherapy as *The Myth of Analysis,* and Aniela Jaffé, in her book, *The Myth of Meaning in the Work of C. G. Jung,* suggests that for Jung the idea of meaning as something apart from human participation is a modern myth.[12] Moreover, in her book *C. G. Jung: His Myth in Our Time*, Marie-Louise von Franz situates Jung's life and work within the context of his lifelong dialogue with the unconscious, which has resulted in a finely honed description of the mythic themes and patterns that connect the inner events of Jung's life with the outer events of the 20th century.[13]

All these threads take and have taken psychology beyond itself as a delimited field of research. Does psychology proper get lost in these ramifications? Is it dissolved? Does it cancel itself out? Is it the end of psychology? Or is a more significant point being made here? Is a proper psychology a science of soul that is all of these threads and none of them? Perhaps, in the end, a science of soul is the living practice of philosophy as the love of wisdom, and/or as the art of consolation in an age of sorrow, as well as the recovery of the need for and a sense of the divine in human affairs. In addition, perhaps a science of soul is the recovery of the ancient arts of alchemy and astrology that do not separate us from the larger forces of creation, and in this respect the creation of a new myth, which acknowledges that at bottom soul and nature are one and that we partake of this wholeness and belong to this web of interconnections.

All of these threads are present within the weave of Jung's psychology and maybe we miss the weave when we see only the end result—psychology! And maybe we miss all the threads that compose the weave when we move too far away from the multiple threads that compose the pattern of soul and slip into the singularity of a psychology. After all, psychology as a special and specialist discipline in its own right is a rather recent invention. Indeed, "[t]he history of psychology reminds us that 'psychology has a long past, but only a short history.'" Psychological curiosity is an ancient interest, as old perhaps as "the inquiring, self-conscious mind of man." It is only in the 16th century that the term psychology is first used, apparently by Melanchthon, a friend of Martin Luther's, to describe a separate field of study. Prior to this development, psychological life was multiple and dispersed. "The studies pertaining to the soul were distributed among metaphysics, logic and physics." Matters of soul were, so to speak, "in the middle of things, and one could find it everywhere and nowhere." But after this development, "... [t]he multiplicity of psychological life gives way to the unity of psychology."[14]

Perhaps, in the end, the self-cancellation of psychology for the sake of reaching its scientific goal is only the recovery of this ancient wisdom. Perhaps, in the end, the end of psychology means the end of any specialist attitude. Certainly this is what Jung suggests when, concerning the practice of psychotherapy, he states, "Although we are specialists *par excellence*, our specialized field, oddly enough, drives us to universalism, and to the complete overcoming of the specialist attitude, if the totality of body and soul is not to be just a matter of words."[15]

A psychology that is not just a matter of words! That is the point of a science of soul that would take psychology beyond itself, and the notion of the psychoid archetype that Jung presents in his essay is the vehicle that disturbs psychology in its comfortable isolation as a singular discipline in its own right. In the sections that follow, I will draw on Jung's seminal essay to show how psychology reaches its goal, becomes what it is meant to be, when it stops being a psychology for the sake of becoming psychological. In the Introduction to this book I said as much when I spoke about a psychology with no name as being less than a formal discipline and more a style or a disposition, a way of being present in and to the world in a psychological way, no-thing as substantive, then, as a noun, but something adjectival, a qualifier to ways of living, loving, and working with soul in mind. All the ramifications that Jung worries about, all those threads of mythology, alchemy, astrology, religion, philosophy, among others that weave the pattern of Jung's work, are so many different ways of speaking about psychology's object of study, the soul. And all are approximations of soul, metaphors that both reveal and conceal soul. I am proposing in this chapter that Jung's notion of the psychoid archetype leads psychology home, back to soul, and that this return for the sake of a new beginning requires a radical shift in how psychology regards its own language about soul. The language of psychology as a special and specialist discipline is also an approximation of soul. It, too, is a metaphor that both reveals and conceals soul. A proper psychology, then, is a science of soul that knows it cannot name soul with any definitive finality. Speaking of the psychoid archetype, Jung says it is a transcendent reality that is inconceivable in itself. A science of soul cannot know, or name as if it knew, the transcendent, but it can remember in its speaking that it cannot.

I want to emphasize in this chapter that the psychoid archetype must of necessity shift how psychology regards its own language. In the face of soul, psychology, I will argue, is humbled into regarding itself as always being an approximate science of soul. In *Psychological Life: From Science to Metaphor* I argued that psychological life is itself a metaphorical reality, and in this context, any psychology that would keep soul in mind would have to remain aware of the fact that psychology is the rational mind talking about the life of soul, that all our psychologies are different perspectives on soul, allusions to soul,

which remains elusive.[16] Psychology has long been conversant with
the metaphor of myth. When psychology goes beyond itself towards
a science of soul, it will have to become conversant with the myth of
metaphor. By the myth of metaphor I mean a shift in consciousness
towards a metaphoric sensibility. This shift would change psychology's
relation to its own language. It would humble psychology by inverting
its relation to soul, by turning that relation inside out. Psychology's
humbling would amount to the recognition that soul is in our
psychologies because our psychologies are within soul.

LANGUAGE AND THE UNCONSCIOUS

My starting point in this chapter is that psychology has a complex
about soul, and in this complex relation, its language is a symptomatic
expression that both remembers and reveals the life of soul and forgets
and conceals it. This complex relation between the discipline of
psychology and its object of study—soul—is present at the very origins
of depth psychology. At these origins we learn that language is itself a
problem because of the difference between the standpoint of
consciousness and the reality of the unconscious, which it addresses
and by which it is addressed. In this regard, a psychologist's conscious
statements about soul always have an unconscious side to them, which
for Jung expresses itself as a "calculus of subjective prejudices." This
"personal equation," which functions unconsciously, always "has a
telling effect upon the results of psychological observation."[17] There
is no perception and no thought that is not mediated by a complex
unconscious perspective, but "not even the psychologist is prepared
to regard his statements, at least in part, as a subjectively conditioned
confession."[18] The psychologist who would keep soul in mind,
however, is charged to mind the gap in his or her research between
his or her conscious claims about the work and his or her complex
unconscious ties to the work.

This hypothesis of the unconscious, Jung notes, "is of absolutely
revolutionary significance in that it could radically alter our view of
the world." It would do so because a serious consideration of the
hypothesis of the unconscious would require us to acknowledge that
"our view of the world can be but a provisional one."[19] Situated in the
gap between consciousness and the unconscious, we live between the

two worlds of collective conscious values, opinions, and prejudices and the values of the collective unconscious. To identify with either one of them is to forfeit the provisional character of our knowing. Jung speaks here of becoming "the ever ready victim of some wretched 'ism'," and even within depth psychology itself, which should know better, the conflict and tensions between schools of thought fall into this category of "isms." One becomes a Jungian or a Freudian, for example, and this leads to "the utter identification of the individual with a necessarily one-sided 'truth'," no matter the validity of that truth. For "[e]ven if it were a question of some great truth, identification with it would still be a catastrophe."[20] In place of knowledge, Jung notes, one would have belief.

A provisional way of knowing requires the ego not only to balance the tension between conscious and unconscious perspectives, but also, and more importantly, to hold off the allure and comfort of being a true believer by falling into either/or ways of thinking. A metaphoric sensibility is a provisional way of thinking and knowing that inoculates one against this temptation, and in various places throughout this text I will describe how an approach to re-search that does keep soul in mind is characterized by this sensibility. In addition, the provisional way of thinking that the hypothesis of the unconscious demands is an ethical command, and in Chapter 13 I will discuss how an approach to re-search that keeps soul in mind becomes a foundation for an ethical epistemology.

This gap, which is also an abyss, between the conscious and unconscious perspectives is a tension, which the 19th-century experimental psychologist Gustav Fechner experienced as a conflict between the "'day-time and the night-time view' of the world."[21] Jung saw this issue clearly in his essay "The Transcendent Function."[22] In that essay he says that the symbol mediates the gap between the conscious and the unconscious. A symbol holds the tension between what is visible and what is invisible, between, we might say, what shows itself in the light and what hides itself in darkness, and as such it requires for its expression a language that hints at meaning and does not attempt to define it or pin it down. Metaphor is such a language, that provisional language mentioned above. A metaphoric sensibility is necessary for a psychology, which, in taking the unconscious seriously, dwells in the gap of the transcendent function.

Poets trade in symbol and metaphor, and we find an elegant example of this issue of the tension between the day-time and night-time views of experience in the Irish poet Brendan Kennelly's memoir, *The Man Made of Rain*, in which he recounts the visitations he had with this figure (the man made of rain) while recovering from quadruple bypass surgery. In his note to this poetic memoir, he speaks of his struggles to write down his experiences with the man made of rain. "I am applying," he writes, "the language of the day to that of night, the language of explanation to the dreamenergised language of being." The issue that Kennelly is raising here is the question of how one writes in the gap between reason and dream, between the conscious attitude of waking life, which would give an explanation, and the fullness of experience, which reaches deeply into the unconscious as dream or vision. "Reason," he says, "must worry itself, chew its nails back to the flesh, to explain the dream beyond its reach." He adds, "If it explains the dream to its own satisfaction, it can tell itself it has the dream in its pocket, snug as a wallet."[23]

A psychology that takes the hypothesis of the unconscious seriously can have no such pockets, because soul as its object of study is always beyond the reach of its languages of explanation. Again, the poet is of help here. Speaking of the man made of rain, Kennelly asks, "What is a vision?" In response, he says, "It is completely normal when you're going through it, odd or tricky when you try to speak of it afterwards." He adds, "The challenge of 'afterwards' is connected with 'afterwords', how to preserve the normality of the visionary moment without being distorted or even drowned in the familiar sea of Dayenglish."[24] If we grant that such visions and dreams belong to the soul about which psychology speaks, then the issue that Jung is raising about the provisional character of the language of psychology is this notion of "afterwords." How does psychology write down the epiphanies of soul in such a way that it does not forget those epiphanies, but re-members them? This was the issue I raised in the Introduction to this book concerning "Green," and it is the issue at the heart of the difference between soul and the complex of psychology.

In his essay regarding the nature of the psyche Jung provides us with an example of this provisional style of knowing the reality of soul when he describes how he came to understand the image quality of the instinct through the fantasy material in dreams. When he was working with patients who needed some intellectual stable point if they were not to get lost in the material, he says, he would qualify his interpretations by "interspersing them with innumerable 'perhapses' and 'ifs' and 'buts' … to let the interpretation … trail off into a question whose answer was left to the free fantasy activity of the patient."[25] He was qualifying what he was saying, giving his words a provisional and tentative quality, binding the image in a meaning and then loosening the meaning. He was making a space as it were between what he said and what the image wanted to have spoken. He was creating a gap between the image and the word, opening a space of difference between the image as an epiphany of soul and the word as matter of psychology's discourse.

What Jung was acknowledging here was that the epiphanies of soul exceed the words that psychology gives to them, that there is always a gap, and perhaps even an abyss, between what psychology says of soul and what soul wants to be spoken. "The moment one forms an idea of a thing," Jung says, "and successfully catches one of its aspects, one invariably succumbs to the illusion of having caught the whole."[26] Psychology suffers this illusion. It makes monuments out of its allusions to soul, which always remains elusive.

In this chapter, I want to undo psychology as a monument to soul by drawing a distinction between the reality of soul and the complex of psychology. In doing so, I will be laying the groundwork for a psychological language rooted in a metaphoric sensibility. Because I will take up this issue in other chapters, for the moment I will just say that a psychological language is a way of speaking in the gap between meaning and the absence of meaning, a way of speaking of meaning as a presence that is haunted by absence. It is a language that bridges that gap between the meaning that is present and whose fate is to be undone, and the one that is absent, whose task is to undo the meaning that has been made. In the gap and on the bridge across the gap between presence and absence our words become an elegy not only for what one must let go of, but also for what has been lost, forgotten, ignored, left behind, or otherwise marginalized, a hymn of lament and thanksgiving, which keeps open a space for a return of what has been forgotten and is waiting to be remembered.

The poet again captures this sense of language as an elegy, as a hymn of lament and praise to presence haunted by absence. Speaking

of the "best and only poem" that he could write for the man made of
rain, Brendan Kennelly says, "Though I appear in the poem, or what
I recognize as my 'own' voice sounds through it, the poem is essentially
a homage to his presence, a map of his wandering discoveries, and an
evidence of my inadequate witnessing of those discoveries and that
presence." Of the man made of rain he says, "He is a real presence in
the poem," yet something of that real presence escapes the poet as an
inadequate witness. In his "afterwords," which are his poem to
remember the man made of rain, he cannot possibly do justice to that
presence, and thus of himself he says, "I am more an absence longing
to be a presence."[27]

   A hint of mourning lingers in this remark of the poet, a scent of
mourning that belongs to his work of remembering. The same scent
lingers with the psychologist who would keep soul in mind in his or
her "afterwords." In the gap between the daylight view of consciousness
and the nighttime view of the unconscious, the psychologist is always
an absence yearning to be a presence because he or she knows that
one cannot write down the soul either in the dark or in the light, that
one has to write down the soul in dark-light. He or she knows that in
that space of transition and transience, where light fades into darkness
and darkness begins to shimmer with light, something of the soul is
always left behind and needs to be mourned. Indeed, the more light
we bring to the unconscious, the deeper the darkness of the
unconscious becomes. The more we come to know, the more we come
to know we do not know. Jung makes this point in the Prologue to
Memories, Dreams, Reflections when he says, "We are a psychic process
which we do not control, or only partly direct." Because of this fact
he adds, "Consequently, we cannot have any final judgment about
ourselves or our lives."[28] A researcher who would keep soul in mind
has to attend, as I said in the Introduction to this book, to the feeling
of mourning for what is left behind in his or her ways of knowing and
expressing and remembering soul.

   The psychologist who would keep soul in mind is, however, no
poet, nor is he or she meant to be. But psychologist and poet do share
the same task with regard to language. Jung, I believe, acknowledged
this fate when late in his life he asked with respect to his work, "Anyway,
why did it have to be the death of the poet?"[29] Where the poet Kennelly
says, "Vision waits for us, ready to give itself; we use countless

techniques to cut ourselves off from it," the psychologist could substitute the word "soul" for "vision" and say the same thing.[30] The epiphanies of soul exceed the words that psychology gives to them. When psychology forgets the difference between its language and soul, when it identifies its language with soul, then it does cut itself off from soul as its object of study. It puts soul in its pocket.

How do we get to this difference between soul and the complex of psychology? Is soul truly other than psychology, or more than what psychology says of it? To answer these questions we have to continue with Jung's essay regarding the nature of the psyche, because in this seminal work he does open the path to this difference, which is essential to an approach to research that would keep soul in mind.

JUNG'S ENCOUNTER WITH QUANTUM PHYSICS: LANGUAGE AND THE INVISIBLE

In his essay, Jung spends a great deal of time on the convergence between his psychology and quantum physics. In both sciences, a principle of complementarity is present. Jung's colleague C. A. Meier describes this principle as the indissoluble bond that exists between the object to be investigated and the human investigator. In physics, this principle is apparent in the study of light. Depending upon the experimental procedure established by the physicist, light shows itself as either a wave or a particle. The question, of course, that this situation raises is: What is light—or matter, for that matter—before the interaction, before light manifests itself as either wave or particle? For physics, the reply is that light, or matter, exists as a quantum potential. In this quantum state, before its collapse into either wave or particle, light is neither one nor the other. It is, on the contrary, the potential to be either one, and in this condition of potentiality, light is, in the felicitous term of the quantum physicist Amit Goswami, a "wavicle." Electrons are wavicles and as such, he says, they are "neither waves nor particles … for their true nature transcends both descriptions."[31] It is important to note here that Goswami says light is neither one nor the other. He does not say both/and. This neither/nor consequence of the principle of complementarity is at the heart of a metaphoric sensibility.

In psychology, there is a similar principle. Jung cites the example of synchronicity, in which an acausal but meaningful connection exists between the material and the psychological realms. This connection requires a redefinition of the archetype as a psychoid phenomenon, which is the subject of the next section. In this section I wish to point out only the epistemological crisis that complementarity in physics and psychology raises.

With respect to synchronicity Jung says, "As soon as a psychic content crosses the threshold of consciousness, the synchronistic marginal phenomena disappear, time and space resume their accustomed sway, and consciousness is once more isolated in its subjectivity." Jung adds, "We have here one of those instances which can best be understood in terms of the physicist's idea of 'complementarity'." Apparently, then, the connection between the physical, material world and the psychological world in synchronistic occurrences is related to the attitude of the subject. Just as the form that light takes depends upon the physicist's standpoint, so synchronistic phenomena depend upon their relation to the subject's standpoint, that is, upon whether the subject is in a conscious or unconscious state with regard to the experience. Something about the unconscious state links psyche and matter. Thus Jung says, "When an unconscious content passes over into consciousness its synchronistic manifestation ceases; conversely, synchronistic phenomena can be evoked by putting the subject into an unconscious state." And lest we miss Jung's point here about synchronicity as an example of complementarity in psychology, he adds, "The same relationship of complementarity can be observed just as easily in all those extremely common medical cases in which certain clinical symptoms disappear when the corresponding unconscious contents are made conscious."[32] Jung then mentions psychosomatic phenomenon, and this suggests that the founding condition in depth psychology of conversion hysteria, in which a psychological experience is also a physical event, could be looked at in terms of synchronicity. In his or her unconscious state, the hysteric's symptoms display an acausal but meaningful connection between body and psyche. When, however, the hysteric becomes more conscious of the symptom, it "collapses" as it were into either a material event of the body or a psychic disturbance of the person. And as Jung said above about what happens to synchronicity when the threshold of consciousness is crossed, the symptom tends to disappear and consciousness is once again isolated in its subjectivity.

There is now a large body of literature on synchronicity as well as on Jung's dialogue with quantum physics. See, for example, Jung's central essay, "Synchronicity: An Acausal Connecting Principle," von Franz's *Psyche and Matter*, the Pauli/Jung letters edited by C. A. Meier under the title *Atom and Archetype*, F. David Peat's *Synchronicity: The Bridge Between Matter and Mind*, Robert Aziz's *C. G. Jung's Psychology of Religion and Synchronicity*, and Veronica Goodchild's "Songlines of the Soul," to name but a few.[33]

It is not my intention, however, to discuss these issues in any detail. Rather, I am citing them because the theme of complementarity raises an epistemological question regarding the relation of our language to reality. Since complementarity demonstrates the insoluble bond between a subject's way of knowing something and the object of his or her study, we need a way of speaking about this connection that remains consciously aware at all times that in its role of co-creating reality something of that reality is always revealed and concealed, something is always made present and visible while something remains absent and invisible, something is always spoken and left unspoken.

This way of putting things does not raise the question of whether some language of the future might be able to capture the totality of its object. The principle of complementarity is not about the failure of language. Rather, it points to the way in which quantum physics and Jung's psychology undercut the dualism of subject and object. It points to the fact that the subject is an indispensable part of the equation of reality. In this regard, I would note in passing that Jung's psychology adds an important dimension to the principle of complementarity in quantum physics in that it brings in the notion of the unconscious. The subject that is an indispensable part of the equation is a complex subject. Therefore, while quantum physics has to acknowledge the presence of the observer, whose trace might be nothing more than the measuring instrument he or she has consciously designed and employed for the experiment, psychology has to go deeper and make a place for the researcher's unconscious dynamics in the equation. This, in fact, is the heart of an approach to re-search that would keep soul in mind, and while this book limits itself to the field of psychological research, there is no reason to exclude other disciplines from this same requirement. Indeed, Jung's work with the quantum physicist Wolfgang Pauli did go in this direction and did consider, for example, the role played by dreams in Pauli's work. In addition, the historian Norman Cohn, in the last two sentences of his book, *Europe's Inner Demons*, in which he researched the massive witch hunts of the 16th and 17th centuries, wrote of the limits of traditional historical research. "But again and again," he writes, "I have felt that beneath the terrain which I was charting lay depths which were not to be explored by the techniques at my disposal."[34] Then, in reference to the postscript, entitled "Psycho-Historical Speculations," he adds: "The purpose of these Psycho-historical speculations is to encourage others, better equipped, to venture further—downwards, into the abyss of the unconscious."[35] Cohn is saying that the historian as researcher should have an awareness of the unconscious, which, I presume, refers not only to the way in which the unconscious has shaped historical events, but also to how the historian's own unconscious shapes a reading of those events.

The issue, then, that complementarity raises is that the indissoluble bond between subject and object means there is always that gap between what one says and what wants to be spoken, between what we are able to make present and what remains absent, whether that absence be the poet's vision of a man made of rain, or the physicist's quantum potential world of 'wavicles', or the psychologist's world of a soul that always eludes the complex allusions of his or her language. In the gap, something is always left out. Something is always lost. Wolfgang Pauli makes this point explicit. Concerning complementarity in physics, he says, "It rests with the free choice of the experimenter (or observer) to decide ... which insights he will gain and which he will lose; or to put it in popular language, whether he will measure A and ruin B or ruin A and measure B. It does not rest with him, however, to gain only insights and not lose any."[36] Complementarity forces us to recognize, not that language fails, but that it succeeds because it fails. Language succeeds when it remembers what it loses; it fails when it forgets that it does always lose something.

In a long footnote that Jung quotes from Pauli, the physicist says, "... [T]he epistemological situation with regard to the concepts 'conscious' and 'unconscious' seems to offer a pretty close analogy to the undermentioned 'complementarity' situation in physics."[37] "Analogy," however, seems too weak a term, and for Jung's colleague, C. A. Meier, there is in fact "'a genuine and authentic relationship of complementarity' between physics and psychology."[38] This complementarity between the two, between psyche and nature, rests upon Jung's re-visioning of the archetype as a psychoid reality. In the next section, we will see that the archetype as a psychoid realm is, for Jung, a non-psychic reality. With the original hypothesis of the unconscious, which, as we saw, Jung termed "a revolutionary idea," psychology moved towards the depth of soul, but it is only with Jung's move away from the archetype as intrapsychic to psychoid that soul begins to be differentiated from psychology. With this change, the unconscious becomes the soul of psychology in place of being the subject matter of a psychology of the unconscious.

In this respect, the psychoid archetype is psychology's quantum revolution. It is the potential realm before the archetype "collapses" into instinct or image. Like Goswami's "wavicle," which is neither particle nor wave, the psychoid archetype is neither matter nor spirit. It is the realm of soul, which is the pivot around which matter and spirit spin, and in this work I am, following Henri Corbin, calling this realm of soul the Imaginal world, which is the theme of Chapter 3.[39] In short, the quantum world is to nature what the Imaginal world is to soul, and just as quantum physics has had to develop a language of probabilities, psychology needs to develop a language of potential and probable meanings, a language of approximations, a language that resists literalizing the visible and forgetting the invisible.[40]

JUNG'S DOUBT

The difference between soul and the complex language of psychology, which I am trying to secure in this chapter, and which is central to an approach to re-search that would keep soul in mind, rests upon a doubt about the psychic nature of the archetypes, a doubt that Jung raises in his essay. He comes to this doubt by way of the three parallels he sees between quantum physics and psychology.

To get at what Jung is struggling with here, imagine the material world that classical physics investigates as a horizontal line. With the rise of quantum physics the line dips, and as the physicist is led deeper and deeper into the darkness of the atomic and subatomic realms, he or she encounters, not physical events directly, but the effects of physical events, which reflect how "a subjective element attaches to the physicist's world picture …." Indeed, as Jung notes, "Physics has demonstrated, as plainly as could be wished, that in the realm of atomic magnitudes an observer is postulated in objective reality, and that only on this condition is a satisfactory scheme of explanation possible."[41] In other words, the observer affects the observed, and there can be no calculus of objective reality that does not take into account how this observer effect actually co-creates the reality observed. To say this in still another way, what physics has demonstrated is that consciousness belongs to the equations of nature. In some unobservable way, consciousness and nature are one. The being of nature is also a way of knowing it.

Now imagine the psychological world in classical psychology, by which I mean psychology without the revolutionary hypothesis of an unconscious, as also a horizontal line. With the rise of depth psychology, the line dips and as the psychologist is led deeper and deeper into the darkness of the unconscious, as Jung was beyond Freud, he or she encounters the same observer effect that occurs in physics. In his correspondence with Jung, Pauli notes: "… [E]very 'observation of the unconscious,' i.e., every conscious realization of unconscious contents, has an uncontrollable reactive effect on these same contents (which as we know precludes in principle the possibility of 'exhausting' the unconscious by making it conscious)." Pauli then adds: "Thus the physicist will conclude *per analogiam* that this uncontrollable reactive effect of the observing subject on the unconscious limits the objective character of the latter's reality and lends it at the same time a certain subjectivity."[42] In psychology, then, the principle of complementarity means that there is an indissoluble bond between the subject, who uses language to speak about the unconscious, and the unconscious, which is the object of that language.

Beyond these two parallels of the observer effect and the indissoluble bond between subject and object, there is a third one between psychology and physics. Just as the behavior of matter in the atomic and subatomic realms is known only indirectly through its effects, the unconscious is known only indirectly through the effects it has on conscious contents. We all know of Freudian slips as an example of this point, but Jung is pointing to something much deeper than the effect the unconscious has on this personal aspect of conscious life. He writes: "Investigation of these effects yields the singular fact that they proceed from an unconscious, i.e., objective, reality which behaves at the same time like a subjective one—in other words, like a consciousness." He is speaking here of the archetypes as an organizing principle that affect conscious life and as such he is saying that this archetypal principle is present or functions as an observing subject. But, and here is where Jung's doubt begins, this archetypal principle that functions as an observing subject is "constituted in a way that we cannot conceive." It is, moreover, "at one and the same time, absolute subjectivity and universal truth, for in principle it can be shown to be present everywhere, which certainly cannot be said of conscious contents of a personalistic nature."[43] Is Jung referring here to the collective unconscious, which underlies his studies of the world's mythologies, which reflect and record the images of the collective unconscious? I think not. He does not say so and in fact the term "collective unconscious" is mentioned only once, and in passing, in this seminal essay in which Jung's doubt about the nature of the archetypes appears. Something more radical is going on here, something that is no less than a total re-visioning of the nature of the psyche, which will, as I am trying to suggest in this chapter, lead psychology into soul.

To get there with Jung, we have to follow the way in which he is thinking outside the box of what he calls the lay mind. "The elusiveness, capriciousness, haziness, and uniqueness that the lay mind always associates with the idea of the psyche applies only to consciousness, and not to the absolute unconscious."[44] I would suggest that in this passage Jung is also referring to the lay mind of psychology, for which the absolute unconscious would be more than just elusive, capricious, hazy, and unique. It would be untenable and inadmissible. Indeed, if the absolute unconscious were to be regarded as admissible and tenable, it would in fact be the cancellation of psychology, through which it would reach its scientific goal of becoming a science of soul.

Jung is thinking outside the box of psychology here. He is thinking of the archetypes as something other than a psychic reality. And so he writes, "The qualitatively rather than quantitatively definable units with which the unconscious works, namely the archetypes, therefore, have a nature that *cannot with certainty be designated as psychic*."[45] We should read this passage slowly and meditate on it. The italics are his.

He is not certain that the archetypes can be designated as psychic. He has a doubt, and from this creative doubt there springs a radically new appreciation of the nature of the psyche and the psyche of nature. The archetype is a psychoid reality, and in this psychoid realm, which is unobservable and is known only by its effects in the material and psychological worlds, the horizontal line of classical physics, which dips into the darkness of matter and encounters an objective quantum world, and the horizontal line of classical psychology, which dips into the darkness of the psyche and encounters the psychoid archetype, not only meet, they are also confused. At the deepest layers of the unconscious, this psychoid reality is not just the union of psyche and nature. Rather, it is the realm that is neither psyche nor matter, a realm where psyche is nature—psyche matters, we might say—and nature is psyche, as evidenced, for example, by synchronicity.

In this psychoid realm, psyche and nature are not two but one, an *unus mundus* that in this book I am calling Soul. The psychoid archetype is the *anima mundi,* the soul of the world. In one part of his essay, Jung goes into a long description of how the alchemists described the soul of the world as a multitude of "fiery sparks" and he writes, "The hypothesis of multiple luminosities rests partly … on the quasi-conscious state of unconscious contents and partly on the incidence of certain images which must be regarded as symbolical." These symbols, he adds, "are to be found in the dreams and visual fantasies of modern individuals, and can also be traced in historical records."[46] In these records these multiple sparks of light are associated with the *lumen naturae,* the light of nature. The soul of the world, then, is the light of nature, a dark-light, a luminosity in the darkness of matter. In this regard, Jung's turn toward the archetype as a psychoid reality to which his studies of alchemy had to lead extends the unconscious into nature. Indeed, in his essay the range of the unconscious that begins with the personal unconscious discovered by Freud goes past the collective unconscious explored by Jung to the unconscious of nature. At the deepest level of the unconscious, the unconscious is nature. The consequence, of course, is that as the psychologist probes deeper and deeper into the psyche, he or she descends into the soul of the world. He or she discovers that at the psychoid level of the archetype, at the level of soul, psyche matters as a matter of the soul of the world. He or she discovers that the unconscious is not just in us but that we are in the unconscious of nature, and that at the deepest levels of our psyches, we retain some dim remembrance of once, very long ago, having been a part of the world's dark-light.

This darkness is an archetypal one that exists at the heart of all our psychologies. We need a psychology of this darkness to balance the light that pervades so much of our psychology. Stanton Marlan has given us such a psychology in his insightful book, *The Black Sun: The Alchemy and Art of Darkness.*[47] He brings insight and illumination to darkness as he brings darkness to light.

The differentiation between soul and psychology that Jung's reflections on the psychoid archetype inspire leads us into this archetypal darkness, which has effects for re-search that would keep soul in mind. Specifically, it has important implications for how we regard the language of psychology, and in the next section I will take up this point. It also has implications for how we write down the soul in writing up our psychologies. How does one write in dark-light? In Chapter 12 I will take up this question.

Before I continue with Jung's reflections, however, I want to offer a reverie of this dark-light. Is it the memory of this darkness from which we have so laboriously extricated ourselves that frightens us still— perhaps by its sweet seduction—into turning on the lights? In the face of this archetypal darkness, do we rush to our in-sights in order to banish the memory? Or, perhaps, is the memory of this darkness a bittersweet one, which leaves in its trace a sense of longing, a desire to return to what was once known, or better yet, inhabited, and has been left behind?

INTERLUDE
THE UNCONSCIOUS OF NATURE: A REVERIE OF RETURN

A few years ago, I took a drive with a colleague to see something of the rugged Oregon coastline. Quite unexpectedly, we encountered an invitation, a sign on the side of the road that said "Sea Lion Cave," so many miles ahead. It was raining and cloudy, as it had been for the four or five days we had been in Oregon, so it seemed like a good idea to have a destination. Along the way, I noticed whales, dolphins, and sea lions swimming down the coast—or at least that was my vision, perhaps colored by the anticipation of what the caves would offer.

At the entrance to the cave is a series of long, winding stairs leading to an elevator that took us the last three hundred feet or so into the depths. By the time we arrived, the day was already quite chilly and the wind, needle-like in its sharpness, whipped our faces as we stood on the outside platform awaiting our descent. Low angry clouds hung close to the water, intensifying my growing feeling of quiet isolation, as if the world, in the physiognomy of this landscape, was silencing the busy ways of human consciousness.

Much of my life's concern for soul has been nurtured by moments like this, and the best that I have been—either as therapist, teacher, or writer—has been only the translation of such moments into word and into image. For this reason, I have felt and known for a long time that at our best moments we are always surprised, and that fundamentally we are never the authors of meaning but its agents—agents of, or witnesses for, soul in its desires for revelation. Still, I was not prepared for this moment, when the door of the elevator opened and we descended the final flight of stairs into the cave. The journey I had been taking in the world found its reflection as a journey of soul.

The sea lions are visible perhaps fifty feet above the hollowed-out inlet—females actually, with their pups born from the last mating. It is the largest rookery on the North American coastline, a deep, wide scar cut into the rocks by the perpetual thrashing of the ocean tides. How long this has gone on it is difficult to say, but one cannot escape the impression of a kind of patient force at work here, a force of wind and tide marked with the index of eternity. Layer upon layer of rock had been sculpted by these forces, and once our eyes became accustomed to the darkness in which we stood, we saw that almost every inch of layered rock was pulsating and quivering, animated by the sea lions that inhabit that place. Actually, long before we saw these creatures, we heard their incessant continuous barking. Deep, throaty sounds already shaped the dark cave, and all around us those sounds and their echoes filled the air with a sense of perpetual, unending hunger. Here, in the descent into the cave, I could hear the insatiable hungers of the animal soul, barking, pounding, rhythmical crescendos of longing, crashing like the tides against the rocks in the darkness of an everlasting night, blind appetites knowing nothing but hunger and its urgencies. Animal flesh: appetitive, instinctual, voracious, and eternal—the terror of the dark and of blind, carnal hunger.

I stood there, mesmerized by the sound, lost within it. Indeed it was only in retrospect, only after noticing another feature of the landscape, that I realized the power of this event and why and how it had affected me as it did. What broke me away from this scene, what freed me, so to speak, from this eternal sea of instinctual hungers, was a dim ray of light that weakly, so very weakly, was struggling to enter the cave from the upper right. I was caught by the light when I saw it, especially by its feebleness, and in a strange way I knew that somehow I was that light in the midst of all that darkness, struggling with the darkness, and perhaps even against it. In that moment, with a feeling of awe, terror, and sadness, I also knew that it was that light that distanced me from those sea lions, that light which placed between them and me an unbridgeable gap … that light, which was—at that moment, and had been, once before, in the dawn of human consciousness—the tremulous bridge we had crossed out of the blindness of those instinctual hungers, out of the darkness of the night.

It was time to leave. As I turned away from this scene, which had given me this gift, I noticed that the sounds had grown farther away. When I rode the elevator up to the surface, the poet Rilke's words came to mind: "And already the knowing brutes are aware/ that we don't feel very securely at home/within our interpreted world."[48]

THE PSYCHOID ARCHETYPE AND THE COMPLEX
OF PSYCHOLOGY

In his work, Jung always insists upon the difference between the archetype and its conscious representations. This difference also applies to his reformulation of the archetype as a psychoid reality. But this reformulation, as we have seen, goes beyond his earlier formulations of the archetype as intrapsychic. Jung even doubts if the psychoid archetype is a psychic reality at all. Beyond this doubt, he suggests that the psychoid archetype is a non-psychic reality.

In this chapter I have been suggesting that the notion of a psychoid archetype takes psychology beyond itself into a science of soul, and I have said that this transition raises an epistemological crisis for psychology. It does so because, as Jung points out, the psychoid archetype, like his earlier formulation of the archetype, is a transcendent reality whose representation in consciousness "differs to an indeterminable extent from that which caused the representation."[49] In other words, the ideas and images in consciousness are always only an approximation of the transcendent reality of the psychoid archetype. The language that we consciously employ to express and interpret these ideas and images, then, always only alludes to the transcendent reality of soul, which remains elusive. In this regard, the words that psychology uses are like the shadows on the wall of Plato's cave. Like those shadows, they point to something beyond themselves. Unlike Plato, however, Jung does not split the transcendent archetype from its effects. He does not split the unconscious transcendent archetype from its expression as ideas and images in consciousness. Jung's archetypes are a dynamic and not just a formal reality, and the ideas and images in consciousness that reveal and conceal the archetypes are as real as the archetypes themselves. They are not illusions, like the shadows on the wall of Plato's cave. Hence in a footnote concerning this issue Jung quotes quite favorably the remark by the physicist Sir James Jeans. Jeans says, "… [T]he shadows on the wall of Plato's cave are just as real as the invisible figures that cast them and whose existence can only be inferred mathematically."[50]

The critical epistemological question that this issue of the transcendent archetype raises is: How must psychology regard its language if its language can only infer a reality that remains invisible and elusive? Moreover, if that elusive reality is the non-psychic realm of the psychoid archetype, which takes psychology beyond itself into a science of soul, then the issue is: How must psychology regard its language in relation to soul? If soul is like a quantum field that "collapses" into either a material event or a psychic feeling/idea/image/

experience, then how can psychology in its language take into account the reality of soul that is neither a material event nor a psychic image/ idea, etc.? In the Preface to the book *Atom and Archetype*, Beverley Zabriskie quotes Jung and Pauli concerning this issue. "For Jung," she writes, "'the common background of microphysics and depth psychology' is as much physical as psychic, and so is 'neither, but rather a third thing, a neutral nature which can at most be grasped in hints since in essence it is transcendental.'" Given this background third, which again in this book I am calling soul, "Pauli sought 'to find a new language that could make the hidden dimension in nature accessible to the intellect.'"[51]

The crisis of language that the psychoid archetype introduces is no less challenging today than the crisis of language introduced with the original notion of the unconscious more than a hundred years ago. And now, as then, this crisis is both a danger and an opportunity. The danger is that if the claims of psychology are too positive in their assertions, or if they are too certain of themselves and too fixed in their assertions, then soul is forgotten. The language of psychology, then, either identifies soul with its words or reduces soul to them. Much of the science of psychology, with its materialistic bias and its causal mode of thinking, regards its language in this way. For example, psychopathology is reduced to and explained as a matter of brain dysfunction and the soul of suffering is forgotten. The opportunity, however, is for psychology to regard its language as metaphorical. Its claims, then, are de-literalized, freed of their demand to be taken at face value, as the whole truth of the matter. Psychopathology, then, as a matter of brain dysfunction, becomes a perspective that reflects the position of the researcher who makes that claim, who "collapses" the field in that way. Moreover, taking a second look at psychology's language in this way does not alter the factual accuracy of the claim that brain dysfunction is implicated in psychopathology. It simply situates the fact within a metaphoric vision, which alludes in this fashion to the soul of suffering, which remains elusive.

In his essay, Jung, I believe, appreciates this crisis about psychology's language. He says, "... [P]sychology is incapacitated from making any valid statements about unconscious states, or to put it another way, there is no hope that the validity of any statement about unconscious states or processes will ever be verified scientifically."[52]

What Jung is pointing to here is the impossibility of an objective validity that does not take into account the presence of the subject, or, in the terms of his essay, the principle of complementarity. Every statement that a psychologist makes about the unconscious is already affected by the unconscious and has an effect upon it. The best psychology can do, then, is always to remain aware that its statements are complex expressions of this interaction. The language of psychology echoes the "calculus of subjective prejudices" of the psychologist as well as the soul of the topic, which effects the ideas and images that the psychologist has and the words that he or she speaks.

An approach to re-search that keeps soul in mind has to make a place for the soul of the work to speak beyond the calculus of a researcher's subjective prejudices. If psychology regards its language from the point of view of complementarity, if it takes a second look at its way of speaking of soul from this perspective of complementarity, it would make place in its research process for the soul of the work to speak beyond the complex presence of the researcher. In other words, it would make a place where it neither reduces nor identifies the soul, the psychoid archetype, with the complex language of psychology, even though soul shows itself only either as a material event or a psychic image or idea, in the same way that quantum physics neither reduces nor identifies the "wavicle" with the wave or the particle, even though the "wavicle" shows itself only as either one or the other. However, psychology cannot develop a mathematical language of soul such as physics has developed for nature, a mathematical language of probabilities rooted in a mathematical sensibility concerned with quantitative relations. Rather, as I suggested in the Introduction, psychology needs to develop a poetics of the research process, a language of metaphoric possibilities rooted in a metaphorical sensibility concerned with qualitative differences. To say this another way, insofar as "Archetypes, so far as we can observe and experience them at all, manifest themselves only through their ability to *organize* images and ideas, and this is always an unconscious process which cannot be detected until afterwards,"[53] the complex language of psychology is in service to soul when "afterwards" in its "afterwords" it remembers soul, as the poet Brendan Kennelly remembers his vision of the man made of rain.

CLOSING TIME

Jung's doubt about the exclusively psychic nature of the archetype and his suggestion beyond this doubt that the psychoid archetype is non-psychic has been the basis for my distinction in this chapter between Soul and the complex of psychology. His doubt and his suggestion beyond his doubt take him beyond psychology and back to soul, and this move, I would claim, is a piece of some unfinished business in his work, which is taken up in this book in the context of doing re-search with soul in mind. Specifically, in the context of the psychoid archetype, an approach to re-search that would keep soul in mind requires a new myth of research, a new approach to research, a new way of imagining the research process, a fresh look at the question of method, and a consideration of the implications of the psychoid archetype for writing down the soul in writing up one's research.

In Chapter 2 I will propose that the myth of Orpheus and Eurydice is an appropriate myth for re-search with soul in mind, and in Chapter 3 I will describe the new approach as an imaginal one. In Chapters 4, 5, and 6 I will describe two characteristics of the research process that flows from an imaginal approach and illustrate them with examples from my graduate students, and in Chapters 7 through 11 I will take up the issue of method. Finally, in Chapter 12 I will describe some of the features of writing that keeps soul in mind.

AN AFTERWORD

I began this chapter with a quote from Jung to the effect that the fate of psychology is to cancel itself out, and perhaps it is not enough for psychology to regard its language in a new way by adopting a rigorous metaphoric sensibility. Maybe, as Jung implies, psychology is doomed to failure and its success is to dissolve itself completely. Maybe psychology as a discipline can no longer serve soul. Maybe the psychologist is unable to bridge that gap to soul with his or her complex language, which always carries with it the shadow of the unconscious from the personal to the psychoid depths. Maybe we need another discipline, one that as yet has no name, to serve soul. Maybe we are beyond the realm of psychology when the epiphanies of soul are breaking through in UFOs, crop circles, and all those other anomalous epiphanies of soul that Veronica Goodchild, among others, is exploring.[54] Maybe the age of psychology is over. Maybe psychology needs a quantum revolution analogous to the one in physics, which moved that discipline beyond its Newtonian phase.

All of this is, of course, speculation, and perhaps for the moment the best way to phrase the challenge raised by these speculations is to recall that physics' quantum revolution conserves Newtonian physics as a special case of the physics of large bodies, of the visible world, while its revolution attends to the subatomic, quantum world of the invisible. Maybe with Jung's re-visioning of the archetype as psychoid, he gives us a quantum revolution of the soul and maybe the Imaginal realm of soul conserves psychology's complex about soul as a special case of soul in its visible appearances, i.e., when it manifests itself as either a material event that becomes the subject matter of empirical psychology, or a mental one that becomes the subject matter of psychological theories and concepts. We should note here, however, the indeterminacy even at this level: is psychopathology a material event of the brain or a mental disorder? We are still confused about this psyche/ matter relation. Von Franz notes, "The psyche/matter problem has not yet been solved, which is why the basic riddle of alchemy is still not solved."[55] Indeed, it was this problem that alchemy bequeathed to Jung and that led him to his reformulation of the archetypal domain as a psychoid realm, that third realm of soul that, as non-psychic, is neither matter nor psyche. And so we are back where we started, needing a way of knowing and being that keeps this reality of soul in mind.

So, for now, I cannot say what a discipline in service to soul beyond psychology might be. I am a psychologist and write as one, and so I limit myself to the epistemological issue of a language that, even as it hints at what it cannot name with certitude, does keep soul in mind, calling for a psychology that has no name, for which psychology with its many names is a special case. This is as far as I can go at the moment, as one who writes as a psychologist in service to soul. A psychology that has no name is a place-holder for a discipline, a way of knowing and being that is yet to be. Within the context of an approach to research that would keep soul in mind, this book is perhaps a very small step in that direction.

CHAPTER TWO

Re-search: Under the Spell of Orpheus

INTRODUCTION

In his now classic work, *Re-visioning Psychology*, James Hillman situates his archetypal approach to those moments in one's life when all seems to be falling apart within a principle and a method articulated by the neo-Platonic philosopher Plotinus. The principle states, "All knowing comes by likeness" and the method is one of "reversion," which is "the idea that all things desire to return to the archetypal originals of which they are copies and from which they proceed." In all things, this desire is "imagined as having the intentionality of returning to an archetypal background." The moments, then, when things do fall apart, when things and ourselves become unglued, have an intelligence about them, or we should perhaps say an *other* wisdom than that of our ego-conscious minds. This other wisdom is an archetypal pattern within every act of behavior and every experience of fantasy within which who I am resembles who I am like when I act and feel in a certain way. "These archetypal resemblances," Hillman notes, "are best presented in myths in which the archetypal persons I am like and the patterns I am enacting have their authentic home ground."[1]

Research also always has its moments of falling apart, moments when the work falls out of the hands of the researcher, when the work seems to resist the conscious intentions of the researcher and begins to twist and turn in another way. Such moments are crucial to an approach to re-search that would keep soul in mind because they signal a shift from the researcher's ego-intentions for the work to the intentions that the work has for itself, a shift from what the researcher wants from the work to what the work wants from the researcher. In these moments of breakdown, the researcher is also swept up into the process of falling apart insofar as the researcher in his or her complex encounter with the soul of the work falls into the work and in the process of working on the work is worked on and even worked over by it. For the researcher who works with soul in mind, then, these moments pose the question of whom the researcher is like when he or she works with soul in mind. In re-search with soul in mind there is always the question of what archetypal pattern or myth informs the process.

In this chapter I want to show that the myth of Orpheus and Eurydice can be regarded as an archetypal pattern that informs re-search with soul in mind. Research that makes a place for the unconscious in the process reverts or is led back to this myth. The researcher who keeps soul in mind works under the spell of Orpheus and Eurydice.

In an earlier book, *Technology as Symptom and Dream*, I described an archetypal pattern behind the origins of an empirical approach to research.[2] That pattern has functioned as a cultural-historical myth, according to which objective knowledge is secured when one behaves like a spectator behind a window, who, taking leave of his or her sensibilities, keeps a dispassionate, impersonal, and distant eye upon the world, which itself is a spectacle for observation and measurement. Of course, we have advanced beyond those origins, and in fact depth psychology, along with physics at the end of the 19th century, played a significant role in "breaking the window." We now know that the researcher is "part of the equation," as I showed in the last chapter, and yet, despite this awareness that the knower is part of the known (that, as hermeneutics has shown, there is a circle of interpretation and understanding between the knower and the known), an approach to research that seriously considers the unconscious participation of the researcher in the research process is still needed. What we also need, of course, is a myth that can serve as the archetypal pattern for re-search that keeps soul in mind, the articulation of whom the researcher is like when he or she descends into the dark-light of the underworld, where the complex patterns of the researcher encounter the soul of the work, its unfinished business.

The psychologist who does re-search with soul in mind is a border figure. He or she stands in the gap between the conscious and the unconscious. He or she takes seriously the notion of the unconscious, which, as we saw in Chapter 1, Jung cited as a most revolutionary idea, an idea that, if taken seriously, would change the world. Certainly, we should take this idea seriously regarding the bodies of knowledge we create about the world. To take it seriously is, in fact, an ethical imperative, a theme I will take up in the final chapter of this book.

In the Introduction to this book I suggested that this gap plays itself out in the tension between what one says and what is always left unsaid, leaving behind the ash of mourning, as it were, in the work of saying and knowing, and making the work of knowing a labor of an-amnesis, of un-forgetting what has been forgotten, and in Chapter 1 I located psychology itself in this gap. There is a gap between the words that psychology uses, its language, and the referent of its words, soul. In that gap, we find the difference between soul and the complex of psychology. To bridge this gap, I called for a poetics of the research process, for an *other* way of knowing soul in addition to our familiar empirical and rational ways of knowing and being. Orpheus is the eponymous poet, the poet whose name is the name of poetry itself, and he is the one who guides us towards a poetics of the research process. He is not only the poet of mourning and un-forgetting, he is also the poet of the gap.

In his extraordinary book *The Orphic Moment*, Robert McGahey presents Orpheus in this fashion, as a figure of the gap, the border, and the bridge. For McGahey the Orphic voice is the moment of the gap "across which language as *poiesis* moves in 'fixing' the experience wherein the god or *daimon* is named." But quoting Plato, for whom the "'marrow of all sciences' is the art of generating 'middle terms,'" McGahey notes that the voice of Orpheus that arises from this gap "fixes" the experience only by letting go of it.[3] Orpheus is the one who comes and goes, the "identity of presence and absence," the one whose presence lingers only for a moment, lightly touching the experience, and whose absence haunts presence.[4] Who better than Orpheus to guide the psychologist/researcher in the gap between the conscious and the unconscious, where he or she is called to "fix" soul by letting go of it? Who better than Orpheus to mediate the tension between soul and the complex languages of psychology? Who better than Orpheus to guide the researcher into the depths of the work, wherein the soul of the work is named? Orpheus is the mythic presence and the archetypal pattern of re-search with soul in mind, the guise of a researcher who, keeping soul in mind, remains aware that his or her work always has an asymptotic relation to soul, who remains aware that his or her work reveals soul and conceals it. Thus, Orpheus is the prototypical figure who liberates psychology from its mimetic addiction to its complex language, the one who, in awakening psychology to its formulaic and repetitive applications of its knowledge, re-members soul. For this ability to be a poet of anamnesis, of the work of un-forgetting, Plato welcomed Orpheus back into the polis, the soul of the city. For the same reason, psychology would do well to welcome Orpheus back into the city of the soul.

THE MYTH OF ORPHEUS AND EURYDICE

In the Foreword to McGahey's book, Thomas Moore asks with respect to Orpheus, "What is it to be dismembered, to sing out of that fragmentation, to be islanded (isolated)?" He goes on to ask, "What kind of necessity compels us to transgress the absolute law and eternally lose our cherished loves and desires to a realm outside or beneath the consoling light of familiar life?" In these remarks, Moore is highlighting some of the themes of the Orphic myth, which we will see are relevant to an approach to re-search that would keep soul in mind. Love, loss, descent into a realm beyond the familiar and known, and dismemberment are some of the Orphic moments of complex research. Before I describe these and some other moments, however, we have to ask along with Moore, "Who is this Orpheus—an historical theologian, a figure of myth, a founder of religion, a poet, or nothing but a figment appearing like a ghost throughout our history?"[5]

Orpheus is a figure who comes out of the mists of time, whose dates belong to the Heroic Age, but generations before Homer and Hesiod. His homeland is said to be Thrace, an ancient land in the southeastern part of the Balkan Peninsula, the location today of modern Bulgaria and parts of Greece and Turkey. It was in this region that the earliest beginnings of Dionysian worship were said to have arisen, and according to E. R. Dodds it was in Thrace that Greek culture first encountered shamanism.[6]

Of his lineage we are told that he was the son of the Muse Kalliope and the god Apollo, although some say his father was Oiagros, a Thracian river god and/or the king of Thrace. His mother, Kalliope, the muse of epic poetry, whose name means "beautiful voice," was, along with the other eight muses, born of Zeus and Mnemosyne. By his birthright, then, Orpheus is a poet/singer whose songs are in service to memory. As such, he is, as McGahey argues and as we noted above, the one poet whom Plato allowed to return to the Polis because unlike the mimetic poets, Homer and Hesiod, whose songs induced in their hearers a life of imitation, Orpheus sang songs that were said to awaken the soul to its forgotten inner melody and to connect the awakened soul to the song of creation. A harmony, a resonance, exists between what Orpheus does and the soul of nature. In response to his melody, the willows would bend and birds and animals of all kinds would gather around him. In having this power to awaken nature, Orpheus sings "the original song to which all creation responds, as if hearing its own inner melody."[7] Unlike the mimetic poets, then, Orpheus is the poet of anamnesis, the poet of un-forgetting.

Already from these few scraps of information, might we say that as the mythic figure behind re-search with soul in mind Orpheus awakens the researcher to what he or she has forgotten about the work? Orpheus awakens the researcher to the song of the work and thus aligns what he or she does on the work with the soul of the work.

Of the character and influence of Orpheus we know quite a bit, but of the incidents of his life we know very little. According to W. K. C. Guthrie, the stories we have of him are "the death of Eurydice, and his journey to the shades to fetch her, the slender tradition of a sojourn in Egypt, the voyage of the Argonauts, and the various accounts of the events which led to his death and the miraculous events which followed it."[8] Of these events in his life, it is the story of him and Eurydice that concerns us here. In an earlier work I traced out the Orphic roots of Jung's psychology and showed how the figure of Orpheus might function as the archetypal presence within Jung's psychology of individuation.[9] Now, in this work, I want to show how this tale of love, loss, descent, and transformation forms the mythic backdrop of re-search with soul in mind. Just as Orpheus comes to us as a mythic figure out of the mists of time, a figure hovering on the border between the timeless realm of myth and the temporal world of history, he also comes to us out of the depths, as a personification for a psychology of the depths in its therapeutic and research functions.

One of the most interesting and important aspects of Orpheus is his journey to the underworld in search of Eurydice. It is this feature of the myth that has inspired the imagination of history. Of all his adventures, including his epic voyage with Jason and the Argonauts, it is this tale of Orpheus and Eurydice that has endured in countless operas, plays, and films, and we cannot help but wonder why. Perhaps it is because that journey to the underworld marks Orpheus as one who knows the secrets of the afterlife, a subject that continues to exercise its endless fascination over us. "The secrets of Hades were in his possession," Guthrie notes, and it is difficult to judge with certainty whether Orpheus "was originally an underworld spirit, to whom was later attached the romantic story of the descent in search of a lost wife."[10] For whatever reasons the link was made, however, it is this connection among love, loss, and descent that has mattered as the myth has evolved. In this evolution, the secrets of the underworld have to do with love and loss, with mourning and dismemberment, and with the transformations that this dismemberment brings. It is this path that we are following, and it is on this path that we will meet the researcher who in service to the soul of the work undergoes a descent and a dismemberment, an experience that transforms the original bond of Eros between himself or herself and the work, much as Orpheus's love for Eurydice is changed after his descent.

Of Eurydice herself, it is only in Roman times that we find the story of her and Orpheus elaborated into the complete tale that we know today. Prior to this, she either is absent from the tale, remains unnamed, or goes by a different name. But with the Roman poet Virgil, and then a bit later with Ovid, Eurydice comes forth. Eurydice was probably a Thracian nymph, who, charmed by the sweetness of Orpheus's music, falls in love with him. In Virgil's account, written around 29 B.C.E., the story of Orpheus and Eurydice is contained as a story within a story in the fourth book of his *Georgics*. I mention this detail because, as Christine Downing points out, a proper understanding of Virgil's Orpheus requires knowledge of the story of Aristaeus, the tale within which the story of Orpheus and Eurydice is told.[11]

Aristaeus, like Orpheus, is the son of Apollo, and in Virgil's story he is a devoted beekeeper whose bees have mysteriously died. The tale of Orpheus and Eurydice thus begins with the loss of something that is loved and itself adds to this sense of loss, for, in his bewilderment over the death of his bees, Aristaeus learns that he is the cause of the death of Eurydice and Orpheus's consequent grief. Fleeing from his unwanted embrace, Eurydice had stepped on a serpent and had died from its bite. In Virgil's account, then, the fate of Orpheus and Eurydice is already established within this forgotten moment in Aristaeus's life. What is of interest here is that something that has been forgotten has to be remembered, and for Virgil it is Orpheus who must do the work of remembering by being dismembered. Orpheus and Eurydice are in Virgil's telling of the tale part of an-other story. They belong to something other and larger than themselves, as we all do when we take that archetypal view of life discussed in the opening of this chapter. It is the same for the researcher who would keep soul in mind. His or her work belongs to something other and larger than himself or herself, and in remembering that aspect of the work, the researcher is dismembered.

In her looking back at Orpheus, Downing points out that Virgil is the first one to give an account of Eurydice's death. "Never before," she writes, "in the tales told about Orpheus had we had an account of his wife's death—only of Orpheus' attempt to undo it."[12] Her point is important because it sets the stage, as we shall see, for Eurydice's perspective on the myth. As we travel from Virgil through Ovid to Rilke's account, we shall see how Eurydice's remaining in the underworld is central to Orpheus's transformation. Orpheus had to look back because the underworld is Eurydice's place, and being there, not only is she freed from being Orpheus's possession, she is also freed into herself. In Jungian terms, she is no longer the projection of Orpheus's anima. On the contrary, because Orpheus does not succeed in returning her to the upper world, he must learn to see life through her underworld eyes. In a similar fashion, the researcher who would keep soul in mind cannot drag the work into the upper world of his or her ego-intentions. He or she has to learn to differentiate his or her projections onto the work from the soul of the work itself, which is not his or her possession. The researcher who would keep soul in mind has to learn to see the work through eyes that have let go of it.

We are, however, still with Virgil and his account of the story. After Eurydice's death, Orpheus is inconsolable, and in his grief, he descends into the underworld to plead with the powers and forces of that realm to release from their grip what he has lost. Downing hints at an important twist in this descent and correctly, I think, describes the psychological condition of that effort. She writes, "In a sense he is pulled into the underworld by his grief: the experience of loss *is* being there."[13] Yes, Orpheus descends, but in doing so he is only enacting what has already claimed him, his love of Eurydice, just as the researcher is pulled into the depths when he or she has lost touch with the sense of the work that has made its claim upon him or her. There are these moments in research, moments that can feel like depression, and if one attends to them, if one keeps soul in mind, then in such moments, when the soul of the work has been lost, one is being drawn into the underworld, the unconscious, of the work.

In descending into the underworld Orpheus wants to bring Eurydice back to the land of the living. He wants to restore what was, to imitate now what was then, rather than remember what has been lost; and through the power of his song, he intends to charm the gods of the underworld into granting him this wish. Virgil does not tell us of the gods' response. We know only that Orpheus appears to have succeeded in persuading them, but at the very moment when the journey to the upper world is nearly completed, we learn of the prohibition that was placed upon him by the gods. Orpheus looks back, and Eurydice is now lost for a second time—this time forever. Virgil concludes the tale with a recounting of how Orpheus mourns for seven months, oblivious to any thoughts of love, until the Thracian women, who feel themselves spurned by his devotion to his wife, tear him apart. His severed head, carried by the river to the sea, continues to say her name, Eurydice, which is echoed back by the riverbanks.

Virgil's account invites us to wonder about the failure of Orpheus to rescue Eurydice from the underworld. It is important to note here that she is first named in Virgil's poem only after Orpheus has turned and thereby violated the restriction placed upon him by the gods. Eurydice, it seems, comes into her own only after Orpheus has lost her again for this second time, only after, we should say, she is no longer the object of his wish to reclaim her, only after she is no longer the object of his broken desire. I am, however, cautious here, because when Orpheus turns, Virgil has Eurydice cry, "What madness, Orpheus, what dreadful madness has brought disaster alike upon you and me, poor soul?"[14] In her complaint, does she share with him the desire to restore and repeat what was? Did the gods of the underworld impose the prohibition against the backward glance knowing that it would be violated? And if so, was the gesture of the backward glance necessary so that both Eurydice and Orpheus would be transformed?

Eurydice wins her name, as we saw, only after the fatal turn is made, and the sad lament of Orpheus's severed head has its cry of "Eurydice" echoed back by the banks of the river, suggesting that in his death and dismemberment Orpheus's voice has now transcended the personal lament of his loss to resonate in harmony with nature, with its own natural cycles and rhythms of life and death. When he first descends into the underworld, Orpheus intends to use the power of his song to achieve his purpose, that is, to assuage his grief and satisfy his narcissistic need for Eurydice. After he has failed, his song becomes an echo of a larger story. As we shall see in the next section, a similar moment marks the soul-oriented re-search process, when the researcher's relation to the work undergoes a *sparagmos*, a dismemberment. In such a moment, the complex character of the work opens onto the unfinished business of the soul of the work. The work that comes through the researcher's complex is no longer about him or her. The wound becomes a work that is part of a larger story when the researcher has been forced to let go of what he or she needs the work to be, when the researcher is compelled to let go of his or her naïve narcissistic attachment to the work.

When Ovid in his *Metamorphoses* re-tells the story, some forty years after Virgil, he makes numerous changes. The architecture of the story, however, remains the same and the archetypal themes of love, loss, descent, the backward glance, dismemberment, transformation, and Eurydice's response are still there. For our purposes, it is not necessary to go into these changes except to note two important points.

First, in Ovid's account, Orpheus's act of turning back does not provoke from Eurydice the sort of complaint found in Virgil. On the contrary, it elicits only one word from her, a final "Farewell." More than anything else, perhaps, there is sorrow in this word, or at least some deep sense of resignation, an acceptance that this turn of events was meant to be. But Downing suggests a third option; she says that Eurydice's "Farewell" hints at the possibility that "the bond between the two ... remain[s] unbroken, perhaps preparing us for the different ending Ovid will give his tale."[15]

Such "farewell" moments often mark the research process, and all three possibilities for that "Farewell" that I have mentioned above are well known to us. For example, in that moment when one loses the sense of his or her work, when it seems that the work has fallen into the underworld, beyond the reach of one's claims upon it, when the work seems to have gone well beyond the measure of one's willfulness, one might begin to feel a sense of resignation and a feeling of surrender to something larger in the work beyond one's will, a shift in one's relation to it that is not without sorrow, and perhaps even on occasion despair, but which is also not without a sense of hope for a different ending, for something that has not been anticipated. In such moments, it might truly be of help to a researcher to remember this larger archetypal pattern in the research process and to know that Orpheus and Eurydice are near.

Second, Ovid changes the ending. In his account, the shade of Orpheus returns to the underworld and there he and Eurydice are again united. Orpheus now knows this place in a way he did not know it before, as if his loss of Eurydice and his failure to regain her have now enabled him to see her and himself with different eyes. And there in the world of shades, as Ovid so beautifully describes it, they walk together, at times side by side, at times with her in front of him, at times with him in front of her, but with no fear of looking back to see her. The relationship has changed. Lost to each other in life, they are now together in that other world. Having lost each other, they have found each other in the world of images, the world of imagination, the world of soul.

Of all the elements in the myth, it is the backward glance of Orpheus that is pivotal. The story turns on that fateful turn. Maurice Blanchot regards "*le regard d'Orphée*" as the central moment in the myth, and in his book *The Gaze of Orpheus*, he writes, "... [E]verything is at stake in the decision of the gaze."[16] Mark Greene notes that in the backward glance there "resides a shattering of Orpheus' former ego and identity."[17] The turn, of course, also shatters Eurydice. She, too, is transformed, and it is the poet Rilke who best captures this change.

In his poem "Orpheus.Eurydice.Hermes," he transforms the complaint of Virgil's Eurydice and the "Farewell" of Ovid's Eurydice into a declaration of her autonomy.[18]

A few stanzas prior to this declaration, Rilke tells us that in her death Eurydice was "[d]eep within herself," and that "[s]he had come into a new virginity." "She was no longer that woman with blue eyes," he says, and then a few lines later, "and that man's property no longer." And so, when Orpheus turns and the god Hermes says "with sorrow in his voice: He has turned around—," Rilke says, "she could not understand, and softly answered / *Who*?"[19]

Who! Just this one word, which the poet italicizes! We are meant to notice something here, some fundamental change not only in Eurydice but also between her and Orpheus. With this question she declares she no longer recognizes him or his claims upon her, and she no longer recognizing him, he, Orpheus, no longer recognizes himself. He had descended, heroically, or perhaps only naïvely, to bring her back, to repeat what they once had, to cancel the loss, to un-remember the love he has lost. Unwilling or unable to re-member, he has to be dis-membered. And in that, he is led to his destiny. But so too is Eurydice. She descends back into the underworld, to her place, to where she is who she is, to where she belongs. The story that began with a fall, with falling in love, turns out to be a tale about the work of love and its transformations.

We know the fate of Orpheus. After his dismemberment, his head and lyre float down the river Hebrus to the island of Lesbos, the home of Sappho and lyric poetry. There his lyre rests within a temple of Apollo until eventually it finds its way into the heavens as the constellation Lyra, while his head, still singing, is buried under a temple of Dionysos. In this destiny, Orpheus continues to shine and sing. In his dismemberment, he is remembered for the ages. Rilke, in his *Sonnets to Orpheus*, says it this way: "O you lost god! You unending trace! / Only because at last enmity rent and scattered you / are we now the hearers and a mouth of Nature."[20]

Eurydice's fate, however, is still uncertain. Her question, *Who?*, still lingers as a piece of unfinished business in this story of love, loss, descent, failure, dismemberment, and transformation. Eurydice still waits in the underworld for that destiny to be honored. In another work, I have argued that the hysteric at the threshold of Freud's and

Jung's consulting rooms is Eurydice's return.[21] When she appears there
in the guise of the hysteric, in the dis-guise of the symptom, she puts
her question again to them, to Freud and Jung, behind whom stands
Orpheus. As Orpheus did, they would follow her into the underworld
and with their "songs" reclaim her by naming her, by giving her many
names: Anna O, Dora, Sabina Spielrein, Toni Wolf, the women of Freud
and Jung, and, perhaps most significant of all, *Anima*. But whom are
we addressing with all these names? Of whom are we speaking? *Who?*
The question lingers, and in it, what we say of her is not recognized
by her. Her question is addressed to us as she once addressed it to
Hermes, the guide who would lead her from darkness into the upper
world of light. *Who?* Laid on the couch of depth psychology, she has
been abducted from her place in the underworld and dragged into
the upper world of psychology's words. In this respect, psychology in
its research and practice suffers, we might say, from a Eurydice complex,
and it needs a way of letting go of its claims upon the soul, a theme
that was taken up in Chapter 1 regarding soul and the complex of
psychology. The Orphic moments of the research process presented
in this chapter describe how the wounded researcher moves from being
claimed by a work to letting go of it.

Who? What Eurydice wants from us with her question is a way of
speaking that does not couch her in our imposed meanings. What she
wants from us is a way of speaking that is not so "cocksure" of itself
when we lay her on the couch. Perhaps, the hysteric at the threshold
of the therapy room should have turned back before she was laid on
the couch, and, like Eurydice, returned to her self in the underworld.
But then who knows? Maybe she has, and maybe what is most
interesting and compelling about Eurydice's place in the myth is this
moment of her question, when the action stops and things turn around.
Maybe that is her destiny—to stop the forward advance of things and
to return them to their source in the afterlife of soul. Maybe Eurydice's
place is in that gap between soul and the complex language of
psychology (described in the first chapter), in that moment when we
are compelled to undo the claims that the language of psychology
makes upon soul. And maybe Eurydice is the one who addresses the
researcher with his or her claims upon the work and with her question
invites the researcher to let go of the work. Perhaps Eurydice is the
one who reclaims and remembers the soul of the work.

In his book *Greeting the Angels: An Imaginal View of the Mourning Process*, Greg Mogenson says, "Everything we see is filtered through the apertures of dead love." "Everything we see," he adds, "we see through the eyes of the dead." "The psyche," he concludes, "is an afterworld of love."[22] What Mogenson is claiming here is that losing an object is the soul's way of finding it. "By becoming absent an object becomes wholly psychological. By losing life it gains the eternal life of the imaginal psyche."[23]

In this book I am adopting an imaginal view of the research process and I am suggesting that the myth of Orpheus and Eurydice is the archetypal background for how research becomes psychological. The myth of Orpheus and Eurydice is about this process of losing and finding, about this work of transformation in which the other becomes a psychological reality, a matter of soul. The work one is called to do is an *other*, and in the process of being claimed by it, of falling in love with it, we learn—by losing it, by letting go of it—to love it for what it is in itself, in its own virginity. Along the way I have suggested several times how re-search with soul in mind might be amplified along the lines of this myth. In the next section I want to give an example of the presence of this myth in the background of this work, and in the subsequent section I will describe in some detail six Orphic moments in the research process, six moments that make the process of re-search one that keeps soul in mind.

THE WOUNDED RESEARCHER: IN THE SHADOW OF A MYTH

The Wounded Researcher had many false starts, which I experienced as dismemberments of the work. At the same time as I was making these many failed beginnings, I was also working on the story of Orpheus and Eurydice for another project. The two projects, however, were unrelated in my mind, and they even occupied separate places in my study. I worked on them independently of each other, and never approached both of them on the same day. Each had its own space and time in this world and each was its own world.

My dreams, however, were telling a different tale and seemed to know there was a connection. In the dream world they seemed to be related, and while I was working on one of those dreams in analysis, it became clear to me that I was forcing the work into my familiar and comfortable academic mold and that the many breakdowns of the work were its way of questioning me, its own version of the Eurydician *Who?* In such moments, and trusting the hints of the dreams—in one of which I was led out of the house of academia by a poet figure, whose guise and demeanor were entirely different from all those in the academy, who were smartly suited-and-tied—I understood that well beyond how I wanted to tie up this work and suit it to my intentions, there was a design that this work had for itself. Where this poet figure was leading the work and me became a disturbing question. Did I have to let go of the work as I had planned it and allow myself to be drawn into the work by him in order to show the issue of research from the soul's point of view?

A moment of dismemberment for the work and for me came when I finally realized that the issue of research was functioning as a cover story and context for describing research as re-search. This difference between research and re-search involves the soul's method or way of learning and knowing. Research as re-search is an e-ducation, or drawing out, of the ego-mind by soul where re-search is a searching again for what has been lost, forgotten, neglected, or otherwise disregarded, a searching again that is a dis-membering of the ego's hold upon the work in order to re-member the unfinished business in the soul of the work. Following the track of the poet in the dream, I had to let go of the work as I had originally conceived it and as I continued to insist upon seeing it, and through the eyes of mourning I began to see that re-search with soul in mind was and remains a piece of unfinished business in how psychology has approached the issue of research. Re-search with soul in mind, research as re-search, is an approach that has been seriously neglected in psychology. To turn to it does not replace or dismiss empirical research in psychology or any of psychology's methods. Rather, research as re-search is a necessary addition that remembers the ways in which soul re-searches, and it opens a space for its method of loosening the ego's hold upon the work for the sake of finding its soul. Following the track of the poet, I began to understand that research as re-search, that re-search with soul in mind, is a work of redemption, a work in service to the wait and weight of history in the work, a piece of cultural-historical therapeutics in which the researcher functions as a witness for what has been left behind.

At this point, I would like to emphasize that I have not imposed this myth upon the work. Rather, I was drawn into this myth of Orpheus and Eurydice as a wounded researcher when, after the dream, I began to ask what this pattern is like of having the work and losing it, of experiencing its multiple failures or breakdowns in the face of my willfulness. In such moments, and trusting the hints of the dreams, I was turned toward and found myself in the shadows of the archetypal background of this work.

In this work, I am being guided by this myth. The myth is the amplification of the work a wounded researcher does, and the story in its pregnant moments describes whom the researcher is like when he or she is working in the depths of soul. I am not, therefore, reducing this myth to this psychological issue, nor am I attempting to explain re-search with soul in mind in this way. This archetypal move is about neither reduction nor explanation. It is about amplification, a work of the imagination, which situates the work of re-search within a larger frame.

To be sure, this archetypal move is a work of interpretation, but, to borrow a distinction from Paul Ricoeur, there is a difference between a hermeneutics in wich interpretation is about the recollection and restoration of meaning and a hermeneutics in which interpretation is an exercise of suspicion.[24] To revert to the myth of Orpheus and Eurydice, then, is to restore, recover, remember, recollect, and perhaps even redeem what has been forgotten in psychological research. It is to restore, recover, remember, recollect, and perhaps even redeem the ways of soul in psychological work. In this hermeneutics of reminiscence I am attempting to turn psychological research toward soul, attempting in this turn to return psychological research to its source in soul, attempting to remind mind of what it has forgotten about research, that as a searching again for what has already made its claim upon the researcher, re-search leads him or her into the depths of the work, where his or her intentions for the work are undone.

The six Orphic moments of research as re-search chart a process of mourning in which the tension between the researcher's desire to possess the work are challenged by the unfinished business in the soul of the work. In this encounter, the movement is from the researcher being claimed by the work via his or her complexes, through the struggles with letting go of it, towards a place of individuation, in which the work is free of the researcher's appropriation of it and the researcher and the work are free of each other. From the first moment when one is claimed by a work, this struggle between holding on to it and letting go of it sets in and each of the five Orphic moments that follow this initial one mark phases in re-search as a mourning process. Certainly for me the many false starts, each of which began with enthusiasm and clarity and ended in ashes, were a slow process of letting go, a slow and difficult process of mourning. Following the track of the poet in the dream, I was led into the soul of the work beyond my original intentions and understandings of it. In this process, my relation to the work and the work itself was radically transformed.

In the next chapter, I will attempt to show that re-search with soul in mind as a process of mourning situates the work of re-search within an imaginal approach. In this endeavor, the Orpheus-Eurydice myth and the imaginal approach supplement and sustain each other, since both myth and approach are about the work of letting go, about mourning as ultimately a work of transformation and individuation. Against the archetypal background of the Orpheus-Eurydice myth, psychological research shifts from being an empirical enterprise to being an imaginal one, and an imaginal approach to research as re-search is animated within this archetypal field.

Six Orphic Moments in Re-search with Soul in Mind

The First Moment: Being Claimed by the Work

The Orpheus-Eurydice tale begins as a story of love. Charmed by Orpheus's voice, Eurydice is taken hold of by him. Re-search with soul in mind begins in a similar fashion. The topic that the researcher chooses has already in a way charmed him or her, and beneath the interest that one says he or she has in the work, there is at play a kind of sweet seduction. Indeed, one's interests are always a complex affair, and like falling in love, in which one is drawn to the other through a complex (love is a complex relation), the researcher is claimed by the work through his or her complexes. In this sense, re-search is a vocation, and in Chapter 4 I will describe this aspect of the re-search process in some detail. For the moment, however, I want only to emphasize that when one keeps soul in mind in the re-search process, one is called into a work by something other than one's intentions. This something other is what I described above as the unfinished business in the soul of the work, the unsaid weight of history in the work that waits to be said.

Jung offers a good example of this moment of being claimed by one's work. In his autobiography, Jung confesses, "In the Tower at Bollingen it is as if one lived in many centuries simultaneously. The place will outlive me, and in its location and style it points backwards to things of long ago." A little further on he adds, "There is nothing here to disturb the dead," indicating that in this place the souls of his ancestors are sustained as he goes about the work of answering "for them the questions that their lives once left behind."[25] For Jung it is the ancestors for whom the work is done. It is the dead of long ago, stretching down the long hallway of time, who ask us to linger in the moment and who solicit from us this turning.

Recently I came across another example of how one is claimed beyond reason by a work. It comes from the work of the photographer Stephen Wilkes and his book, *Ellis Island: Ghosts of Freedom.*[26] In October 2006, I had the opportunity of viewing a selection of his photographs, which were on display at the Monroe Gallery in Santa Fe, New Mexico. Apart from the stunning beauty of the photographs of this abandoned place, which once was the portal to freedom for so many immigrants who had come to the U.S. with their hopes and dreams, I was struck by the description he gave of how he had come to this work. "For two weeks after shooting the first group of pictures of Ellis, I was obsessed. I couldn't sleep. I couldn't erase the buildings from my mind. So I went back, many times every chance I could. What began as a one-hour editorial assignment became a five-year passion. Somehow, it felt as if I was chosen to do it: to document the light and the energy and living spirit of this place."[27]

Wilkes's interest became a passion, and when one looks at his photographs it is easy to see that his passion was in response to those "ghosts" who still lingered there waiting for their stories to be told. Claimed by them through his passion, Wilkes documented with his camera the haunting presence that is still felt in those ruins. When I add to Wilkes's account my own reaction to his work, I also understand why I was drawn to that exhibition in Santa Fe and felt compelled to return to it a second time. My father had passed through the rooms and halls in those photographs and had been in those buildings nearly eighty years earlier. Looking at Wilkes's photographs, I was seeing for a moment through the eyes of the dead. I was seeing my father in a different way, and in the light of those photographs he was for a moment released from those claims of love that link father to son in so many complex ways. He was no longer just my father. He was that young man of 17, there with all those other ancestors who had made the same journey. Through those photographs I could see that he had already turned away from me and had walked back into that world of his hopes and dreams from which I was born.

Earlier I quoted Mogenson, who describes the soul as an afterworld of love. It is an apt statement about love and its shadows because it succinctly says that what begins with love and the claims it makes upon us must end with a radical transformation of that love and its claims. What we love we lose, and in that moment we begin to see the love that claims us by means of our complexes through different eyes. We also lose what claims us in re-search. What claims us we cannot possess, and it is this shadow of love as possession that is transformed. This is the path that the myth of Orpheus and Eurydice takes and it is the path of re-search with soul in mind that begins with being claimed by the work. Before I move into that second moment of loss, however, I want to offer one more example of how re-search with soul in mind begins with being claimed by the weight of history that waits in the soul of the work.

As I began writing this book, I was aware of the dead who were gathering around me. Not only was I aware of the anonymous dead, the ungrieved multitude of the 20th century, from the trenches of World War I, those slaughterhouses of the soul, where the dreams of European Enlightenment revealed their dark shadow, to the horrors of the Holocaust, whose morbidity still haunts us today, to the too-numerous genocides of the last three decades that continue, but I was also aware of the death we have visited on our oceans and trees, and the animals and plants with whom we share this home. All of them seemed to require my attention and all of them seemed to be connected to this work on re-search with soul in mind. So many unfinished lives and untold stories have accumulated as the weight of history that we bear. In the beginning of the work, had they gathered to re-mind me not to forget that research is re-search? Had they gathered to re-mind me that we have a responsibility to these anonymous dead, who are the weight and the wait of history?

In the shadows of history, in earshot of those unfinished tales, we live our lives and think our thoughts in the presence of a haunting absence. Research as re-search begins here in the presence of this haunting absence, in service to what claims us. Claimed by a work through his or her complexes, the wounded researcher sees the work through the lens of those ancestors who linger with their still unanswered questions, the ancestors for whom the wounded researcher becomes a witness and a spokesperson. Research as re-search is, as we shall see as we follow the track of the myth, a work of an-amnesis, of un-forgetting. But to re-member what we have forgotten, we must first lose or let go of what we would possess.

The Second Moment: Losing the Work/Mourning as Invitation

What we love we lose, and mourning is thus an inevitable aspect of love. Research as re-search is about loss, and it demands mourning, whose first phase is an invitation to release what has been lost. In re-search that keeps soul in mind, this phase of mourning has to do with the ego letting go of its hold upon the work. This invitation into mourning is the beginning of a transformation of the ego's complex ties to the work. To illustrate this second moment of the re-search process, I want to give three examples in which mourning presents itself as an invitation to let go of what has been lost.

The first two examples come from my own experience of the loss of a loved one, described in my book *The Soul in Grief: Love, Death and Transformation*.[28] In that book, I recounted the long descent into the abyss after the unexpected death of my first wife, to whom I had been married for 25 years. Writing that book some seven years after her death, I gave many examples of the early phase of mourning, in which I was invited to acknowledge the loss. One of those examples was a dream, the other a piece of synchronicity.

The dream occurred within the first few days of my wife's death. In the dream,

I knock on the door of my friend's house, where a party or celebration of some kind is taking place. The rooms are filled with many guests and I

see my wife, who is dressed in a beautiful green gown adorned with peacock feathers. Her smile is radiant and she is moving among the guests with a kind of flowing motion, as if not weighed down by gravity. She looks happy and all the guests notice her. This is her place, and in it I seem to have become invisible, as if I were the one who has died.

This dream was an early invitation to acknowledge the loss and to let go of my own refusal to do so because of my own needs. In the dream, she has come into her own virginity, as it were, and there, in the underworld of death, she no longer sees me. The image through which she is presented in the dream was, in a way, a preview of the *telos* of the mourning process. But it would take a very long time for me to accept that invitation into mourning, because mourning is a tricky business— a business in which the desire to restore what once was and has been lost outweighs the hard task of re-membering the loss.

The second example comes from much later, some nine months after the dream. It was a piece of synchronicity involving a bookshelf in my study, where I had intended to work. Many months had passed since my wife's death, and I had hardly ever entered that room during that time. One day, however, I was awakened from a deep afternoon sleep by the sound of a crash in that room, and upon investigation, I discovered that the shelves of the one bookcase that held a collection of my publications had collapsed. Wearily, I put the shelves back in place and arranged the books in the original order of their dates of publication. That order was a kind of track of my life, a kind of timeline frozen in place, something of the past to hold on to. A few days later, the shelves collapsed again, and again I repeated the same process. Whereas I had felt only a weary sadness at the collapse the first time, this second time I felt an angry resistance against allowing this destruction of the old order and a stubborn determination to fight against it. My stubborn will, however, was no match for this call from the world to let the old order die, this call to surrender and mourn the loss of my wife. She had died, but I could not let go of her. Or, more to the point of mourning, I could not let go of my need of her. The collapsing shelves, however, were insistent and when they crashed for a third time, I replaced the books at random, just as I picked them up off the floor. I let go of my stubborn attempts to keep the old order as it was, and the shelves did not collapse again. It was an early moment of change, a moment in which I also began to re-member the loss and suffer it rather than try to maintain the order that had been.

The third example, also a dream, was related to me by a young woman whose brother had died in a skiing accident. Here is the dream:

> *I am hiking alone behind the North Star Ski Resort when I come across some ancient caves. They are blue and cavernous and deep. I rappel down through chamber after chamber, following the blue light. When I reach the end, there is a room with nothing but a fireplace, which is lit, and a rocking chair. My brother is sitting in the rocking chair. He looks strange because he has a very long, gray beard and his hair looks scraggly. I also notice that his fingernails are grotesquely long. He looks very sad. Once again, I go through the feeling that he is not really dead, but has just been here the whole time. I am not angry, though. I ask him what he is doing here. He tells me calmly that he is "stuck here" and that I need to tell Mom to "let him go."* [29]

I do not doubt that the connection between these examples and the doing of re-search might not be readily apparent. But the examples suggest that just as re-search is part of life, life is also a process of re-searching. Life lived with soul in mind, like re-search done with soul in mind, involves loss, and all three examples indicate that loss requires a transformation in one's relation to the other who has been lost. We lose what we love, and in that losing we have to let go of what we have loved. Orpheus loses Eurydice, but as we shall see, she comes into her own, and the two of them come into their own together, only when Orpheus has lost Eurydice again, only when he has failed in his efforts to re-establish the old order that had existed between them when she was his possession. Like the figure in the dream saying to the dreamer that she has to tell Mom to let him go, the work that initially claims us and that we would then make our own, that we would possess, takes leave of us in this second moment of research as re-search, in this moment when it feels as though the work has collapsed despite our best efforts to restore it, when it feels we have lost sight of it and no longer control it. In such a moment, the work is inviting the researcher to mourn the loss and let go of the work.

Before I move on to the third Orphic moment in re-search, I want to note in passing that the dream is a fine example of research as re-search because it calls the dreamer back to what is being neglected and forgotten, and has been lost. Indeed, I am inclined to say that the dream is the best way to illustrate research as re-search, because, as a form of knowing, it asks the dreamer, just as the researcher who keeps soul in mind is asked, to let go of the ego's hold on things. We might say then that research as re-search is a way of dreaming a work with awareness. This does not mean that dreams are the content of one's research, though they might well be. Rather, it means that the dream's relation to the ego is a good analogue for the work's relation to the researcher. Indeed, it means that the dream has a place in a re-search method that would keep soul in mind. I will take up this issue in Chapter 11.

To follow a dream is, however, no easy task, nor is it easy to follow the track of the work when it invites us to let go of it. The gap between a dream and its enactment in life is often very wide, as was the seven-year time gap between the collapsing of the shelves and the completion of the book on grief. The grief book was a piece of re-search. It was the transformation of a wound into a work, a process that required a descent into the abyss, where the loss could be re-membered. The researcher whose work has collapsed and resists all efforts to restore it falls into such an abyss. It is the dark night of the work. It is the moment when loss becomes a descent into the as-yet undreamed possibilities in the work, a descent from the researcher's hold on the work to the soul of the work. It is a descent into the complexities of the claim that the work has made upon the researcher and a descent into that place where this complex claim might be dissolved and transformed into the unfinished business in the soul of the work.

The Third Moment: Descending into the Work/Mourning as Denial

Mourning, as I said above, is a tricky business because it requires of the one who grieves a loss a radical transformation of his or her relation to what has been lost. Mourning a loss can get sidetracked in a continuing refusal to let go of what has been lost, so that the one who grieves grieves for himself or herself, and in the process attempts to hold on to what was. The mourning of loss then becomes a process of denial of that loss and mourning encloses itself in rituals of repetition in place of re-membering. In this phase of mourning, one mourns, not the loss of the other, but rather, only what the other has meant to oneself; one mourns what he or she has lost of himself or herself.

The myth of Orpheus and Eurydice tells us that Orpheus descends into the underworld in pursuit of Eurydice. His intention is to persuade the gods to release her back into life, and, confident of his abilities as a poet, he thinks he can accomplish this feat through the use of his powers of song. Apparently, however, he is not willing to die with her. He is not willing to stay there in the underworld with her. Indeed, Plato criticizes Orpheus precisely on this point: his motives have more to do with his own loss and with his attempt to restore things to their former condition than they do with Eurydice. Orpheus wants a second chance. He wants to return to the life he and Eurydice had before her death. He wants things to be the way they were.

In this respect, Orpheus is still quite naïve, and perhaps even too much in awe of his own gifts. Naïve and perhaps too narcissistically involved in his own powers of song, he has not yet been transformed by his loss. The loss of Eurydice has not yet sunk in, and indeed he has not yet let her go. And so he does persuade Hades and Persephone to release Eurydice, and this sets the stage for his loss of her for a second time, a loss that will radically transform him, her, and the relation between them.

The myth of Orpheus and Eurydice lingers in the background of research as re-search, like the cosmic background radiation of the Big Bang that lingers in the story of the universe. For the researcher, there is a trace of this Orphic moment of descent when for a second time his or her hold upon the work is challenged. After one has initially lost a feel for the work, after one has initially lost his or her sense of it, one often responds by re-doubling one's efforts to keep the work on track, to bend it to one's will, to shape it, and shape it again, along its original lines. The sacrifice that the initial loss of the work invites is understandably resisted. One has put time and effort into the work. One has invested oneself in it and the proof of that investment sits there on one's desk, a piece of work that has been made. How can that be sacrificed, edited, torn apart, dismembered and re-membered? The researcher would not only save what has already been done, he or she would continue the work along the same lines. A kind of stubborn willfulness is still present, a stubborn resistance against surrendering to the deeper currents of the work.

One of my graduate students, Debbie Greenwood, provides a good example of this Orphic moment of research and of the phase of mourning as denial. Her work entitled, "Resting at the Crossroads: Working with Women's Narratives and Art-making,"[30] was a successful attempt to bring together her vocation as an artist and her vocation to her research on women's narratives. The tension between these two vocations formed the complex core of her work. Weighed down by the responsibility she felt to both of these vocations, she struggled to find a way to reconcile the two. Not unlike me in my own earlier description of how this work on research and my project on the Orpheus-Eurydice myth eventually found a shared place in my study, Debbie eventually made a space for art-making in the same office where she was writing her dissertation. In her research for her dissertation, she was asking her subjects to construct a narrative of their lives by re-membering themselves through the making of art, specifically the making of a book, and now she was enacting this same process. Spending some of her days making books or art, she found that her writing progressed more rapidly.

And yet something of an imbalance between her two vocations lingered. Was she an artist or a researcher? Claimed by her work on women's narratives through art-making, was she in her commitment to the research losing touch with herself as an artist? The tension surfaced over the issue of having to edit a particularly important piece of her dissertation. Advised by a friend who was familiar with her work that it had to be edited, she struggled one evening to cut out some parts of the work, to let go of them. But she could not do it. She could not sacrifice parts of the dissertation that she had worked so diligently to construct. It was her work, and she had to keep it as it was, even if the work itself was demanding a change. That night she vomited several times, and the following morning she knew that what she had so far written was too much and that she would have to edit it. So, "I worked," she said, "to find a way to say more with less." Reflecting on this struggle over editing, she came to realize that the struggle was the work's way of calling her to attend to it. The project itself, she concluded, was reminding her that the excess material was not there for its own sake, but rather to satisfy her need to defend herself against her fears that her work as a researcher might not be accepted as valid. The conflict over editing was a struggle between her presence to the work as an artist and her presence as a researcher. Making the work more than it needed to be in order to satisfy her own needs, she was denying what the work itself needed to be. Her struggles over the editing process were a way of denying the loss of her control over the work, a form of mourning as denial.

I should note that this process of mourning as denial, this attempt to avoid mourning her loss of the work and of her control over it continued to express itself symptomatically. Near the end of the dissertation process, Debbie developed a case of acute tendonitis in her right shoulder. Working within the transference dialogues (discussed in detail in Chapter 5), she discovered that in this instance the symptom was the work's way of reminding her not only to slow down, but also to acknowledge her limitations, in her words, in "integrating and holding the compelling stories and images that were entrusted to me." The enforced slowing down was, she said, "a boon I didn't want to recognize at the time." The slowing down forced her to realize that the work was integrating itself, even as she was struggling to integrate it on her terms.

In the descent into the work, in this Orphic moment of research, the body of the work is made through the researcher's embodied presence to the work, as numerous examples from my graduate students attest. Re-search that would keep soul in mind is a matter of the flesh and one is drawn into research as re-search not as a disembodied and dispassionate mind, but as a full flesh-and-blood human being. One has to have the heart and the guts for the work as well as a nose for the scent of its sense. Orpheus is drawn into the abyss, and though he at first still resists the necessity to let go of his Eurydice, the work of love and loss, which this myth celebrates, will have it otherwise. Orpheus will suffer the loss and be changed by it. His mourning will require not only his separation from Eurydice, but also his carnal dismemberment as the price of transformation that brings him, Eurydice, and their work of love and loss to completion. In the same way, the researcher who works with soul in mind is the work. He or she lives it as it is being done, suffers it and in the end is transformed by it. Working on the work, the researcher who keeps soul in mind is worked on and even worked over. Like being claimed by a work and suffering its loss, descending into a work is not just an idea about research. These processes are living moments in re-search, moments that are amplified by the Orpheus-Eurydice myth.

*The Fourth Moment: Looking Back at the Work/Mourning
as Separation*

In the Prologue to this book, I quoted a passage from the Roman
poet Virgil. It is appropriate to repeat it here:

> ... faciles descensus Averno:
> noctes atque dies patet atri ianua Ditis;
> sed revocare gradum superasque evadere ad auras,
> hoc opus, hic labor est.

> ... easy is the descent to Avernus:
> night and day the door of gloomy Dis stands open;
> but to recall one's steps and pass out to the upper air,
> this is the task, this is the toil.

Orpheus fails to find his way back with his Eurydice. Having
secured her release from the god and goddess of the underworld, he
disobeys their command not to look back. At the very moment when
he is about to achieve his purpose to restore himself and Eurydice to
their former life together, he turns to see if she is still following his
lead. Is it doubt that makes him turn? Perhaps! Fear? Perhaps! Or
perhaps, as Virgil describes it, it is some sudden frenzy, a moment of
delirious madness at the prospect of completion, an uncontrollable
passion. Whatever the motive, what is crucial here is that in his fatal
turn a second loss occurs.

Myths, like fairy tales and dreams, are particular in their repetition
of certain details, and so we must ask why this story repeats the loss.
Why a second loss? If we stay with the myth, then we know that
Orpheus was enacting a fate that was already imposed upon him by
the gods and goddesses. It seems, then, that this second loss is an event
of necessity, an event which in the end forces Orpheus to re-view
Eurydice through different eyes, through the eyes of his failed attempt
to restore his original view of her as his possession. What the powers
of the underworld know, that Orpheus does not, until this second loss
occurs, is that he *has to* look back so that in this transformative review of her he can see her again through the memory of his loss. In his
imaginal view of the mourning process, Mogenson says, "The meaning
of life is something we find through the mourning of life lost."[31] In
that backward glance, Orpheus loses Eurydice for a second time, and

in this second loss they are separated again as each goes his or her own separate way, she back into the underworld and he to journey on alone, more bereft than ever. Until that fateful turn when he loses her again, Orpheus does not know who Eurydice is in her own right, and thus he cannot mourn his loss of her.

Re-search that would keep the underworld of soul in mind requires this transformative backward glance when the work is freed into itself and freed from the researcher's narcissistic attachment to it. In this moment of glancing back, what is in question is the work as a means to some end for the researcher. Not unlike the parent who must eventually let go of his or her child as a means to some end for himself or herself, the researcher in this moment of the backward glance has to let go of the work as a means to his or her own ends. He or she is forced to separate his image of what end the work serves for him or her from the work in its own right.

A good example of this moment was given to me by a colleague and friend who had lost the sense of his book. The work had fallen into an abyss, and in his descent into the darkness of this abyss, he sought to retrieve it and restore it to its original form. But he had become mired down in his efforts to cast and recast the original chapters into some form that would repeat his original intentions for the work. Should he, therefore, merely shorten the chapters, many of which had become too long? Or should he draft a new outline and perhaps start again? Something of the core of the work seemed to be missing, something that would gather the work into another form. Since he had lost his sense of the book and was not willing to surrender to some other possibility for it, the work languished, and for all intents and purposes came to a halt.

But in this moment, after all efforts to redraft the original plan of the work have failed, when the work has come to a standstill, the work is also about to begin. For this colleague, the moment of his backward glance coincided with a piece of active imagination with the work in which he discovered the specific end for which his book was serving as a means. At the deepest root of his complex attachment to the work he discovered the inflated demands he had been unconsciously projecting onto the work. He was writing this book, he said, to save a neglected aspect of Jung's psychology as a means of saving himself from the attacks of a harsh internal critic, who constantly devalued his abilities. While his book and his talents were exceptional, his own moment of looking back at the work made it clear that the work could not go on until he was able to separate the book from his need for it to be a means to that end. When he did so, the work began again.

The moment of the backward glance is often not as dramatic or as clear as this one. Indeed, it is more often the case that this moment marks the lowest point in the research process, the moment when the work seems to be over. The irony, however, is that the work ends and begins again just at this moment, when all seems lost, when the work is no longer the ego's possession. The backward glance is, therefore, a pivotal moment, the moment when the work turns, when it turns away from the researcher, like Eurydice turning away from Orpheus, and re-turns to itself, like Eurydice returning to the underworld. Now the researcher is no longer in charge, no longer in the lead, commanding the work. Rather, he or she is being led by the work. This pivotal moment is a shift from the original claim that the work made upon the researcher via his or her complex, from that original moment when the researcher was abducted by the work, through the first sense of its loss, to this moment when the work itself takes the lead. It is a shift in the research process from being the author of the work to becoming an agent in service to the work. One student described this moment as a change of tune, a change that required a reversal of who was leading the dance and who was following the lead.

The image of the blindfolded alchemist being led into the mountain of the adepts is an apt image for this moment. Commenting on this image, Marie-Louise von Franz says, "The blindfolded man represents the stumbling search for truth."[32] Until the researcher is forced to regard the work on its terms and to let go of it as a means to some end for himself or herself, he or she is like this blindfolded man. The researcher sees the work only on his or her terms and is blind to what the work is in itself, blind to that unfinished business in the soul of the work. Before this turn that turns the researcher toward the work and returns the work to itself, the researcher stumbles forward, and what looks like clarity in the research process is, from the point of view of the work, on its terms a sign that the researcher has not let go of the work. The moments of the descent and the backward glance that follow it are a blinding. They are moments when clarity of mind yields to the dark-light of the work and the blinded researcher begins to follow its lead. In the illustration in which this blindfolded alchemist appears, there is also another figure, who is following an animal into the mountain of the adepts. According to von Franz, this figure represents a way into knowing that follows the natural instincts. For the researcher who would keep soul in mind, the backward glance is an invitation to follow the soul of the work. But to do so is no easy task. Indeed, it requires that change of tune, which is a kind of dismemberment of one's familiar and comfortable style.

The Fifth Moment: Dismembered by the Work/Mourning as Transformation

After his descent into the otherness of the underworld and his failure to bend the forces of that world to his will, Orpheus is changed. Orpheus now sees life through the eyes of death, through the eyes of loss, and in remembering that loss he has let go of his original claim to return Eurydice to the upper world, where he once was in possession of his gifts and of her.

The myth tells us, however, that this transformation is radical. Orpheus's mourning following the second loss tears him apart. He is dismembered. But the myth also tells us that this dismemberment is the condition of his transformation. In Ovid's telling of the story, Orpheus and Eurydice are reunited in the underworld of shades, in the world of the image, in the imagination of the soul. And in this transformed state it is sometimes Orpheus who leads the way and no longer has any need to look back, and sometimes it is Eurydice, and sometimes they walk together side by side. What the image suggests is that Eurydice was lost to Orpheus, but also not lost. Indeed, the image tells us something more. It tells us that truly letting go of someone or something is the way to find what has been lost, to be with it beyond the need to possess or control it. "By becoming absent," Mogenson writes, "an object becomes wholly psychological."[33] In losing each other and suffering the loss, Orpheus and Eurydice experience mourning as a creative act of transformation in which each is freed into his or her own destiny. For Rilke, it is because Orpheus is dismembered that he is re-membered and hence remembered. "O you lost god! / You unending trace! / Only because at last enmity rent and scattered you / are we now the hearers and a mouth of Nature."[34]

Orpheus still sings, his voice still echoes through us, who do not forget him. And regarding Eurydice, it is her question "*Who?*" in response to the god Hermes informing her that Orpheus has turned that releases her from his grasp. I will say more on her question in the next section, when I consider the sixth Orphic moment.

In the art of doing re-search with soul in mind, the work begins to come into its own and becomes wholly psychological with the dismemberment of the researcher, who has let go of the work. Working on the work, the researcher is also worked on and perhaps even worked over, and the work, which, from the ego's point of view, has been lost, is now, from the soul's point of view, in the process of being found.

Unable to hold on to the work and dismembered by it, the researcher who lets go of the work begins to imagine it in a different way, from *its* point of view, beyond his or her possession of it. He or she, we might say, begins to see it with underworld eyes as he or she begins to attend to the unfinished business in the soul of the work. Through the process of dismemberment, the researcher's initial complex relation to the work is transformed. The complex wound becomes a work and in this transformation the researcher finally becomes a witness and spokesperson, not for himself or herself, but for what has been left unspoken, unsaid, neglected, marginalized, or otherwise forgotten. The work is no longer about the researcher. It is about the weight of history in the work that has been waiting for its voice.

In this sense, research as re-search is truly a work of an-amnesis, a work of un-forgetting, a work against forgetting, and as such the work that is made from the wound becomes a cultural-historical therapeutics. Mogenson notes, "The mourning of losses and the making of culture are synonymous activities."[35] The wounded researcher, the researcher who has been dismembered by the work, knows this connection between mourning what he or she has let go of and the art of creating a work. He or she has lent himself or herself to the work, and by letting go of it and mourning that loss, he or she has continued the work of soul in culture.

Research as re-search has, therefore, a different orientation. As a work of mourning, its first direction is not forward into new areas of knowledge. Rather, its first move is backwards, towards what has been lost, forgotten, or left behind. As a work of mourning, research as research is a work of anamnesis, which advances by remembering. It moves forward by stepping backwards to regard, recover, redeem, and renew what has been left behind, and in this orientation it opens a space for a new beginning. Re-search with soul in mind thus transforms what we uncritically take for granted by returning to origins for the sake of an *other* beginning.

A fine example of this fifth Orphic moment in re-search is present in the work of one of my graduate students, Johanna Treichler. Her dissertation is entitled "Walk Your Own Walk," and the initial core complex that drew her into the work was her experience of her brother's paralysis.[36] In response to one of the questions I asked her, just as I have asked all the students who have worked with me to keep soul in mind in their dissertations, she noted that this initial core complex had to be dismembered in order to get to the soul of the work, to what in the work wanted still to speak beyond her own designs upon it. My question to her was about how, in becoming more conscious of the complex vocation that drew her into the work, she, and the way she did the work, had changed. Here is her reply:

> For me the question should really be: How hard was it to identify or pinpoint the vocational aspect? Even though I was following the original vocational call of "walking my own walk," there were layers and layers of material to be sorted out through the alchemical process of *separation.* It took five more years of analysis, active imagination, dialogue, painting, writing, walking, and grieving to finally identify the core complex of the unacknowledged, and unappreciated feminine, that wanted to be seen and honored through my work. What seemed to be a manageable complex turned into a major life-review for me and my Swiss female ancestors. Yes, this final discovery was most helpful. Even though I seemed to walk my walk, for too long I could not make sense of where I was going, as I was circumambulating the core complex of the call. Many of my ancestral relatives must have felt "walked on." ... Once I made the connection, acknowledged my core calling, the mental fog lifted. I am now able to ... walk my own walk on a deeper level.

Her statement is actually a summary of many of the Orphic moments: being claimed by the work through the initial personal wound of her brother's paralysis; losing that sense of the work as multiple layers beneath that personal complex began to open up; going through the process of descent and separating out what belonged to her complex and what belonged to the work; and arriving at that transformation in which what at first seemed manageable turned out to be a major life-review, which was nothing short of a dismemberment. Beyond the summary, however, what stands out in her statement is how, through these various moments, her ability to let go of the work as she had imagined it, the ability to allow herself to be dismembered by what the work wanted, enabled the unfinished business in the soul of the work to speak. The personal complex wound of her brother's paralysis, which is what initially drew her into the work, was the portal through which the ancestors for whom the work was being done could enter the work and speak. It is these ancestors for whom the work was being done, that unacknowledged and unappreciated legion of her Swiss female forebears who could not walk their own walk, who wanted to be seen and honored through her work. In the end, then, a dissertation about walking one's own walk, which began with the memory of a brother in a wheelchair, became a march or parade of sorts, a march whose purpose was to remember those who have been left behind. It has been a work of un-forgetting, a work of anamnesis, and, as such, a piece of cultural therapy.

The Sixth Moment: The Eurydician Question: Mourning as Individuation

> Who's turned us round like this, so that we always,
> do what we may, retain the attitude
> of someone who's departing? Just as he,
> on the last hill, that shows him all his valley
> for the last time, will turn and stop and linger,
> we live our lives, for ever taking leave.[37]

This is the image with which Rilke ends the eighth Duino Elegy. It is, perhaps like all images are, both existential and archetypal. We are all like that singular figure of the one who in the gesture of the backward glance lingers for a moment before departing. In such moments of letting go, we cannot, try as we might, take with us what is left behind. Or, to be more accurate here, we can take what we leave behind only insofar as it is transformed, and in this, the backward glance of the one on the hill, is the completion of the backward glance of Orpheus. The backward glance that would hold on to what is being left behind becomes a gesture of release, a way of mourning what is left behind by carrying it in the imagination. Mourning, here, is a creative process that frees the one who mourns as well as the one or thing that is mourned from their claims upon each other. Thus, mourning is an act of individuation in which the one who leaves and the one that is left behind both come into their new virginity.

A strange word, this word "virginity," to use here to describe this sixth Orphic moment of re-search, but a fitting one because it is the word that belongs to Eurydice in that moment when she is freed of Orpheus's possession of her. Recall her response to Hermes when he tells her that Orpheus has turned. It is the question "*Who?*" With that question Rilke confirms that in her death "[s]he had come into a new virginity."[38]

This Eurydician question stands also at the end of re-search. In the beginning of re-search, the researcher has been claimed by the work and in the end he or she is addressed by the work with this question, which invites him or her to let go of the claims that he or she has made upon the work, even the claims of authorship and ownership. Of course, in a nominal sense one *is* the author of the work, but in an archetypal sense one has been merely an agent for the work that has come through one but is not about one, and in this respect Eurydice is the one who reclaims the soul of the work , the one who returns the work to itself. One no more possesses, at the end of the work, what has been made than one did at the beginning. Indeed, a work that begins as a vocation ends with the recognition that to be claimed by a work is to be in its service and that in the end we have to let go of it again, but this time with awareness that we never really possessed it. Research as re-search has been a journey of companions whose ending is a mutual farewell, not unlike that farewell that Ovid has pass between Orpheus and Eurydice before they are reunited in the land of images, as the researcher and the work are in the place of the imagination. Freed from the researcher, from the time-bound world of his or her claims and needs, like Eurydice freed from Orpheus, the work enters the realm of the living imagination, the timeless realm of soul, where nothing is ever lost until it is no longer re-membered, and where the work waits again with the weight of its history of unfinished business, waits for what remains unsaid to be spoken by another who will be called into the work.

So many of my students have described this moment of the ending of the work in this way, as a bittersweet moment of deep mourning, a strange mix of joy and sorrow at the recognition that having been in service to something other than themselves, they are now, as the work takes leave of them, released back into their own lives, perhaps to await another summons. This is, perhaps, the archetypal root of that depression that often follows creative work, and perhaps, in recognizing that in all creative work we are from beginning to end in service to the unfinished business of soul, the leadenness of depression is transmuted into the gold of the bittersweet mourning of this Orphic moment.

Writing of the relation between mourning and the creative process, Greg Mogenson makes the following point:

> The dark impulses which guide creative work are of a kind with the impulses that compel the work of mourning. Just like the writer or artist who sits down to work without knowing in advance exactly what his labors will give birth to, we mourn in suspense of the autonomy of the image. A thought upon waking scribbled into a dream-journal, a fragment of a remembered conversation, a feeling of dread in the pit of the stomach: any of these experiences may be recognized as a call away from life, a call from the beyond. But if we are to find the pattern in the collage of our grief we must actually make the collage.[39]

Yes, we must actually do the work that summons us from a place beyond ourselves, and in the end we must let it go back to that place as we are called back into life. This is the archetypal rhythm of an imaginal approach to re-search that keeps soul in mind, a pulse that finally, at the end of the work, registers the difference between what has been said in the work and the soul of the work that remains unsaid.

CHAPTER THREE

An Imaginal Approach to Re-search

Countless millions crowd the depths of the psyche waiting for
the imagination to give them wings. [1]
—Greg Mogenson

INTRODUCTION

This book is an exercise in imaginal psychology. Specifically, it
offers an imaginal approach to psychological research. The term
imaginal was coined by Henri Corbin to differentiate a region
of reality that is intermediate between sense and intellect and that
mediates between them. Quoting Corbin, the literary critic Harold
Bloom writes in the Preface to one of Corbin's major works, "… [T]he
imaginal world is by its essence the intermediate world, and the
articulation between the intellectual and the sensible, in which the
Active Imagination as *imaginatio vera* is an organ of understanding
mediating between intellect and sense and as legitimate as these latter
and that world itself."[2] In Jung's work and in the work of James
Hillman, this intermediate world is the world of soul, which has its
own ontological status as a domain of reality between the domains of
matter and mind. Referring to psychology, Hillman says, for example,
"We have lost the third, middle position which earlier in our tradition
and others too, was the place of soul."[3] As this middle term, soul is
neither a matter of fact nor an idea of mind, although it lends itself in
our psychological traditions to being measured as a fact or
conceptualized within a system of ideas. Soul is in our psychologies

CORBIN'S MUNDUS IMAGINALIS
& JUNG AND HILLMAN

because all our psychologies are within soul. Each of our psychological traditions is a perspective on soul, and since a perspective never gives us a complete picture, there is always a gap between what a psychological tradition says of soul and what soul is. Moreover, insofar as a perspective identifies its point of view with the totality of what is, it functions as an unconscious complex within a tradition. Thus, I argued in Chapter 1 that psychology has a complex about soul. Each complex perspective of psychology reveals something of soul and conceals something of it. What is concealed remains as the unfinished business of soul in all psychological work.

Greg Mogenson has applied an imaginal approach to the mourning process, and in this work I am applying an imaginal approach to a process of re-search that would keep soul in mind.[4] With respect to research, my argument is that the completion of a work by a researcher is not the end of the work. Something of the unfinished business of the soul in the work lingers, and it is attention to this unfinished business that characterizes an imaginal approach to research. In the next chapter I will describe how this unfinished business makes its claim upon a researcher through his or her complexes. Research, then, is a vocation, and within an imaginal approach, the researcher is called into a work so that what lingers in the work as a piece of unfinished business can work itself out through the work. The issue here is not what the researcher wants from the work so much as it is what the work wants from him or her. An imaginal approach is a shift from an ego perspective on research to the soul's perspective. Within this approach to research, a researcher is in service to something other than himself or herself.

This shift lends a tone of mourning to the research process, since the ego is called upon to let go of its hold upon the work. In the Introduction I said that the mood of mourning threads itself throughout this work and that it belongs to what I called a poetics of the research process. In the poetics of the research process, mourning is a natural activity of soul, an activity in which the ego is not the center of the work. An imaginal approach to research is a poetics of the research process in which the researcher has to "die" to the work so that the unfinished business in the soul of the work can speak.

Mourning was also central to Chapter 2 in the discussion of the Orpheus-Eurydice myth. In that chapter I argued that this myth is the archetypal background for an approach to re-search that would keep soul in mind. Since an imaginal approach is one that keeps soul in mind, this myth is the archetypal background for this approach. Within the context of this myth, the imaginal approach to research is about finding the unfinished business in the soul of a work by letting go of one's hold upon the work.

RE-SEARCH AS UNFINISHED BUSINESS

In the previous chapter I showed how Virgil's version of the Orpheus-Eurydice myth unfolds within the larger story of Aristaeus, the bee keeper. Within the context of this myth, which is the archetypal background for an imaginal approach to research, to do re-search with soul in mind is to be attuned to the fact that in one's work one is already being claimed by an-other story, that one's work is already situated within a larger pattern, and that in one's work, one is in service to something other than oneself. Within an imaginal approach, that larger tale to which one is in service is the unfinished business in the soul of the work, which makes its claims upon a researcher through his or her complexes for the sake of continuing that work. This unfinished business in the soul of the work lingers, for a complex researcher, within the shadows of culture as the weight of history. It lingers as a weight that waits for its voice to be heard. Within an imaginal approach, a researcher has to undergo, like Orpheus, a process of dismemberment, a kind of death in relation to the work, which is a letting go of his or her egoic position in relation to the work, a surrendering of his or her claims upon it. To be in service to the unfinished business in the soul of the work, to come to know the ways of the soul in the work, is for the ego to die to its claims upon the work, its possession of it. It is for the ego the ordeal of letting go of the work, even to the point that at the end of the work, when in that moment of looking back at it the researcher is faced with the Eurydician question, "Who?," he or she realizes that all along the path of the work he or she has been the agent for, and not the author of, the work.

Jung's psychology is a clear example of an imaginal approach to the soul. The depth of his scholarship and the range of his reflections rest upon an Orphic gesture, a variation of a backward glance that functions as a kind of style or attitude for re-searching the ways of soul. We saw in the last chapter that the tower at Bollingen is the ecological context for his work, the place where his psychology is nurtured in the soil of the ancestors for whom his work is done, and in the present context, it is worthwhile to return to that tower for a moment to listen more fully to what he says.

> In the Tower at Bollingen, it is as if one lived in many centuries simultaneously. The place will outlive me, and, in its location and style, it points backward to things of long ago. There is very little about it to suggest the present. If a man of the sixteenth century were to move into the house, only the kerosene lamp and the matches would be new to him; otherwise, he would know his way about without difficulty. There is nothing to disturb the dead, neither electric light nor telephone. Moreover, my ancestors' souls are sustained the atmosphere of the house, since I answer for them the questions that their lives once left behind. I carve out rough answers as best I can. I have even drawn them on the walls. It is as if a silent, greater family, stretching down the centuries, were peopling the house.[5]

Jung's backward glance here, we might say, is a maturing of the Orphic gesture, a ripening of it. Everything except the lamp and the matches point backward, and, in the ambience of such things, Jung returns to the past, not for the sake of repeating or holding on to it, but for the sake of attending to it. The mood of that place and Jung's attunement to it describe a moment of re-collection and re-cognition, a moment of realization and release, a moment of transformation and surrender. What Jung is saying here is that his work is and has been situated within an-other story, within a larger story. If we regard his tower as an image and symbol of who Jung was and how he worked, if we regard his description of that landscape as a way of describing himself and his way of working, then what we are being told is that Jung and his psychology have been in service to something other than himself. There is in his description a surrender of the egoic position that would claim ownership of the work. There is in his description a recognition that he and his thoughts have been in service to those questions of the ancestors left behind and unanswered. There is in his description a deeply felt sense that he and his work have been in service to the unfinished business of the ancestors. Indeed, in his autobiography, Jung describes the audience for his work as consisting of the "Unanswered, Unresolved and Unredeemed."[6]

This attunement and devotion to the unfinished business of the ancestors in one's work is a key aspect of an imaginal approach to research. By ancestors I do not mean, nor do I think Jung means, only the personal ancestral line that lies in the work. The ancestors are that silent, greater family that stretches down the centuries. They are the weight of history that lingers as a shadow in the margins of our individual and collective thoughts and dreams, the weight of unanswered questions that wait to be addressed. This is what an imaginal approach to re-search attends to, this unfinished business in the soul of one's work.

But to do re-search in this imaginal way, one has to put oneself in that kind of mood and ambience that Jung describes. One has to attune oneself and be responsive to what lingers and haunts the present in this way. One has to have, so to speak, an eye for the invisible in the visible, or that third ear that is sensitive to the whispers of those unanswered questions that make their appeal to us. Jung indicates as much when he says, "We are very far from having finished completely with the Middle Ages, classical antiquity, and primitivity, as our modern psyches pretend." Continuing along this line, he adds, "The less we understand of what our fathers and forefathers sought, the less we understand ourselves," and, contrasting what he calls "Reforms by advances" with "Reforms by retrogressions," he reflects on the spirit with which he has written his autobiography, this backward glance of re-collecting who he has been and what he has done:

> In this book, I have devoted considerable space to my subjective view of the world, which, however, is not a product of rational thinking. It is rather a vision such as will come to one who undertakes, deliberately, with half-closed eyes and somewhat closed ears, to see and hear the form and voice of being. If our impressions are too distinct, we are held to the hour and minute of the present and have no way of knowing how our ancestral psyches listen to and understand the present—in other words how our unconscious is responding to it. ... Inner peace and contentment depend in large measure upon whether or not the historical family which is inherent in the individual can be harmonized with the ephemeral conditions of the present.[7]

One does not necessarily have to subscribe to Jung's notion of a collective unconscious to appreciate what he is saying here. One has only to acknowledge that we are historical beings and that time, as we live it, is neither a line nor a measure but always a present moment that is haunted by the living horizons of a past and a future. In every present moment, we live in the light and the shadows of a past, which we re-member in the context of a future we imagine and dream. What we want to become shapes what and how we re-member what we have been. The other side of the coin is also true. How we re-collect the past informs how we imagine the future. In other words, the past re-membered comes to us through the future imagined, just as the future imagined re-collects the past.

Attending to the unanswered questions of the ancestors, then, is essential to the ongoing activity of a human life, and an imaginal approach to re-search serves this activity. In the unfinished business of history, the researcher finds the progress in his or her work. An imaginal approach to research that works towards re-collecting what has been left behind in order to continue the work is fundamentally different from an empirical approach to research with its emphasis on prediction and control. The former moves into the future through the past, while the latter moves from the present into the future. This difference is not a judgment about which is more true or valid. Rather, important in itself as difference, it arises when one makes a place for the movement of soul in research, which, as Jung points out, is a matter of "reforms by retrogressions." In this way, a researcher who attends to the business of what has been left behind adds to the progression of human knowledge. He or she, Jung notes, begins to see and hear the form and voice of being, which we might rephrase by saying the form and voice of the unfinished business that lingers in the soul of the work and that presents itself to one who undertakes this work with half-closed eyes.

But what are we to make of this curious phrase about half-closed eyes and the injunction against being too distinct in our impressions of the present moment? I would suggest that this way of putting things is a way of describing an attitude of reverie, a way of dreaming the world with one's eyes "wide shut." In the Introduction I indicated that the question of reverie as a legitimate way of knowing the ways of soul was an important question in this book, and now I am saying that it is vitally important to an imaginal approach to re-search. Reverie is the mood of the poetics of the research process, and, as such, it is a paradoxical way of knowing the world, whose mood is neither oneiric nor rational. In reverie, we are in that middle place between waking and dreaming, and, in that landscape, the borders and edges of a work become less rigid and distinct. They melt somewhat, and the work becomes a porous membrane through which the ancestors might slip into the work, just as the Man Made of Rain, as we saw in Chapter 1, slipped into the gap between the language of the day and that of the night for the poet Brendan Kennelly. In reverie, the work takes on a symbolic character and is freed of its literal and factual density. The work becomes many-layered and is laden with numerous meanings, which require interpretation. It is laden with possibilities, which require understanding.

Where there is a symbol, there is a need for interpretation, and, in this respect, an imaginal approach to re-search that would attend to the unfinished business of the ancestors in the work is a hermeneutical science and not an empirical one. Or, to put this in more precise terms, there is an aspect of psychology and psychological research that requires a hermeneutics of understanding rather than an empirics of explanation. In Chapters 10 and 11 I will describe in detail a specific style of hermeneutics that has arisen alongside an imaginal approach to re-search, and so for the moment I will limit myself to two remarks. First, the hermeneutic method of an imaginal approach is about anamnesis, and this approach returns to its archetypal roots in the Orphic myth. As we saw in Chapter 2, Orpheus is the poet of un-forgetting, and, because of this ability, he is the one poet whom Plato allows to return to the soul of the city. The imaginal approach to research is about the re-collection of what has been forgotten, left behind, neglected, marginalized, and unfinished, and, for this reason, it has a place in the city of the soul. In addition, the gesture of this imaginal approach is the backward glance, which Jung adopts in the ambience of his tower. It is the gesture or style of working that returns one to what still calls out to be done and re-members what has been forgotten for the sake of a new beginning. Second, an imaginal approach to re-search complements an empirical approach—it does not replace it. It stands alongside the empirical approach to psychology and research and is entitled to that place.

If Jung's psychology offers an example of an imaginal approach to psychological work, so too does phenomenology. Although it is true that phenomenology has won a place within the science of psychology, that place has largely been for its qualitative methodologies. Nearly forty years ago now, Amedeo Giorgi published his groundbreaking book, *Psychology as a Human Science*, which laid the foundation for phenomenologically-based research methods, and over the years he, as well as the psychology department at Duquesne University, have honed those methods.[8] However, as valuable as these contributions have been for bringing phenomenology into psychological research, they sacrifice the broader scope of phenomenology and thus mute its impact for a psychological science. Thus, it is not this path of phenomenology as method that I am following here. Rather, I am concerned with how, as Merleau-Ponty says in the Preface to his seminal work, *The Phenomenology of Perception*, phenomenology is first a style of thinking and being, before it is a system of philosophy or, we might add, a methodology.[9]

That style of thinking and being is an attitude that situates one between the two extremes of subjectivism and objectivism. For a phenomenologist, the world that we perceive and as we perceive it is not already an object complete in itself waiting for its laws to be discovered and explained by a conscious subject who is apart from it and not a part of it, a subject who floats, as it were, above or beyond the world, like some disembodied spectator mind. On the contrary, phenomenology begins with our entanglement with the perceptual world, the world that makes sense as we sense it. From this starting point, the task of thinking and knowing "consists in re-learning to look at the world." It is a work that invites one "to take up this unfinished world in an effort to complete and conceive it."[10] In his reflections on Merleau-Ponty's work, therefore, John Sallis aptly describes phenomenology as a return to beginnings.[11] As we re-learn to look at the world again, phenomenology becomes a work of re-turning with regard to the world in which we are enmeshed for the sake of coming to know with awareness those bonds that tie us to existence. We might say that phenomenology is a kind of homecoming, a return to what we already know without knowing that we know it. Between those extremes of subjectivism and objectivism, phenomenology is the work of mind finding that mind matters, that thinking is an embodied act, and that the body is a pre-reflective mindfulness of the world.

Sallis, however, makes it quite clear that phenomenology as a return to beginnings is always a project. The thought that returns to its beginnings in the perceptual world is not the same thought that has it beginnings in the perceptual world. Because it takes an act of thinking to find that thinking has its foundation in perceptual life, the beginnings to which thinking returns are not secured and fixed. The very work of phenomenology, therefore, circles back on itself. It is a way of working that perpetually returns to itself. If phenomenology is a work of homecoming, then the home to which it returns is made in the very acts of returning. For the phenomenologist, origins are a destiny. The phenomenologist, as Merleau-Ponty notes, is a "perpetual beginner."[12]

As a return to beginnings, then, phenomenology is essentially about attending not only to the unfinished business of knowing the world, but also to business that is always unfinished. Phenomenology is a work that is an *opus contra naturam*, a work that works against what phenomenology calls the natural attitude, which would take the world as something already finished in itself and would regard our ideologies about the world as established truths. In this process, the major task of the phenomenologist is to loosen the grip of our preconceived and taken-for-granted ideologies, whatever form they take—be they political, economic, scientific, philosophical, or psychological. This theme runs throughout the work of the phenomenological psychologist, Erwin Strauss. For him, the perpetual task of phenomenology is to unravel the unwritten constitution of everyday life.[13] Hence, I would argue that the phenomenologist works under the spell of Orpheus, because, like Orpheus, this work of return is a work of an-amnesis, a work that, in unraveling the unwritten constitution of everyday life, is one of un-forgetting. Indeed, one of the descriptions of Orpheus is that of the loosener, the one who frees us from the mimetic life of repetition and forgetfulness. Orpheus awakens the soul to what it has forgotten, and the phenomenologist as one who returns us to beginnings does the same. Here, phenomenology and Jungian psychology converge.

At the end of his book, Sallis notes that this return to beginnings, to what Jung calls the unanswered questions left to us by the ancestors and what we might call the unspoken and unfinished business that lingers within our traditions, is a circling around the beginnings. This circling, he says, is the holding of a sustained tension between the two beginnings, the beginnings that are an origin and the beginnings that are made again in the return. There is a difference that separates these two beginnings, and the philosopher, the lover of wisdom who practices phenomenology, situates himself or herself and is situated in "the strife of the difference." Referring to philosophy, he says, "One of the names that the tradition has given to the power of persisting in that strife is imagination." As the final statement in his book, he writes: "The question is whether there can be a philosophy of imagination which is not also a philosophy of the *cogito*."[14] In other words, can there be a legitimate way of thinking that holds the tension between thinking and imagining?

An imaginal approach to research affirms not only that this task is possible, it also indicates that it is necessary. In the Introduction to this book, I cited the necessity for a poetics of the research process to complement the empirics of that process. If we take phenomenology as one foundation of psychological work, then a poetics of research that is grounded in a way of thinking that opens itself to the imagination is essential. An imaginal approach that seeks to respond to the unfinished business in the work is a return to a *cogito*, to a way of thinking that is able to imagine those still unanswered questions that are left to us by those who have come before us and who have spoken before us. To linger in the shadow of the beginning, in the shadow of those unanswered questions that haunt one's work and by which one is claimed, is to re-imagine those beginnings as an-other possibility.

J. H. van den Berg is one of those individuals whose work exemplifies this movement of phenomenology as a return to beginnings. He calls his work *metabletics,* a theory of changes, and in numerous books he has demonstrated how changes in humanity's psychological life are mirrored through changes in the cultural-historical milieu. Van den Berg's metabletics is an argument against the immutable character of psychological life and the natural world, and a defense of differences. Thus, for example, van den Berg argues that people who lived in the Middle Ages not only lived a different existence, but also lived within a world where matter itself was different. However, because we believe in what he calls the principle of constancy, according to which, for example, the way matter is now is the way it has always been, we soon forget the difference. The consequence is that we fall into regarding the way we are now and the way the world is as a natural fact, when in fact who and how we are now and the way the world is is the outcome of a cultural and historical transformation in the human psyche.

The issue of the nature of matter offers a clear example of van den Berg's approach. In an article entitled "Phenomenology and Metabletics," van den Berg raises some intriguing questions about the the 20th-century splitting of the atom, whose power was made visible for all to see with the detonation of the atomic bomb in 1945. Noting that "[n]othing of the kind had ever been accomplished before, for the simple reason that no one had ever been able to release nuclear forces," he asks if that was in fact the only reason. He acknowledges, of course, that the physicists brought about nuclear fission, but again he wonders if that is the complete and sufficient explanation. The principle of mutability, which lies at the heart of his metabletics and which says that psychological life and the nature of the world change and do so together, opens these provocative questions: "Why should not matter itself ... 'have known how to bring it [nuclear fission] about?'" He goes on to ask, "Is it really so certain that medieval matter would have allowed this artifice?"[15] In response to these disturbing questions, van den Berg says that medieval matter would have allowed it if the 'physicist" of that time had had at his or her disposal the theory and the apparatus of the physicists of the 20th century.

But with this reply, is van den Berg finished? Is it only that the "physicists" of the medieval world knew less than we do today, that they were simply ignorant of the true facts about the nuclear nature of matter? If this was all that van den Berg was saying, his metabletics would be only another argument for progress situated within an immutable world, within a world whose laws have always been what they are and are simply waiting for the advancement of knowledge. Van den Berg, however, is arguing for something much more radical here.

Returning to his question, van den Berg wonders about the achievement of nuclear fission in our time. "But who is to say," he asks, "that the theory and the mechanical requisites do not belong to a realm of efforts which have been made possible by a different sort of matter, a matter which was new, which was modern?" If the theories and equipment had been available in the medieval world, then matter would have split because it would have already been the matter of today. Van den Berg makes this point in the following way: "Conveying the mechanical contrivances to the Middle Ages would then imply changing medieval matter, whereupon it would be reasonable to assume that the atomic bomb could also have been invented in the Middle Ages."[16]

But, of course, nuclear fission was not accomplished in the Middle Ages because medieval matter is not modern matter. This is van den Berg's point. Medieval matter mattered in a different way. It was a different matter. Although van den Berg would not use these terms, I would argue that his metabletics is an example of how an imaginal approach as a return to beginnings is about attending to the unfinished business in the soul of the work. In this example, the unfinished business of modern physics is about the psychology of matter; it is the unfinished business in the soul of matter left over from the medieval world. For an imaginal approach to the psychology of matter, this leftover business, which has come to fruition in the nuclearization of matter, most horribly expressed in nuclear weapons, raises some interesting questions. One question might be what is it that matter is asking of us in this process? Another question, perhaps more disturbing in its implications, might be what the creation of weapons of mass destruction says about how we have responded to what matter has been asking of us?

Jung, as we saw, also commented on the Middle Ages, and in his remarks he noted that we are not done with that period. Its history lingers in our souls as so many yet-to-be-answered questions. To appreciate both Jung and van den Berg, one has to get beyond the temptation to project onto the past one's present view of things. Thus, van den Berg considers if his argument is refuted by the nuclear explosions that fire the stars and are comparable to the nuclear explosion of our atomic weapons. "One is inclined," he admits, "to presume that in the Middle Ages the same explosions took place."[17] But again, he points out that we have regarded the celestial realm in this fashion only in modern times, in that same time frame when matter itself became so explosive. This is in fact not so surprising. It really only indicates the subtle connections between above and below. When the stars become nuclear furnaces, the Earth begins to matter in a different way than it did before, just as when the Earth begins to matter in a modern way, the stars of heaven become the nuclear furnaces of the cosmos. We should note here the difference and not disregard it. The sky of heaven is not the same thing as the cosmic sky of exploding stars. For the man and woman of the medieval world, heaven was above them, and to die was to be taken up to that place. Well, heaven is no longer above us, and it cannot be, because then to die would be to go into a nuclear night, a fate that seems unthinkable. My point here is that when earth and sky matter in a modern way, heaven and the angels who have dwelt there have to lose their place.[18]

To re-iterate this last point, the stars of the medieval sky were not nuclear furnaces, nor, for that matter, was the star that guided the wise men to Bethlehem a nuclear matter. What risks do we run if we disregard this difference? "Is it permissible," van den Berg asks, "to transport to the past the scientific knowledge of the present?" If we do, are we not saying that the people of the Middle Ages lived in a false world? He goes on to ask, "Is it permissible—without any reservation, without even a question—to presume that this knowledge is valid also in the past which was not able to bring this knowledge forth?" Not able to bring this knowledge forth because such knowledge belongs to a different world, because it matters in a different way. Van den Berg says, "Nothing justifies this transportation other than the unjustified and unjustifiable principle of constancy" according to which "matter is immutable and remains constant through all ages."[19]

What risks do we run if we transport what and how we know the world and ourselves today back in time? We risk not only not knowing ourselves but also not knowing the ancestors who have bequeathed to us their unfinished business. They become merely pale copies of us. Moreover, in erasing the differences between us and the past, in making the past one unbroken line of progress towards us and who and what we have become, we risk being dismissed in the same way by those whom we are already dreaming. Concerning our modern knowledge of the stars in relation to the medieval stars, van den Berg says, "Yet, if we open a book written during that period, no mention whatever is made of such happenings. One can read other stories about the stars, and these stories must after all be taken seriously, if ever we expect future generations to take us and our words seriously."[20] In our presence to the world and the ways in which we know it, we belong to that same silent, greater family, stretching down the centuries that Jung has described, a line that stretches in both directions. And, in that procession, we are in service to the unfinished business of those who precede us as we will one day be the ancestors whose questions are still to be answered by those who follow. We can only hope, therefore, that they who come after us will remember us and in so doing imagine forward what we have left behind.

The two examples of Jung's psychology and van den Berg's phenomenology as illustrations of an imaginal approach to psychological research suggest that this approach has significant implications for our cultural existence. What we naïvely take for granted as the natural character of our present cultural moment has at its depths the unfinished business of those who have gone before us and whose presence lingers as those unanswered questions in our work. When one attends to this unfinished business, one's work becomes a moment in an ongoing cultural-historical therapeutics. To make this point another way, under the spell of Orpheus, phenomenology and Jungian psychology re-imagine our idea of progress in research. Progress in knowledge coincides with the ongoing task of making the collective unconscious of humanity more conscious.[21]

Jung attests to the therapeutic aspect of research, when it is indeed in service to the unfinished business of culture and history, in the following passage from his autobiography:

> When I was working on the stone tablets, I became aware of the fateful links between me and my ancestors. I feel very strongly that I am under the influence of things or questions which were left incomplete and unanswered by my parents and grandparents and more distant ancestors. It often seems as if there were an impersonal karma within a family, which is passed on from parents to children. It has always seemed to me that I had to answer questions which fate had posed to my forefathers, and which had not yet been answered, or as if I had to complete, or perhaps continue, things which previous ages had left unfinished. It is difficult to determine whether these questions are more of a personal or more of a general [collective] nature. It seems to me that the latter is the case. A collective problem, if not recognized as such, always appears as a personal problem, and in individual cases may give the impression that something is out of order in

the realm of the personal psyche. The personal sphere is indeed disturbed, but such disturbances need not be primary; they may well be secondary, the consequence of an insupportable change in the social atmosphere. The cause of disturbance is, therefore, not to be sought in the personal surroundings, but rather in the collective situation. Psychotherapy has hitherto taken this matter far too little into account.[22]

What Jung says in that last line suggests that the unfinished business and unanswered questions of the ancestors, issues and questions that are more collective and cultural than personal and familial, apply to therapy as well as research. Therapy is a mode of research, and research is a mode of therapy when each is a matter of re-search, of searching again for something that has already made its claim upon one. In both instances, we are in service to something other and larger and different than ourselves, to some collective cultural story whose work is to be continued.

TWO CASE EXAMPLES OF AN IMAGINAL APPROACH TO RE-SEARCH

In this section, I want to give two examples of re-search as unfinished business. The first is an example from Jung, and the second from a graduate student at Pacifica.

In his autobiography, Jung reports a dream, which he says first led him to the idea of the collective unconscious. In reporting this dream, Jung also notes that at the time he had this dream, he was working with Freud and that he was somewhat dissatisfied with Freud's way of interpreting dreams. The dream is of a house, and it goes as follows:

> I was in a house I did not know, which had two stories. It was "my house." I found myself in the upper story, where there was a kind of salon furnished with fine old pieces in rococo style. On the walls hung a number of precious old paintings. I wondered that this should be my house, and thought, 'Not bad.' But then it occurred to me that I did not know what the lower floor looked like. Descending the stairs, I reached the ground floor. There everything was much older, and I realized that this part of the house must date from about the fifteenth or sixteenth century. The furnishings were medieval; the floors

were of red brick. Everywhere it was rather dark. I went from one room to another, thinking, "Now I really must explore the whole house." I came upon a heavy door, and opened it. Beyond it, I discovered a stone stairway that led down into the cellar. Descending again, I found myself in a beautifully vaulted room which looked exceedingly ancient. Examining the walls, I discovered layers of brick among the ordinary stones blocks, and chips of brick in the mortar. As soon as I saw this I knew that the walls dated from Roman times. My interest by now was intense. I looked more closely at the floor. It was of stone slabs, and in one of these I discovered a ring. When I pulled it, the stone slab lifted, and again I saw a stairway of narrow stone steps leading down into the depths. These, too, I descended, and entered a low cave cut into the rock. Thick dust lay on the floor, and in the dust were scattered bones and broken pottery, like remains of a primitive culture. I discovered two human skulls, obviously very old and half disintegrated. Then I awoke.[23]

Jung goes on to report that what most interested Freud about the dream was the two skulls, and he notes that he strongly resisted Freud's view of the dream as the repression of some death wish. But, wanting to learn from Freud, he associated the two skulls to his wife and sister-in-law, and he notes, "Freud seemed greatly relieved by my reply." Jung concludes, "I saw from this that he was completely helpless in dealing with certain kinds of dreams and had to take refuge in his doctrine." He then goes on to say, "It was plain to me that the house represented a kind of image of the psyche—that is to say, of my then state of consciousness, with hitherto unconscious additions." The different levels of the house presented different levels of the psyche, and, in his understanding of the dream in this fashion, Jung notes that he became increasingly aware of the keen difference between himself and Freud in terms of their intellectual attitudes. He explains his position by saying, "I had grown up in the intensely historical atmosphere of Basel at the end of the nineteenth century, and had acquired, thanks to reading the old philosophers, some knowledge of the history of psychology."[24]

What is of interest here is not the actual meaning of the dream. I am not making a case here for either Freud's or Jung's interpretation. Rather, there are four issues in this material, each one of which bears upon the question of re-search as unfinished business.

First, it seems clear that Jung is speaking about the role of complexes in the work of understanding. Without using the term "complex" in his remarks, he alludes to its presence in his observation that Freud, in response to his dream, took refuge in his theory about dreams. Of course, no one is immune to the influence the complex has on all observations and interpretations, including Jung himself, as we saw from his remarks about the complex in Chapter 1. A complex is a kind of wounding, and for the wounded researcher it is both the obstacle and the pathway into the unfinished business in the soul of his or her work.

Second, when Jung refers to the historical atmosphere of Basel, where he grew up, he is in effect confessing that his sense of his dream has its complex roots in that atmosphere. That atmosphere, he seems to suggest, formed a kind of vocational setting for his work, and indeed in the next chapter I will take up this issue of research as a vocation that calls or pulls the researcher into his or her work through his or her complexes.

Third, when Jung tells us that this dream was his first inkling of the collective depths of the unconscious, he is not only confessing his difference with Freud regarding the unconscious, he is also suggesting, I would argue, that his psychological work, his explorations into the nature of the psyche and the unconscious, was funded by the unfinished business of soul in Freud's psychology. Depth psychology, which began with Freud's dream book, was and is a psychology of the unconscious, and Jung's dream indicates that within this beginning there was leftover business, the "Eurydician" question that soul always poses to our psychologies. Thus, Jung's dream affords us a good example of how an imaginal approach to research is indeed about the unfinished business in the soul of the work. Below the personal repressed unconscious, Jung's dream was an invitation of soul to go deeper into this work.

Fourth, and finally, that Jung was given the idea of the collective unconscious through a dream indicates that the unfinished business of soul in one's work, the unanswered questions, can address one as much through the dream as through reason and speculation. An approach to re-search that would keep soul in mind should make a place in its methods for these possibilities, and this is what an imaginal approach to re-search does. It makes a place for dreams as well as other a-rational and unconscious states as portals into research. Within an imaginal approach, the dreams of soul are as valid as the ideas of mind for finding the path into one's work. I will go into this matter in detail in Chapter 11, but for the moment I should note only this one stipulation: dreams as portals into research are not the data of research. Jung's dream of the collective unconscious was not the datum of his work, but he was led into his ideas and theories about the collective layers of the unconscious through that dream. It was the doorway into a lifelong program of re-search into the collective symbols of the unconscious. The dream was, so to speak, the back door into the house of his work.

The second example of re-search as unfinished business is from one of my graduate students, Paul Jones, who wrote a dissertation entitled "City and Psyche: An Exploration into the Archetype of City." Paul came to this work from his work as a city planner, and it was through a sense of the aridity of that work that he was drawn into some of the unfinished business about the city. He writes:

> By the time I entered Pacifica, I was convinced I wanted to leave city planning behind. Twenty-five years of working in that field, along with land development, master planning, project management, and civil engineering had left me feeling arid and brittle. I had lost faith in the way this kind of work is usually practiced, and its reliance on linear thinking, pragmatism, analytical problem solving, and ego-control no longer held any interest. But over the next nine months a series of seemingly unrelated conversations and events had circled me back toward the city again, yet in a very different way. Almost against my will, the first hint of a topic centering on the city as a psychological, even archetypal phenomenon began to emerge.[25]

All of Paul's long years of service as a city planner had left something out of his relation to and understanding of the city, and something else of the city was beginning to ask for his attention. So, as he writes, "In my second summer at Pacifica I was moved to explore what I thought of as the shadows of my home city, Flagstaff, Arizona." But, he adds, "I did this by stealth since my work for the local government was well known in the community, and I was anxious about my Pacifica work being 'discovered' in a way that might prove damaging to my position and relationships throughout the community." Here is a clear instance of how the claims that a work makes upon a researcher, its unfinished business, can deeply challenge his or her investment in the work. The shadows of the city wanted to speak, but Paul first had to overcome years of immurement in certain ways of thinking about the city and working with others.

In such a circumstance, I have found, it is often an event that turns up the heat of the work that wants to be done, and in Paul's case it was a pivotal tragedy that steered the project "toward an emphasis on losses the city sustains when soul is ignored or marginalized." He writes, "A troubled young man who had fallen into mental illness shot and killed a popular young police officer in the darkest hours preceding dawn." This event, he says, affected him deeply: "... [T]he image of the young man, now a murderer, became burned into my own awareness, and colored everything I found and wrote that summer." The city in its darkness before dawn, the city in its shadows, the city in its marginal areas untamed by the linear thinking and pragmatism that had earlier so shaped Paul's work on the city, now spoke to him through this event. It would be an overstatement to say that it spoke to everyone in that way, for we know that such events do not. But it touched Paul because it was a place where his own complex struggles with the city encountered some of the unfinished business that the city had with him.

Paul was being drawn into another vision of the city, and two other events furthered this process. One was the destruction of the World Trade Center, and the other was a symptom. Several months after the destruction of the World Trade Center, Paul was diagnosed with prostate cancer. The removal of the gland left, he states, "a literal void inside," which reflected for him the void left by the events of 9/11. In addition, he says that the removal of the prostate "left me feeling dry and bereft," echoing his earlier language of aridity to describe his life as a city planner. I am not suggesting that our symptoms are caused by what we fail to regard, nor am I even hinting at the symptom's presence as some moral failure to become more conscious. The point is that a researcher is an embodied presence who brings to the work the fullness of who he or she is and who carries the work as more than a matter of mind. In Chapters 5 and 6 I will attend to this issue of the symptomatic side of re-search that keeps soul in mind in order to point out some of the dangers that arise when one opens oneself to the unconscious depths of the work.

Paul did not shy away from working with these events and the symptom. Indeed, he makes it quite clear that they finally deepened and moved the work in the direction towards that unfinished business with the city. He writes, "I suppose the by then firm hold of this topic, and a more imaginal way of moving through it, became more obvious when, after six months of strenuous effort, I could not make the early chapters work the way I originally imagined and planned." He was stuck. The work wanted something else from him. He had failed to bend it to his will and ideas. But, "[t]his failure," he adds, "opened a space for an unexpected and quite different structure and narrative voice to appear as I feverishly wrote the chapter on water at a lush and quiet retreat in nearby Winslow, in the middle of the worst drought in 50 years, in less than a week." The aridity of the city as he had known it in his professional work was now being watered as the city as an archetypal phenomenon began to unfold its origins and long history in connection with water. "It was as if a dam had broken." And indeed it had for the researcher and for the work. Paul discovered as he moved into the deep waters of the work that the original town site of Flagstaff had been located at that site in Winslow where his work began to flow. Here is how Paul describes that place and that moment:

> The tiny trickle glitters in the sunlight, moving according to its own wishes, downhill as is its nature. I scoop out a tiny, wet puddle of this water and touch it to my lips, reflecting on the profound gifts it gives us, especially in this arid land. I wonder about where this precious water came from, and how it made its way to the surface in this particular spot, and why and how something so important to this city could have been so orphaned and forgotten. ... The water itself has become magical; in it I can see worlds both inside and outside my own time and place-bound life. ... Despite the clamor and congestion of the city built all around it, the little spring still bubbles up into life and dream, whether anyone of us notices or not.

Conclusion

That little spring is the image of the unfinished business in the work that Paul was drawn to do. It was, we might say, the dream of the work. Doing his work, Paul was re-membering the dream of that little spring and, beyond it, the dream of water in relation to the founding of cities. His recovery of this piece of unfinished business is a work of imaginal history, a work that is not just some antiquarian interest in a dead past. Rather, it is the re-animation of a past that slumbers and waits in the present as the weight of history, whether we notice it or not. Imaginal history as psychological work is a work of re-membering, a creative act whose backward glance under the spell of Orpheus moves the work closer to its unfinished destiny.

PART II

Process

CHAPTER FOUR

Re-search as Vocation

Introduction

In the last chapter, I noted that within an imaginal approach to re-search, the work wants something from the researcher as much as the researcher wants something from the work. I called what the work wants from the researcher the unfinished business in the work, and I gave several examples of it. In this Chapter, I want to explore how this unfinished business in the work claims a researcher through his or her complexes. Then, in Chapter 5, I will describe the ways in which a researcher can and must differentiate his or her complex relation to the work from the work's unfinished business, if the work is to be more than a personal confession of the researcher's complexes, an unconscious projection of his or her biases onto a work.

As we shall see over the course of these next two chapters, the attempt to take into account and to account for a researcher's complex unconscious draw into a work is no easy task, and at the end of the day one can never be quite sure about the results. Nevertheless, the effort is worth the risk, because without any systematic attempt to assess the presence of unconscious dynamics in research, these dynamics function anyway in an invisible manner. I cited Jung to this effect in Chapter 1. A psychologist's conscious statements about soul always have an unconscious side to them, which Jung called a "calculus of subjective prejudices." This "personal equation," which functions unconsciously, always "has a telling effect upon the results of psychological observation." There is no perception and no thought that is not mediated by a complex unconscious perspective, but "not even the psychologist is prepared to regard his statements, at least in part, as a subjectively conditioned confession."[1] After more than a century of evidence for the existence of the unconscious and its formative influence on all aspects of human life, it seems naïve in the extreme not to take it into account in our ways of knowing and researching.

A true sense of objectivity, then, has to include these subjective dynamics. Objectivity is not secured by denying the presence of the researcher in the process. It is not secured by the fiction of the neutral observer, who is apart from his or her observations, an observer who is split off from what he or she observes. Nor is it secured by including the researcher's conscious assumptions about the work by bracketing them as phenomenology does[2] or by incorporating the researcher's experience of the work as Moustakas does in his heuristic approach.[3] As valuable as each of these approaches is for having bridged the chasm between the neutral observer and what is observed, for having undone the illusion of the neutral observer, neither one attends systematically to the unconscious participation of the researcher in the research process. Assumptions that can be bracketed are not the same thing as complexes that are unconscious. A bridge thrown across the divide between subject and object has to sink into the depths of that "abysmal" divide. Indeed, in Chapter 13 I will argue that a reliable foundation for any ethical epistemology must include ways of assessing these unconscious factors in the research process.

PRELUDE: REFLECTIONS ON THE "VULNERABLE OBSERVER"

In the opening chapter of her marvelous book, *The Vulnerable Observer: Anthropology That Would Break Your Heart*, Ruth Behar, a cultural anthropologist, cites the ethno-psychoanalyst George Devereux's 1967 book, *From Anxiety to Method in the Behavioral Sciences*, a work that has, for the most part, been sadly neglected. Reflecting on Devereux's book, Behar points out that "observers in the social sciences had not yet learned how to make the most of their own emotional involvement with the material." To rectify this state of affairs, she notes, Devereux insisted that "[w]hat happens within the observer must be made known ... if the nature of what has been observed is to be understood."⁴ Then, quoting Devereux, she adds that for him the subjectivity of the observer "influences the course of the observed event as radically as 'inspection' influences ('disturbs') the behavior of the electron." The observer "*never* observes the behavioral event which 'would have taken place' in his absence, nor hears an account identical with that which the same narrator would give to another person."⁵ Then, approaching the heart of the matter, Behar notes, "Yet because there is no clear and easy route by which to confront the self who observes, most professional observers develop defenses."⁶ For Devereux, these defenses go by the name of "methods [that] reduce anxiety and enable us to function efficiently."⁷

What Behar and Devereux are suggesting is that method functions to control and contain a researcher's involvement in his or her work. Method allows distance and functions as a defense against emotional entanglement. As far as it goes, this is a legitimate aspect of method, but it becomes problematic when the functions of control, containment, distance, and defense get in the way of the "calculus of subjective factors" that Jung spoke about. To suggest that this "calculus" must be kept in mind is to raise the dual question of what purpose is served by its inclusion and how one goes about including it.

With regard to the first question, Behar notes: "Although he [Devereux] acknowledged the subjective nature of all social knowledge, for Devereux self-reflexivity was not an end in itself."⁸ Research is not about the researcher. It is not just a memoir or confession. Rather, it is about a topic that is other to the researcher but which nevertheless finds itself and speaks itself through him or her. Attending to this chiasm between an interested and involved observer and the observed was, for Devereux, a "means to a more important end—achieving significant forms of objectivity and therefore truly 'true' science."⁹ For Devereux, then, inclusion of the subjective factor was for the sake of developing a "true" science for all socially constructed forms of knowing. Moreover, as we saw in the last chapter's discussion of van den Berg and modern physics, even the so-called hard sciences are socially constructed. Thus, the inclusion of the knowing subject in the object to be known is an inescapable demand for any body of knowledge that would be truly objective.

But the second question, how one goes about this inclusion, still remains. And finding the answer is really a matter of determining at what level or depth the subject is to be included. In other words, the discussion on inclusion has to involve a consideration of how one understands subjectivity. A truly objective science requires inclusion of the unconscious dynamic factors in the research process, a necessity that Devereux acknowledges with his emphasis on the observer's countertransference reactions to his or her work.[10] Behar, however, does not go down to the level of the unconscious in her notion of subjectivity. Her "*vulnerable* observer" is not the "*wounded* researcher." The vulnerable observer merely seeks to bridge the gap between subject and object. The wounded researcher, on the other hand, is meant to go down into the terrain beneath the bridge, into that abyss that the vulnerable observer attempts to bridge. The difference is that while the vulnerable observer includes only those subjective factors that he or she is conscious of, the wounded researcher delves into his or her unconscious complexes, which he or she then strives to make conscious.

Although Behar makes no place in her scheme for the emotional vulnerable observer as a complex wounded researcher, I agree with her that any inclusion of the subjective factor in research, whether it be conscious or complex issues, raises a concern. "Should we be worried," she writes, "that a smoke alarm will blare in our ears when the ethnography grows perilously hot and 'too personal'?"[11] This is a concern, but the issue is not one of choosing between being too hot and personal and being too cold and impersonal. In the depths below the bridge that is thrown between subject and object, the wounded researcher has to be neither too hot nor too cold. In this in-between place, in this place between research as a personal confession and research as a distant observation, the wounded researcher is not, however, lukewarm. Rather, he or she embodies the paradox of detached involvement, which is perhaps better expressed by the quote from Devereux mentioned above with which Behar begins her book:

> It is customary to call books about human beings either
> toughminded or tenderminded. My own is neither and both,
> in that it strives for objectivity about that tendermindedness
> without which no realistic behavioral science is possible.[12]

Objectivity about tender-mindedness is the key point in Devereux's work, and it is the point at which his work regarding the observer's countertransference and the efforts of the wounded researcher to make the unconscious factors in research more conscious converge. This tender-mindedness refers to the subjective emotional component of the researcher, to the ways in which one is drawn into the work through his or her passionate attachment to it. Or, we might describe this tension between tender-mindedness and tough-mindedness as that between the tender heart and the tough mind. But, however we describe it, Behar has no reservations that "the emotional and intellectual baggage the anthropologist takes on the voyage" needs to be included in his or her work and in a very direct way. Indeed, in her forceful defense of this point, she criticizes Devereux for approaching this issue of inclusion "with only half a heart."[13]

For Behar, a full-hearted inclusion of the researcher's emotional and intellectual baggage moves research towards memoir insofar as a central place is made for the inclusion of the "I" in research. As an example, Behar cites with approval the work of the psychiatrist Kay Redfield Jamison, who co-authored a standard medical text on manic-depressive illness, and then published a memoir, *An Unquiet Mind*, in which she confessed that she herself was a wounded healer who suffered from that illness. In her work, Behar says, Jamison "refuses to conceal her transformation of anxiety into method." Describing her encounter with Mogens Schou, the Danish psychiatrist who introduced lithium into the treatment of manic-depressive illness, Jamison notes that it was his question to her, "Why are you *really* studying mood disorders?" that challenged her. Initially hesitant to respond to this question, Jamison was eventually encouraged to include her own experience in her research by Schou's admission that he himself was studying these mood disorders because of the presence of them in his family history. Jamison realized that "[i]t had been this strong personal motivation that had driven virtually all of his research."[14]

Jamison does not shrink from the anxiety of her stance to include her own presence in her work. "It is," she says, "an awful prospect, giving up one's cloak of academic objectivity."[15] Behind that cloak, one can pretend to be the neutral observer, the observer who is dispassionate about what he or she observes. Letting go of it, one becomes the vulnerable observer. About letting go of it, however, Behar asks, "But surely this is not the anthropology being taught in our colleges and universities? It doesn't sound like the stuff of which Ph.D.s are made. And definitely it isn't the anthropology that will win you a grant from the National Science Foundation." And, as if this indictment is not enough, she adds, "Nor, to be perfectly honest, is it the anthropology I usually tell people I do."[16]

A strange dichotomy is at work here. Behar's discipline of anthropology does not coincide with what she does as an anthropologist. The discipline makes no place for her in the work. But doing the work not only makes a place for her, it also forcefully insists upon it, upon a practice of anthropology that breaks the heart, as the subtitle of her book says. Might we not say the same thing about the discipline of psychology, in which the doing of psychology seems to leave out so much of the psychologist who is doing psychology? Moreover, insofar as depth psychology has taught us that the "I" of the researcher is complex, that the "I" who has feelings and ideas about the work is a multilayered presence, should we not acknowledge that much of the practice of psychological research makes no place for the unconscious factors that shape, inform, and influence the psychologist's research?

The purpose then of including the "I" of the researcher in the work is to overcome this strange dichotomy. But doing so does not, or at least should not, force us into a choice between being either a tough-minded observer/researcher, who excludes his or her emotional draw into the work, or a tender-minded vulnerable observer, who veers towards research as memoir and confession. Devereux wants to eschew this dichotomy, and indeed any truly objective science has to do the same. Research that would be objective about the researcher's subjective presence to and in the work has to make a place for that subjectivity as well as for the complex roots of that subjectivity if the work is to be more than an unconscious confession of one's complexes. The latter is Devereux's goal, and hence, I would suggest, it is Behar who approaches the inclusion of the subject in the work with only "half a *mind*." She leaves out the unconscious depths of the conscious "I," somewhat like approaching being in love with only half a mind, that is, with only the rational mind. But love, like work, is a complex affair, and one brings to such moments all the emotional and intellectual baggage that one brings to a work. For both, we need more than half a heart and half a mind.

"The beliefs and behaviors of the researcher," Sandra Harding says, "are part of the empirical evidence for (or against) the claims advanced in the results of research. *This* evidence too must be open to critical scrutiny no less than what is traditionally defined as relevant evidence."[17] The critical scrutiny that Harding speaks of here requires ways of assessing the unconscious aspects of those beliefs and behaviors, of assessing what Devereux calls the countertransference of the observer. *The Wounded Researcher* shares this goal. The wounded researcher is a complex witness who, by attending not only to the conscious but also to the unconscious subjective factors in his or her research, seeks to transform a wound into a work. The work comes through the wounding, which makes one, as it did Behar and Jamison and Schou, vulnerable and open to the work, but without letting the work become merely a confession about the wound. The wounding is a way of being present, and what this presence requires from a truly objective researcher is the sustained commitment and the capacity to open that wound to inspection so that the work it addresses can be differentiated from it. Such work is a complex affair.

Speaking of the work of philosophy, Nietzsche says, "It has gradually become clear to me what every great philosophy has hitherto been: a confession on the part of its author and a kind of involuntary and unconscious memoir."[18] His remark captures the confessional/memoir aspect of research as well as the unconscious aspect of it, and this is the task of the wounded researcher. We need an approach to research that does indeed make a wholehearted place for the "I" of the researcher, for what I will describe below and in the next chapter as the researcher's reveries of the work, even as such research might approach memoir, as my Introduction to this book illustrates. But we also need research that attempts to make a place for the tough-minded task of making the unconscious of that wholehearted "I" more conscious, and in the next chapter I will describe this as making a place for the soul of the work.

THE COMPLEX CHARACTER OF RE-SEARCH AS VOCATION

No investigator, however unprejudiced and objective he is, can afford to disregard his own complexes, for they enjoy the same autonomy as those of other people. As a matter of fact, he cannot disregard them because they do not disregard him. Complexes are very much a part of the psychic constitution, which is the most absolutely prejudiced thing in every individual. His

constitution will therefore inexorably decide what psychological
view a given observer will have. Herein lies the unavoidable
limitation of psychological observation: its validity is contingent
upon the personal equation of the observer.[19]

I called the previous section a prelude because the real play begins
with the acknowledgment that the vulnerable observer is a wounded
researcher whose heart for the work is rooted in complex unconscious
dynamics that tap into the soul of the work. As noted above, for Jung
the nature of psyche is complex, and it is this complex character
of psyche that decides inevitably what view of things a given observer
will have. This complex influence operates in life as well as in research
because all researchers belong to life. Given this, either we consciously
find ways to include the complexes of the researcher in the process, or
we try to contain, within the format of method, the anxiety they cause
when the researcher's complexes are touched by some aspect of the
work, a stratagem that amounts to allowing those complexes to
function unconsciously.

The first step in acknowledging the complex character of research
is to recognize that it is through the complex that one is drawn into a
work. The image of the neutral observer and/or the dispassionate
researcher is built on the fiction of the complex-free person, whose
neutrality and dispassion separate him or her from that which he or
she studies. It yields a simplistic psychology that leaves the complex
psychologist out of the picture. The point I wish to make here is that
it is, in fact, through our complexes that we are initially drawn into
life, love, and work. Jamison's story given above is an example, and in
the last chapter, when I discussed how the imaginal approach to
research takes up the unfinished business in the work and I gave several
examples of this from Jung and others, I was heading in this direction
of the complex character of imaginal research. For, in truth, the
unfinished business in the work claims the researcher through his or
her complexes. The ancestors that Jung speaks of are the ones who linger
in the work, and it is their unfinished business that makes its appeal
to the researcher. It is for this reason that I would argue that re-search
that keeps soul in mind, complex re-search, re-search from an imaginal
approach, is a vocation. A topic chooses a researcher as much as, and
perhaps even more than, he or she chooses it.

The work that the researcher is called to do makes sense of the researcher as much as he or she makes sense of it. Indeed, before we understand the work we do, it stands under us. Research as a vocation, then, puts one in service to those unfinished stories that weigh down upon us individually and collectively as the wait and weight of history. As a vocation, research is what the word itself indicates. It is re-search, a searching again for what has already made its claim upon us and is making its claim upon the future.

The Wounded Researcher: A Reverie of Origins

The story of this book's origins is a good example of re-search as a vocation. I speak of origins here and not beginnings because the beginnings of a work are often easier to identify. The beginnings of a work have to do with events in the world that present the occasions and opportunities for its inception. The origins are often more difficult to pinpoint because they have to do with the psychological depths of that weight and wait of history within which both the book and the author of the book are conceived, where in fact the author is made ready as the book's agent, author-as-agent, conceived by the book as its voice, as the expression and fulfillment of its dreams. Recall my earlier remarks about the painting on this book's cover. The figure in that image is the "stranger" who is writing this book, the composite of myself and that other who guides the work, who shepherds its dreams.

In relating this example of research as vocation, I am veering towards memoir. I am engaging here in a reverie of origins, which sets the boundary of the value and the limits of this approach to research. This backward glance, this piece of re-collection, situates and contextualizes this work within my own subjectivity, within the feeling tone of this work that has captured me, and in the exploration of the depths of this subjectivity (via dreams and symptoms, for example), the soul of the work, its unfinished business beyond my complex relation to it, finds a place.

The beginnings of this book date from 1991, when Pacifica Graduate Institute invited me to build an approach to research that would be in accord with its stated mission, "To be in service to the soul of the world." The challenge was to develop a way of doing research that remained faithful to the tradition of depth psychology's commitment to soul. The response to that challenge over the years was not, however, a direct one. Indeed, the response has been a journey into the origins of this work, some of which precede its beginnings by almost twenty years and even more.

Recovering origins is always a work of an-amnesis, a work not just of remembering but also of un-forgetting. The difference here is between a horizontal journey in time, back to a past that has been left behind, and a vertical descent into moments of time, in which the past still haunts the present. Anamnesis is that Orphic work explored in Chapter 2. It is that work of making more conscious what was, and still is, unconscious in a past that weighs down upon and waits within the present. In this Orphic return for a second look, the task is not simply that of making explicit what was previously implicit. On the contrary, as a work of an-amnesis the path of this book has been a process in which the unfinished aspects in earlier work, the thoughts that were un-thought in them, have been deepened, re-figured, and re-membered here.

To cite a personal example, the theme of my first book (published in 1982), the metaphorical character of psychological life, is deepened, re-figured, and re-membered in this work within the context of an imaginal approach to research.[20] Within this imaginal approach (the theme of Chapter 3), the image quality of metaphor, whereby it is neither a thing nor a thought, neither a fact nor an idea, becomes the ontological ground of psychological life, while the metaphoric quality of the image becomes its epistemological strategy, the way of saying and writing down the soul (the theme of Chapter 12).

Both of these thoughts were un-thought in my earlier work, and without the context of this present work they would have remained so. Those not-yet thoughts, those remainders of an earlier thinking that lagged behind itself, lie at the origins of this work, haunt it as the weight and the wait of unfinished business. But in this reverie of origins, this backward glance at them, it becomes evident that those origins were also a destiny that was already ahead of that earlier work, soliciting it, dreaming it forward. Those un-thought thoughts about metaphor as the epistemological strategy of psychological life and image as its ontological ground were not like some notes left over in the drawer of one of my desks waiting to be gathered up and made use of in this work. They were living presences, shadowing my thinking, teaching, and writing, slowly becoming more conscious in essays, lectures, late night ruminations, and dreams. Only in 2001, for example, in the Afterword written for the re-publication of that first book, did I bring together this connection between the ontological character of psychological life as image and the epistemological expression of the image through metaphor.[21] Only afterwards in an Afterword, after all the words had been spoken in that first book and spoken again in the new edition after nearly twenty years! Only then, slowly, was the weight and wait of the unfinished story of that first book redeemed. Only then were the dreams of that earlier work dreaming itself through me completed, at least for the moment. Projecting itself ahead of me, drawing me and this work towards them, e-ducating that earlier work by leading it and me beyond itself and myself, seducing me and it to become what it and I were meant to be, those dreams have become the site where the metaphoric character of psychological life now unfolds itself as the poetic realism of the soul's imaginal life and the poetic process of research, whose ways of knowing include the mood of reverie, making re-search with soul in mind as much a matter of the tender heart as of the tough mind.

The consequences of a way of knowing the world that erases its shadow, an idea that was un-thought in my second book, *Technology as Symptom and Dream*, is another example of the origins of this book as a work of un-forgetting and thus of research as vocation.[22] In *The Wounded Researcher,* those un-thought implications re-present themselves as an approach to research, which, in keeping soul and its complexes in mind, moves towards an ethical way of knowing and being (the theme of Chapter 13). Many of the essays written in the decade of the 90s and collected in *Ways of the Heart: Essays Toward an Imaginal Psychology* were already on the path, moving towards and leading me in the direction of this work on research as an ethical way of knowing and being, preparing me and making me ready for it.[23] The essays on reverie, hospitality, cardiognosis (or the place of the heart in knowing), alchemy and the subtle body of metaphor, and the role of the witness versus the critic in psychological work were not consciously written with this work on research in mind. All were written independently of each other for some specific occasion, with no conscious relation to some larger idea or theme that would bring them together. But in a way that is beyond reason, they were dreaming about the wounded researcher, and as I catch up with the unfinished business in those essays, I begin to remember, for example, that the wounded researcher doing re-search with soul in mind is a witness who in reverie lingers in the moment of the work being done with an attitude of patient hospitality, which not only allows, but even encourages the work to unfold as itself and for itself, without any anxious concern on the part of the researcher for its outcome, or even its purpose or utility. These moments, by the way, are a large part of the joy of writing.

What I am trying to illustrate here is that elusive quality in my experience of looking back, and, in a moment of un-forgetting, like waking to a dream, becoming aware for the first time that what was un-thought by me in these earlier works was still thinking itself through me. In this Orphic glance, it would be easy to assume some smooth line of progression in all this, but that is not how the experience was lived. Reason would make this whole process of re-search as vocation into a straight line and would thereby miss the meandering ways of soul that draw one into his or her work. So, I stay with the phenomenology of the experience to show that in each of the examples cited above, I did not know what was un-thought in those earlier works, but those thoughts not yet thought by me knew me. What I am trying to describe here is that twist in which ego-consciousness comes to know that in the work of remembering it is being re-membered. When I say, therefore, that the unfinished business in those earlier works has been deepened, re-figured, and re-membered in this one, I do not mean that I have done this deepening, re-figuring, and re-membering. Or rather, I do not mean that I have done it alone. The active agent in these processes is not that clear or simple when one acknowledges that re-search is a vocation. On the contrary, these processes seem to take place somewhere in a third, imaginal space between author and work, in the intersection where it is never quite so clear if I am re-membering the earlier work or it is re-membering me, or both. All that seems clear is that in re-search as vocation, the researcher does not so much make the work as it makes him or her.

The "wounded researcher" was there in the un-finished business of those earlier works, and not there. He was there waiting for the moment and the context, the occasion and the opportunity, ahead of me, waiting for me to catch up with myself, the dream of the soul of those earlier works waiting for me to become its voice. In this respect, the "wounded researcher" is one of the archetypal images of the unfinished business in the work that has claimed me these past twenty years and more. Re-membering those subtle connections between this unfinished business in my earlier work and this book, I am trying to illustrate that re-search as vocation is a process in which I have had to catch up with the Wounded Researcher, whom I did not yet know— or did not yet know what "he" knew —and had to wait for this occasion to become aware of that.

In this sense, re-search as a vocation is a journey of transformation. What the knower comes to know changes who the knower is. It is an alchemical process in which one knows only insofar as one lets oneself be known, a process that is an Orphic dismemberment of the researcher by the work that has called him or her into its service.

In writing this book, I must confess, I have become the very thing that I have been writing about. I have become the wounded researcher who is telling the tale of the Wounded Researcher. For sure, we can know things because someone has told us of them. And we can know things because we have experienced them directly. But there is another level of gnosis, which Henri Corbin describes as knowing something by becoming it. He calls these different ways of knowing different hermeneutical levels. "Level A," he says, "is theoretical certainty," in which someone hears, for example, about fire and what it is like from someone else, as a child might when his or her parents warn him or her of its dangers. "Level B," he says, "is the certainty of eyewitness testimony," in which one comes into contact with fire directly and personally, as one might, for example, at a campfire. Then, there is Level C, in which the certainty is lived; that is, at this level of gnosis and understanding, "one becomes the fire, or is consumed by the fire."[24]

While Corbin sees this third level of understanding and gnosis as a spiritual journey, I am suggesting that it is a journey that begins with the descent into the soul of a work that has solicited one into the journey. It may very well be the case, however, that re-search as vocation is a spiritual process. Perhaps we should admit, or at least consider the possibility, that all modes of research have a spiritual component to them, that even the most tough-minded empirical style of research has a transcendent quality, perhaps even a numinous aspect, and maybe even a hint of the sacred.

Corbin understands the relationship between these levels of gnosis and understanding as one in which each level takes up and transforms the previous one. Each level draws the one below it into itself and transforms it, raises it to a higher level just as the Wounded Researcher has drawn me towards it and in the process has transformed me, has fired my ideas into flesh, has drawn them out of the very body of my being so that in one very real and deep sense I would have to say that I have suffered the work by bearing it along the way. Thus, research as re-search is a searching again, not only for what one has already known in some way but has forgotten, but also a finding that is a re-finding of what has already found you, a claiming that is a re-claiming of what has already claimed you, and a calling that is a re-calling of what weighs upon you and waits for you. As I said earlier, the topics that we think we choose in fact choose us as much as, and probably more than, we chose them, and the intentions that the researcher has for the work are ensorcelled by the dreams of the soul in the work. In light of this, how much a book is a product of one's reason and how much a product of its dreams remains unclear.

This ambiguity nurses the element of grief within the heart of re-search as vocation, because the researcher in the work is neither the exclusive maker nor the owner of the work. The researcher already claimed and dreamed by the work does not own it in the beginning. Nor does he or she own it at the end, for in the end and at the end of the work, a researcher can hold on to the work only by letting go of it. The book that is finished is already dreaming itself beyond the boundaries of what has been said, and there lingers around its horizons another weight and wait of history. If there is compensation for this Orphic sense of loss when one works with soul in mind, then it lies perhaps only in the fact that the one whose name is on the book gets the royalties.

The element of grief is not, however, bought off so easily in this way, and a sense of loss always haunts re-search done with soul in mind, a sense that arises in the gap between the subjectivity of the researcher and the soul of the work. This Orphic sense of loss may be especially true of psychology, when we consider that all our psychologies are complex approximations of soul, in which we succeed because we fail. Soul is always the unfinished business left over in our psychological work and, as such, is the vocation that calls us into re-searching it. One may, therefore, become the living embodiment of his or her work, as suggested above. One may become a living witness for it, but that does not mean that now one possesses the work. On the contrary, the work that is done leaves the researcher behind, as Eurydice does with Orpheus.

Mourning, as I said in the Introduction, is the way of the soul and a theme that threads itself throughout this approach to research. Knowing something begins in awakening to loss, as the origins of depth psychology indicate. The hysteric, Freud said, suffers from reminiscences. But little did I know, when I wrote of my own experience of grief in *The Soul in Grief: Love, Death and Transformation,* that this book, too, like the others described above, was already gathering me for this encounter with the Wounded Researcher, who attends to the weight and the wait of history so that what has been lost might be re-membered, so that what is unfinished might be attempted again.[25] Each work leaves a symptomatic residue that becomes the vocation of not just another work, but also an *other* work. *The Soul in Grief* was and is such a residue that is re-membered in this work.

This reverie of origins suggests there are no lines that lead in a direct way from the idea of a project to its completion. Nor are there any straight lines from the origins to the beginning of a work, or, indeed, any clear traces that lead back from the beginnings of a work to its origins. The work, like a dream, has you as much as you have it, and, in one very true and deep sense, research as a vocation always faces a researcher with the question of "whom does the work serve?"

Whom does this work serve? For whom is it being done? With these questions I am drawn deeper into the origins of this work, perhaps even beyond the archetypal figure of the Wounded Researcher discussed above, to places that, like the archetypal figure of the Wounded Researcher, are beyond my own complex relations to them, to the weight and wait of history that originate this work and that have come to me only in dreams and the ritual ways in which I have sought to give form and voice to those dreams in this work. In the dedication of this book, I named the ancestors and a dream figure. They are also the ones who have carried the unfinished business at the origins of this work, the ones who have haunted those earlier works with their unanswered questions, the ones who were calling me into this work towards the Wounded Researcher. They are the ones who, along the long path of this book, have always checked and undone my subjective plans for the work, my numerous outlines and multiple drafts, teaching me along the way that research as a vocation is nothing less than a process of being undone by the work, and this coincides with the recognition that the one(s) for whom the work is being done does (do) not coincide with the one who does the work.

Working with a Western-trained physician who was also a shaman, trying to make sense of some recurring gastrointestinal symptoms, I learned in a direct and powerful way that I had been very distant from my ancestors and that in my symptoms lay much grief and fear about loss. In the ceremony of throwing the bones, however, I also learned that one ancestor, my father's mother, had been and was close to me. After the ceremony, I was instructed to continue the work, and I began to collect photos and other mementos of my grandparents on both sides of the family. As this work progressed, I built a small altar, on which I placed all these items, and I made it my practice to start my day with a ritual in honor of these ancestors. One day, as I was engaged in greeting them, I was struck by a deep sense of sadness while looking at a photograph of my father's mother. In this picture were present my grandmother, her husband, and another man, who was the brother of either my grandmother or grandfather. My father's older brother stood by his father, while my father, less than a year old, was seated on his mother's lap. How many times I had looked at the picture and how many times I had missed what I saw and felt that day! In that moment, I felt my grandmother's tears, and I remembered the one story that my father told me over and over about her death.

The story was about his parents returning to Europe in July 1914 to sell some land after being informed by their relatives of the worsening political situation. Ultimately, my grandfather died in that war, but my grandmother died before he did, and it was this story of her death that my father told me many times. Lying in a field on the farm where he was living with his mother and brother, he saw a star fall from the heavens. He knew at that moment, even as a very young boy, that his mother had just died.

Remembering that story, I felt my grandmother's sorrow. She was leaving behind, in very uncertain circumstances, two young children who were destined to become orphans. In my own life, my work, and my writing, this theme of the orphan has haunted me. It has been an archetypal dominant in my work about forgotten origins and the need to return and remember. In that moment, I knew why my father's mother had been close to me. Her story needed to be remembered. Her story, and that of my ancestors, needed a sense of an ending.

As strange as it might seem, this book on research is that ending. It is through this story, this piece of unfinished business, through the archetypal figure of the Orphan that I have been led to understand how research is re-search, a work of an-amnesis, of un-forgetting and re-membering what has been lost. As such, the work of re-searching, the work of knowing, is a work of mourning. And maybe in the dark-light of the soul, when compared with the bright light of the mind, myths of loss—from those about Paradise and the Fall to that of Orpheus and Eurydice—encode for us the insight that the price we pay for wanting to know is a sense of loss.

We do work in the dark-light of the dead when we work with soul in mind, when we attend to the weight and the wait of history. The work that we are called to do is in service to the ancestors, and it is through our archetypal blessings or wounds and our personal complexes that we make the work, which comes through us but is not about us. Indeed, it was only after this experience, seeded by the work with the shaman and the daily rituals, only after I had engaged and was engaged by the story of my ancestors and its presence in my life, that this book began. The photographic images were not something to look at—they were something to see through, portals through which to enter into an *other* world. For more than a decade, this work had slumbered and at times had false starts. But, in the afterlife of the image, as Mogenson describes it, a complex history and an archetypal inheritance have been transformed into a work that redeems that history.[26] I am reminded here of the poet, T. S. Eliot, who says in "Little Gidding," the last of the *Four Quartets*,

> We die with the dying:
> See, they depart, and we go with them.
> We are born with the dead:
> See, they return, and bring us with them.
> The moment of the rose and the moment of the yew tree
> Are of equal duration. A people without history
> Is not redeemed from time, for history is a pattern

Of timeless moments. So, while the light fails
On a winter's afternoon, in a secluded chapel
History is now and England.[27]

Research as vocation is against forgetting. In the afterlife of the image, where my ancestors lingered as the weight and wait of history, their story asks to be re-membered. Their longing for a sense of an ending has coincided with an ending that this work marks for me, at that threshold to which a dream figure has led me.

Some time after this experience with my ancestors, I had the aforementioned dream, in which a street poet leads me from the house of academia into the streets of life. This street poet, a dark-skinned figure, tanned by the sun, with teeth stained brown by the long use of tobacco, is casually and even sloppily dressed. He is a rough, even crude, figure of back streets and alleyways. In the dream,

I enter a large Victorian-style house where a group of colleagues and academics are gathered for a conference on Jung's work. All of them are pale-skinned and appropriately suited-and-tied, and have their backs turned toward me, so that I am unable to connect with any of them. I wander through the house, and, in the back part of it, I meet the street poet. This figure escorts me to a screen door and opens it. Beyond the door is a landscape that reminds me of my boyhood days. I can see a field of grass situated in a park, and there are many people milling about in a leisurely fashion. I can feel the soft air on my skin, and I can smell the scent of spring. The scene has a sense of life and freedom, in sharp contrast to the room where my colleagues and other academics are gathered. With a gesture of his arm, the street poet shows me this landscape. But we do not enter it. The dream ends with both of us standing on the threshold.

I have been drawn into this work on research; it has been a vocation, and the Dedication in this book marks how it has been in service to the figures of history and dream, these companions who ask for their stories to be told. For the past fourteen years, as I have been thinking and writing and teaching about this work, I have also been working slowly on a book of poems, reveries, and reflections called "Dark Light."[28] The title has always intrigued me, and, in truth, I am not certain from where it comes. I know only that in the soul's dark-light I am trying to catch up with a dream, to catch up with it before it is too late, because dreams do not wait forever.

But, as I began this book again, I was persuaded about a connection between "Dark Light" and *The Wounded Researcher*. They meet in that dream, where this book on the Wounded Researcher is about an ending, while the book about dark-light is about a beginning. This dream is an alchemical vessel in which the transmutation of philosophy into poetry begins, or, perhaps more cautiously, where the logos of philosophy, as Martin Heidegger and, more recently, Peter Kingsley note in their work, returns to its roots in the poetic.[29]

It is this transmutation, this return, this recollection, this remembering, this tension between the philosophic and the poetic that shapes this book as a way of knowing and doing re-search that keeps soul in mind. It is, if you wish, another way of speaking about that tension between the tough-minded and the tender-minded. With soul in mind, we turn slightly away from the brightness of the light of reason and its rational and empirical ways of saying the world as we are turned toward a way of seeing the world in the soul's dark-light and speaking it poetically. This last remark does not mean that the researcher becomes a poet, nor does it mean that we as researchers abandon the virtues of empirical and rational modes of discourse and research. It means only that we allow ourselves to recover something that we have lost along the way, that we remember and allow ourselves to be re-membered by this one simple fact: that we are called into speaking by the aesthetic appeals of those unfinished stories, where the word "aesthetic" taps into its etymological roots, which tie it to feeling and sensing, particularly to the sense of hearing. For research as vocation, then, one needs to have a good ear for the work as much as good insights about it.

In the dark-light of this book on research, the threads that connect it to a living past, which lingers as the weight and wait of those unfinished tales, have become clearer, and I find that the "I" who has written this book has needed that shaded clarity. When the weave between complex and archetype was woven, the work began, and, in this sense, it was only when "I" had a sense of the ending of the book that "I" could begin it. In this respect, a work is finished before it is done, and indeed it is never done. And this makes research as vocation a journey of homecoming, a journey that is never completed. It also makes it a kind of redemption. Research as vocation is not only about the unfinished business of the work, which carries its archetypal motifs that make their claim upon a researcher through his or her complex relation to these themes, it is also about the researcher who, in taking up the work, transforms a wound into a work.

Research as vocation places the researcher within a context that is larger than his or her intentions for the work. Indeed, the work is the site where the complex pattern of the researcher's history and the unfinished business of the ancestors meet, where the complex and archetypal dimensions in the work meet, where the time-bound and the timeless qualities of the work encounter each other. We are born with the dead, the poet says, and so is the work that claims us. A researcher who keeps soul in mind, who works in the dark-light of soul, is like an eavesdropper who listens in on the conversations of those for whom the work is done. To be sure, one's name is always appended to the work. My name will be on the cover of this book. I have written it, and I have become, as suggested above, the wounded researcher. But, as also suggested above, I am the wounded researcher, and I am not the wounded researcher. We part company when the book is finished so that it can continue to be done. Thus, the "I" who has written this book has been suspended between the "I" who has been drawn into the work and the ancestors for whom the work is done, between me and the dream of the work. So, again, my name is on the book, but the figure in the image on the cover seems closer to the reality of who has been the author of the work, someone who is neither me nor the ancestors, but someone who is a threshold figure, the eavesdropper who, neither inside nor outside the process, has written down both sides of the conversation.

In this larger context, psychological life and work, of which research is a part, is a turning that re-turns to what has taken hold of one for the purpose of re-garding, re-membering, and re-animating what has been left unsaid. This re-turning is for the sake of an-other beginning. It is for the sake of saying what, in still needing to be said, haunts the shadows of the reasonable mind. This book is an example of such a vocation. It is a work that is done at the threshold, where the psychologist who keeps soul in mind is neither the philosopher/ academic nor the poet of the street.

The dream ends at the threshold, where the sense of ending and beginning are held in tension. Holding this tension between the work whose unfinished business still waits to be done and the work that is finished by the researcher is what an approach to re-search that makes room for soul requires. In the end, it is an exercise in exorcism, a kind of exorcism not of what is evil but of what has been forgotten, abandoned, and betrayed, a ritual of mourning that gives the weight and wait of history its proper burial, or, if that is too much, then at least this much: a writing that is done in graveyards and in the dark-light of soul while lingering with the ancestors whose lost worlds and values—those worlds and values of soul—solicit us, draw us out of ourselves, and are not to be forgotten either in life or love or work. It is a book, then, that is dedicated to being against forgetting.

I have taken some time to present a reverie of the origins of this book. In doing so, I have illustrated how re-search done with soul in mind is not separable from all those complex entanglements described above. We do not work in isolation from the complex character of our lives. We work through it, and, to work with soul in mind, one has to work through the complex by working through it, by making it more conscious. In addition, I have taken this time in order to demonstrate that, for better or for worse, the reverie of origins, this archaeology of the complex vocational roots of one's work, sets the limit and marks the boundary of the work. In this reverie of origins, there is no disguise in either method or theory that would mask the complex roots of this book in my own subjectivity, and thus the value of this book can be understood and weighed in relation to that limit. Through this reverie of origins, this work is, in fact, liberated for the reader as well as for me from its complex origins, and in this respect, as I will show in the next chapter, reverie is a way of letting go of the work insofar as it makes one's complex relations to it more conscious.

A STUDENT EXAMPLE OF RE-SEARCH AS VOCATION

It would be a mistake to present only my own description of research as vocation as an example of this process. Therefore, I now offer a detailed example from the work of one of my graduate students, Kerry Ragain, whose dissertation was a phenomenological study entitled "Archetypal Threads in the Experience of Being Adopted."[30]

Throughout his three years of coursework, Kerry struggled with the deep split that he felt between his passionate love of history and his psychological studies. He often seemed to have a faraway look in his eyes, as if his consciousness were attuned to something outside the

moment, and there was a profound sense of melancholy in the air when
one was with him, as if he were mourning for something that had been
lost or left behind.

Kerry was adopted, and in his daytime job he worked as a
counselor with children who had been placed in foster homes. He had
this job, this occupation, but his vocation seemed always to be towards
the past. During one of our many conversations outside of class, he
once said to me that if he could, he would pursue a dissertation in
history rather than psychology, and, indeed, on one of these occasions,
he even named a particular interest: medieval techniques for preventing
the rusting of armor. On another occasion, after returning from a trip
to France, he wrote an essay for one of my classes in which he described
how in the medieval part of one city he felt strangely at home and yet
more alienated from himself than ever before. He was not just living
in two worlds. Rather, he was lost in two worlds, not at home in his
day world and far away from those medieval landscapes that seemed
to beckon him to come home.

Kerry was stuck between these two worlds, and he was stuck in
his dissertation process. He knew that his agency would not continue
to support his education if he did a dissertation in history, but he could
feel no connection between his passionate longing for a lost time and
place and his current work with foster-care children or with his own
history of having been adopted. Was there some archetypal pattern
threading together his work, his history, and, as he says it, "my
longstanding preoccupation with the particular images, places, and
events situated in medieval history"? As he stewed in this uncertainty,
he began to sense "how the well of grief and sadness around the many
genealogical disconnections associated with my own adoption were
part and parcel of my interest in studying, and almost wanting to re-
live, certain aspects of life from a long time ago." Slowly, he began to
see, as he puts it, "how my interest in history might be part of a
metaphor illustrating a desire on a deeper level to connect with my
own personal history, which had, in too many ways, been lost due to
having been adopted." But something still seemed to be missing.

Here was a complex root of Kerry's work, but it was disguising
itself as an intellectual passion for the places and times and images
and events of the Middle Ages, for a history that belonged to a time
beyond him, and as a mood of melancholy. In this complex form, the

work had taken hold of him as a symptom does, as a tension between remembering something that is too vital to forget and forgetting it because it is too painful to remember.

With respect to the former side of the symptom, he was keeping this complex, symptomatic presence of the work alive by playing with it, by engaging it with music. Never knowing fully why he did it, Kerry would nevertheless bring his bagpipes to class, and in the evenings he would play them. He writes: "I used to play the bagpipes down in the building's basement, at night, directly under where we held the class that day." Was he being drawn at night to the depths of what was taking place and being spoken about above during the day? Was the work being cooked here between the demands of the ego and the demands of the soul of the work, between what Kerry the researcher was constrained to do in the day world of work and occupation and what the work itself wanted to be done?

The imaginal approach to research that this book defends would reply to these questions in the affirmative. The vocational aspect of the process attends to these subtle complex interweavings between a researcher and the work, and it acknowledges that the work is indeed made between the two. Piping the work into existence in the nighttime basement, Kerry was enacting an aspect of the research that counts in the genesis of a work as much as his daytime forays into the library to play the keys of the computer did. He was embodying the process by which a work begins, continues, and moves towards a finish between a researcher who is both author of and agent for the work. Or, it is perhaps phenomenologically more accurate to say that Kerry was creating that generative imaginal place in re-search with soul in mind where a researcher is neither author nor agent, where this distinction is always slipping away so that one is never able to answer with final clarity if it is "I" who is doing the work or those for whom it is being done who do it, just as one is never able to say with finality whether one's left hand is rubbing one's right hand, which is being rubbed, or one's right hand is rubbing the left, which is being rubbed. A chiasm exists between the two hands, just as a crossing so subtle but real exists between the researcher and his or her work.

The nighttime forays into the basement were offset by the other, symptomatic side of the complex. Kerry felt a strong resistance to exploring any connection between his draw into history and his own biographical wound of having been adopted and having lost so much of his own history. The claims that the images, events, places, and times of the medieval world made upon him left him with a deep sense of grief and sadness, and he did not feel he wanted to open those same portals with an exploration of his biographical wounds. So, he resisted the connection between the two. His own sense of a lost past was kept separate from his melancholic draws into the lost past world of the Middle Ages, while the nighttime piping in the basement of the work went on. Forgetting this complex root of his work had a foreseeable consequence. "The resistance appeared in the form of an academic paralysis which impeded creative movement."

About this paralysis, Kerry notes, "For the next few years, I sought to find an image in the music which could lead me to a topic, but nothing came. Meanwhile, that basement cloister became a crepuscular chamber where I immersed myself in the music after class. As I continued to pipe my way through the Ph.D. program, the didactic piece of the work began drawing to a close, and I nevertheless found myself at an impasse with regard to ascertaining a dissertation topic." What he had was his passionate interest in the Middle Ages and its history, which claimed him through a mood of melancholy and longing, his piping, which was like a series of ongoing reveries that drew him into those times and places, his job of working as a counselor with children in foster care, and the traumas of his own early adoption. He had four pieces of a complex puzzle, but without any overall image to hold them together and from which to craft a work.

In the last quarter of his program, Kerry arranged a meeting with me, in which it became clear that nestled within his interest in the historical past of the medieval world was an orphan in time. Yes, he belonged here and now to this world of his job with foster children and with his own wounds about having been adopted. But at another level, he belonged to another time and place, and this, in the deepest sense, made him a orphan in this world. Here was the key he needed. "As we sat together that day, tending the coals, I began to grasp more fully the archetypal significance of the connections among my musical interests, my preoccupation with the past, my daily clinical work with foster children, and my own history of having been adopted; it was the Orphan who was guiding my images and actions." It was this figure of the archetypal Orphan for whom the work was being done.

I present this one example of the vocational character of research in some detail because it says so clearly that a work that keeps soul in mind is a complex tapestry woven of many threads: of passionate intellectual interests, of wounds that linger in complex ways that draw one into a work, of archetypal blessings, of daily work in one's profession, and of other daily practices and rituals that might seem disconnected to a work but which actually carry something of its depth that is not to be forgotten. All of these threads were woven together in Kerry's work. He went on to do a systematic phenomenological study of six adopted individuals, in which he explored numerous dimensions of their experiences of being adopted, including the question of their relation to time and history.

What he found was not only that the existential orphan carries some sense of being an archetypal Orphan in time, but also that in some sense we all are, within the context of being historical beings, Orphans in time. Under the guidance of this archetypal motif of the Orphan in time, and through his own complex of being adopted, Kerry crafted a psychological study of the experience of being adopted. He transformed a wound into a work in which this piece of unfinished business in being adopted, this sense also of being lost in time, when one has lost one's own temporal history, was addressed. Not only did he deepen the psychological aspects of the experience of being adopted by getting to its archetypal core, but his study also suggested that the archetypal Orphan, as the one who is adrift in time, is present in those who have a deep, abiding, and feeling sense of history.

His own words here are perhaps the best testimony and the best way to make this point and to conclude this example:

> Every day while writing I felt as if I were in close proximity with the world where the scent of history lingers, where our ancestors once put leather shoeprints in the dust outside of their cottages. I could almost feel the mud of the field under my fingernails. I believe this sense of connection and potential is far beyond the window of my temporal existence. I felt as if it were a privilege to have been called as an imaginal witness through my vocation into this project around the links among history, loss, and adoption.

Conclusion

There are many other examples from my graduate students who have worked in this fashion, either with me as an advisor or with one of my colleagues, Veronica Goodchild. But it would easily double the length of this chapter to present them, and so I conclude merely with a list of those studies. The reader who is interested in attending to the vocational process in his or her work might find in these dissertations some markers left by those who have already passed this way.

A Bibliography of Dissertations

Barrett, Deborah. "Through the Forbidden: Journeys of Suffering and Transformation." Ph.D. dissertation. Pacifica Graduate Institute, 1996.

Bennett, Jacqueline Pisani. "Reverie and the Recovery of the Ancestral Landscape." Ph.D. dissertation. Pacifica Graduate Institute, 2003.

Callan, George. "Temenos: The Primordial Vessel and the Mysteries of 9/11." Ph.D. dissertation. Pacifica Graduate Institute, 2002.

Campbell, Terri. "Death: A Dialogue between Freud and Jung." Ph.D. dissertation. Pacifica Graduate Institute, 2006.

Fisher, Jack. "Factual Fictions/Imaginal Truths: The Space between the Objective and the Subjective in Texts That Connect Theory with Experience." Ph.D. dissertation, Pacifica Graduate Institute. 2004.

Gratz, Conrad. "The Experience of Living with Enchantment." Ph.D. dissertation. Pacifica Graduate Institute, 2007.

Greenwood, Deborah. "Resting at the Crossroads: Working with Women's Narratives and Art-Making." Ph.D. dissertation. Pacifica Graduate Institute, 2006.

Harrell, Mary. "Journey to Imagination: A Woman's Lessons about Life and Love." Ph.D. dissertation. Pacifica Graduate Institute, 2003.

Hunt, James. "When Memory Comes Calling: Ancestors, Archetypes, and Incarnational Imperatives in the Therapeutic Context." Ph.D. dissertation. Pacifica Graduate Institute, 2004.

Jones, Paul F. "City and Psyche: An Exploration into the Archetype of City." Ph.D. dissertation. Pacifica Graduate Institute, 2003.

Killinger, John Eric. "Between the Frying Pan and the Fire: The 'Intermundia' of Clergy Transitioning out of Parish Ministry." Ph.D. dissertation. Pacifica Graduate Institute, 2006.

Knapp, Carly. "Eros and Thanatos: A Figuration of Death as an Imaginal Presence in Dialogue with Depth Psychology." Ph.D. dissertation. Pacifica Graduate Institute, 2005.

Langhans, Dennis. "An Odyssey of the Heart: A Return to the Place, Rhythm, and Time of the Imaginal Heart." Ph.D. dissertation. Pacifica Graduate Institute, 2002.

Macfarland, Ellen B. "Discovering the Healing Power of Nature: A New Perspective for Healing the Wounds of Childhood Abuse." Ph.D. dissertation. Pacifica Graduate Institute, 2004.

Orodenker, Judith. "The Voice of the Goddess: The Reemergence of the Archetypal Divine Feminine." Dissertation in progress.

Rowe, John. "The Experience of Mystery in Enduring Love: Embracing the Soul of Marriage." Ph.D. dissertation. Pacifica Graduate Institute, 2005.

Sadownick, Douglas. "Homosexual Enlightenment: A Gay Science Perspective on Friedrich Nietzsche's *Thus Spake Zarathustra*." Ph.D. dissertation. Pacifica Graduate Institute, 2006.

Sgarzi, Julie. "In the Labyrinth of the Secret: A Meditation on the Nature of the Secret." Ph.D. dissertation. Pacifica Graduate Institute, 2002.

Todd, Jo. "Grieving with the Unborn." Ph.D. dissertation. Pacifica Graduate Institute, 2006.

Tomlinson, Kay. "Conversations with the Ladies: Art-Making in Collaboration with Imaginal Figures." Dissertation in progress.

Treichler, Johanna. "Walk Your Own Walk." Dissertation in progress.

CHAPTER FIVE

The Transference Field between the Researcher and the Work

… [A] complete psychology must reintegrate with the human that which detaches itself from the human ….[1]

—Gaston Bachelard

INTRODUCTION: OUTLINES AND THREADS

There is, I believe, a difference between an outline, which one sketches out for the body of a work, and the more subtle body of the work that threads itself throughout the process of the work. The outline one makes projects the work so that one always seems to be writing from that place where the work is imagined as finished. The thread of the work, on the other hand, runs beneath the outline and always seems to call one back to the beginning so that each phase of the work seems to have already been imagined from that beginning, already prepared by what has gone before, as if a particular moment in the work has already been dreamed and imagined. Outlines and threads both matter, and the one who makes a work stands between an ending that is imagined and a beginning that is always calling to be re-membered. Indeed, we see the end clearly enough to the degree that we re-member the threads that pulled us towards it. In such moments, outlines are re-membered and the ending is imagined again.

So it is with this particular moment in the book, with this chapter, whose threads tie it to the chapters that have preceded it. In the Introduction to this book, I spoke about the tension between what is said and what is always left unsaid, about the remainder that asks not to be forgotten; and in Chapter 1 I followed that thread into the gap between psychology and soul. In that gap, psychology as a complex about soul is always ahead of itself, and being beyond itself in this way, it becomes forgetful of its source in soul as its object of study, a forgetfulness that makes psychology always a work of return so that what is unsaid in its complex words about soul is not forgotten. In Chapter 2 I picked up the thread of Orpheus, and in the myth about him and Eurydice I found a story to describe the tension of having something in hand, whether it be a love or a work, and then losing it and having to find it again. In that process of losing and finding, what is found again is not what was once had or said, what was once possessed or named and supposedly tamed by one's words. Orpheus and Eurydice are both redeemed into their own otherness only after he loses her, just as a work is redeemed into its own otherness, into itself from the researcher, only after he or she has let go of his or her claims upon the work, has surrendered to the work and been addressed by the claims it has already made upon him or her. In Chapter 3 I called this otherness to which one always has to return, this unsaid dimension, the unfinished business in the soul of the work. Indeed, this unfinished business is the thread that holds together the subtle body of the work, that body that is other than one's outline for the work, that other in the work that lies beyond one's ego involvement in and plans for the work; and in Chapter 4 I followed that thread into that place where one is called into a work and its unfinished business through one's complexes. In this complex relation between the researcher and his or her work, in this gap between what is said and what is left unsaid, the researcher, I suggested, might finish the work, but the work is never done.

This is where the thread lies at the beginning of this chapter, and it marks a place so different from the many outlines I have sketched for it. Like a high tide taking back the land that one had gained for a moment, even as it erases the marks one had traced upon the sand, replacing them with markings of its own brought up from the depths, the unfinished business in the soul of a work—that sense of its otherness beyond one's intentions for it and claims upon it— continually takes back into the depths the outlines one has made, the words one has written and imagined as permanent, and leaves traces from those depths that hint at another beginning. So we follow the threads that have been left behind as a work begins again, for re-search that would keep the depths of soul in mind needs to acknowledge these rhythmical tides that flow between the ego of the researcher and the soul of the work, tides that, in fact, make a work of soul always a perpetual beginning, and make every effort at beginning again, as we heard before from the poet Eliot, a wholly new start and a different kind of failure. Progress in psychology, then, is by way of these acts of return, and failure is not our business, because for us there is only the trying again and again to make the marks upon the sand/page while the tides have, for the moment, receded. Indeed, this rhythmical process is a kind of play, and, as I will explore below, the transference field between a researcher and the work is therefore a space of play.

Re-search that would keep soul in mind needs to create, as part of its process, a space that acknowledges the tension between the said and the unsaid, a space that ensures that the unsaid is not forgotten or left behind and that invites a way of holding on to a work by letting go of it, a space, moreover, that attends to the unfinished business in the soul of the work, and that finally offers a way of differentiating the researcher's complex ties to the work from that unfinished business in the work itself. These are the threads left behind from the previous chapters, and it is these threads that make up the fluid subtle body of this chapter.

OPENING A SPACE/MAKING A PLACE

In the last chapter, we explored the idea that research as a vocation means that a topic chooses a researcher through his or her complexes as much as, and perhaps even more than, he or she consciously chooses it. The researcher is always in some complex, myth, dream, or fantasy about the topic, and an unconscious dynamic is therefore always present between the researcher and his or her work. This dynamic plays itself out within a transference field; and, indeed, there is in the re-search process that would keep soul in mind an awareness that a transference field exists between the researcher and his or her work as much as it exists between a therapist and a patient, a lover and a beloved, a teacher and a student, a parent and a child, a writer and an editor, a reader and a work.[2] Perhaps the most important aspect of an imaginal approach to research is that it calls for a process that specifically acknowledges this dynamic field between the two and establishes procedures that attempt to make this unconscious field as conscious as possible.

This does not mean, however, that research is therapy, or that it should be. While research that attends to unconscious dynamics generally has a therapeutic effect upon the researcher (and I will explore this issue later in this chapter as well as in the next chapter), my intention is not to make research into therapy or to confuse the two. Re-search that would keep soul in mind is no more a form of therapy than education is, but education can be, and often is, therapeutic. Perhaps, if we invert the relationship, we will come closer to a phenomenological experience of this issue. If we regard therapy as a form of education, then we can regard education as a form of therapy. Similarly, if we regard therapy as a form of research, then we can regard research as a form of therapy. But, however we imagine this issue, the point here is that for re-search that would keep soul in mind an effort must be made to differentiate what the complex researcher brings to the work from the work itself, just as a therapist must differentiate what he or she brings to the patient from who the patient is in himself or herself, or just as a lover must differentiate what he or she brings to the other in the relationship from who that other is in the relationship. Without such efforts, the complex presence of the researcher, the therapist, or the lover functions as a projection. And while the presence of such unconscious projections into research can never be completely eliminated, just as they can never be completely eliminated in therapy or love, there is, I would argue, an ethical imperative to make the complex process of research as conscious as possible, just as there is in therapy, in love, and in life.

In the next section, I will describe those procedures for carrying out this difficult but necessary task, but first I want to explore in this section the space of this transference field and describe the place it opens up for these procedures. I want first to describe this space before describing the ways in which we work in this space.

To attend to the complex transference space between oneself and one's work is to lose oneself for the sake of the work. When Orpheus loses Eurydice, that loss happens to him. The loss that I am referring to here is an active choice. It is a conscious decision whose intention is to loosen one's hold upon the work. One enters into the transference field between oneself and the work with the sense that one no longer knows what the work is about. Indeed, the transference space is created through this act of humble submission. One begins to wonder and to ask, "what is this work really about?" But what is the response to such a question? What does one do? With the question, one has carved out a space of possibility. One has carved out a potential space, an imaginal space, for the work. But how does one then proceed to make it into a place of action?

In the chapter of his memoirs entitled "Confrontations with the Unconscious," Jung describes that moment when, after his break with Freud, he was at a loss about himself and his work. In response to this situation, Jung recounts, he said to himself, "Since I know nothing at all, I shall simply do what occurs to me."[3] One of the things that he did was play. He returned to his childhood game of building with blocks, and in that space he made a place for allowing himself to be addressed by the unconscious. Out of those potential spaces of play, those free exercises of the imagination, Jung discovered what he would later call the process of active imagination.

When the researcher allows himself or herself to let go of the work, he or she is making a space that can be a place for playing with the possibilities in the work, that is, with the aspects of the work of which he or she is ignorant. The researcher willingly surrenders in such moments to the question, "What is this work really about?" In this spirit of play, the researcher engages the unfinished business in the work. From within that question, the potential space of the transference is made into a ritual place of play in which the ego not only temporarily steps aside, but also is temporarily put aside as one becomes more at home in this place. In this ritual place of play, the researcher steps out of his or her ego position in relation to the work and steps with it into an imaginal landscape, which is neither the world of nocturnal dreaming, nor the world of focused daytime wakefulness.

The transference dialogues, which are modeled on Jung's notion of active imagination, are an invitation to play in this imaginal landscape. It is a landscape of Winnicottian transitional phenomena, in which the differentiation between the researcher and the work, his or her separation from it, is mediated by the fantasies and reveries and images of the work that emerge within this landscape. In his excellent article, "Active Imagination as Imaginal Play Space," August Cwik shows clearly the relation between Jung and Winnicott, and he notes that the transitional process of play remains as a necessity throughout life in order to "relieve the strain between the inner fantasy world and the outer real world." Cwik says that for Winnicott "all of life consists of a transitional interplay between self and reality."[4]

According to Rose, the transitional process of play "can be observed in the creativity of everyday life."[5] Play is one of the soul's ways of managing the difference between oneself and the other, between oneself and the world, and between oneself and one's work. An approach to re-search that would keep soul in mind needs to make a place for the soul's need to play. The transference dialogues make a place for this to happen. In this place, a researcher is as detached as possible from the outcome of the process in order to be as passionately involved as possible in the process.

Research is serious business, but if one is to do re-search that keeps soul in mind, one cannot be deadly serious. A spirit of play that invites the as-yet-unimagined possibilities in the work to speak has to hover over the field between the researcher and his or her work. Only when the researcher is able to play with the work can the unfinished business of the work find a place in the work.

Before I proceed to the next section to describe the procedures for playing with the work in the transference field, I want to note two things. First, a researcher's ability to play with the possibilities of the work seems to be directly related to the ego's ability to let go of the work, to surrender its position of control. My experience with this work, both personally and with hundreds of students over the years, has been that such surrender is more often than not very difficult. Numerous resistances arise, not the least of which is the feeling of embarrassment when one enters into dialogues with the "strangers" in the work who carry and become the spokespersons for the unfinished business in the work. Jung himself attests to this fact regarding the childhood games he played. "This moment," he says, "was a turning point in my fate, but I gave in only after endless resistances and with a sense of resignation." He then explains why these resistances were so persistent and strong: "For it was a painfully humiliating experience to realize that there was nothing to be done except play childish games."[6] For Jung the man, the games of childhood were childish. For the grown up and serious-minded researcher, the invitation to play with and be confronted by the still undreamed possibilities in the work can feel the same way. The process can feel foolish, a waste of time, inefficient, and completely beside the point. In an experiment I did almost twenty years ago, when I first imagined this theme of a complex relation between the "researcher" and the work, I noted numerous examples of this kind, and other forms of resistance.[7]

Resistance abounds because the ego does not play; it does not want to get lost in the play, and that is the challenge. As one student once put it, to get lost in this way, to give up for some moments one's sense of control over and direction of the work, one has to be able to allow oneself to feel dumb, or at least a bit stupid. But I have become a firm believer that soul welcomes these moments of stupidity, whether we call it playing or dreaming or falling in love. So, when the transference dialogues begin to feel difficult and foolish, when the critical ego wants to dismiss all this, the question is: Have we forgotten how to play?

The second point I want to make is that active imagination is generally situated within a therapeutic framework. Its purpose is to deal with the unconscious, to come to terms with it, in Jung's words. Indeed, for Jung, there is a very close relation between this process and the notion of individuation. In this book, I am making use of Jung's procedure of active imagination within the specific context of research. The reader, I believe, has every right to question whether this is a legitimate extension, as well as whether it is even a good idea, because of the many difficulties and dangers associated with confronting the unconscious. I have wrestled with these questions myself.

With respect to the first issue, I would argue that it is a legitimate extension. The researcher is no less a complex involvement with his or her work than the therapist is a complex involvement with his or her patient, or two lovers are complex presences to each other. The unconscious is a dynamic presence in all aspects of life. When the researcher designs his or her study, he or she does not somehow step outside of life. The laboratory belongs to the world as does the library and the study where one writes. The researcher does not miraculously transcend the unconscious. The unconscious is a dynamic presence in research as in life, and we cannot nor should not ignore it.

With respect to the second issue, I will consider in the next chapter how this process of transference work can be a dangerous one. For the moment, however, I will say that the intention behind the application of active imagination to the context of research sets a kind of limit. The intention of these dialogues for the researcher is not to ask what they say about him or her, but what they say about the work. Of course, this distinction is only relative because there is no absolute split between a purely subjective and uninvolved researcher and an objective work. Nevertheless, there is a difference, and the researcher can and must hold to this difference between himself or herself and the work. The researcher will always be challenged in his or her complex positions relative to the work, and this will have personal effects. But, and this is the key point, with the intention to keep the focus of these dialogues on the question of how they speak about the work, the researcher is not only maintaining his or her ego stance in relation to the work, but he or she is also always bringing the process back to a focus on the work. Always returning to the work, the researcher at least sets a limit to the process. The research process is not therapy, although it might pose therapeutic challenges and have therapeutic implications that invite exploration in another context.

LETTING GO OF THE WORK

In this section, I want to describe two procedures for working in the ritual space of play. These procedures are two phases in the process of letting go of the work. This phrase—letting go of the work—refers to the researcher's conscious relation to the work, to the ways he or she has claimed it and has been shaping it according to his or her intentions for, and ideas about, the work. In this process of "letting go," the researcher surrenders his or her outlines so that he or she can be addressed by the threads that tie him or her more subtly to the work. Before I describe these phases and their subdivisions, I want to outline them in a schematic form. This outline might help the reader/researcher by offering a map of the terrain to be explored.

Phase One: The Ritual Space of Reverie

Phase Two: Transference Dialogues

    Step 1: Setting the Stage

    Step 2: Invitations

    Step 3: Waiting with Hospitality

    Step 4: Engaging the "Others" in the Work

       First Moment: Giving Form and Being a Witness

       Second Moment: Critical Regard

         (1) The Way of Aesthetics

         (2) The Way of Understanding

    Step 5: Scholarly Amplification

Phase One: The Process of Reverie

Engaging in reveries of the work is one way of letting go of it, and in the last chapter I gave the example of Kerry Ragain who, through the playing of his bagpipes, was drawn into the depths of the work that he did not and could not consciously imagine. Reveries of the work are the ways in which, to borrow a phrase from the last chapter, the tender heart of the tough-minded researcher finds a place in the work. In these moments of "time out" from the work as consciously intended, a researcher makes a place for the unconscious sense of the work to speak. These reveries attach the landscape of the work to its subterranean depths. They bring the depths of the work to the surface, where they float like islands arising from the volcanic depths of the sea.

Who does not think of islands now and then and dream of them as places of respite and refuge from the mainland of life? Gaston Bachelard, in his reflections on reverie, claims that one of the functions of reverie is "to liberate one from the burdens of life."[8] Reveries of one's research perform the same function. They free the researcher for a moment from the burdens of the work. They liberate him or her for a moment from shouldering the burden of being its author. In his or her reveries, the researcher surrenders to something/someone *other*, which is authoring the work. It may be a memory that surfaces and comes unbidden from who knows where, a memory that often feels as if it is as much a fantasy as it is a recollection of a long-vanished past. It may be a longing for some vague place or time that seems to hold one, just as Kerry's pipings opened him to a yearning for the lost times and places of the medieval world.

Reveries are the way that the soul of the work turns the ego's conceptions of it into fantasies, and fantasies are the bridge that spans the gap between the unconscious depths of the work and the researcher's conscious understandings of it. Joan Chodorow notes the important role that fantasy played in Jung's confrontations with the unconscious. She points out that by attending to his fantasies, which arose spontaneously, he was able to translate the emotions that threatened to overwhelm him into images that calmed and reassured him. Jung, she says, paid strict attention to his fantasies and indeed tried various ways to drop or fall into them. For example, "sometimes he imagined climbing down a deep descent; other times he imagined digging a hole, one shovel-full of dirt at a time."[9] Jung's imaginings were invitations into reverie, just as Ragain's descent into the basement with his bagpipes was an invitation. And, just as Jung discovered images in his fantasies, Ragain discovered the archetypal Orphan in his bagpiping reveries in the basement of his work. Working with one's reveries, one might discover "who" is in the work beyond one's own complex participation.

The researcher can set the stage for reverie to take place, as Jung did with his procedures, or Ragain did with his descent into the basement to play his bagpipes. But reverie is something one falls into. Reverie happens to us. One can set the stage for its appearance, but one does not direct the action. Indeed, even when one does nothing to establish the conditions for its appearance, reverie can happen spontaneously. Reveries come unbidden and arise spontaneously, as, for example, when one is reading a text and suddenly becomes aware that for the last few minutes one has been daydreaming. Bachelard captures this moment when he says: "I am a dreamer of words, of written words. I think I am reading; a word stops me. I leave the page."[10]

He leaves the page! Yes, Bachelard is correct, but perhaps it is closer to the experience of that moment to say that he is taken from the page. That is to say, reverie is a kind of abduction. One is drawn elsewhere. But where? Where is one taken when one is abducted from the page?

The alchemist before his fire offers a reply. Jung regarded his psychology as being in a direct line with alchemy, and he found in alchemy direct expressions of the unconscious. Imagine, then, for a moment an alchemist before the fire. He is dreaming, but he is not asleep. Then he sees a salamander roasting in the flames, or a green lion devouring the sun. Where is the alchemist in this moment? What is he doing?

Von Franz notes that the alchemists were performing their experiments on matter with no specific program in mind. She writes, "Thus there exists in alchemy an astonishing amount of material from the unconscious, produced in a situation where the conscious mind did not follow a definite program, but only searched."[11] There in front of his fire, with no conscious plan or intention, the alchemist is neither dreaming nor fully awake, and in this condition he is drawn into matter through the images of the unconscious. Bachelard says that the "psychology of the alchemist is that of reveries trying to constitute themselves in experiments on the exterior world."[12] In the context of research, these experiments are ways of dreaming the subject matter of one's work with one's "eyes wide shut." They are, as Bachelard says, reveries.

It seems, then, that reverie is a pathway into the unconscious depths of the moment, whether that moment is one of reading a book or gazing into the flames of a fire. The researcher in front of his or her work knows this kind of moment of abduction, this moment when one is led away from the work into the depths of the unconscious in the work. Such moments seem to favor the occasions when one's work seems on the verge of becoming overwhelming, or, more frequently, when the work seems to be stuck. In either case, such moments are times for reverie, for stepping back so that the fantasy images that arise in the quasi-narratives of reverie can either calm the work or disturb it enough to get it moving again. These moments are opportunities to attend to the depths of the work, which might otherwise be forgotten.

Reveries hold the secrets of the work, secrets that the researcher does not yet know. One of my former graduate students, George Callan, provides a rich example of the place and use of reverie in research. The dissertation she finally wrote, "Temenos: The Primordial Vessel and the Mysteries of 9/11," had its origins quite literally in the margins of her thinking, in a place outside her conscious thoughts, when, through her hands, she gave herself over to moments that can only be described as moments of reverie.[13] The following is a description of those moments in her own words:

> It happened that in my first year of doctoral studies, while my conscious mind focused intently on the material delivered in the classroom, that my right hand, having a mind of its own, strayed from its note-taking responsibilities. It idly scripted

doodles in the margins of the page—spontaneous calligraphy, meaningless flourishes and scribbles. In the second year of my studies, these unbidden images became distinct, taking the form of sacred objects from my childhood memory: chalices, tabernacles, grottos, shrines, elaborate candlesticks. By the third year, the notes had been relegated to the margins and the pages were filled with iconic images: ornate boxes, baskets, bathtubs with wings, decorative envelopes, apothecary jars, teacups, circus tents, towers with whimsical spires, wardrobes on wheels, clocks in their casings, with little nooks and drawers and glass knobs. They all had something in common. They were vessels— containers. While the pure flow of the drawing soothed the intensity of academia's demand, I gave no particular value to these images. It had not yet entered my consciousness that I was being pursued. The messenger in the form of revelatory image had arrived from the margins, passing through the threshold of the right brain while the left brain still clung to the linear content at center stage.[14]

Eventually, however, Callan caught up with herself, with where the work had already led her. She caught up with herself at the margins of the work. Until that moment, she was the object of the research. She was pursued by the work and invited to engage it in a form of creative play. The dissertation began, she confesses, when she consciously agreed to collaborate. It began when she recognized the value of those marginal reveries, and acknowledged being claimed by the work. In this move towards collaboration, Callan was entering more deeply into the reveries of the work.

In time, I came to heed the insistence of the messenger, and a daily practice emerged. I began to nurture those whimsical images, draw them on fine Italian paper, touch them with color, refine the details of their embellishments. It became clear to me that I had to empty out the erudite notions and abstract ideas of academia, and release my soul from what Ficino saw as the Saturnian and melancholic inclinations of the scholarly life. Theory and analysis would eventually be invited back, but only under the wise tutelage of the imagination.[15]

Earlier I said that reveries hold the secrets of the work, and Callan suggests that these secrets, which wait at the margins of the work, seduce the researcher's imagination. Reverie, then, opens up the imagination of the work beyond theory and Saturnine "analysis." It is not that theory, reflection, analysis, and scholarly investigation are supplanted and have no place in the work. Rather, it is that imagination has a place as well and is a complement alongside them.

Called into the work from the margins through the doodled reveries of her right hand, Callan was being drawn into a work about the mysteries of enclosed spaces, some of which, like the tabernacles and chalices, had a hint of the sacred and a scent of the transformative powers of these spaces. She was set to write about this when her complex relation to this work was addressed by an event in the world—the tragedy of 9/11. A synchronicity? Perhaps! But, however we regard this moment, the fact remains that with 9/11 the work went beyond her own intentions and plans for it. The reveries at the margins of the work prepared her for this aspect of the work beyond her own vocational complex relation to it, just as the nighttime bagpipe reveries of Kerry Ragan had prepared him as described in the last chapter. Played in the basement of the classroom where his daytime consciousness was busy with attending to the lectures, his musical reveries, like Callan's marginal ones, attest to the important place that reverie has in re-search that would attend to soul. Both examples show how reverie draws the researcher into the unconscious depths of a work and leads him or her beyond his or her conscious aspirations for the work. Both examples show how reveries are ways of dreaming the work with one's eyes "wide shut," opening a place for the depths of the work to enter into that imaginal space between nocturnal dreams and daytime awareness.

Phase Two: Transference Dialogues

A second way of letting go of the work is for the researcher to engage the work directly and systematically in the transference field that exists between himself or herself and the work. This second procedure, like the first one of reverie, is designed to make a place for the unconscious in the work. But whereas reverie happens to the researcher without his or her intent (one falls into reverie, as Ragain and Callan did in the course of their daily activities), the transference dialogues have an intentional quality to them. To say this in another way, reveries are a more passive form of letting go of the work, while the transference dialogues are a more active way of doing so. In addition, whereas reverie tends to challenge the personal complex that underpins the researcher's unconscious relation to the work, these dialogues extend the range of the unconscious in the work. Notwithstanding these differences, both reveries and dialogues are ways of letting go of the work. They share a common intent: to differentiate what the work wants for itself beyond the margins of what the researcher wants from the work.

Recall that in Chapter 2 I noted that Jung's notion of the psychoid nature of the archetype extended his understanding of the unconscious to the point where it became for him a *sui generis* reality, a reality on its own terms beyond not only its personal but also its collective-archetypal depths, beyond, in other words, the personal and transpersonal depths of the psyche. "At this level," as I have written elsewhere, "the researcher is engaged by those autonomous figures of the soul, by what I sometimes call the strangers who carry the dreams of the soul in the work. Here we are beyond a psychology of projection and are in the presence of those for whom the work is done, for those ancestors, for example, whose unfinished stories seek expression through us. Here the researcher is addressed not only by the complexities of psyche as an underworld, but also by the epiphanies of soul as an-other world."[16]

This difference between the underworld of psyche and the other world of soul is present throughout this work, and it is central to the transference dialogues, whose four levels, described below, open a place where the researcher encounters not only his or her complexes but also the "others" in the work, the "strangers" who carry the unfinished business of the soul of the work. To express this difference in another way, what the researcher encounters in the transference field is his or her complex realities that are subjectively real and the "others" in the work who are imaginally real. This difference between the subjectively and the imaginally real is from Andrew Samuels, who discusses it in an article in which he shows that the countertransference field between an analyst and a patient can be the epiphany of the imaginal world described by Corbin. For Corbin "the imaginal world is by its essence the intermediate world ... between the intellectual and the sensible." Intermediate between the world of intellect and the world of sense, the imaginal world is also an intermediary world where, as we saw in

Chapter 3, imagination as *imaginatio vera* is "an organ of understanding mediating between intellect and sense," and which is as legitimate a mode of understanding as either one of them.[17]

Drawing upon Corbin's work, Samuels notes that like the *mundus imaginalis*, the transference field is an intermediate landscape between the world of sense and that of intellect. Samuels employs Corbin's notion to suggest "that two persons, in a certain kind of relationship, may constitute, or gain access to, or be linked by, that level of reality known as the '*mundus imaginalis*.'" He expands on this with the observation that "[f]or the patient, the analyst himself *is* an in-between, a real person and also a transference projection. For the analyst, the world he shares with the patient is also the patient's own imaginal world."[18]

In this work, I am extending the range of the transference field as an intermediate landscape to the research process. For the researcher who would keep soul in mind, the work is an in-between. It is a real text within the broadest sense of this term within a tradition that stirs the researcher's emotional complexes, and a text with a history carried by the "other" in the work as its unfinished business. Between the researcher and a work, then, the transference field is a complex and imaginal intermediate place where imagination as a mode of knowing plays with the possibilities of the work. The key point to remember here is that in the dialogues in the transference field between the researcher and the work, imagination is a legitimate way of knowing. It is the mode of access to those subtle realities of the imaginal world that neither make sense in that they do not impinge upon the sensory apparatus of the researcher, nor are a matter of mind. For ego-consciousness, this is indeed strange terrain. We trust what we can measure, calculate, and observe, and we define this realm as objective over against feelings, fantasies, images, and intuitions, for example, as subjective. Within this dichotomy, not only is the imaginal realm denied, but even its possibility is dismissed. Between sense and intellect, then, an abyss is opened and the fate of soul and its imaginal landscapes has been to fall into that abyss. To descend into that abyss requires a different way of seeing and knowing. The researcher who keeps soul in mind knows this. He or she knows that there is more to seeing than meets the eyeball and more in heaven and earth than we might dare to dream of in our philosophies.

The psychological dialogues between researcher and topic take place at four levels of the transference. In the previous section, I described this space as a ritual place of play, and elsewhere I have noted, "This creation of a ritual space serves the same function in re-search with soul in mind that the creation of the ritual space of experimentation serves in empirical research."[19] The transference dialogues serve the same function for an imaginal approach to research that an experimental design serves for an empirical approach to research. It is a praxis that must be learned, and the complex researcher who would keep soul in mind has to learn this practice of transference dialogues, just as the experimental researcher has to learn the laboratory practices that characterize his or her work.

The attitude that an experimental researcher brings to his or her work—an attitude of neutrality, for example—shapes and is visible in the experimental design. In the same fashion, the attitude, mood, and style that a complex researcher brings to the work shapes and creates the place for the transference dialogues and even makes them possible. However, whereas empirical research makes a place for the researcher to take charge of the work, an imaginal approach makes a place for the researcher to let go of the work. "With these dialogues the researcher's perspective on the work is loosened, deepened and transformed." The place of the ego in the work is temporarily suspended and is inverted, as it is in dreams. "These psychological dialogues de-centre the researcher's position and invite him or her to listen to the stranger's point of view on the work."[20]

Step One:

The first step in the transference dialogues is creating the space and setting the stage for the dialogues to happen. The mood that helps to create this space is reverie, whose features, which I described in the last section, apply here. Reverie, then, is both a way of letting go of the work and the mood of the space of the transference dialogues. The only thing I would add is that this mood of reverie is another way of thinking, which is analogous to what Jung describes as non-directed thinking. In non-directed thinking, "[w]e no longer compel our thoughts along a definite track, but let them float, sink or rise according to their specific gravity."[21] We might say that in the mood of reverie, the complex researcher stops thinking and gives himself or herself over to being thought. He or she follows the track of thinking into paths that he or she has not made.

This mood of reverie fosters a specific attitude, which further articulates the space for the transference dialogues to take place. It is the attitude of "negative capability," a term coined by the poet John Keats, who defined it as the ability "of being in un-certainties, Mysteries, doubts, without any irritable reaching after fact & reason."[22] Negative capability fosters the capacity to remain open to experience without judging whether it is true or false, and in this respect it is the poetic counterpart to what phenomenology describes as the *epoché*, the practice of attending to experience as experienced without judgment about its truth or validity or even its meaning. Such judgments come later, only after one has attended to what presents itself and how it presents itself. Negative capability is also the poetic counterpart of the depth psychologist's attitude toward the dream. The dream is simply what it is, an experience that presents itself. To ask first what does the dream mean before one has attended to its presence is to refuse to stay with its mystery and ambiguity. It is to irritate the dream into meaning. "For poet, phenomenologist, and depth psychologist," I wrote, "presence does precede meaning because of a patience which can linger in the moment and wait for the presence in the present to appear."[23]

Negative capability, then, is the antidote to impatience, and, as such, it allows meaning to unfold itself out of presence and one's attention to it. In negative capability, meaning is not imposed, it arises as a surprise. Mogenson makes a similar point when he speaks about "the pattern in the collage of our grief." Speaking of the image and the meaning in the pattern, he cites Jung: "Image and meaning are identical; and as the first takes shape, so the latter becomes clear." The images that present and hold one's experience of grief inform the meaning. They are its figuration, and the images and meaning belong together. The meaning is in the image, and it will become clear if one can refrain from becoming impatient and attempting to irritate the image into meaning. Hence, as Jung adds, "the pattern needs no interpretation: it portrays its own meaning."[24]

The researcher who enters into the transference field with this attitude of negative capability, then, is open to what the "strangers" in the work have to say. He or she does not judge whether these "others" who comment on the work are real, autonomous presences or projections, nor does he or she impose a meaning upon what is spoken. On the contrary, the "strangers" in the dialogue are welcomed, like Jung welcomed Philemon. They are welcomed with a style of hospitality whose gestures create a place for an encounter between the researcher and the "strangers" in the work, a place where the unfinished business in the work can be spoken. In writing about hospitality, I said that its gestures are a mode of soul-making, which I illustrated through the story of another Philemon and his wife Baucis, told by Ovid in his *Metamorphoses*. These two old people, who welcomed into their home the gods Jupiter and Mercury disguised as travellers, practice soul-making "by lingering in the moment, by staying with the strangers who are made guests without judgments, evaluation or criticism."[25] And, because they do so, the gods in the end reveal who they are. The gestures of hospitality that Philemon and Baucis practice toward the two strangers result in an epiphany of the extraordinary that lingers in the ordinary when one is able to remain in uncertainty, mystery, and doubt, without any irritable reaching after fact and reason. What epiphanies, then, await the researcher who invites the strangers in the work across the threshold into the space of the transference? What epiphanies might arise when we practice such soul-making with our work, when we keep soul in mind?

The mood of reverie, the attitude of negative capability, and the gestures of hospitality create the ritual place of play for the transference dialogues between the researcher and his or her work. Taken together, they inform a way for the researcher to be in this place. They are his or her practice, no less important for re-search with soul in mind than the practices of measurement and observation are for the empirical researcher. Taken together, they create an ambience perhaps best described by another poet, Samuel Taylor Coleridge, as a "willing suspension of disbelief," an attitude "directed to persons or characters supernatural ... so as to transfer from our inward nature a human interest and semblance of truth sufficient to procure for these shadows of the imagination that willing suspension of disbelief for the moment, which constitutes poetic faith." Amplifying this notion, Coleridge spoke of the danger of contaminating the imaginative visions of a poetic faith with literal fact. Poetic faith is a "negative faith" that allows the images of a poetic realism to work by their own force, "without either denial or affirmation of their real existence by the judgment," an appreciation that would be "rendered impossible by their neighborhood to words and facts of known and absolute truth."[26] In other words, the willing suspension of disbelief is the attitude that makes a place for the imaginal others to do *their* work on the work.

In citing Coleridge here, I am not suggesting that research is poetry. But I am saying, as I did in the Introduction, that there is a poetics to the research process when one keeps soul in mind, a poetics that complements an empirics of research. Within a poetics of the research process, Coleridge's description points to that willingness to allow an experience to be what it is without either denial or affirmation of its real existence by some act of judgment that would measure the experience against some preformed notion of the real versus the imaginary. In this respect, the ritual place of play in the transference field between the researcher and the topic is a place where the researcher is willing to be a witness before becoming a critic.

To be a witness, however, is no easy task, as I showed in an essay on the reality of angels in medieval painting.[27] To appreciate fully the experience of angels in medieval painting, one has to be a witness who practices a willing suspension of disbelief, which is not simply a willingness to believe, but is the more challenging willingness not to disbelieve. It is one thing to declare that one either believes in the reality of angels or does not believe, and quite another to say that one does not disbelieve, because the latter indicates that one has at least made an effort to confront one's prejudices against such a reality. A witness, then, is one who is able to be responsible to some work because he or she has listened, because he or she has opened himself or herself to being addressed. With regard to the transference dialogues, then, the willing suspension of disbelief is not simply a willingness to believe in the process and the content of the dialogues. Rather, it is the willingness not to disbelieve them, that is, a willingness to suspend for a moment the categories and prejudices of the ego-mind that would work against the process. It is, then, a willingness to be addressed by the "others" who carry the unfinished business in the soul of the work and who, in doing so, challenge within this ritual place of play the researcher's complex relations to the work.

Step Two:

Adopting the mood of reverie, the attitude of negative capability, the gestures of hospitality, and the willingness to be a witness rather than a critic, the researcher is ready to take the second step in the process of dialoguing with the "strangers" in the work. In this second step, the researcher extends an invitation to those "others" who have a stake in the work, to those ancestors, for example, for whom the work is being done, or who wait with and hold the unfinished stories in the work.

While the form of the invitation is specifically tailored to each of the four levels of the transference field as listed below, at each level the researcher begins by announcing the topic that he or she is engaging. Over the years, I have found that it helps to overcome the sense that this process is only an interior monologue with oneself if one speaks aloud. Doing so lends some weight to the feeling that a dialogue with an *other* is about to happen. The forms of the invitations presented below are not formulas to be followed. They are suggestions, guidelines, and each researcher has to find his or her own words in this process.

I should also note here that these psychological dialogues, which continue throughout the research process, are not scheduled in any specific order, and I caution researchers that the "others" in the work who respond to their invitations might not be from the level of dialogue that the researcher has chosen. Surprise is often the case, and the researcher has to be prepared to welcome the strangers who actually respond. This element of surprise is, after all, another way in which the researcher is being chosen by the work.

- **Personal Level:** "Who is there in my family, biography, and/or history who has something to say about this work?" "Do my parents have a voice in this work?" "My siblings, etc.?"
- **Cultural-Historical Level:** "Who is there from another historical period and/or a different culture who has something to say about this work?" "Is there someone from another race, gender, socio-economic class who has a voice in this work?"
- **Collective-Archetypal Level:** "For whom is this work being done?" "Who are the guides or ancestors who are directing this work?" "Whom does this work serve?"

- **Eco-Cosmological Level:** "What do the other creatures with whom I share creation have to say about the work?" Do the animals have a voice in it?" "The plants, the trees, etc.?"

In each of these levels of dialogue, the researcher is engaged in the process of differentiating what he or she brings to the work from the work itself, not unlike what a lover and a beloved have to do within the dialogues of life that form their relation. In this work of differentiation, the researcher is being charged to stay with the work as it challenges his or her complex relations to it, and to be open to the unfinished business in the soul of the work that the "strangers" carry, which takes the work beyond the researcher's complexes. It is important to say again that an imaginal approach to research respects the work's autonomy. The levels of the dialogue, then, reflect a range that addresses both the complex psychology in the work and the soul of the work. The levels correspond roughly to the range between soul and the complex of psychology discussed in Chapter 1, although I am reluctant to make this correspondence into a formula. Quite often, a dialogue at the personal level, at which one might expect a great deal of complex material to appear, surprises the researcher with the appearance of an archetypal figure who does not belong to the researcher's history. I have often seen a wise old woman, or Crone, for example, or a gathering of silenced women take their place in lieu of the grandmother to carry the researcher's complex relation to the work.

Step Three:

After the invitation is extended, there is nothing for the researcher to do but wait. Impatience for something to happen is an early danger in the process, and at this juncture one needs that patience that belongs to the attitude of negative capability described above. One has to learn in this moment how to be still and, as the poet Eliot says, how to "wait without hope / For hope would be hope for the wrong thing." Eliot goes on to advise that one must also wait without love or faith, and perhaps that, too, is required. But the important point here is what he concludes: "But the faith and the love and the hope are all in the waiting."[28]

In this moment, one has to learn to wait without desire of any sort. I have found over the years with my students that this practice of patient waiting for whatever will happen is most difficult. One's internal critic begins the assault with accusations—that one is wasting time, for example, or that this process is only a piece of foolishness, or that this work is only a narcissistic involvement with oneself, or that the work itself is no good. Such criticisms are to be noticed, but not engaged in some defensive counterattack. One has to be careful here not to judge the criticism negatively, and one has to learn to ask, "Who is making the criticism?" One has to move from the idea of the internal critic to the personification of the criticisms.

One of my former graduate students, Jo Todd, provides a good example of this moment. Her dissertation, "Grieving with the Unborn," is a hermeneutic study of the polar positions of pro-life and pro-choice in the abortion debate.[29] Todd came to this study via the backdoor, since her initial forays into her work were around the issues of death and grief, both of which seemed to have followed her throughout her life. These themes were a complex in which she was caught. She was haunted by memories of death, such as that of her father the day after her tenth birthday, and by images of death and the rituals surrounding it. So, for a summer field-work project, as part of her coursework, she "embarked on a rudderless three-month mission entitled, 'Images of Death.'" For this project, she photographed cemeteries, tombstones, and other monuments of death and then presented them in a slideshow to her class. After the presentation, however, she confessed that the project had no "juice" for her. Her images of death had no life. Of this time she writes, "Adrift, drowning in unfathomable affect, I was lost, unconsciously possessed by Death and Grief." Coincidental to this moment was the internal-critical voice of her deceased mother, which chided her for being consumed with such dark issues, which no one would want to hear about. She was doing what she had always done: delving into things better left unspoken.

Jo, of course, could have persisted against this criticism and pushed ahead with the work, but she did not. Indeed, the criticism seemed to reflect her own feelings of lifelessness about the images of death. The internal critic was questioning the work and even attempting to stop it, as she herself was questioning it and feeling stuck. Was there something to hear in the criticism? Was this not the work she was supposed to do? Was there another work that was hiding in the shadows of Death and Grief?

Jo found her dissertation in those shadows. Through her transference dialogues, she encountered, in her words, the "Old Woman" who "revealed my unconscious relationship with Death and Grief through my discarded abortion experiences." One of the dialogues she presented in her study makes this point quite dramatically:

> You have missed the opportunity to bring life into the world, and there is no way to fix that. ... You have not truly grieved this very deep loss and it is something you must do. You have looked at the loss of your mother, father, grandparents, friends, and extended family, but you have not looked at the fact that you murdered two children that God gave you and that you decided to destroy.

There is no mistaking the tone or the content of this dialogue with the "Old Woman." Her words speak the language of pro-life, which was antithetical to Todd's strongly and stridently held pro-choice position. In her dissertation, she was challenged to re-imagine both of these positions and to find between them and beneath their rhetoric a third way, which would speak of and to the soul's perspective on the abortion debate. This piece of unfinished business in the cultural soul of the abortion debate became her work. Through her scholarly explorations of the cultural history of the abortion issue she discovered that the rhetoric of faith within the pro-life stance and the rhetoric of scientific reason within the pro-choice stance cloaked a shared yearning for some re-connection with nature, the feminine, and the archetypal image of the Divine Child. Jo Todd discovered in her work that beneath the polarized rhetoric of the public debate on abortion one could be in service to the sacred dimensions of life without being anti-choice.

Jo Todd was thus led into her work through that early critical voice that was opposed to her initial sense of the work. Beyond the images of death and grief, she was asked to reclaim her own complex relation to her own discarded abortion experiences and, through her relation to them, to become a witness for what remains unfinished in this issue.

Earlier I said that after the researcher extends his or her invitations to dialogue about the work, there is nothing to do but wait. But what is the researcher waiting for? Is he or she waiting for a clear and distinct idea to form, for some thought to arise to give a sense of direction to the work? No! He or she is waiting for something more subtle than conscious thoughts.

These invitations to dialogue are, as we saw, like the process of active imagination, and, as Cwik notes, "The starting point of active imagination can be a mood, a dream image, or any spontaneous visual image."[30] To these I would add bodily sensations. In this third step, the researcher welcomes these phenomena, even though they may seem marginal or irrelevant to the process of research, which is, after all, supposed to be subject only to the powers of the critical mind. But they have come, and, with gestures of hospitality and the attitude of negative capability, the researcher enters into dialogue with them. If it is a mood, such as anxiety, or a bodily sensation, such as discomfort, one enters into it as fully as possible.

Regarding the mood, Cwik says, "The participant *sinks down* into this mood *without reserve*."[31] The same act of surrender is true also for a bodily sensation. One has to remember here that in this space of transference where the dialogues take place, one is playing with the possibilities in the work, and the "strangers" who might carry those possibilities come as they are in response to our invitations, and not as we wish. If they come as mood or feeling rather than as thought or idea, then this is how the researcher is being engaged by the unconscious depths of the work. Would a researcher who had invited a colleague to come to his or her house for a discussion about his or her work turn that colleague away at the door because he or she was not garbed as the researcher had expected? Would anyone? Such an action would be inhospitable to the colleague, and it would be equally inhospitable to the "strangers" in the work. Indeed, such an inhospitable act would make it more likely that neither would come again.

Working with students over the years, I have found it helpful to suggest that within each mood or feeling there is an image and/or a gesture, and that in giving oneself over as fully as possible to the mood or the feeling the researcher might find an image in the mood or a gesture in the feeling. Indeed, I would say that image, mood, and gesture are a triad and that where one is present so are the others. Mood, image, and gesture bring one into the unconscious depths of the work and any one of them can open the researcher up to the possibilities in the work. But again, one must attend to these epiphanies of the work without judgment or criticism. Cwik notes that the one who enters into active imagination "willingly and consciously produces an *abaissement du niveau mental*, an altered state of consciousness,"[32] which

I have described as reverie, and which certainly characterizes the consciousness of one who is at play. Playing with the possibilities in the work requires, as Jung notes, the suspension of all criticism. As strange as it may seem, therefore, if research is to keep soul in mind, then it must acknowledge that the researcher's mood and body belong to the body of his or her work and that his or her work is embodied. One's work settles into one's flesh and indeed is spun out of one's flesh. The curious thing here is that empirical models of research often assume that the researcher is a dispassionate and disembodied mind. But the pain that one might feel in one's gut as the work tightens up can be an expression of what is being ignored or rushed past in the work, an invitation to slow down and to inquire who or what is addressing the work and/or what is asking to be digested further in it. In this manner, transference dialogues bring the body into the work. They heal the split between body and mind. They engage the researcher fully as an embodied mind. With soul in mind, one truly does "suffer" the work. One bears it, and one endures its cost.

Step Four:

Having set the stage, extended the invitation to the "strangers" in the work, and waited for an image, mood, or bodily sensation in response to the invitation, the researcher is now ready to take the fourth step. In this step, he or she actively engages the "strangers" in the work. There are two related but distinct moments in this step of engagement, which Jung first described in his essay "The Transcendent Function," and which he first called "active imagination" in his 1935 lectures at Tavistock and continued to elaborate over the years in many other works.[33] Cwik presents a comprehensive overview of these sources and offers a fine summary of these two moments.[34]

The first moment in this fourth step is the moment of reception, with its requirement to give some concrete shape or form to what takes place in the transference field between the researcher and the "strangers" in the work. Cwik notes the importance of this moment for Jung: the "actual ocular evidence effectively counteracts the ever-present tendency to self-deception and helps to prevent the contents from slipping back into the unconscious."[35] Indeed, one of my graduate students used different stones to symbolize the "others" in the work. Through those stones she was able to feel herself in dialogue with an *other* and to bracket her self-conscious sense that the dialogues were just conversations with herself. In some respects, those stones functioned as transitional objects, mediating the tensions between her psychological states and the material world.

To give form to the process, the images that appear or the moods that are evoked or the bodily sensations that are felt can be drawn, painted, sculptured, or written as a dialogue between the researcher and the "others" in the work. Which method the researcher chooses here depends largely upon his or her individual type. Those who are more visually inclined might prefer to draw or paint the "other," while the more verbally inclined might actually write down the dialogue that takes place between himself or herself and the "other." In this latter form, the dialogue, Cwik says, "appears as a script written between two characters."[36]

Here, the attitude of the researcher towards these products is important: he or she has to practice that willing suspension of disbelief described above. In this first moment, the researcher has to be present more as a witness than as a critic. He or she simply has to be present to what is, without judgment or evaluation. He or she is required not to disbelieve that the drawing or the painting or the script is the outcome of the engagement between the "I" of the researcher and the "others" in the work, the "strangers" who have come in response to the invitations to speak about the work. The researcher is required not to disbelieve that these dialogues occur between the "I" of the researcher and what Mary Watkins calls the "invisible guests" who are present in imaginal dialogues.[37]

The transference dialogues, as I said earlier in this chapter, belong to an imaginal approach to research. In the context of Watkins's work, the dialogues take place in that imaginal realm where the unfinished business in the soul of the work unfolds. The four levels of these dialogues are, moreover, consonant with how over the years she has broadened her understanding of the range of these imaginal dialogues to "embrace not only our relations with others, but also our relations with the 'beings of nature and the earth, and that which we take to be divine.'"[38] The "strangers" whom the researcher encounters in these imaginal dialogues are the deepening of the work, just as the *other* as difference or stranger that we encounter in life is the deepening of the self. The researcher who would keep soul in mind and who practices this process is one who, in lending an ear to the "others" in the work, opens the work to being addressed, challenged, broadened, deepened, and changed.

Dialogue as openness to the other is a radically ethical way of being and living in the world. In his essay "The Transcendent Function," Jung says, "The present day shows with appalling clarity how little able people are to let the other man's argument count, although this capacity is a fundamental and indispensable condition for any human community."[39] The transference dialogues are a way of letting the "other's" argument count. It is an ethical way of doing research, an issue I will consider in the final chapter of this book.

In the second moment of Step Four, after the process of engaging the "other" in the work has been made concrete in one form or another, the researcher moves away from being the witness and towards becoming the critic. Becoming the critic does not, however, mean that one becomes judgmental about the previous moment. Rather, it means that he or she takes a critical stance towards the products of that first moment by posing the question, "What do they say about the work?" How are the drawings, or paintings, or scripts related to the work? This is the work of reflection, as opposed to the work of reception in the first moment.

Over the years, I have found that this moment of reflection is best served when it is separated clearly from the moment of reception. Certainly, during the first moment, reception, the work of reflection is to be postponed. I often suggest to my students that they wait some time, often even a day or two, before reflecting on the relevance of the products for the work. I encourage my students simply to be with the "strangers" in the work during this interim period between the two moments, that is, to stay with what has been brought to them as one would with a companion, just as one might carry a dream into life and walk alongside it before trying to make sense of it. When a dreamer does this, he or she is allowing the dream first to make sense of him or her, before he or she attempts to make sense of it. In like manner, the intention behind creating this little space between reception and reflection is for the researcher to hold the products of the dialogues alongside his or her more conscious thoughts and ideas about the work, to allow a time and place for them to rub up against each other. I have also found that more often than not, when the moment of reflection begins, the stage is also being set for another dialogue, establishing a rhythm of sorts between receptivity to the "strangers" in the work, and reflection on their contributions to the work.

In this moment of reflection, there are two critical ways of dealing with the products that arise in the moment of reception. "One is the way of creative formulation, the other the way of understanding."[40] Jung notes that each of these principles has inherent dangers if one is allowed to predominate to the exclusion of the other.

When the principle of creative formulation is dominant, the individual tends to focus on the aesthetic aspect of the product. "The danger of the aesthetic tendency," Jung says, "is overvaluation of the formal or 'artistic' worth of the fantasy-productions; the libido is diverted from the real goal of the transcendent function and sidetracked into purely aesthetic problems of artistic expression."[41] The real goal of the transcendent function that Jung speaks of here is that third thing—the drawing, or the painting, or the script—that mediates the gap between conscious and unconscious and is a byproduct of their interaction. When the researcher falls into this aesthetic danger, then he or she judges the product in terms of its artistic worth and loses touch with the meanings that it has for the work.

On the other hand, when the principle of understanding is dominant, the individual tends to focus on the meaning of the product. "The danger of wanting to understand the meaning is overvaluation of the content, which is subjected to intellectual analysis and interpretation, so that the essentially symbolic character of the product is lost."[42] When the researcher falls into this danger, then he or she loses touch with the specificity of the image or the dialogue. Overvaluation of the meaning prematurely forecloses any sense of wonder and ongoing curiosity about how a particular image in a drawing or painting or a particular dialogue informs the work.

Regarding these two ways of coming to terms with these products, Jung notes that "the ideal case would be if these two aspects could exist side by side or rhythmically succeed each other: that is, if there were an alternation of creation and understanding."[43] Cwik notes that Jung himself is the prototype of this rhythm. Jung, he says, "painted or sculpted his fantasies, and, at the same time, amplified these emerging images intellectually through his understanding of myths and alchemy."[44] The same task is demanded of the researcher who has entered the transference field. He or she has to give form to what is received in the process and explore the meanings of the images and dialogues produced as they relate to the work. As Jung's statement shows, however, the researcher also has to attend to the images, symbols, and fantasies on their own terms, and this way of understanding leads to the fifth step in the process of transference dialogues. Before I describe this fifth step, however, I want to underscore the point that the drawings or paintings or scripts that arise in the transference field are not the data. They are pathways into the unknown in the work, portals into the work's undreamed possibilities. They are the ways in which the work is redeemed into its own otherness beyond the researcher's conscious intentions and plans. It is not enough, therefore, for the researcher simply to give form to these possibilities, or even to reflect upon their meanings for the work. In addition, the researcher has to amplify the possibilities presented by researching the images that accompany the dialogues.

Step Five:

In this fifth step, the researcher amplifies the material of the dialogues through scholarly work, and in doing so, he or she aligns himself or herself with the traditional researcher. It is important, however, not to lose sight of the fact that the path to the library has been through the deep subjectivity of the researcher. The wounded researcher meets the traditional researcher as one who has made the attempt to make his or her unconscious presence to the work more conscious and as one who is in service to the unfinished business in the soul of the work. The imaginal approach and the transference dialogues do not replace scholarly modes of research—they add an important and neglected aspect to them.

An example from one of my graduate students illustrates this point. It is from the work of Linda Lauver, who, even as I write this passage, is in the process of doing her work. In her research on Mayan culture, the image and figure of the jaguar has appeared in her dialogues. Writing the dialogue, she has also reflected on its meanings for her project. What also needs to be done, however, is scholarly amplification of the image through myth and symbol and an exploration of its presence and significance in Mayan culture as noted by other scholars. Jaguar, we might say, is the guide who has been leading her deeper into the work, and she has to research who and what Jaguar is, not only in relation to her work, but also in relation to Jaguar as the "other" in the work, to Jaguar on its terms. Only in this way is the work truly redeemed into itself. Only in this way does one truly let go of the work.

The value of these psychological dialogues between the researcher and the work in the transference field between them is that they slow the work down. This slowing down of the work will, of course, run counter to the ego's position in the work, but re-search that would keep soul in mind is a kind of alchemy. And, in alchemy, things have to cook a bit, and the heat under the flask where the work is being done has to be turned up if the stone as the goal of the opus is to be achieved.[45]

An Additional Consideration

Before I close this chapter, there are two additional questions to be considered. First, how does one decide *what* to include of the transference material, and, second, *how* does one incorporate the transference material into the work?

With regard to the first question, it is important to note that not all of the transference material is to be included. If it were, the work itself would be overwhelmed. Two criteria guide the choice of material. First, does the material bear directly upon the researcher's complex relation to the work? Second, does the material illustrate how the work was transformed by the researcher after he or she made his or her complex relation to the work more conscious? Of course, these two criteria are subjective judgments, and such judgments themselves are complex matters. There is really no way around this subjectivity, but there are some things that a researcher can do to address it.

Over the years, I have discovered that the element of surprise can play a useful role in selecting the material, and I advise my graduate students to pay attention to those parts of the transference material that go against their expectations. Something is always at work in these moments, something "other" that overturns one's preconceived notions about the work.

In addition, a researcher can, and in fact should, draw upon the same commitment initially made to make a place for the unconscious in the research process. That the researcher has in fact been engaging the work in this way indicates that he or she is dedicated to the ethical task of letting himself or herself be addressed by the "other" in the work. Reminding oneself of this dedication at this stage of the process can provide one with a strong incentive for not spoiling the work, but continuing it in an ethical, honest, and courageous fashion.

Finally, one should not discount the effect of the benefits one has received along the way as a motive for continuing to confront the other in oneself when making the choices of what to include of the transference material. There is a quiet kind of joy that comes from seeing more deeply into the work because one has seen through one's complex relations to it. A researcher who has had glimpses of the unfinished business in the soul of the work is changed by these epiphanies. There is an inner sense of having been deepened into oneself by this work. There is an alchemy to this process in which the researcher is centered more fully in himself or herself to the point where the work has been released more fully into itself.

With regard to the second question, how to incorporate the transference material into the work, I have found over the years that the material becomes a living part of the work when it is organically stitched into the body of the work. Incorporated in this fashion, the transference material functions as a kind of resting place or oasis, where the researcher's complex ties to the work are nourished by the unfinished business in the work. To mark off the boundaries of these oases, the transference material is set in different type. In addition, the material is presented in a digested form. Having made his or her decision about what to include, the researcher presents just enough of the material to show how it advances the work beyond his or her complex relation to it. In other words, the researcher provides a clear indication of how the transference material that is included is related to the work. He or she has already done the hard work of reflecting on these connections, and all that remains is to show what they are.

CLOSING TIME

In this chapter, I described active imagination as a ritual space of play between the researcher and his or her work. I also outlined the two procedures for letting go of the work and I started off a discussion on what one should include of the transference material and how it might be included it in the body of the work. Throughout the chapter,

I have referred to the work and experiences of my graduate students to illustrate this material. Chapter 6 extends these examples. It provides numerous descriptions of the experience of students who have used reverie and transference dialogues in their work. These examples are a working model of these processes, and they demonstrate both their value and their limitations. Despite the past fifteen years of effort on my part, my understanding of how one makes a place for the complex unconscious presence of the researcher in re-search is still a work in progress,

CHAPTER SIX

The Transference Field:
Student Examples

Catch only what you've thrown yourself, all is
mere skill and little gain;
but when you're suddenly the catcher of a ball
thrown by an eternal partner
with accurate and measured swing
towards you, to your centre, in an arch
from the great bridgebuilding of God:
why catching then becomes a power—
not yours, a world's.[1]

—Rainer Maria Rilke

INTRODUCTION

In this chapter, I want to give some examples from my graduate students of their experiences in using the transference process in research. The examples are grouped around a series of questions I sent to them, to which they replied as they reflected on the process. All quotations are personal communications from the students. At the end of this chapter, I will also make a few remarks about the dangers of this process and some things a researcher can do to set limits on these dangers.

STUDENT RESPONSES

Question #1: Describe how you did the dialogues. How did they change your work? Did they change you, and if so, how? At the

end of the research process, how was the work different from what you initially imagined? How were you different?

Kerry Ragain, whose dissertation is entitled "Archetypal Threads in the Experience of Being Adopted," described the dialogues as a "corporeal portal into a way of being which is hospitable to the figures of soul" in the work.[2] He compared this description to the experience of Philemon and Baucis, who welcomed into their home the gods Jupiter and Mercury disguised as travelers, and who, for their generosity and hospitality towards the strangers, were rewarded with an epiphany of the divine. Ragain is referring here to the attitude of hospitality, which we described earlier as an essential condition for establishing the ritual space of play for these dialogues to occur. Hospitality toward the "strangers" in the work has the potential to open what otherwise might remain disguised. It has the potential to reveal something unexpected and well beyond one's ordinary concerns. "The dialogues," he says, "can be seen as an entry point into a new way of knowing and being that is humble and gets one beyond the gravitational pull of one's self, and beyond the small grouping of concepts or perceptions that one thinks he or she knows." Describing the ritual space of the dialogues, Ragain noted that the room of his study "became a convention center where I and the figures could sit together and convene." He is suggesting that over time the practice of the dialogues transformed the strangers in the work into companions who accompanied him on the journey.

Jo Todd, whose dissertation is entitled "Grieving with the Unborn," does not so much describe the way she did the dialogues as how they changed her and her work.[3] She credits the dialogues with helping her to become more conscious of her complex identification with her pro-choice perspective on the abortion issue. Indeed, until she was able to enter into the space of these dialogues, her work was not progressing. She was stuck. "At the beginning of the study," she writes, "I worked with the transference dialogues because there was no other way into the subject." As she entered more deeply into them, she notes, they "consistently revealed unacceptable and undigested perspectives." In addition, they "constellated unanticipated affect." And yet, as she worked with these unpleasant "surprises," the dialogues proved to be "the key into the heart of the debate," where her "normalized certainty" about her pro-choice view was "relegated to the dubious position of a perspective." "The dialogues," she writes, "reminded me that I am always in a perspective," and this idea, she adds, "challenged the popular myth of objectivity, that comforting place of certainty," by which she means that place of dispassionate non–involvement with the work. Indeed, what Todd's work demonstrates is that a true sense of objectivity must take into account the indissoluble link to a subjectivity that has become somewhat conscious of its own unconscious complexes. She writes concerning the dialogues, "Without their help I could have continued unconsciously justifying the rightness of my [pro-choice] perspective." Then, the pro-life perspective would have remained at odds with her pro-choice one, and the work that was asking to be born would have remained unborn. "Instead," she writes, "the dialogues with *Others* re-viewed the work." They cast into a different light the areas she was able to re-search, and they helped to situate the polarized perspectives in a wider field. "Remarkably," she says, "the study revealed the abortion controversy as a cultural container," a vessel that exposed in each position some deep-seated archetypal energies. In her research, she uncovered, for example, that the conflict in the abortion debate between scientific rationalism and religious fundamentalism is a response to a deep sense of loss of Soul in Western culture, and she demonstrated that with this loss, the "possibility of the birth of the Divine Child was aborted" in each perspective, where it continues to linger symptomatically in the rhetoric about the unborn child. In this dialogue work with her transferences to the topic, Todd was embodying the ethical attitude towards research discussed in Chapter 13.

Todd is clear that the dialogues sometimes "took time to digest." They required, she notes, "an other-than-ordinary state of mind," which was "not constructed or destructed by objective facts or academic research." Her words here recall the mood of reverie, the attitudes of negative capability, and the willing suspension of disbelief required to construct the space for these dialogues. In this space, she entered into an-other relation with her work. There, "I could slow down," she writes, "soften my gaze and listen patiently." These moments, she makes clear, were not substitutes for her academic research and its scholarly demands. They were a complement to them. "As a result of the transference dialogues," she concludes, "I was stretched, sometimes beyond recognition." She was, in effect, different at the end of the work from what and who she was at the beginning, and the work, too, was different from how it had initially been imagined and planned. Of herself, she says, "I am less certain, more thoughtful, and yet paradoxically stand on more stable ground." The work also was stretched beyond its original frame. Uncovering some of the archetypal energies hidden within the rhetoric of the two polarized positions on abortion, she "emerged with an enhanced sense of its possibilities for the generations to come and for our current global and cultural situations."

Question #2: What value do you see in these dialogues? Were some of the levels more valuable than others?

In his dissertation, "Between the Frying Pan and the Fire: The *Intermundia* of Clergy Transitioning out of Parish Ministry" (2006), Erik Killinger not only made use of the transference dialogues himself, he also asked his research participants to engage in the process, a procedure that Kerry Ragain had pioneered in his study.[4] Ragain attempted to explore archetypal motifs such as that of the Orphan in the background of a person who had been adopted. From his own transference work with the topic, he was aware of the value of the dialogues in releasing unconscious aspects of the experience. Reporting on his extension of this procedure to his subjects, he said it proved helpful because it showed them that "there are ways of understanding and gaining information about themselves that are beyond their conscious sphere of awareness." In effect, then, Ragain trained his subjects to be co-researchers in this process, and this gave them an experiential sense of the archetypal motifs associated with being adopted. Through this process, they were able to participate in the study at a level that was deeper than an intellectual understanding of the work.

Killinger, on the other hand, was less enthusiastic about this extension of the use of dialogues. Of the four subjects he employed in his phenomenological design, three made use of the dialogues. One of these three found the dialogues to be "inflated," while the other two dialogues by the subjects had for Killinger a monologue quality, and this suggested to him some avoidance by his subjects of the "strangers" presence in the process. This result is not surprising, since the process of dialoguing, which is modeled on Jung's procedure of active imagination, makes a severe demand upon the ego's sense of control and hence meets with resistance. The procedure itself, moreover, is not easy to do, and it takes commitment and a strong sense of motivation to engage it. What might motivate a research subject to make the effort is as mysterious as what motivates people to pay attention to their dreams.

The transference dialogues led Killinger into "the deepening spiral of the work." They were valuable, he says, because "I was encouraged, pricked, goaded, invited, led, and cajoled to work through the work rather than simply intuit its course *sans* an experiential aspect." The dialogues, he is suggesting, are valuable because they give the researcher a felt sense of the work, as Ragain's "co-researchers" discovered. They deepen the work beyond intellect into feeling. In addition, the process of dialoguing moves the ego out of the work in different ways, some of which are as gentle as encouragement and some as forceful as a prick or a goad.

As to the relative value of the levels of the dialogues, Killinger remarks, "I do not know that some levels were more valuable than others." Nevertheless, he reports an interesting observation about the first level. "Despite my hesitance to stipulate the value or helpfulness of one dialogue over another, it is worth pointing out that the initial transference dialogue in my experience marked the location, initiated the digging, and opened the way for the other three levels to emerge as they did." This observation fits with my own experience over the years with many students who report that the personal level of the dialogues is the easiest to do. Perhaps this is so because within this field one is meeting more-or-less familiar others who belong to one's biography and history. Be that as it may, Killinger adds that on the basis of this initial dialogue "a space was made for encounters with other *numinosa,* or figures of soul." Commenting on the value of these encounters, he adds, "I discovered the extension beneath both the complexity of my knowledge and the knowledge of my complexity enfolded by fantasy and reverie." In short, for Killinger, the value of the dialogues lay in their deepening of the work and himself in relation to the work. In these depths the work spoke through him without being just about him. A differentiation occurred without a splitting-off from the work. The objectivity of the work was secured in the deepened awareness of its subjectivity.

Debbie Greenwood, whose dissertation, "Resting at the Crossroads: Working with Women's Narratives and Art-Making," has already been cited in Chapter 2, says quite directly, "Yes, they were very helpful."⁵ She elaborates by saying that the dialogues helped her "to look beyond texts—the written word—for answers." What she means here is that the dialogues got the work moving again when she and it were stuck. They freed her and the work from that tension she felt in the work between being an artist and needing to be also the scholar who was doing a Ph.D. dissertation.

Indeed, this was the tension at the heart of her project—how to bring women's narratives through artwork into the open and at the same time situate her research within the scholarly tradition regarding narrative, the work of memory, and the role of storytelling in re-membering the unfinished business in a life. Only when these two were in rhythm did the work seem to move more smoothly. Quite frequently, however, she experienced doubts about her scholarly voice in the work. Was it being overwhelmed by the artistic aspect of the work? In these moments, the dialogues helped to give a place to the artistic voice in the work. Her own words are eloquent testimony to this process: "Doing my own art process (making collages and books) before working with the women," she says, "opened me to my own fears and the places my own voice felt frozen." Her own art process situated her in a place of reverie where she could rest more easily with this aspect she was bringing to the work, and in the dialogues she found a way to be open to the value of listening to what the "others" have to say about the unfinished business of a life that needs to be re-membered. She writes, "So, I worked toward listening. I learned to wait on an idea, to sleep on it, rest with it for a while." One value of the dialogues was that they slowed the process down; they mitigated somewhat the ego's impatient anxiety about the work. This is an aspect of the dialogues that many of my students reported on, and I have come to regard it as a sign that these dialogues aid the researcher in letting go of the work and resting with it within a larger field that has its own rhythms and pace. "It wasn't easy," she adds. But, "it has changed me."

On the relative value of the different levels, Greenwood is clear that while for her the first three levels were generally helpful throughout the project, the collective-archetypal level proved particularly helpful at the specific moment when she was at an impasse in the work and feeling paralyzed by it. She was struggling with her inability to make the narratives of her subjects coherent. Overwhelmed by the richness and complexity of the data, she says, "I was not able to hold together the elements of my research to form a line of reasoning I could articulate." Stuck in this way, she was incarnating the burden of the work. "My sleep was poor," she writes, "my energy non-existent." Entering into a dialogue, she asked, "Who is there that can help me understand this?" After a few moments, an old woman in a wheelchair appeared. It was the same woman who earlier had appeared in one of her dreams. Now, she wondered about the old woman's name and thought to herself that it was Helga, but the old woman corrected her and said, "No, it is Hilda." It is worthwhile to quote a portion of this dialogue, not only to illustrate this point, but also to show how the actual scripting of the dialogues takes place.

> Hilda (H): "What do you see?"
> Debbie (D): "An old woman in a wheelchair."
> H: "No, what do you see?"
> D: "Someone with a disability."
> H: "What does that mean to you?"
> D: "You have limitations."
> H: "What kind of limitations do you mean?"
> D: "Well, there are some things you can't do—like play basketball."
> H: [*Laughing*] Some people do. This isn't a disability, it is a perspective. It gives me a point of view, this wheelchair. I see things in a different way from this side of the experience.

Reflecting on this dialogue, Greenwood says, "I found this image of the old woman in the wheelchair helpful." In the dialogues, this old woman is not frozen by her limitations. At another point in the dialogue, the Old Woman in the Wheelchair says to Debbie, "You are worried about what you see as your limitations, your affliction," referring to Debbie's concern about her ability to hold the tension between the scholarly demands of the work and the creative aspects of it. Debbie was questioning whether she had the ability to hold the work together, and of her doubt she says, "I had lost the inspired side of the research." Feeling her sense of limitation, she says, "I found myself running ahead of the project, judging the quality of the work before its time." Is it not interesting how the presence of the Old Woman in the Wheelchair in the transference field serves as a counterpoint to Debbie's felt sense of running ahead of herself? The Old Woman in the Wheelchair moves in a different way, more slowly. As such, she reminds Debbie that in moving too fast she has been losing touch with the work. "Instead of letting myself succumb to the natural timing of the project and the interrelationships between the art-making and the theoretical side of the project," Debbie adds, "I felt I had to manage the data and my time." The old woman's presence, however, changed all that. "Her aliveness and assertiveness penetrated the dreary existence I had made for myself."

In the previous chapter, I indicated that in addition to understanding how what one is given in the dialogues relates to the work, one must also research the meaning of the material on its own terms. Debbie did that with the name of the figure who had eased her felt sense of limitation. The name Hilda had surprised her, because, as she notes, "I was not fond of Scandinavian names." Researching the origins of the name, she discovered that "Hilda" means "protector" and "woman warrior," and with this awareness she was led more deeply by this figure into the work. "At first glance," she writes, "the name and her physical disability created a paradox." How could someone with such an obvious limitation be a protector, much less a warrior? It was the same question that Debbie was facing in herself. How could she with her limitations and doubts forge ahead with the work? But then she remembered Hilda's message. "Her affliction was part of her strength," she writes. "I had felt so tired and beat up by the difficulty of pulling ideas together that I welcomed her spirit," she adds. Hilda thus became for her a companion. "Traveling so broadly through various disciplines to investigate my topic had brought me into contact with the scholarly ideas of many remarkable people," Debbie writes, and "[i]t had made me aware of my limitations." Before Hilda's appearance in the dialogues, she says, "I had begun to walk too lightly and humbly when exploring these important works, not entirely appreciating what my perspective might bring to the discussion." Hilda helped Debbie to see her limitations as a perspective and to appreciate what she could bring to the discussion about ritual, memory, narrative, and other themes in her work. "A woman warrior and protector was exactly what I needed to further support my work."

Greenwood used a dream image to open a space of dialogue where she encountered the Old Woman in the Wheelchair. But what can we say of this figure? Who is this "other" in the work? Referring to Hilda, Greenwood says, "It was the first time that I thought of myself as having an ally in the process." As ally, mentor, and guide, Hilda led Greenwood into the depths of the work and out of her places of being stuck; and, in this respect, the Old Woman in the Wheelchair is an example of the autonomous stranger who acts something like the *spiritus rector* of the work. One value of the dialogues, then, is that they can offer these opportunities, which not only slow the work down and deepen it, but also relieve the researcher of some of his or her anxieties, which, if we recall the work of Devereux mentioned in Chapter 4, are too often covered over by a flight into method, and which Debbie tried to cover over with a flight to finish the work. Hilda slowed her down, called her back to herself and back to the work. For Debbie, that was one real value of the dialogues.

Question #3: What limitations do you see in working with the dialogues?

Jo Todd, whose dissertation has already been described above, speaks to the "ever present danger of getting lost in the dramatic affect generated by the presence of archetypal energies." As the researcher gets drawn into the work through a complex, the dialogues, which are intended as a means of letting go of the work, can actually translate into his or her becoming sucked into it. Todd offers an apt image of this connection between the complex of the researcher and the archetypal energies of the work. "The researcher's woundedness," she says, "which invites the vocational call, can create a quagmire." Instead of the dialogues helping to differentiate the complex relation of the researcher to the work, they overwhelm him or her. "It is possible," Todd says, "for the dialogues to invite the researcher into the deep faster than he or she is able to descend." This is one of the real dangers of this process, and hence one if its serious limitations. The dialogues are not for everyone, and those who do engage in them need lifelines outside the work. Todd makes this point herself when she says that the dialogues "are not for anyone who wants immediate results," highlighting again that this process slows down the work and deepens it by forcing the researcher to come to terms with his or her unconscious projections onto the work. She also adds that because of the dangers, the process "require[s] the presence of a mentor or guide." This notion of a mentor or guide arises with many of my students, and it re-configures the role of the mentor in the academy. The mentor has to be one of those lifelines who stands with and for the work but not in it. I will address this theme in greater detail later in this chapter.

In spite of this limitation and the dangers involved, Todd affirms the value of these dialogues. "If differentiation occurs, then personal woundedness, complexes, and biases can stand in service to cultural healing." For Todd, this benefit was worth the risk and danger. The slow and at times painful process of working through her complex identification with the pro-choice position on abortion made it possible for her to become a spokesperson and witness for the unfinished business in the soul of this debate.

Another major limitation of the process is the challenge it offers to the ego's desire to control and be in charge of the work. This limitation expresses itself in the form of resistances to the dialogues, which I will take up in the next question. But here, it is worth quoting some of the remarks made in response to this question regarding limitations. Kay Tomlinson, whose dissertation, "Conversations with the Ladies: Art-Making in Collaboration with Imaginal Figures," is currently in progress, says, "This way of working is often frustrating, often slow, always more complex."[6] Here the limitation of the dialogues concerns the issue of time. The slowing down of the work by the dialogues serves the interests of the work, but not necessarily those of the ego. From the ego's point of view, this slowing down is a significant limitation on its timeline for the work. Thus, what is of value for the soul of the work becomes a limitation for the ego, in much the same way as any victory for the Self is experienced by the ego as a defeat.

Ellen Macfarland makes a similar point. In her dissertation, "Discovering the Healing Power of Nature: A New Perspective for Healing the Wounds of Childhood Abuse," she drew upon her encounters with nature as a healing mechanism for her own experience of abuse.[7] In addition, in her work as a therapist, she had seen how the healing power of nature worked for her patients. These were two of the roots of her complex vocational draw into the work, and although she had in her own life and work experienced the effects of nature on the healing process, she still found the dialogues difficult to sustain, because they were drawing her into some unfinished business in the work about abuse. She observes that in dialogue with "the horse nation, the tree nation, and the dolphin nation I became intensely aware of the trauma that these species have experienced at the hand of the human nation." These guides into the depths of the work were stretching the work beyond her original intentions. They were challenging the ego position she was bringing to the work, which would have circumscribed the work within the borders of the therapy room. Thus, she says, "My ego always had a plan for how the active imagination dialogues were supposed to go." With such plans in mind, she adds, "I tended to dismiss the dialogues as not being real."

Over time, however, she was able to let go of her intentions regarding the work, and indeed the final effect of this process was a marked transformation in her life and her work. Having become acutely aware of the unfinished business in the work, aware of how the abuse of children connects with the larger story of our abuse of nature, she has become an advocate for cultural healing. She writes:

> Rather than continuing as a therapist, I closed my practice and have worked to become an author and a teacher. Finding a new path to follow has not diminished my call as a healer for those who have been traumatized. The importance of my work on my dissertation has allowed me to hope that those who have been traumatized may well be the ones who can change the course of our culture's inability to care for all the other species of the planet.

What was initially experienced as a limitation became a portal into a new way of being and working. Again, therefore, we might say that what is viewed as a limitation from the ego's point of view is seen to be of value from the soul's point of view. Keeping the soul of the work in mind by attending to the limitations inherent in the dialogues, one might become a witness and spokesperson for the unfinished business in the work. In Macfarland's case, as well as in the case of Jo Todd discussed above, the scope of the work expanded beyond the narrower limits of the ego's position. In each case, the researcher, stretched beyond her original complex identification with the topic by the dialogues, has become an agent of cultural healing.

It would be a mistake, however, to champion only the idea that what the ego experiences as a limitation of the process is of value for the soul in the work. It would be a mistake to lose the ego's point of view here, to forget Todd's image of the quagmire. The limitations of the process protect the researcher and the work from that quagmire.

Dennis Langhans, whose dissertation, "An Odyssey of the Heart: A Return to the Place, Rhythm and Time of the Heart" (2002), makes this point quite directly.[8] His work is a piece of cultural therapeutics, which goes beyond his original intentions for the work. "In seeing that the mechanistic heart of the scientific viewpoint had become the dominant 'reality,' I experienced the sense of loss," and, he adds, "I set out to find the lost human heart." What Langhans set out to find in his work was "The Heart's other ways of knowing and being, which had become the discarded, the devalued, the forgotten." But in the journey which the dialogues initiated, he says, "something *other*, something unexpected found me." What found him was this realization: "The heart, it would seem, is not limited exclusively to the human realm." What found him was the devalued, discarded, and forgotten heart of the ecosystem.

In one section of his dissertation, he gives a beautiful example of a reverie, which, as we have seen, is also a way of letting go of the work. This reverie, entitled "Facing the Heart of San Elijo," was, he says, "a fulcrum moment, a pivot point in the dissertation." "Some numen spoke here," he remarks. "It spoke both through me and to me." Here is a portion of his reverie:

> As I stood in this place of San Elijo, reflecting on images of the human heart, I was struck by the likeness between prevalent diseases of the human heart and those of the ecosystem. The lagoon suffered from a combination of atherosclerosis and congestive heart failure. Its arteries were constricted, blocking the flow of the salt water to its body. Moreover, the organ of its salty blood, the heart, was drowning in its own stagnant fluids.

This reverie changed the work. It expanded it beyond his original journey in search of the lost human heart. Here was the heart of the ecosystem crying out for a voice, and in his work and in the dialogues, he gave a place for that voice. Langhans, however, is quite direct about the labor required to do so. It is not helpful or wise to remain in reverie, where one can fall into the quagmire of the archetypal energies of the soul of the work. Addressing the issue of limitations, Langhans says, "The work of dissertational research rightly requires the rational or critical element." In evaluating the place that the imaginal approach gives to non-rational elements in the research process, elements such as the dialogues themselves and the dreams that often serve as a starting point for the dialogues, he pulls no punches: "To take only a non-rational approach strikes me as a form of romantic denial." The limitations of the transference dialogues are for him a reminder of the need to find a way to marry the rational and the non-rational in re-search that would keep soul in mind. "So," he says, "I see a need to bring the ego and the rational into the tent of dialogue." He sees the need to take the limitations seriously as a way of remembering. "The witness needs the critic; the *orare* seeks the *laborare*."

The transference dialogues are indeed a laboratory in which both *labor* and *oratory* take place. Earlier, I described the space of these dialogues as a ritual space of play, and in this space both the witness and the critic belong. If re-search with soul in mind strives to make a place for the witness, it is because, as Langhans notes, "in our culture the critic is well known and appreciated, while the witness, on the other hand, is decidedly less appreciated." In the previous chapter, I described the witness as one who is able to be responsible to some work because he or she has listened, because he or she has opened himself or herself to being addressed. This is precisely what is asked of the researcher in the transference field. He or she is addressed by the "others" in the work, by the "strangers" who carry its unfinished business. The witness waits on presence for the epiphany of meaning. The critic, however, has a different task. The critic is the one who brings judgment into the field and the one who is charged with exploring the multiple meanings of what is given in the dialogues. The critic is also the one charged with situating what is given in the dialogues within the established tradition of scholarship pertaining to the work. Both stances operate in the transference dialogues, and this is Langhans's point. One has to be able to wait and evaluate what is given. The limitations of the dialogues invite both stances. One has to wait within them if one is to discover the weight of the unfinished business in the soul of the work. But one also has to weigh in the balance of scholarship and its judgments what one has received in the waiting.

Question #4: What resistances did you feel to the dialogues? What was the source of these resistances? How did you work with them?

For Jo Todd, the very first dialogue pushed her into "an unknown, dangerous territory" concerning her experiences of and positions on abortion. In this place, she was "overwhelmed by chaos, bewilderment, and despair." Her complex response to abortion had been a "self-righteous defense of a woman's right to choose," which had not taken into consideration all the undigested affects around her own abortions. "The material was so hot," she said, "I could not work on it at all." Indeed, the undigested affects buried themselves so deeply within her body that she "experienced physical symptoms from disowned embodied knowing."

Here she was, a researcher, who, while knowing a great deal about the abortion debate and passionately defending its pro-choice position, was living out its complex roots in a symptomatic way. I have found this symptomatic embodiment of the work to be a constant feature in this approach that attempts to keep the soul of the work in mind, and it is a danger that goes with the processes of letting go of the work. But what choice do we really have? What Todd's experience of the process reveals so bluntly is that the body knows what the researcher does not yet know about the work, just as in the transference field between patient and analyst, the body of the therapist registers what is in the field before the therapist has words to describe it. As I have noted elsewhere, the transference field in therapy is a gestural field, and the same gestural field is present between the complex researcher and the strangers in the work who carry its unfinished business. Of the place of the gestural body in therapy, I have written, "Haunted in our gestures by significant others, shadowed by the ancestors, we are in and through our gestures stitched into and held by a tradition."[9] The same applies to the research situation. In and through his or her body, the researcher is brought into the depths of the topic, stitched into its tradition, which runs deeper than his or her complex relation to the work.

So, as challenging, and even dangerous, as this process can be, I would ask again: what other choice do we have? Do we avoid acknowleging the presence of the body of the researcher in the work by making a mental flight into method (a strategy that would safeguard the researcher against his or her anxieties by splitting him or her in two)? Even with such a flight into method, do we not still suffer the work, bear it in our flesh, and even spin it from blood and bone and gut and heart? And if we do, then is it not better to do so with as much conscious attention to this process as possible? Instead of denying the body's role in knowing, would we not make some advance if we admitted it at the outset and were thus more prepared to work with the symptomatic side of the research process? Moreover, as we have seen, do we not also gain some important insights into the unfinished business of the soul of the work when we take into account the limitations of and resistances to the transference dialogues, insights into the depths of the work that we might otherwise lose?

Todd gives us another example of how her resistance to the process manifested itself. Recall her statement that in the beginning the material was so hot that she could not work with it. Well, two months after the official beginning of her study, she reports, "I found myself, perhaps synchronistically, in a life-threatening fire." A coincidence? A random event unrelated to her work? Perhaps, but then again, perhaps not! Reflecting on this event, Todd wondered if Jung's warning that what we refuse to embrace from within can come back to us from the outside as fate was applicable here. However one chooses to interpret the fire Todd was in, what Todd says about it is instructive: "Certainly over the next five years I sometimes felt as if I awoke to an unexpected fire in the work that threatened to devour me."

As to the question of how she worked with these resistances, Todd says only that she continued to step into the transforming field of the dialogues. As the dialogues proceeded, she was able to approach them less and less as a victim and "with a more kindly and tolerant view" of her own abortion experiences, and she was able to moderate her former demonization of the pro-life side of the debate. What she leaves unsaid, but what is to be noted, is that it was not necessary for her to do the dialogues. She made a conscious choice to use the technique. Her choice required that she have the courage to stay committed to the vocation that drew her into the work. In his essay, "The Development of Personality," Jung cites choice, courage, and vocation as key elements in the process of finding one's own way in life.[10] These same elements apply to the researcher who would find his or her way in the work, and who, in doing so, finds a way into the life of the work.

Kay Tomlinson is very specific about her resistances to the dialogues. She says they took three forms. "The first," she writes, "was simply a kind of performance anxiety." Afraid to fail, she wondered if she could do it and do it right. This is not an uncommon source of resistance. Conrad Gratz, whose dissertation is entitled "The Experience of Living with Enchantment," says it quite simply: "The resistance of the ego and its desire to comply with cultural demands for such things as 'getting the job done on time' and 'making good sense of what I was doing' surfaced many times."[11] The dialogues are an *opus contra naturam* with respect to the cultural conventions of the ego: this resistance is rooted particularly in the ego's having to relinquish its control over the process and especially over the work. In the transference dialogues, one is thrust into unknown territory, and in this unfamiliar place one is inclined to convince oneself that one's old wineskins are up to the task of containing the new wine. The challenge here is to divest oneself of the more familiar role of critic and take on the less familiar role of witness, and it is the ego's fear of being stripped bare of its familiar critical stance that nurtures the resistance. In the face of this resistance, there is nothing to do but cultivate those attitudes of negative capability, willing suspension of disbelief, and hospitality, described in an earlier chapter.

The second type of resistance is stronger because it goes to the heart of the question of who the "others" are in the process. What is their status? Are they, as Tomlinson says, "not really there?" In the world of sticks and stones, as she describes the "real" world, she finds it difficult to avoid the feeling that "I am somehow making it all up." In the world she was brought up in, she would have to regard these "strangers" in the field as "a figment of my imagination." They would be projections and would have no authority or autonomy of their own. Kay adds an interesting point here when she speculates that this type of resistance is particularly a problem for women in our culture, since they have been taught from very early on to distrust their own ways of knowing. While I do not necessarily disagree that gender can play an important role in this type of resistance, I have found that it also poses a problem for men, who have, after all, played such a large role in defining reality in terms of sticks and stones. For both genders, the problem may lie in the culturally generated resistance to accepting that even the world of sticks and stones can and does manifest itself in subtle ways, that even that world is a subtle reality, that the imaginal is real because the real is imaginal.

Over the years, I have begun to call this type of resistance, which is also quite common, the "anti-Philemon factor," in reference to Jung's encounters with the figure of Philemon, whom he regarded as the one who taught him about the autochthonous character of the psyche. To be sure, there are complex projections at play in the field, but there are archetypal and psychoid dimensions as well. I have found over the years that it is best not to make judgments about who is what, but to welcome the "others," the "strangers" in the work, with hospitality. In any case, the difference is often apparent without judgment, and, more to the point, in the end it does not really matter. The dialogues are a creative endeavor in which the complex, which one can always find in the work, is transformed, if all goes well, into the work. The transference dialogues are an expression of the soul at play, specifically at play in transforming complex events into symbols, into a work. The transference dialogues are a field in which a wound can be made into a work.

The third type of resistance that Tomlinson experienced speaks to this difference and to the reality of the imaginal "others" in the work. Tomlinson is inhibited by fears that these "others" "really are there." This possibility, she says, is "daunting because it implies a responsibility to them if I recognize them as real persons, in the same way that I am responsible to beings in the sticks-and-stones world." Tomlinson correctly sees that an ethical obligation accompanies this possibility, and, as a friend of Jung, she notes his remarks on this issue.

> It ... is a grave mistake to think that it is enough to gain some understanding of the images and that knowledge can here make a halt. Insight into them must be converted into an ethical obligation .... The images of the unconscious place a great responsibility upon man.[12]

This form of the resistance is important because its exploration reveals that knowing and understanding the "strangers" who carry the soul of the work into the dialogues is not enough. Re-search that would keep soul in mind and would therefore make use of the dialogues imposes an ethical obligation upon the researcher to take up the unfinished business in the soul of the work. In the final chapter of this book, I will take up this conjunction between the wounded researcher and the ethical character of re-search with soul in mind.

As to the differences between the complex and archetypal and psychoid levels of the field, Tomlinson notes that she feels her ethical obligation to the latter more keenly than to the former. "There is a difference between those folks, whom I consider friends and equals, and the Others, like some of my guides, and especially Merlin, who often appear in active imagination." With the latter, the serious work of her work becomes even more serious.

In addition to these three types of resistance, Tomlinson notes that even as she has progressed in her work, the resistances have not faded. One form that this continuing resistance takes very frequently is "the call of the domestic." Tomlinson writes, "I will be working at my desk or in my studio, deeply involved in writing or doing my art work, and suddenly, out of nowhere, I'll remember that I was supposed to do laundry today, or that I need to make a phone call, or that the cats need to be let in or out." Who of us has not experienced these welcomed distractions that invite us to surface from the depths of the work? And who has not at times followed the same path as Tomlinson? "Off I will go to the task," she says, "leaving my dissertation work behind, sometimes for days at a time, and feeling guilty and torn apart all the while." And with this form of resistance, as with the others, the wisdom in it is to be honored. With respect to the dialogues, I encourage my graduate students always to work within a boundary of time and then beyond that boundary allow oneself to be drawn back into the daily round of life. Clothes still have to be washed, bills need to be paid, and the researcher has to move away from the desk and walk in the world. What I am saying here is that in the transference field, the "others" in the work are only one half of the dialogue.

Debbie Greenwood, amazed by the many guises that her resistance took on, corroborates Tomlinson's observations: "A dirty house, laundry that piles up and suddenly must be done—or else" was one form for her, as was "the small dog who wants your attention and wants to be let in and out of the house an inordinate amount of times just when you need to take time to reflect." In addition, Greenwood echoes Todd's remark about the symptomatic body as a form of resistance. Resistance "came to me in the form of an illness," she writes. She got pleurisy twice, and became extremely depressed at times and quite anxious on a few other occasions. Reflecting on these times, Greenwood suspects that they functioned to slow her down so that she could more easily digest the material she was confronted with in the dialogues. In her dissertation, she was inviting her subjects to take the time to gather the forgotten shards of each of their histories through the process of making art. The dialogues, she admits, brought "many things to the fore that I had put aside" concerning the loss of a sense of one's past. "I needed to learn," she notes, "to take more time with the information I was given."

Regarding how she worked with her resistances, Greenwood says, "I developed a variety of strategies." Sometimes, she studied the library videos from my classes on research. On other occasions, she just "got out of the house" and away from the work, and in still other situations, "I would invite synchronicity in by some other means." Posing a question such as, "What might I want to consider in relation to my work today?," she would "pull a rune or a tarot card or go to the library for fun and to see what turned up." In all these activities, she was working with her resistances by paradoxically taking an active part in surrendering to something beyond her willfulness. She was working with her resistances by engaging in play.

Judith Orodenker, in working on her dissertation, "The Voice of the Goddess: The Reemergence of the Archetypal Divine Feminine,"[13] offers a fascinating image and description of the dialogue process, which is the counterpoint to her resistances: "As I moved into the phase of the research that involved engaging with the artwork and the transference dialogues and gathering of data, I felt myself slowing down." This is a feature of the dialogues we have encountered before, and it seems to be one of the primary characteristics of the process. Orodenker goes into some detail about this felt sense of slowing down. "It was," she writes, "as if my body and mind together were moving through a thick substance, something like honey," a description not unlike that of the state of reverie, in which one's "words seem to drip with the blue honey of the world"[14] as time slows down. In the process of slowing down, the dialogues situate the researcher within an *other* landscape and in this "honey world," Orodenker says, "My thoughts became less organized, and although my thoughts felt thick and oozing with honey, they were not dense, but light, and my focus, or rather what I was able to pick up on and take delight in, were the associations between things." What she seems to be suggesting here is that in the landscape of the dialogues, one notices not the leaves on the tree, but the spaces between the leaves. Or, to put this more prosaically, in the "honey world" landscape of the dialogues where one is slowed down, one's consciousness becomes less convergent upon a point and more divergent as it encompasses a wider field.

Orodenker hints that this way of being is one of reverie, that way of being in the world between waking and sleeping. She writes, "I began to dwell in contemplation for long periods of time … sitting … with my eyes closed, not asleep, but again, contemplating." The mood of reverie is, as we have seen, the mood of the transference dialogues, which opens one to an *other* world, to that imaginal world where the "others" in the work wait with their unfinished business.

But this way of being in dialogue with the work is precisely what sets up the resistance to it. "At times," Orodenker writes, "I became impatient with my state of being, trying to force my will on the process, saying to myself, "Come on, come on, you've got to get going faster." Eventually, however, she recognized the source of this resistance. In moving into the "honey world" of her dialogues, "I realized," she says, "that I was moving into a way of being that was non-linear, involving non-linear thought." The spaces between the leaves became the focus, the associations and connections among things. This way of being with the work, she adds, "was a necessary part of the process, and wisdom from within was guiding me into it." What better way is there to say that in the transference dialogues one is invited to let go of the work so that one can be guided into it?

Orodenker tells us one other thing about her resistance. It is a rather oblique point, but nonetheless valuable. Even after embracing the dialogues as a necessary process and feeling more comfortable within them, Orodenker says, "I still felt unsettled and even a little resistant." The form of this continuing resistance, she discovered, was "feelings of fear and sadness." The fear she attributed to her complex about "trusting my own intuition and inner guidance; a fear of bringing what I know to be true out into the world." This, too, is not an uncommon aspect of the process. The transference dialogues invite the researcher to enter into the work through his or her subjectivity and in that process to attend to how he or she is to be a spokesperson and witness for the unfinished business in the work. Such a process runs counter to the mainstream tradition of scholarly work, which, in principle, rules out the subjective element from the equation. It is not surprising, then, that one would feel some fear around trusting one's own voice.

Of the sadness, however, Orodenker says nothing, and here is the oblique point about resistance to these dialogues. The transference dialogues open one not only to the "others" in the work, but also to their landscape of the imaginal world. The researcher gets a glimpse of the soul of the work and of the reality of soul. Then, one has to come back to psychology and to the hard work of transforming what one has been given into language. One has to mediate the gap and endure the tension between soul and the complex of psychology as described in Chapter 1. One has to suffer the loss between what one says and is able to say and what still remains to be said. One has to mourn the difference between green and the greening of the world as discussed in the Introduction. One has to know that after every sentence one writes there trails behind the last word the word "and." The sadness to which Orodenker alludes, then, is, I would argue, an expression of re-search as a mourning process.

To close the discussion on this question, I want to cite a remark made by Langhans, which, I believe, enters deeply into the shadow aspect of research as a process of mourning, and thus into sadness as an oblique form of resistance. "I see the process of dialogue," he says, "as a rumination, a chewing; it is the grinding of the *prima materia* of reveries, dreams, and reflections." Continuing the analogy, he reflects: "Food is chewed because it resists digestion; it resists its descent into shit." For Langhans, the transference dialogues are about transformation, the goal of which is the metamorphosis of previously undigested material—reveries, dreams, reflections (to which I would add complexes)—into something that can be digested. The transformation on the way to this goal requires "[c]hewing, a tearing apart, a dismemberment," which "produces another mess which is, of course, the digestible food." And this mess, he adds, "is made flesh and dwells within us." In effect, we eat at the work that eats at us, sometimes quite disturbingly as it upsets our sleep and rumbles in our guts, but all on the way to becoming us. We do the work that does us, and in the end we are the work, its living embodiment. Other students as well have commented on this aspect of the re-search process that keeps soul in mind: they have experienced it as a process in which one is made by the work as much as, and perhaps even more than, one has made the work. They have spoken about the alchemy of this process through which one is changed.

But here Langhans descends into the shadows of this process of transformation, wondering what one gets or has as a result of chewing on the work and being chewed on by it in the dialogues. Meditating on the dialogue process, he writes:

> It all feels so blah—so meaningless. There is no point, so what is the point? Terrible tautology—terrible labyrinth—caught in an endless circuit. So here I write in some ways hoping that it will break something free so I can resume the slow tortuous process of writing the dissertation. What the fuck am I doing in all this? I feel so utterly lost. It is an emotional and social paralysis. It is like ALS—a slow degenerative disease. What is the point? The question wants some causality, some teleology as an answer. But there probably is no answer, only the wretched question. And it passes in thought that this whole exercise, this writing, this life is nothing but a pathetic, narcissistic scene in a play never written. So what is the point? There is no point.

There is an unmistakable tone of sorrow in his words, but sorrow covered over by the "black dog of sorrow," which is despair, and which radiates from the work of the dialogues to the writing and to life. This radiation happens because the researcher is a complex presence to the work, and when a complex is touched, the entire scope of one's world is seen through it. And yet there is deep wisdom in sorrow, and even out of despair, the "black dog of sorrow," Langhans attests to the wisdom found in it. He writes, "In traveling back through the dialogues, I am struck by the unconscious coincidence between the different levels of woundedness and their presence to the work." In this revelation, he has his own Orphic moment. "Only now," he says, "in this backward look, do I see so many of the connections which were to unfold themselves later in the work ... connections between wounding and work." Just as Orpheus's loss of Eurydice frees both of them into themselves, so also, only when Langhans has lost the work does it become a work.

What these dialogues indicate so clearly is that we make the work out of our wounds, which certainly are in the work, but more importantly, are transformed as the work. To bring the "subjective factor" into research is not to reduce research to confession. On the contrary, it is to ensure a radical objectivity that, by taking the researcher's complex presence into account, illustrates not only the creative capacity of soul to transform a wound into a work, an event into a symbol, but also its desire, and perhaps even need, to do so.

Question #5: How did these dialogues help you to get in touch with your own complex presence to the work, without which that presence might have unconsciously informed and influenced your ideas about the work?

Erik Killinger replied to this question by describing the transference space of the dialogues as an openness that "afforded me explorations of material I had not known before—or, rather, forgot I knew." In this process of re-membering and being re-membered, the work of the dialogues, he says, "changed me by at once maturing me and bestowing upon me a childlike naiveté." Without this effort, he adds, "[m]y understanding is that the work I did would be incomplete at best." Killinger seems to be saying that as a result of this process of coming to know his own complex presence to the work more fully, he became the completion of the work, an agent of its fulfillment. Recall here that his dissertation was a phenomenological study of members of the clergy transitioning out of parish ministry, an investigation that led him to an exploration of what he termed the *intermundia*, or the world between the former world of parish ministry and the world outside it. Killinger says, "My part in the work was to grow more attuned to that in the work which called to me out of my own darkness that was waiting for me in the between."

Erik himself had made such a journey. He had left parish ministry and had found himself in that *intermundial* place, but there were aspects of it which, without the dialogues, would have remained in darkness. Erik had a strong vocation to this work, which called to him through his own complex journey out of parish ministry. Without the dialogues, the darkness in that complex would have been projected into the work, and he would have found in the interviews with his subjects confirmation of his own prejudices. Interpretation of interviews is never "free." It is always a complex process.

In addition, Killinger suggests a more general way in which the dialogues helped him to get in touch with his own complex presence to the work. He writes that "perhaps the biggest change was learning to wait for the work to communicate on its own time." Citing an old Zen proverb, he says he learned that it was not his place "to push the river." "I have learned," he adds, "[that] it will come when I have waited a little while, and I better appreciate the kairotic moment." Killinger is referring here to what we have said before about this process slowing the work down, but he seems to be adding another subtle twist to this point. The reference to not pushing the river suggests that the slowing down is in fact an inversion. It is not just that the ego learns to become more patient in the process, but rather, that the ego's position in the process and in the work is radically altered. From pushing the work to letting oneself become immersed in its flow, the researcher discovers, Killinger is suggesting, that the transference dialogues reveal not only the complexes of the ego in the work, but also the ego itself as a complex in the work. With its impatience to "push the river," with its desire to retain control over the work, with its inability to let go of it and to become its agent rather than its author in this process, the ego of the researcher gets in the way of the process and in the way of attending to the "others" in the work, who bring its unfinished business. The process of transference dialogues can be viewed as a way for the ego to get out of the way, just as it must with the dream, as Hillman so clearly demonstrates in *The Dream and the Underworld*.[15]

Kerry Ragain's work with the dialogues confirms their value in making more conscious his own unconscious complex relation to the work. (Recall that his phenomenological study explored the archetypal dimensions of the experience of being adopted.) In response to this question, he commented, "Through the transference dialogues I caught glimpses of the woundedness, which, first of all, accompanies my own experience of being adopted." The process of the dialogues "brought up material I would have rather not faced," he admits, "The images and affects that arose during these times were raw." But by engaging these raw images and emotions, which formed a large portion of his complex draw into the work, he was able to work out his own wounds without imposing them upon the work. About the dialogues he writes: "[T]he manifest resistance I felt when engaging the dialogues made more sense." Kerry notes that with the complex of his own adoption experience becoming more conscious, he was less disturbed and was made less anxious by the initial descriptions of his subjects. Not having to filter what they were describing about their experiences of being adopted through his own complex relation to the material, he was better able to be present to the experiences of his subjects in the interviews.

I should note here an important contribution that Ragain made to the research process. Making his own complex relation to the material more conscious in the transference dialogues, he found that some of his uneasiness in the interviews was not the product of his own complexes, but the result of his subjects' complexes, experienced by him in the form of projective identifications. In his study, Ragain made use of projective identification as part of his method. It became for him one way of understanding the unconscious depths of his subjects' descriptions and another source of data. This idea is worthy of further exploration in relation to the method that arises from an approach to re-search that would keep soul in mind by making the unconscious of the research process more conscious. It is also an indication that the imaginal approach to research, the processes of vocation and transference dialogues, and the method that flows from these are still, in spite of fifteen years of effort, a work in progress. *The Wounded Researcher* finishes the work—for a moment—but the work is not done.[16]

Jo Todd, whose study on the abortion debate we have cited on several occasions, makes a very clear statement about the effect of the transference dialogues on her work. She writes, "The Old Woman's dialogue which initiated the study challenged my certainty that the abortion experiences were resolved." Todd is referring here to her two abortions and to the pro-choice position she had adopted. Was that position a defense against her "unborn grief" over the abortions, a phrase that echoes the title she gave to her work, "Grieving with the Unborn"? At the start of her study, before the dialogue with the Old Woman, Jo was certain that her pro-choice position was more than correct. She was certain that it was the only right position in the debate. But now she could grapple with the possibility that defending it with the same self-righteous zeal that she found in the pro-life position was her way of warding off the grief she would not allow.

Earlier, I cited a portion of this dialogue in another context. Now I want to cite it again in this context.

You have missed the opportunity to bring life into the world,
and there is not a way to fix that. ... You have not truly grieved
this very deep loss and it is something you must do.

Reflecting on this dialogue, Todd says of the Old Woman, "She
showed me my unconscious complexes influencing the work."
Engaging in the dialogues with the Old Woman, the issue of death,
which is at the heart of the abortion debate, became less abstract for
her. As she was led into her grief over her two abortions, death became
an intimate companion in her struggle between the two opposing
points of view. "I discovered," Todd writes, "Death's personal character
... as an effect of engaging in these dialogues."

The Old Woman of the dialogues had framed Jo's abortions in
terms of the life that was lost. She had placed the issue of death within
the context of life. Commenting on the effect of this reframing, Todd
says the later dialogues "revealed that from a cultural-historical
perspective, I had unconsciously absorbed Pro-Life's images." These
images, deeper than her convictions, she says, "were subtly and
unconsciously challenging my initial Pro-Choice perspective." "My
rigid one-sidedness," she adds, "fueled an unconscious, defensive self-
righteous certainty at odds with this changing idea." Rounding the
circle of her growing insight into her complex relation to her work,
Todd notes, "If this unconsciously constellating tension had remained
undisclosed, it would have created a very different study." "I would
have remained," she adds, "committed to pursuing with increasing
militant certainty the Pro-Choice point of view." Instead, she
concludes, "the transference dialogues disclosed my unconscious,
unfinished business. I began to see that I had dissociated and projected
it onto the radical Pro-Life movement."

Having acted as her advisor, I want to say once more that this
process of making one's unconscious complex relation to the work more
conscious is no easy task. Jo Todd's determination to do so, a
determination found also in the work of all those other students who
have done the same, takes courage. It is a courage that is matched only
by the effect of this process, which is to bring to research a deep ethical
sensibility. In the transference dialogues, a researcher is committing
herself or himself to owning, as best she or he can, the shadow that
she or he casts upon the work.

Question # 6: How did these dialogues help you to get in touch with the soul of the work beyond your own complex relation to it?

This question is really inseparable from the previous one because, as Todd's example illustrates, the process of making one's unconscious relation to the work more conscious opens the work to its own unfinished business. This is no different from what happens in a relationship between two people. When one becomes aware of the complex ways he or she has been relating to the other, that other deepens into a new mystery. So, too, does the work deepen into its own mystery when the researcher becomes more conscious of his or her complex projections onto it. I want to close this part of the chapter, however, with a few specific responses to this question. In the background of each reply is that difficult work of having engaged one's complex relations to the work.

Erik Killinger offers a good example of how the work opened into unexpected areas as a result of the transference dialogues. Of his work on the transitioning of clergy from parish ministry, he writes, "I had not expected to be reading theoretical physics in the area of zero-point energy, mathematical papers on toroidal topology, or even papers on metasystem theory." But that is where he was led by his exploration of the topology of the *intermundia* or between-world in this transition. Perhaps closer to the topic, he adds, "I granted that readings in the Old and New Testaments would find their way into the work," but even here he was surprised. He did not expect that he would be reading these texts in "the Kabbalistic way, whereby it was no longer the task to undertake the usual methods of exegesis in which I had been trained." The work itself required of him a different way of reading, "of reading each letter, each word, phrase, complete sentence, paragraph, and/or pericope as though I was backstage of it, as well as reading the spaces between and playing with the letters in the dance of black fire on white fire." In short, what Killinger is telling us is not only did the work move beyond his initial complex expectations of it, not only did it change, but also he changed and had to as a consequence of its change.

Kerry Ragain, whose dissertation on the archetypal threads in the experience of being adopted has been cited above, is very direct about the role of the dialogues in opening the work beyond his own complex ties to it. He says, "I believe that the dialogues helped me understand the archetypal dynamics behind my own experience of being adopted, which required deepening the relationship between my conscious perspective and the archetypal layers beyond it." These dialogues he describes as "a tunnel into a world beyond myself, where the experience of the Orphan is situated at the horizons of history." He adds, "I think, overall, I can see how my engagement in the dialogues helped me understand that my own pain associated with being adopted is really part of the Orphan's experience, and as such is a layer of human experience, which has been re-created since the dawn of time." When we recall here Kerry's descriptions of his bagpiping in the basement of his daytime classroom work in search of some lost, bygone era, and his poignant description of himself in such moments as someone who felt lost in time, it seems as if the figure of the Orphan in his work on adoption was waiting for him on the other side of his woundedness about having been adopted. The Orphan, it seems, was waiting there in the basement of the work, waiting with this piece of unfinished archetypal business in the experience of being adopted. And lest we miss the point about how these dialogues, in working through the researcher's complexes, open to the unfinished business in the work, Kerry tells us, "I think without the dialogues, the woundedness perhaps would have entered the work in other ways, as a specter lurking in the margins." "And this outcome," he concludes, "would have merely recreated in the work a mirror of my own wounds around being adopted."

To conclude this part of the chapter, I offer this example from the work of Ellen Macfarland. Recall that her dissertation was on the healing power of nature in childhood abuse and that it was her own experiences of abuse and her work as a therapist with abused patients that drew her into the work.

> I am taken back to a time when, on a morning walk through my neighborhood, I came upon unbelievable wreckage from a violent storm .... Suddenly, I turned a corner and the street ahead was littered with downed trees, broken branches, and a strong energy of shock and tragedy. As I walked through the debris, my heart cried out to the trees that were still standing with gaping wounds left from their broken limbs.
>
> I am aware that ... by looking through the wounds of the broken trees, I am taken to a place of connection with the

universe. I wonder as I walk through the chaos if my soul's pain brings comfort to these broken trees. I have to hope so—for they offer so much to us as wounded beings.

The next part of the journey into the tree world happened two days later. I had decided to return to that street and again was stunned as I turned the corner. The street was back to "normal." There were a few piles of neatly stacked wood. There were a few trees that still had visible wounds from where their limbs had been torn away. I was overwhelmed by feeling because the scene indicated that in a two-day period of time it had all been cleaned up, taken care of, and forgotten.

As I walked along this path of forgotten devastation, I could not help feeling so angry as I compared it to what happens to the devastation caused by child abuse. In so many ways it seems that we, in our culture, are doing the same thing with this shadow of family life. There is a collective collusion to clean up what happens to these children, take care of the obvious needs, and then forget.

This reverie, as she calls it, was actually a dialogue with the trees, and it indicates that the transference field between the researcher and her or his work can take place through events engaged in the world. Indeed, her reverie suggests that there is no hard-and-fast differentiation or rigid boundary between reveries and transference dialogues as ways of letting go of the work. In reverie, events become mirrors that reflect the researcher's complex ties to the work and, in this case, the heretofore unrealized depths of the work itself. As Macfarland says, "This reverie moved the work forward beyond what I had initially conceived as the scope of the research."

The numerous student examples that I have given in this chapter indicate that reveries and transference dialogues, as two related ways of letting go of the work, change the researcher and the work. The researcher at the beginning of the work is not the same as at the end of it, and the work that is finished is not done. There are always both more complex shadows that linger in the margins and more unfinished business in the work. Macfarland again is a good witness on this point. She, who in her life and practice has experienced the healing powers of nature for the wounds inflicted by child abuse, has now become a spokesperson for the wounds of nature inflicted by us.

> I would add that the work is not complete once the research is
> completed. I am now over two years beyond the completion of
> my dissertation and the work has deepened and continues. I
> am now studying the wolf nation and the struggles that they
> have had to survive complete annihilation on this continent.
> This life-changing aspect of the work should not be discounted.

We are drawn into our work through our wounds and drawn
beyond those wounds to create a work that takes up the weight of
history that waits in the work as unfinished business.

Reflections on this "Most Dangerous" Process

In a recent article, I pointed out two dangers of making one's
unconscious complex relation to the work more conscious. "One
danger," I said, "is for the researcher to ignore the complex character
of research." When this happens, the researcher is much more likely
to project his or her complexes onto the work. Then, "soul work that
is done in service to the world can easily degenerate into an ideology."
"The second danger," I wrote, "is for the researcher to identify with
the claims that the work makes upon him or her." Here, the danger is
"for the ego of the researcher to claim the work that claims him or her,
with the result that the complex character of the work becomes a work
about the researcher's complex, a work that is not only an ideology
but also a bad confession." In the face of these twin dangers, I
nevertheless argued, "The opportunity and the challenge of doing
research with soul in mind are to create an epistemological strategy
that allows a researcher to be consciously in service to a work without
being unconsciously identified with it."[17] This argument, I believe, is
still valid. Notwithstanding these dangers, there is an ethical demand
for the researcher to make his or her unconscious relation to the work
more conscious.

There is, however, a third danger in this process of confronting
the unconscious in research. It is a danger we have already described
in this chapter. The danger is for the researcher to become
overwhelmed by the contents of his or her complex relation to the work
and/or to become flooded by the archetypal energies that can be
released in the transference dialogues.

More than a quarter-century ago one, of my graduate students,
who was working on a dissertation about an epic poem from an ancient

civilization, was flooded with the material he was exploring. The epic poem began to take on an unbounded significance with the consequence that the focus of the study became blurred and was never completed. He was swamped by the archetypal energies released in the work, and he lost his way.

I cite this example because it indicates that working with material psychologically can be, and often is, psychoactive. To use an analogy here, the researcher who works psychologically with material that becomes psychoactive is like the physicist who works with radioactive material and becomes exposed to its radioactivity. The material is hot, as Jo Todd indicated above, and the researcher can get too close and get "burned." So, whether we keep soul in mind or not, this third potential danger can and often does become a reality, and because it does, we are, I would argue, on safer ground, or at least better ground, if we are as conscious as possible of the dangers and have procedures, such as the transference dialogues, to deal with them. In the case of the graduate student cited above, I had at that time no inkling of this danger, and I wonder at times if his experience has been in some way a seed for this work on the Wounded Researcher. Be that as it may, the dialogues, which can be the triggering agent of this third danger, can also be the boundary that contains it.

I have already cited above some of the manifestations of this danger encountered by my graduate students. One form it has taken with some of them has been the creation of bodily symptoms. Debbie Greenwood, for example, twice developed pleurisy, which she understood as her body's way of slowing down the research process, asking her to breathe more deeply and deliberately into the work instead of racing ahead with it and getting out of breath. In commenting on this, I suggested that the body of research that the researcher explores is connected to the body of the researcher who is doing the exploring. The symptomatic body is, or can be, an indication that the body of the researcher knows something about the process of the work that the researcher does not yet know.

Linda Lauver, whose dissertation on Mayan culture I cited in the previous chapter, offers another example of the presence of the symptomatic body in research. Before she was able to begin her work, she suffered for several weeks from a skin condition, which she described as a burning from within. This eruption disrupted the work, and in her reflections on it, she discovered its connection to the Mayan rituals of purification. To begin the work, something in her had to be burned away. In Chapter 11 I will go into this example in some detail.

Erik Killinger, whose work is described above, has also suffered the work bodily. He writes, "From a choking incident that revealed several interrelated gastrointestinal ailments of which I was unaware to a bout of pleurisy, I experienced necessary Dionysian fragmentation—cleansings, purifications, if you will." I find it telling that he speaks here of a necessary fragmentation because it indicates his own deep understanding of the body's presence in the work. In his case, he understood not only that he needed to slow down and rest within the work, but that the work he was undertaking also would require him to digest it in ways that were painful.

I, too, know this place, for while I have been engaged in working on this book, it has been working on me. I, too, have suffered gastrointestinal symptoms of more than a mild nature and have had to confront my own willfulness and impatience with the work, as if I were trying to digest something too quickly. Indeed, this work has been one of the things that, prompted by a dream of it, has sent me back into Jungian analysis. While I am not advocating analysis as a prerequisite for doing re-search with soul in mind, I do want to make the point that the analytic process, which has a slowing down effect, has had its parallels in this work, in which I have had to learn to take the time to digest this work and to let it digest itself at its own pace. In addition, regarding the place of the symptomatic body in research, I am not suggesting here for myself or for the other researchers a causal connection. Nor am I suggesting that the interpretations are final. I do not even know if they are correct. But that is not the issue. The issue is to become curious about what they might be suggesting, and to treat such symptomatic expressions as an invitation to engage the work in another way. For myself as well as the other researchers, this attitude has proved helpful, especially with regard to how one is engaged in the process of the work. In attending to the unconscious in the research process, does one discover that he or she is being too willful and impatient? Does one need to slow the process down? Does one need to digest the material at a more leisurely pace?

Accidents are another form in which the third danger of this process manifests itself. I already cited Jo Todd's example of being caught in a fire, which she related to how hot the material she was working with in the dialogues had become. Erik Killinger also provides several examples. During the course of his work, he had three laptop computer crashes, a car collision, in which he was blindsided by another driver, and a fall down a flight of stairs, which cracked two of his ribs. Are these only coincidences, unrelated to his work, in which he was exploring the unfamiliar landscape of the *intermundia*, the between-world for parish ministers who were making a transition out of that world? Perhaps! As I said above regarding the symptomatic body, one cannot be sure, either of their relevance to the work or their meaning. But again, one can adopt that attitude of negative capability and at least remain open to their possible meaning. Killinger adopted such an attitude. "Were these incidents," he wondered, "the work's way of telling me I was on the wrong track?" Did he have to lose what he had written—three times—to find what wanted to be written? Do we not engage in a similar process when, perhaps with a little more awareness, we discard earlier drafts of the work? Was he too narrowly focused so that he had to be blindsided by what was being left out of his field of vision? Was he stepping into the work in such a way that required a fall? When and if one keeps soul in mind and is open to the unconscious factors in the research process, these questions are not inappropriate. As for Erik, in reply to his own question about perhaps being on the wrong track, he discovered through these incidents an answer that was more subtle than either a negation or an affirmation. "I came to know and understand," he says, "that I was on track, but that I could not freely make intuitive leaps within the process of the work without working through the work experientially." Moving too fast, he could lose his footing, and flying too high, he could fall. The "accidents" seem to have brought him back to the body of the work through his body, so that what he was coming to know about the *intermundia* landscape of ministers transitioning out of parish life was also a felt knowledge.

In his book, *Inner Work*, Robert Johnson describes clearly the use of active imagination for personal growth. However, he articulates an important precaution: "Before starting active imagination be sure that there is someone available for you to go to or call in case you become overwhelmed by the imagination and can't cut it off." In addition, he advises, "In the rare cases of people who get easily lost in the fantasy realm and can't find their way back, it is better that they do not do Active Imagination but find cooler ways of relating to their inner world."[18] While Johnson is offering this caution and advice within the context of using active imagination for personal growth, the caution and the advice should also be noted and taken to heart in using active imagination in research. Along the lines of Johnson's advice, I would point out, as I have done before, that the use of transference dialogues in research is not for everyone. As for his words of caution, I would agree that for those who employ the dialogues, it is important to have others with whom one can speak about the process.

Of course, the ideal other for the researcher who would keep soul in mind and engage the unconscious in the work is the analyst, but, as I noted above, this is hardly feasible as a requirement. However, it is not unreasonable to expect that the researcher's others will include his or her advisor and committee members, friends who know about the work and have an interest in it, and colleagues with whom he or she has discussed or can discuss the work. In addition, I would point out that the use of active imagination in the transference dialogues for research already establishes a different landscape from that involved in its use for personal growth. The focus and intention are different, and while, as I said earlier, the researcher and his or her work cannot be separated, they can be differentiated. I advise my students to remember that the transference dialogues establish a ritual space and that within that space the focus is on the work. Whatever complex material and/or archetypal energies arise, the focus remains on the work with the understanding that whatever else might be stirred up can and should be dealt with in another context. The analogy that I sometimes use here is the classroom. It is not as uncommon as we might like to think that a teacher stirs up complex and archetypal energies in the transference field between himself and or herself and a student. When this happens, both the teacher and the researcher have an obligation to know what is happening and to set and hold the boundary around the work. Whatever else might get constellated in this field outside the work can and should be taken elsewhere.

Finally, I would add here that one must always remember that the position of the ego in the transference dialogues and the work of active imagination is the other pole in the process. The ego's presence is neither to be dismissed nor diminished by comparison with the unconscious in the work. As Jung noted, "The position of the ego must be maintained as being of equal value to the counter-position of the unconscious, and vice versa."[19] It is helpful, I believe, to understand that one's work is bounded by one's life, which is the larger circle. The researcher has to go back into life, and indeed it is inevitable that he or she will be drawn back into it. If, at certain moments, one pours one's life into a work, it is important to counter that move and allow the work to yield, and perhaps even offer it up with a conscious sense of sacrifice, to the ordinary vicissitudes, demands, joys, and sorrows of everyday life. Outside the study and away from one's desk, there are always those dishes to be done, those bills to be paid, those friends to telephone, that novel to read, as well as the simple pleasure of being useless for a moment while sitting in the garden.

Exits and Entrances

An imaginal approach to research is one that attends to the unfinished business in the soul of the work. To do so, it is necessary to differentiate what belongs to the work from what the researcher as a complex presence to the work brings to it. The use of reverie and transference dialogues are two ways of facilitating this differentiation. On the one hand, they invite the researcher to become more conscious of his or her vocation to the work and the ways in which that call into the work is webbed into his or her complex projections onto the work. On the other, in so doing, they open a space for the researcher to attend to the weight of history as unfinished business that waits in the work. In the chapters on the imaginal approach, on research as vocation, and the two chapters on transference, I have given numerous examples of these themes.

Although the vocational dimension and the processes of reverie and transference dialogues can be used with any approach and with the methods that arise from those approaches, a specific method has grown up alongside the imaginal approach and the processes of research that flow from it. It is called alchemical hermeneutics, and it is the subject of the next five chapters. It is a method that, having its roots in the imaginal approach, furthers the task of making a place for the unconscious in research. In alchemical hermeneutics, approach, process, and method all converge upon this issue of the unconscious and are in service to that ethical demand to take into account the dynamic and complex unconscious factors in research.

Before I conclude this chapter, there is one final point to make in reference to the above remark about how the vocational dimension and the processes of reverie and transference dialogues can be used with any approach and with the methods that arise from those approaches. My point is that this approach to research and especially the processes that flow from it, as well as the method that has arisen from it, should be used alongside and in conjunction with other approaches and methods, such as the empirical approach, the phenomenological approach, and traditional hermeneutics. I move from the statement that they *can* be used with other approaches to the statement that they *should* be used in conjunction with other approaches, and I do so for two reasons.

First, they do not replace other methods and forms of research. They add something to them that is generally neglected—the deep subjectivity of the researcher, which is required for a true sense of objectivity. Second, inclusion of the unconscious factor in research is an ethical issue, because its inclusion situates the bodies of knowledge we create within a framework that keeps one from taking up his or her perspective as an unexamined truth and making use of it as an ideology. The ideology of the true believer is the death of true thinking. True thinking requires that the thinker take into account his or her shadow. Just as the body of the researcher casts a shadow, so too does the thinking of the researcher. There is always something un-thought in one's thinking, and a thinker who would be true to his or her thought and to the task of true thinking has to attend to its presence. Maurice Merleau-Ponty says it this way in his essay, "The Philosopher and His Shadow":

> To reflect (Husserl said in *Ideen I*) is to unveil an unreflected dimension, which is at a distance because we are no longer it in a naïve way, yet which we cannot doubt that reflection attains, since it is through reflection itself that we have an idea of it. So it is not the unreflected which challenges reflection; it is reflection which challenges itself.[20]

It is through consciousness that we come to understand that there is an unconscious shadow in our thinking. The ethical demand here is to establish procedures that take reflection's challenge to itself deeper into that challenge. The ethical demand here is to secure procedures that help consciousness descend into that dark-light that is one's thinking. Phenomenology by itself does not achieve that; it points the way. The phenomenologist has to meet the depth psychologist at the abyss for this descent.

> *... faciles descensus Averno:*
> *noctes atque dies patet atri ianua Ditis;*
> *sed revocare gradum superasque evadere ad auras,*
> *hoc opus, hic labor est.*

> ... easy is the descent to Avernus:
> night and day the door of gloomy Dis stands open;
> but to recall one's steps and pass out to the upper air,
> this is the task, this is the toil.[21]

PART III

Method

CHAPTER SEVEN

Recovering the Soul of Method

Introduction

When we think of the issue of method, we usually think of it as a series of procedures designed not only to ensure the objectivity of one's results, but also to allow other researchers to repeat the work and to check the reliability and validity of the results. Method, as such, is part of the scientific ethos, which was first developed as part of the sciences of nature, beginning in the 16th century, and was later applied, in the 19th century, to the social sciences. When, therefore, we declare that psychology is a science, the generally unspoken idea here is that it follows the scientific method. However, in his insightful book *Jung and the Making of Modern Psychology*, Sonu Shamdasani subtitles his work *The Dream of a Science*. The making of modern psychology, then, has been the dream of becoming a science, and essential to that dream has been its emulation of the methods and procedures of the natural sciences.[1]

In 1892, William James, while reflecting on the status of this dream, claimed that psychology was still "only the hope of science." It was for James still only the hope of being a science because, as he added, "at present psychology is in the condition of physics before Galileo and the laws of motion, of chemistry before Lavoisier and the notion that mass is preserved in all reactions." James, however, appears to have had no doubt that one day the dream of psychology to be a science would be realized. He wrote, "The Galileo and the Lavoisier of psychology will be famous men indeed when they come, as come they some day surely will."[2]

Looking back on that high hope of more than a hundred years ago, Shamdasani wonders if there has been any progress towards the goal of that dream. He wonders "whether the founding separations of psychology from theology, philosophy, literature, anthropology, biology, medicine, and neurology had successfully taken place—or whether psychology today is in any better shape than James' estimation of its standing in the 1890s," when it was still only the hope of becoming a science.[3]

Notwithstanding Shamdasani's remarks, my intention in this chapter is not to argue the point of whether or not psychology's dream of becoming a science has been realized. There is no doubt that psychology cannot be separated from other disciplines, as I argued in Chapter 1, or that psychological processes have biological conditions. Nor is there any doubt that psychological processes can be and have been successfully investigated according to the scientific method. Even Jung's theory of the complex began with measurement, when he designed his word association experiment. To some degree, the dream has been realized and the hope has been fulfilled. The point to be emphasized here is that the realization of this dream has rested upon an image of psychology as a unitary discipline, whose unity is secured by adherence to the idea of method as it has been developed in the natural sciences. In this regard, the subject matter of psychology has been made secondary to method. The subject matter of psychology has been, we might say, held hostage by psychology's commitment to method. The question of whether psychology has realized its dream of becoming a science might, therefore, more profitably be phrased as whether the realization of that dream has been of value.

In the Introduction to their book *Entering the Circle*, Martin J. Packer and Richard B. Addison argue in the negative. Citing empiricism and rationalism as the "[t]win perspectives [that] have come to rule research and theory in contemporary psychology," they show in detail how these two perspectives have provided "the taken-for-granted background assumptions that run throughout modern psychology, from empiricist approaches such as social learning theory and positivist experimentalism to rationalist approaches such as structuralism and much of cognitive science." These approaches, they add, are ways of talking about psychology, and "[a]long with ways of talking they regulate techniques of inquiry." In other words, empiricist and rationalist approaches become programs for method. On one side, "[e]xperimental manipulation of variables and the prediction and testing of observable associations are empiricist programs." On the other side, "[c]omputer simulation and formal modeling are rationalist lines of attack." Packer and Addison make no bones about their judgment of these techniques of inquiry. Hermeneutics, they argue, "provides a *better* perspective on the world than the traditional twins."[4]

Comparing and contrasting these three modes of inquiry, Packer and Addison show how each of these three perspectives regards the subject matter of psychology in incompatible ways. For empiricism, psychology's domain of inquiry consists of independent entities with absolute properties. For example, "people can be described in terms of objective properties such as personality traits, intelligence quotients, or attachment strengths, that are assessed in categorical or quantitative terms with psychometric tests and measures." Securing this point, they add, "Modern psychometrics assumes the mental and behavioral worlds are each made up of independent entities that can be collated and measured." Packer and Addison make it clear that in this mode of inquiry, psychology has modeled itself on the sciences of nature as inaugurated by Galileo in the 17th century. They also make it clear that "[t]here are, perhaps, excuses for the belief of the time that the true way of understanding reality had finally been achieved by the new 'scientific method.'" Nevertheless, they argue correctly, "There is no longer any excuse for this naïve realism of 17th century empiricism to continue unabated in contemporary psychological research." Taking their point one step further, they add, "It is time to acknowledge that so-called objective reality is a product of human invention."[5]

I agree with Packer and Addison's description of empiricism in psychology. In *Psychological Life: From Science to Metaphor*, I described in historical detail how the origins of modern psychology as a science did model itself on the rise of the new sciences in the 17th century, and, in *Technology as Symptom and Dream*, I showed that the idea of an objective reality apart from the human subject had its genesis in the cultural and historical invention of linear perspective vision, which quickly became a cultural convention, a habit of mind.[6] But I do not agree with the conclusion that Packer and Addison draw regarding the inadmissibility of empiricism and rationalism as modes of inquiry in psychology. I will return to this point later.

With regard to rationalist approaches in psychological research, Packer and Addison state that the rationalist domain of inquiry is the formal structures that underlie appearances, and they name Descartes and Kant as two of the philosophical forebears of this approach. Each of these philosophers "took on the task of reconstructing human knowledge in its entirety, and determining the conditions for and limits to genuine knowledge." In psychology, this philosophical vision has informed structuralist researchers, who deal with "more restricted subdomains" of human experience.[7] As examples, Packer and Addison cite de Saussure's and Chomsky's studies of the formal structures of language that underlie everyday acts of speaking, while Piaget's studies do the same for intelligence and Kohlberg's for moral judgments. Common to all of these examples is the abstraction from the actual performances encountered in daily life for the sake of explaining them in terms of the syntactic rules that regulate the formal structures. So, for example, a child's behaviors in the context of situations designed by Piaget to test the child's operational intelligence are explained in terms of the schemas of assimilation and accommodation, which are abstracted from any context.

For Packer and Addison, both empiricist and rationalist modes of inquiry are "Rube Goldberg devices designed to enable people to escape from what they fear is a vicious circle: the circle of interpretation, the hermeneutic circle." In other words, empiricist and rationalist methods function as a defense against anxiety, which was the same point that Devereux made, as we discussed in Chapter 4. For Packer and Addison, the source of this anxiety that generates method is the same as it is for Devereux. It is the presence of the subject in the work. "Researchers working in the empiricist stance," Packer and Addison write, "fear that if their search for a method that achieves objectivity fails then relativism must be an inevitable result, and inquiry will reflect only subjective opinions." With regard to the rationalist perspective, Packer and Addison observe that "when those who have embarked on the never-ending rationalist quest for total explicitness become confronted by the recognition that there is unavoidable ambiguity in human affairs and understanding, their fear is a similar one, that this ambiguity will be a total one, leading inexorably to the same relativism."[8] Method as technique, then, is designed to replace the presence of the researcher as subject. Commenting on the empiricist and rationalist approaches, Packer and Addison declare: "In both stances method is considered a matter of procedure or technique, involving analytical operations that require no involvement of human judgment and valuation."[9] Method, we might say, is designed to erase the circle of interpretation that surrounds the researcher as subject and the subject of his or her research. Or, in the language we are developing in this book, method, we might say, is designed to exclude the transference field between a researcher and his or her work.

In their defense of the hermeneutic mode of inquiry, Packer and Addison assert that "our understanding of method must change,"[10] and the intention of that change is to erase the erasure of the presence of the researcher in research. I agree with this inclusion of the researcher in the research process, although I side here with Devereux, who argues for the inclusion of the unconscious depths of the researcher. The researcher who belongs to the research process is a wounded researcher, and in this respect an imaginal approach belongs to the hermeneutic tradition even as it transforms it. Taking into account the unconscious aspects of the researcher, an imaginal approach refigures and deepens the hermeneutic circle into a hermeneutic spiral. I will have more to say about this matter in the next chapter.

Earlier I said that while I agree with Packer and Addison's descriptions of empiricist and rationalist perspectives, I do not agree with the conclusion they draw from their critique of these two modes of inquiry. In their defense of the hermeneutic method of inquiry, they dismiss empiricist and rationalist procedures on philosophical and historical grounds, but they fail to take into account the psychological aspects of these methods. To be sure, any mode of inquiry that attempts to exclude the researcher's presence stands today on shaky philosophical grounds, and, with the excavation of the historical foundations and cultural contexts of empiricist and rationalist modes of inquiry, it is clear that they are human inventions, which should not, and cannot, be divorced from the contexts in which they arose. Thus, Packer and Addison are correct when they declare that "empiricist inquiry involves a hidden, and indefensible, assumption that an observer has direct, unproblematic access to the real world," and when they claim that "[r]ationalist inquiry involves an equally suspect assumption that we can have accurate intuitive knowledge about the operation of some portion of our cognitive apparatus." Of the former, we should say it is indefensible because it forgets that the world that we call objectively real is a way of designing the world and interpreting it. And, of the latter, we should note that Packer and Addison say, "Psychologists especially should doubt this!"[11]

But what is it that psychologists especially should doubt? They should doubt, I would say, any mode of inquiry that fails to take into account the psychological complexity of human subjectivity, a complexity, as we have seen throughout this book, that is rooted in the various levels of the unconscious, which range in their depth from the personal through the cultural-historical and collective-archetypal to the eco-cosmological realms of the psychoid archetype. What is of interest, however, is that Packer and Addison's remark about what psychologists especially should doubt is placed in parentheses. It is a parenthetical remark, something off the main line of inquiry, a digression. With respect to method, then, what the psychologist especially should doubt is any approach to method that would leave out of the picture its complex psychological meanings, and this doubt should be part of the main discussion of method.

Psychology has been dreaming of itself as a science since its very beginnings, as we saw in the opening of this Introduction. A major aspect of that dream has been its commitment to defining itself less in terms of its subject matter of soul and more in terms of method. That psychology as a science has endured, and even been successful, strongly suggests that this way of attempting to realize its dream by committing itself to method has indeed served soul in some way. The dream of being a science has been of value. Empiricist and rationalist methods of inquiry have revealed something of soul even as they have concealed something of it, and in this respect, if one is to be truly psychological about psychology and not just philosophical in one's judgments of it, one does need to appreciate method as something more than just a set of procedures and techniques.

To understand psychology's dream of being a science requires that we move into the question of the method of psychology by moving into the issue of the psychology of method. The psychological question regarding method is how empiricist and rationalist methods have been in service to psychology's dream of being a science. If we question method in this way, we might better understand not only the value, but also the limits, of psychology's realization of its dream of being a science through its commitment to method.

METHOD AS METAPHOR

In this section, I want to propose that method as a series of rules, procedures, and techniques is rooted in a metaphorical vision of one's subject matter. The design of a method, in other words, reveals what the researcher already imagines about his or her subject. In this respect, method is a perspective, and in this sense it functions primarily and essentially as a metaphor. To unfold how method is a metaphor, I will begin with an example.

My first book, *Psychological Life: From Science to Metaphor*, ends with a photograph of an experimental psychologist who is researching dreams.[12] What the picture shows is that the dream is already defined by his way of approaching it, something that is evident from the equipment he is using. In the photograph, the psychologist is wearing a pair of goggles, which is wired to a recording device that sits atop his head. The lenses of the goggles, however, do not open to the world outside. Rather, they focus on the inside. They are turned inward to record the psychologist's eye movements. From the recording device atop his head it is clear that the psychologist is looking for the dream inside the brain. The way in which he is studying the dream, therefore, already defines what the dream is that he is studying. This psychologist already believes that the dream is a function of eye movements that register brain activity, and his method incarnates and enacts that belief. His method has taken the measure of the dream as a matter of measurement. His method says in effect that a dream is what is measured, and the "is" in the statement is regarded as an identification of the dream with the measurement and an explanation of the dream by the measurement. The dream counts in his psychology because it can be counted, and this is what his method reveals. To be specific here, his method reveals the dream as a material event, as a biological activity.

But suppose we become curious about what he might be dreaming in studying the dream in this fashion. Suppose we begin to wonder about the content of his dream. We might be tempted to say that his way of studying the dream exemplifies his dream that psychology is a science. And yet no measuring device would reveal that particular content of the dream. The meaning of the dream is concealed by this method. Indeed, the method conceals an even more important point, namely, that dreams are meaningful. No measuring apparatus with goggles that record the dreaming brain will ever find the meaning of a dream. What the psychologist's method hides is that there is more to dreaming than what meets his eyeballs.[13]

I am not arguing here that this empirical method for measuring dreams is wrong. Dreaming does depend upon brain function just as thinking does. I could not think the thoughts to write these passages if I were brain dead, and if someone like our psychologist in the photograph were to wire me to a similar recording device, there is no doubt that my thinking, like his dreaming, would measure brain activity. No, my point is not that this method is incorrect. Rather, I am arguing that method is a way of making some things count while discounting other things. Method is a perspective that both reveals a topic and conceals it. What I am suggesting is that a method is an enacted metaphor. Just as a metaphor tells us what something is by implying that it is not what it is, this empirical method tells us that dreams are a brain function because they are also not a brain function. The metaphorical "is" is also always an "is not." Thus, if we are such stuff as dreams are made on, then this stuff is and is not brain tissue.

The metaphoric "is" not only establishes an identity between dreaming and brain activity, it also alludes to a difference between them. Identity and difference are the two poles in metaphoric action, and in method as metaphor. With respect to the identity pole, the claim that this method makes, that dreams are brain activity, is a fact. But with respect to the difference pole, this fact rests upon a metaphoric vision within which it is a fact. The fact that this method establishes has its roots in this metaphoric way of seeing the dream.

Without a metaphoric sensibility in psychology, we get stuck in either the identity pole or the difference pole, and each has its own consequences for psychology. On the one hand, if we get stuck in the identity pole, then we become trapped in one or another form of realism regarding soul, and psychology becomes a discipline that reduces soul to either biology, or to social forces, or to historical causes. On the other hand, if we get stuck in the difference pole, then we lose the concrete and specific relation of soul to body, culture, society, and history. Soul then becomes only a symbolic reality, and psychology becomes a discipline with no grounding in body or world. Psychology becomes a discipline in which everything can be symbolized out of existence. A metaphoric sensibility is necessary because it holds the tension between concrete and symbolic modes of thinking.

My point, then, regarding method is that it is always necessary to remember this metaphoric tension. Thus, while this empirical method is excellent in revealing the material conditions that are necessary for the dream to manifest itself, when the metaphoric tension is slackened, dreaming is identified only with brain function. In this identification, the metaphoric root of the method is forgotten and dreaming is reduced to brain activity, which becomes the cause that explains dreaming. Then, the dream as meaning is lost, in the same way that the complex would be lost if one reduced its expression to those physiological signs that Jung measured in his word association experiments. When this happens, method, I would argue, functions in a discipline as a symptom.

In their symptomatic character, methods are to epistemologies what symptoms are to individuals. In their epistemological guise, methods as symptoms are shared neuroses, expressions of a collective, cultural unconscious, which forgets something that is important to remember. In the case of our example of the psychologist in the photograph, what the method forgets is that physiological phenomena, whether of brain activity in dreaming or of reactions to certain words in word association experiments, are ways in which soul reveals and expresses itself as body, and indeed *is* body. The physiological measures are not the way in which soul is reduced to and explained by the body. Body is not the *explanation* of soul; it is its *expression*. To say that soul is body is, then, to speak metaphorically. It is to say that it is true and not true. If and when the metaphoric character of "is" is forgotten, however, if the metaphoric character of "is" becomes unconscious, the methodological claim becomes a complex projection in psychology about soul. The metaphoric statement then becomes a claim that is taken to be true. My point, then, is that symptoms are complex projections whose generative metaphoric roots have been forgotten. Or, to say this more simply, symptoms are unconscious metaphors. This is so for individuals, cultures, and epistemologies.

But if we are to remain true to the psychological meanings of this method, then, in addition to asking what this method forgets about soul, we have also to ask what the metaphor of method as measurement remembers about soul. Doing so, we transform the symptomatic character of method back into metaphor.

The success of psychology as an empirical science indicates that its methods of taking the soul's measure are indeed serving something of the soul's desires. Without going into a long discussion of this point, I would offer two examples of how these methods are ways of remembering soul. Empiricist methods are ways of remembering soul's desire for anonymity on the one hand, and its desire for repeatability on the other.

The measure of dream as brain activity is applicable to you and me, as well as to all who dream. Measurement and numbers are a cloak of anonymity, the ways in which soul hides by being applicable to everyone and anyone, and therefore to no one in particular. Measurement and numbers serve the soul's desire not to be identified with the personal dimension of human life, not to be reduced to and explained by the biographical and social contexts of the individual. Measurement and numbers serve the soul's desire not to get enmeshed in a psychology that amounts to a "personology." To be sure, all these contexts do matter, but they are not all that soul is about. To appreciate fully the strength of this desire, we have only to recall that in Jungian psychology the archetype serves the same desire of soul for anonymity.

In a similar fashion, empirical modes of inquiry that take the soul's measure serve the soul's desire for repeatability. The psychologist in our example can have his experiment repeated and his results affirmed or contested because his method is easily reproducible. One can repeat the experiment again and again, thereby ensuring that replicability, one of the primary features of the scientific method, is served. But something else is being served here beyond this service to science, namely, the soul's desire for repetition. We see this in the child who asks over and over again for the same story to be repeated, and we see it in traumatic dreams, which repeat the trauma in the service of mastering it. In addition, we see this desire for repetition in the repetition compulsion, and, indeed, Freud showed us the relation of repetition to remembering as well as to the comic and the uncanny, and its role in bringing the illness into treatment through the transference. Repetition serves many functions for soul, and both scientific psychology and depth psychology have responded to the soul's desire for it. Is it a wonder that in these instances of repeatability and anonymity, empirical psychology and depth psychology should, in their respective studies of soul, converge on it from different places? It is not a wonder, I would suggest, when and if we take the time to regard method psychologically. It is not a wonder when we look at method again from the point of view of what it serves for soul, because, as we saw in Chapter 1, all our psychologies have a complex about soul so that soul is in all of our psychologies; each psychology serves soul in some way.

In its regard of method as metaphor, an imaginal approach to research is method-friendly. Holding the tension of identity and difference, an imaginal approach values each method for what it is able to reveal about soul while remaining aware of what it also conceals or forgets. Every method, then, is always incomplete, and in this context we might turn to the etymology of the word "method" to experience more fully an important implication of this fact.

The etymology of the word "method" links it to the images of a path and a journey. A method is a way into one's work. It is a way of going to work on one's work, the making of a path that one follows into one's work. When one designs a method, one is mapping out the journey that one will take from that place of not knowing one's topic to that place of coming to know it. And, as with all other journeys, how one goes along the path informs what one will experience of the topos—the topic or place—where one arrives, and how one will experience it. If I plan to go to Paris, I can journey there by ship or airplane. In both ways of going, I will get to where I want to go, but how I go there will shape how Paris reveals itself to me. If my path is by ship, I might find that Paris opens itself as a place of leisure and romantic settings, whereas if I go by plane, I might find a Paris of a very different sort. Neither Paris is the right one or the real one. Both are real and right in relation to what path has been taken. Of course, this is only an example to illustrate the connection between methods as paths and how the *topos*—topic or place—is revealed.

The implication that I see here is that psychology needs a plurality of methods. Indeed, I would argue that unlike the sciences, which it has dreamed of emulating, psychology might very well be a discipline that does not define itself in terms of method. It might very well be the discipline where content or the subject matter of soul and not method is the priority. The need for a plurality of methods in psychology begins to make sense when we consider for a moment how wide the range of soul is. One finds soul in the complex fantasy that psychology has about the brain, and, in Richard Tarnas's book *Cosmos and Psyche*, one finds soul in the movement of the planets.[14] How could one method suffice to cover the wide expanse between Descartes's fantasy of the pineal gland in the brain as the seat of the soul and the great wheel of the stars, between that microcosm of nerve tissue and the macrocosm of the heavens? Soul is revealed by the architect and the poet, by the playwright and the film-maker, by the politician and the physician. No one method or way of going into these domains can suffice, nor can one impose a particular method on all of these expressions of soul in the world. How does one "read" a building? How does one explore a myth? How does one understand the rhetoric of the politician or the vision of the film-maker? All of these things might be measured and mapped, but none of them can be reduced to their measurements.

Earlier in this chapter, I asked if psychology's dream of becoming a science has been of value. Taking a psychological approach to the value of this dream, which gives method priority over subject matter and makes method the message, we have been led to a deeper appreciation of the role of method in psychology.[15] First, we have seen that the methods of psychology as a science are incomplete. Second, we have recovered method as metaphor. Third, we have seen that psychology is a discipline whose subject matter or content takes precedence over method. And fourth, we have been led to acknowledge the need for a plurality of methods in psychology because of the wide expanse of soul as its subject matter.

Given this need for a plurality of methods, an imaginal approach to research rests in part on the recognition of the absence of and the necessity for a method that makes a place for the more subtle and non-traditional modes of knowing, such as feelings, dreams, symptoms, intuition, and synchronicities alongside a researcher's ideas, observations, and measurements. Within an imaginal approach to research, the former ways of knowing are equally legitimate methods of opening a path into one's work. In the Introduction to this book, in the soft meditation on green, I tried to give expression to the feeling quality in the way of knowing that keeps soul in mind, and in Chapter 2 I described how one of my own dreams informed this book. In Chapter 6 I gave some examples from the work of my graduate students to show how they made a place in their work for the symptomatic body, dreams, and synchronicities. The Old Woman in the Wheelchair, who figured prominently in Debbie Greenwood's transference dialogues, first came to her in a dream, and Linda Lauver was also, to use her own word, "initiated" into her work by a dream. In addition, she, as well as Greenwood, Jo Todd, and Erik Killinger, highlighted the role of the symptomatic body in their research process, and Todd and Greenwood described what appeared to them as moments of synchronicity in their work. But, in all these examples, these expressions functioned unofficially as a way into the work, and in Chapters 10 and 11 I will propose a method that will make such expressions more official. This method is called alchemical hermeneutics.

But why alchemical hermeneutics? What does the term "alchemical" add to the tradition of hermeneutics? Before we can reply to these questions, we need to understand some key themes in hermeneutics. This is the subject of the next two chapters.

CHAPTER EIGHT

Hermeneutics and the Circle of Understanding

Introduction

Hermeneutics refers to the act of understanding and interpreting symbolic texts of whatever source or kind. A shard of pottery found buried beneath an ancient city is as much a text as an historical document, but so too is a dream and a set of data gathered in research. In each of these instances, and in the respective disciplines of history, archaeology, and psychology that take these texts as their objects, hermeneutics exists because these symbolic texts are ambiguous. Where there is ambiguity, there is need for interpretation, and interpretation is needed because there is ambiguity.

Tracing the origins of hermeneutics, Palmer writes that the word *hermeios* refers to the priest at the Delphic oracle—the temple of Apollo, the god of oracles, dreams, and prophecies. "This word," he says, "and the more common verb *hermeneuein* and noun *hermeneia* point back to the wing-footed messenger-god Hermes, from whose name the words are apparently derived." Thus, in the hermeneutic act we are in the presence of Hermes, who is "associated with the function of transmuting what is beyond human understanding into a form that human intelligence can grasp." Hermes, then, is the mythic figure who inhabits "the process of bringing a thing or situation from unintelligibility to understanding."[1]

Already in these brief remarks it is clear that the philosophical ground of hermeneutics rests within a mythological context. Hermeneutics belongs to Hermes. But so, too, do Orpheus and

Eurydice belong to Hermes, inasmuch as he is their guide between the underworld and the upper world, their guide between life and death. Moreover, when Heidegger says that Hermes "'brings the message of destiny' ...," which is a presenting and explaining of "... that which was already said through the poets, who themselves according to Socrates in Plato's dialogue *Ion* are 'messengers of the gods ...' ,"[2] hermeneutics, under the aegis of Hermes, aligns itself with the view that an imaginal approach is a poetics of the research process. This term "poetics of research" does not mean that research is poetry. It means, as we saw in the Introduction, that a researcher is attuned to the gap between what is said and what is always left unsaid, the gap between conscious and unconscious, which is bridged by the symbol as the expression of the transcendent function. The poet Orpheus, as we saw in Chapter 2, stands in the gap, and now we see that Hermes is the one who translates that gap. In an imaginal approach to research, Hermes, as the one who brings the message of destiny, is the figure who brings into understanding the destiny of the work.

Insofar as re-search with soul in mind is under the spell of Orpheus, it is also an approach to research that has its roots in the "Hermes process," in the art of translation or movement between worlds. Hermes is the one who guides the wounded researcher in the six Orphic moments of the journey between himself or herself and the text, the one who is charged with making the complex unconscious presence of the researcher to the text more conscious, and the one charged with mediating the difference between what the researcher wants from the work and what the work wants from the researcher. Hermes is the guide in the work, the one who stands between the researcher, who would bring the soul of the work into intelligibility, and the work itself, which, like Eurydice, belongs with its perpetual unfinished business in the underworld—this is why, as I said in Chapter 4, the work is never done, even though it is finished. Hermes is the one who is always leading the work back into its depths, and who does so with all those countless tricks and deceptions involved in the process of making a work. Was he the one who made the noise that distracted Orpheus from his goal and caused him to turn? Is he the one who is near, when the work suddenly no longer makes sense to us, when it faces us with its own variation of the Eurydician question because it no longer recognizes itself in our words and interpretations? Is he the one who keeps the soul of the work in mind by forcing us to turn and to look at it again? Such questions, of course, are not meant to be answered. They are spurs to the imagination and invitations not to forget the depths of the work. Hermes is the face of the alchemical hermeneutic method, the one who connects this method and the vocational and transference processes of the imaginal approach to research. He reminds us that an alchemical hermeneutic method is a natural outgrowth of this approach and its processes.

Because of the ambiguity of the symbol, hermeneutics begins with a distinction between presence and meaning. This distinction does not separate presence from meaning. On the contrary, it emphasizes that meaning is an unfolding within and out of presence, which takes place in dialogue with a witness who is present to presence. This genesis of meaning can be described as a turning from the phenomenon that presents itself to understanding that phenomenon, a turn that is always returning to itself in the work of interpretation. Said in another way, this hermeneutic turn describes the hermeneutic circle, which embraces the knower and the "text" to be known. Within the embrace of this circle of understanding, the knower approaches a text with some foreknowledge of it, which in turn is questioned and challenged and amplified by the text, thereby transforming the knower who returns to the text with a different understanding of it. In principle, the process is never finished; that is to say, hermeneutics is always an ongoing enterprise. The hermeneutic act is infinite in its horizon because the text is what it is only in relation to and as a relation with a "reader." Thus, hermeneutics is about the co-creation of reality.

Hermeneutics as a method of engagement between a reader and a text or a researcher and a work is on the way towards an alchemical hermeneutics. Alchemical hermeneutics shares with the philosophical tradition of hermeneutics this emphasis on the relational character of the hermeneutic act. There are, however, some key differences between them, especially regarding the nature of the subject who engages and is engaged by the text. To make a bridge between this chapter and the ones that follow, I will describe seven of these key differences. In doing so, I am also answering, at least in part, the question raised at the end of the last chapter regarding what alchemical hermeneutics adds to the tradition of hermeneutics.

ATTENDING THE DIFFERENCES

The Hermeneutic Spiral

Insofar as the alchemical hermeneutic method is an outgrowth of the imaginal approach, with its research processes of vocation and transference dialogues, it continues the work of deepening the relational aspect by making a place for those other subtle unconscious connections between a researcher and his or her work expressed in dreams, intuitions, feelings, symptoms, and synchronicities. One task of an alchemical hermeneutic method is to deepen the hermeneutic circle by twisting it into a spiral. The researcher, then, follows the arc of the hermeneutic circle, but in such a way that the engagement of the two takes into account the unconscious aspects of the researcher and the work. One consequence of this deformation of the hermeneutic circle is that alchemical hermeneutics is not about making its method more philosophically valid. Rather, it is about making philosophical hermeneutics more psychologically aware.

Indeed, that was my intention when I did an experiment on complex knowing.[3] The intention was to develop a hermeneutics of the depths as a psychological gnosis, a hermeneutics with soul in mind. Von Franz, in her book *Alchemy*, makes a similar point when she discusses the relation between Jung's psychology and the new physics.[4] She acknowledges that in order to appreciate their convergence, it would be necessary for analysts to learn physics and for physicists to be analyzed. Her point, I believe, is that the factor of the dynamic and collective unconscious cannot be ignored in our epistemologies. In this context, the task that confronts psychology is to make the unconscious dynamics in our sciences and philosophies more conscious. Moreover, what von Franz suggests regarding the sciences has also been suggested with regard to history. As I noted in Chapter 1, the historian Norman Cohn, in a postscript to his fascinating book *Europe's Inner Demons*, makes this explicit confession: "But again and again I have felt that beneath the terrain which I was charting lay depths which were not to be explored by the techniques at my disposal. The purpose of these 'Psycho-Historical speculations' is to encourage others, better equipped, to venture further-downwards, into the abyss of the unconscious."[5]

The disciplines of history, philosophy, and physics, it would seem, would benefit from becoming more psychologically aware. The development of an imaginal approach to research, with its processes and its take on method, is a contribution to the task of developing such an epistemology.

Loitering in the Vicinity of the Work

In the philosophical tradition of hermeneutics, the work of understanding begins with the foreknowledge that a reader brings to a text, or a researcher brings to his or her work. One enters into a text or a work with a question, and, as the one who brings the question is questioned, the circle of understanding gets constituted. Alchemical hermeneutics stays longer, as it were, with the moment of being questioned by the text. Less immediately reactive, alchemical hermeneutics remains more receptive, more inclined towards the poet John Keats' notion of negative capability, which, as we saw in Chapter 5, characterizes the process of transference dialogues. In this respect, the alchemical hermeneutic method complements that process and continues with that way of being with the work. Not so impatient to engage the work in any conscious way, not so quick to irritate the work into meaning, the researcher who uses the alchemical hermeneutic method is content to dream with the text, to linger in reverie in the moment of being questioned, as one might, for example, linger for a while in the mood of a dream.

Lingering in reverie at the beginning, alchemical hermeneutics is almost opposite in its spirit to the philosophical tradition of hermeneutics. Something of this difference is captured when we deepen the spirit of lingering into loitering. To loiter is to linger aimlessly. It is to stand idly about, something that in the culture of ego-consciousness is usually prohibited. "No Loitering," says the sign, which in the context of research is the ego's prohibition against idly wasting time.

Alchemical hermeneutics, however, does linger and loiter in the moment of being addressed, and in doing so adopts an attitude that is so at odds with the culture of ego-consciousness that the usual prohibition against loitering betrays its roots in the soul. Etymologically, there is a connection between loitering and bulimia. For an ego-mind impatient to get on with the hermeneutic task, then, to loiter in one's research is more than prohibited. It is pathological. Focusing on the starting point of being addressed, lingering and loitering there, however, alchemical hermeneutics embraces this pathology for what it precisely is: the speaking of the soul of the work. Loitering in this moment when one is being addressed by one's research, alchemical hermeneutics bears witness to the fact that mindfully feeding the work is not enough. The work hungers to be fed also by soul.

Thus, the alchemical hermeneutic researcher begins with a kind of emptiness. It is an emptiness that has the qualities of patience and hospitality, which leave the researcher continuously open to surprise, an openness that, in having no plans, simply invites the text—the work—to tell its tale. The story of Philemon and Baucis, which we told earlier in this book, is a good example of patience and hospitality as attributes of a method or way of opening a path into a work.

The Symbol in Alchemical Hermeneutics

A third difference between alchemical hermeneutics and the philosophical tradition of hermeneutics is the relation to the symbol. Hermeneutics, as we have seen, is required because human beings exist in an ambiguous world, in a world of symbols. A symbol is a reality that yokes a presence that is visible with one that is invisible, just as, for example, the mighty wings of angels in medieval paintings hint at the invisible realm where their function as messengers between the human world and the divine is enacted. A symbol is also a reality that holds together a tension of opposites, which is Jung's description of the transcendent function, in which the symbol is the spontaneous presence of a third between something that is conscious and something that is unconscious. In addition, we could say the symbol is a reality in which presence is haunted by absence, a reality in which absence is a presence and presence is an absence, as it is, for example, in a work of art. When one looks at van Gogh's "Starry Night," for example, one realizes that the brilliant night sky is and is not there. It hovers, as it were, on the edges and margins of the shapes and colors, showing itself through them without being in them. The power of the symbol here is that through the painting we are escorted into that world that is present through its absence.

Beyond these descriptions, however, depth psychology adds a significant dimension to the notion of the symbol. Freud's example of the *fort-da* game in *Beyond the Pleasure Principle* indicates that symbols arise from the ground of traumas and losses.[6] In his analysis of a child's invented game, Freud shows how the absence of the mother is expressed symbolically through the creation of this cultural achievement. Through the game, the mother who is absent is present again. The symbolic game overcomes a loss. Similarly, the human cultural world, with all its rituals and symbols, might be regarded as a hymn to loss and reconciliation.

To situate the symbol within this context is to introduce an irreducible element of grief into the Hermes process, the hermeneutic act of interpretation, because there is always a remembrance—conscious or unconscious—of the gap between the original presence and its symbol. Interpretation is always a "failure" because what is present in the symbol remains haunted by what is absent. Alchemical hermeneutics is, therefore, always an act of mourning, which, as we saw in the Introduction, is central to the imaginal approach to research. A hermeneutics of the depths is always an expression of longing, and in this respect it differs from philosophical hermeneutics. Interpretation at the level of soul is not just about deciphering a hidden meaning, it is also about a hunger for the originary presence that still lingers as an absent presence. For a psychological hermeneutics, it is this lingering absence that fuels the hunger for interpretation, that unfinished business of soul that waits as a weight in the work beyond the words we use in our psychologies to write up the work.

We can deepen this difference by recalling the archetypal and mythic background of the god Hermes within the hermeneutic act and recalling as well his associations with Aphrodite and Eros. It is the gods and goddesses who linger in the symbol, or, if you prefer, a sense of the sacred that lingers as an absent presence in the symbol. Thus, we might say that one has to have a nose for hermeneutics, a nose for detecting the scent of the gods who linger in the ordinary. Hermeneutics, then, is about a longing to return to the originary presence of the Divine which haunts the human world, a longing for a restored connection to the sacred, to the gods, who, Heidegger says, have fled and whose radiance, therefore, no longer shines in human history, and to the gods, who, Jung says, have become our diseases. In this latter context, hermeneutics as a longing for the sacred is for the sake of healing. When we link Hermes with Aphrodite and Eros, we see also that the healing aspect of the hermeneutic act comes through the expression of love.

I am suggesting that an alchemical hermeneutic method opens a path to knowing that is healing and redemptive. A contemporary cultural example illustrates this point. At the site of the 9/11 tragedy, one of the designs that was considered to commemorate the event is called "Reflecting Absence." It features a large reflecting pool, which mirrors trees and other features of the site, but not the missing Twin Towers. Like the missing towers, the event, which is absent, is nevertheless made present again in a symbolic fashion, and the absent ones who died there and who now haunt the memorial that is present are remembered and redeemed. The weight and wait of their histories, their unfinished business, encounter remembrance and redemption.

Alchemical hermeneutics (as a path of re-turning in a healing act of loving re-membrance) is practiced by one whose consciousness has become attuned to a mythopoetic way of knowing the world and being in it, a way of knowing and being that is attuned to the guise of the wholly, holy other in its dis-guises, since Hermes, we should not forget, is a trickster, a master of disguises. He is also a thief and a liar, and this means that the researcher must always take into account the shadows that darken the light of interpretation, the complexes that linger in the transference field between the researcher and the topic. Alchemical hermeneutics is a way of remaining present to the fact that the wholly and holy other is present in the complexes that haunt our concepts, as well as in the myths that haunt our meanings, in the dreams that haunt our reasons, in the symptoms that haunt our symbols, in the fantasies that haunt our facts, in the fictions that haunt our ideas, and in the images, like those of 9/11, that dwell in events.

From Wound to Wonder: The Time-Bound and the Timeless

Memorials are like archetypes insofar as both haunt the time-bound world with the timeless. Not only does the 9/11 memorial situate the event within the moment of that wound, which is deeply embedded in time, but the date itself has become a symbol of an event that is now also outside of time. In a similar way, archetypes are present as an absence in every temporal moment, and for Jung they carry the numinous and timeless realities of the soul. I have always understood Heidegger to be saying the same thing in philosophical terms. Being shines through beings, and as such every ontic moment has a trace of the timeless in it. Jung's psychology and Heidegger's phenomenology converge towards the same tension between the temporal and the timeless, and the alchemical hermeneutic method of an imaginal approach to research has its roots in this convergence. It is a method, which, with its roots in this convergence rather than in the sciences, asks a researcher to remain open through his or her wounds to the wonder of the timeless spirit of the work. Soul in Jung and Being in Heidegger may hold a place for the same concern: to rescue the timeless realm of soul that haunts and shines through the wound in presence, but is and has been forgotten in a metaphysics of presence, which, as David Michael Levin points out, is a metaphysics of the surface.[7]

An alchemical hermeneutic method as a hermeneutics of the depths challenges this metaphysics of the surface. It is a method or a way of going into the work that moves from a time-bound wound to the timeless wonder of the work. Recall here the earlier discussion of Freud's *fort-da* game, in which the child who has suffered the wound of his mother's absence transforms his wound into a symbolic game. The alchemical hermeneutic method is this same art of transforming a wound into a work. It asks the researcher to attend to his or her wounds and through them to make the work that takes the wound beyond itself.

Lending an Ear to the Work/Being Addressed by the Work

Earlier I spoke about how a researcher who takes up an alchemical hermeneutic method lingers with the work and loiters near it. He or she is like the alchemist tending the fire, slowly, without impatience, watching the flames as the work heats up to its proper temperature. This is careful work because, if the work is rushed and the heat is too high, the vessel cracks. On the other hand, the alchemical texts always warn of the danger of falling asleep, especially as the goal of the work is approached. The researcher who loiters near the work is always in danger of becoming so beguiled by his or her fantasies of the work that he or she neglects to tend the fire and it goes out unnoticed. The researcher is then left with only the cold gray ashes of the work.

What I am trying to suggest here is that the practice of the alchemical hermeneutic method requires a balance between two ways of being present to one's work. In Chapter 5 I already described these two ways in terms of the figures of the witness and the critic, who structure the transference field between the researcher and the work in two distinctly different ways. The transference field is the alchemical vessel in which the complex researcher and the unfinished business in the soul of the work are mixed. Those dialogues are part of the process of an imaginal approach in which the complex wounds of the researcher are transformed into a work that comes through the researcher but is not about him or her. These two ways of being present as witness and critic appear again in the method, and in this respect the method is a continuation of the process, which, as we saw, is applicable to all methods.

In the alchemical hermeneutic method, the researcher as witness attends to the flames without any premature concern about the results. He or she is present to what the work presents of itself before becoming critically concerned with its meanings. In the guise of witness, the researcher respects a basic phenomenological truth of experience, which says that presence precedes meaning and that, indeed, meaning arises out of being present to what presents itself. This fidelity to presence is a style or posture in which the witness leans into the work and lends an ear in order to hear better how he or she is being addressed by the work. The researcher as witness is poised to get an earful, as it were, because he or she knows that the unfinished business in the soul of the work is continuously trying to address him or her, to get his or her attention before he or she starts to address it by focusing his or her attention and imposing his or her conscious intentions, plans, worries, and concerns on the work. I am not, here, splitting presence and meaning. I am, on the contrary, saying only that in the alchemical hermeneutic method the act of interpretation begins with being summoned by the work, and that one speaks out of being present to this summons and speaks on behalf of it, on behalf of those for whom the work is being done.

Paul Ricoeur, one of the few philosophers who has taken into account in a rigorous way the impact of the unconscious on traditional hermeneutics, acknowledges this shift between hermeneutics as a form of addressing a text and as a form of being addressed by it. In the next chapter I will have more to say about Ricoeur's important work, especially with regard to how an alchemical hermeneutics differs from his view, but here I want to note only that in his serious encounter with the unconscious in Freud's work, he emphasizes this shift. "After the silence and forgetfulness made widespread by the manipulation of empty signs and the construction of formalized languages," he writes, "the modern concern for symbols expresses a new desire to be addressed."[8] What is being acknowledged here, I would suggest, is the illusory foundation of a consciousness that would believe itself to be self-contained as something other and apart from nature. What is being acknowledged by this desire to be addressed is the recognition that before one speaks about the world, the text, or the work, one has already been called into speaking through the ear.

Alchemical hermeneutics begins in the ear and not on the tongue, and in this respect it has implications for language. Before I speak to those implications, however, I want to cite an image from alchemy that shows how knowledge is born in an act that delays the impatient desire to fulfill an impulse for the sake of knowing. It is the story of the goddess Isis, who is lustfully desired by one of the angels of the first firmament. Before she will give herself to him, however, she wants the angel to give her the alchemical secret. She demurs, therefore, and the angel promises to return with one greater than himself who will impart to her the secret. Isis knows what she wants and she has her question—"Will you, the angel, tell me the alchemical secret?" But she also knows that beyond this beginning question she must hold back her impulses. She knows she must become silent and wait. And in exercising that patience she is rewarded, for the greater angel who comes does tell her the secret of alchemy.[9]

The researcher who is too impatient in his or her desire to know the secret of the work will go beyond the initial question (which, after all, is simply the declaration of an interest in and an invitation to the work) with continued questions, which will only deafen the researcher to how he or she might be addressed. What I am suggesting here is that beyond the vocation that draws a researcher into a work with a question, the researcher who would practice the alchemical hermeneutic method has to learn that speaking in fact begins with being addressed, that it is a response to having heard. One who practices the alchemical hermeneutic method knows that the words one gives to the work are born in an act of obedience, in the obedience of having listened. Indeed, it is not surprising that the Latin root of "obey" is "to listen." In listening to what addresses us, we are obedient to something other than ourselves, and we obey when we listen to what addresses us. In alchemical hermeneutics, this obedience is in service to the soul of the work, the angel of the work, we might say, in reference to the Isis story.

The implication for language in this shift from hermeneutics as a form of addressing a text to hermeneutics as a form of being addressed by a text, i.e., a hermeneutics that takes into account the unconscious, is that language is a gift. We speak because we are called to do so. "Are we, perhaps, here just for saying: House,/Bridge, Fountain, Gate, Jug, Olive Tree, Window,—/possibly: Pillar, Tower?"[10] These few lines from the ninth of Rilke's *Duino Elegies* should make us pause for a moment. That one word "perhaps" tells us how radical this shift from tongue to ear can be. We say these things perhaps because they want to be spoken of in that way. We say these things because we have listened to them. And what about that other singular word—"possibly"? What does that say to us? Does it not suggest how fragile this bequest of language can be and how careful we must be in saying what has spoken to us? Consider how easy it is to conquer the dream with our "dayenglish," to recall here the words of the poet Brendan Kennelly cited in Chapter 1.[11] Alchemical hermeneutics is a method that takes this matter of language to heart, and in the chapter on writing down the soul I will go into this matter in some detail. How does one faithfully write down the soul of the work by which one is addressed? How does one avoid the temptation to impose upon the soul of the work the pre-formed language of one's ideas, the language of psychological jargon that gives a meaning but misses the experience?

Alchemical hermeneutics, we might say, is the art of ventriloquism. As a hermeneutics of and for soul, it is, we might say, a hermeneutics for dummies. Perhaps we are, as researchers, here just for saying what the work wants to be said. Possibly we are, as researchers, called to be spokespersons for the unfinished business of the ancestors in the work.

Sophia alongside Hermes

In his seminal text *Answer to Job*, Jung tells us in rich historical and archetypal detail how Sophia, the feminine counterpart to Yahweh in the act of creation, has been lost.[12] The art of hermeneutics is a work of co-creation between the reader and the text. The reader, however, is too often imagined without his or her feminine counterpart, and hermeneutics needs the presence of the anima, of the soul, in its ways of reading. Gaston Bachelard acknowledges this point when he says, "I am not the same man when I am reading a book of ideas where the animus is obliged to be vigilant, quite ready to criticize, quite ready to retort, as when I am reading a poet's book where images must be received in a sort of transcendental acceptance of gifts." And, having noted this difference, he adds, "Ah! to return the absolute gift which is the poet's image, our *anima* would have to be able to write a hymn of thanksgiving."[13]

I am not arguing here for a split between an animus and anima hermeneutics any more than I was arguing earlier for a split between the witness and the critic or between presence and meaning. Rather, I am only suggesting that alongside a hermeneutics that would take hold of and command the text, we also need to have a hermeneutics that would be an act of thanksgiving. Without genderizing the issue, I am suggesting that alongside a hermeneutics that privileges intelligence and reason, we also need to have a hermeneutics that gives a place to intuition and feeling as ways of knowing a text and being addressed by it. The alchemist in front of his fire was accompanied by the *soror mystica,* just as Yahweh in his acts of creation was beside himself with Sophia, and just as Freud and Jung were invited to be beside themselves with Dora, Toni Wolff, and a host of others. Yahweh forgot Sophia, with rather disastrous consequences, according to Jung, and Freud and Jung, as I have argued elsewhere, did not lend their ears as they should have to their Sophianic companions.[14] The alchemical hermeneutic researcher should learn a lesson from all this. The alchemical hermeneutic researcher has to be beside himself or herself with the anima.

An alchemical hermeneutic method would re-imagine the art of interpretation as a longing for the return of Sophianic wisdom. A key aspect of this wisdom is the art of receptivity, the art of allowing oneself to be addressed, impregnated, like the Virgin of the Annunciation, the art of allowing the critical mind to become virginal for a moment, free of its preconceptions, plans, and intentions, so that it might be inseminated by the soul of the work. When our hermeneutics falls too much on the side of the critic with his or her questions, and does not allow sufficient time for the witness to linger and loiter in the moment of being questioned, the voice of Sophia can easily be silenced. When our hermeneutic arts begin too early and too quickly with our questions for the topic, when our hermeneutic arts do not allow sufficient time for us as researchers to be questioned by our topic, drawn into its voice, we lose the feminine element in our arts of understanding.

Alchemical hermeneutics makes a place for Sophia in the arts of understanding, in which one is asked to lend an ear to the work. There is much work to be done here, but I will content myself for the moment with noting that this work would have to work out the many ways in which hermeneutics is deepened and changed when Sophia and her tradition stands beside Hermes and his tradition.

The Embodiment of Understanding

The introduction of Sophia into the arts of interpretation leads to a seventh and final difference between alchemical and philosophical hermeneutics. It is a difference about the place of the body in understanding and is closely allied with the notion of lingering as the attitude of the witness in a state of virginal receptivity.

To linger and even loiter in the presence of what is present is to recover the animate flesh. It is the lived body that lingers in an erotic conspiracy with the world, and hermeneutics must always start on the ground of this con-spiracy, where the researcher breathes in harmony with the work, where the moment of inspiration by the work is the beginning. To enter the hermeneutic circle and to tumble into the hermeneutic spiral is not an act of mind. Or, if it is, then one's hermeneutics is too much on the side of the critic, who is in the fantasy of breathing life into the work. No, to begin with the ensouled body and its gestural fields is to acknowledge that between one's flesh and that of the work, like the relation in the transference field of therapy between the flesh of the therapist and that of the patient, a secret dialogue has already been in progress, a dialogue that now poses its questions to the researcher.[15] The embodied witness is the one who interprets on the grounds that he or she has already been interpreted. He or she makes sense and derives meaning on the grounds of how he or she has already been made sense of. The witness does not enter the circle, because he or she has already been encircled. The witness, loitering in virginal receptivity in the presence of the work, is the one who is questioned, while the critic is the one who already has a question. It is a difference between a masculine style of breaking into a work, impregnating it, and a feminine one of being impregnated by the work and nurturing the fruit of that impregnation. To let Sophia join Hermes in the hermeneutic act challenges the usual position of the critical ego-mind in the research process. Alchemical hermeneutics is a joint affair, an animated hermeneutics of reveries and hospitality akin to the kind of presence that the alchemist and *soror mystica* of old brought to their work.

SUMMARY OF THE DIFFERENCES

Before I conclude this chapter, I want to summarize the seven differences between philosophical and alchemical hermeneutics.

First, alchemical hermeneutics deepens the circle of understanding between a reader and a text into a spiral of engaged confrontation. The difference of form points to the presence of a deep subjectivity in alchemical hermeneutics. This engaged subject enters a spiral of descent in which meanings that arise from presence are continuously undone. Alchemical hermeneutics is not, therefore, only about arriving at meaning as a solution. It is also about the continuous dissolution of meaning over time in relation to the unfinished business in the soul of the work. In this respect, alchemical hermeneutics taps into a deep root of alchemy. According to Edinger, one of the key operations in alchemy is the *solutio,* and, indeed, he quotes one source to the effect that "*Solutio* is the root of alchemy." In addition, he says, "In many places the whole opus is summarized by the phrase 'Dissolve and coagulate.'"[16] The Orphic myth, which enfolds the imaginal approach to research, is present in this work of dissolution. In the spiral of descent, the researcher who practices this alchemical hermeneutic art lets the work draw back, with Eurydice, into the underworld of soul, into that afterworld of love.

Second, in alchemical hermeneutics the researcher lingers with his or her question to the work so that he or she might be more deeply questioned by the work. In this mode of lingering, the alchemical hermeneutic researcher consciously tries to slow down the impatient ego's desire to get on with the work. Lingering and even loitering in the vicinity of the work, the alchemical hermeneutic researcher is content to be idle for a while and even to dream alongside the work. Or, perhaps, it is better to say that the researcher only appears to be idle, since lingering and loitering have their own styles and rhythms of being engaged, which are so different from the styles and rhythms of the ego-mind.

Third, alchemical hermeneutics deepens the sense of the symbol by showing how symbols arise from the ground of loss. Thus, an element of mourning accompanies the hermeneutic arts. In the attempt to recover the original presence that has been lost and to which the symbol points, alchemical hermeneutics suggests that research is a work of reconciliation, redemption, and healing both for the researcher and for the ancestors who linger as the unfinished business in the soul of the work.

Fourth, alchemical hermeneutics situates the researcher in that place between his or her time-bound complex wounds, which draw him or her into a work as a vocation, and the timeless soul of the work. In this sense, alchemical hermeneutics is a method or way of transforming a wound into a work without reducing the work to the wound of the researcher. The method of alchemical hermeneutics aligns itself here with the process of transference dialogues.

Fifth, alchemical hermeneutics reverses the emphasis on the issue of questioning and being questioned by a text. In this reversal, alchemical hermeneutics emphasizes that questioning begins in the ear and not on the tongue. It emphasizes that the art of questioning begins with the art of allowing oneself to be questioned. In alchemical hermeneutics, the researcher lends an ear to the work and as a witness opens himself or herself to being radically and continuously addressed by the work. Here again, the method of alchemical hermeneutics continues the process of an imaginal approach to research. The process of transference dialogues are the alchemical container in which the researcher is continuously questioned by the work, in which he or she continuously lends an ear to the "other" in the work, who carries its unfinished business. While this process of transference dialogues is applicable to all methods, the alchemical hermeneutic method is especially suited to it and is a natural extension of it.

Sixth, alchemical hermeneutics brings a feminine presence to the arts of interpretation and understanding. In this method, Hermes is beside himself with Sophia. Sophia's presence in the hermeneutic act transforms the critical ego-mind of the researcher into a virginal receptivity that allows the researcher to be continuously open to and inseminated by the voices of soul in the work. Alchemical hermeneutics is the art of nurturing the fruit of this impregnation. It is the art of learning how to carry to term the work that is asking to be born.

Seventh, alchemical hermeneutics gives a central place to the body as the starting point of the hermeneutic process. In and through the body of the researcher, the complexes by which one is called into the work become the ground of the continuing erotic dance of desire between the researcher and the work. The complex body of the researcher is the site that invites the original seduction by the work and the ongoing play of it.

CONCLUSION

In this chapter I have described a few key themes in hermeneutics, and I have indicated seven ways in which alchemical hermeneutics differs from the philosophical tradition of hermeneutics. These seven differences do not betray the tradition of hermeneutics; rather, they add to it by taking into account the unconscious, which has been the province of depth psychology. In a sense, we might say that alchemical hermeneutics is the offspring of the encounter between the tradition of hermeneutics and depth psychology. But, however we might express this point, what cannot be denied or avoided is that the unconscious is a challenge to the hermeneutic tradition. Speaking to this point, the philosopher Paul Ricoeur writes:

> For someone trained in phenomenology, existential philosophy, linguistic or semiological methods, and the revival of Hegel studies, the encounter with psychoanalysis constitutes a considerable shock, for the discipline affects and questions anew not simply some particular theme within philosophical reflection but the philosophical project as a whole.[17]

In the next chapter I will consider how this statement of Ricoeur's goes to the heart of the issue regarding the nature of the subject in the hermeneutic act. The subject in the hermeneutic circle is one who goes into a text or a work by going down and through his or her own complex relations to the text or the work. We might say in this regard that the way into a work is the way down and through the subject.

CHAPTER NINE

Towards a Hermeneutics of Deep Subjectivity

INTRODUCTION

As we saw in the last chapter, Paul Ricoeur has noted that the unconscious poses a challenge not simply to one or another philosophical theme, but to the whole enterprise of philosophy itself. But what is so for philosophy actually applies to all human endeavors insofar as all such endeavors involve acts of thinking. In other words, the unconscious presents a challenge to the task of thinking in whatever disciplinary form it takes. How a historian thinks about the past, or an economist thinks about money, is no less informed by unconscious issues than it is for how a philosopher thinks about thinking or how a researcher thinks about his or her work. We need, therefore, a method that takes the unconscious into account. Alchemical hermeneutics is that method, and, as we saw in Chapter 8, it differs from traditional hermeneutics in seven fundamental ways. All of these differences, moreover, arise because of the place that alchemical hermeneutics gives to the unconscious. Has the unconscious, therefore, generally been absent from hermeneutics? With few exceptions, the answer to this question would seem to be in the affirmative. In the next section, I want to give an historical example of how the unconscious has been more or less absent in hermeneutics.

Posing a Question

If the unconscious has been more or less absent in hermeneutics, then what does a hermeneutic method that makes a place for the unconscious in the work of interpretation and understanding look like?

In 1883, Wilhelm Dilthey published *Introduction to the Human Sciences,* in which he made an important contribution to the field of hermeneutics based upon his distinction between the methods for the natural sciences—*naturwissenschaften*—and the human sciences or, as is sometimes translated, the sciences of mind or spirit—*geisteswissenschaften*. For Dilthey, the subject matter of the latter was the *geistige Welt*, the objective world of spirit or mind, which H. P. Rickman notes was, for Dilthey, based upon, but distinct from, both the mental world of the person and the physical world of matter. For example, such things as "the English language, the play Othello, the game of chess and the Napoleonic code ... are creations of individual minds but confront us with an objective existence of their own."[1] They are symbolic realities, expressions of mind as it has incarnated itself in material form, and for Dilthey, how one understands such things and interprets their meanings differs from how a physicist or biologist or chemist understands the phenomena of his or her discipline. *"Die Natur erklaren wir, das Seelenleben verstehen wir,"* Dilthey said.[2] We explain Nature, while the life of mind or spirit is understood.[3] Dilthey's point, then, was that the objects of these two sciences were so different that the laws that apply to the natural sciences do not apply to those human sciences, like art and history, which require different ways of knowing and being. A researcher, for example, cannot fully or truly understand an historical event, or a work of art, or a dream through modes of explanation which apply in the natural sciences. A work of art, or a dream, or an historical event requires more than cause-effect analysis or reductive explanations. They require description and interpretation, which stay rooted within the human experience and the cultural-historical contexts of its expression.

Dilthey proposed that psychology as a human science was to replace psychology as a natural science, and he went further in suggesting that such a human-science psychology was to be the foundation for the sciences of mind or spirit in general. As it stands,

Dilthey's distinction between the natural and the human sciences was valid in its time, and it has proven to be helpful in numerous ways. But advances in the sciences, particularly in physics and psychology, especially Jung's elaboration of the psychoid archetype, expose three problems with it.

First, the distinction between methods of explanation and methods of understanding, which belong, respectively, to the sciences of nature and those of mind or spirit, leaves a void between nature and mind or spirit. In other words, the distinction accepts this dualism as a fact. In this respect, something of the ghost of Descartes haunts Dilthey's project. Since the life of mind or spirit does not lend itself for him to the methods of the natural sciences, psychology in its own right and as the foundation for those sciences of the mind or spirit can only be a human science. Soul, however, is the third term between nature and mind, and yet, in this void or Cartesian abyss between nature and mind, soul is missing, and with it the possibility of psychology as a science of soul is gone.

Since Dilthey's time, however, we have come to understand that explanation and understanding, as two distinct methods for two distinct sciences, are not so clearly separated because nature and the life of mind or spirit are not so clearly demarcated. In quantum physics, for example, the explanation of nature cannot be divorced from how the personal equation of the experimenter informs his or her understanding of the nature he or she wishes to explain, and in Jung's psychology the psychoid nature of the archetype suggests, as we saw in Chapter 1, that at the deepest level of the psyche, soul is a reality where nature and mind are one. The complex reality of soul is present, therefore, in both explaining nature and understanding the excrescence in material form of the life of mind or spirit. But, as said above, between psychology as a natural science and a human science, Dilthey leaves no room for a science of soul.

The tradition of psychology as a human science has been plagued by this absence. In 1970, Amedeo Giorgi published his ground-breaking book, *Psychology as a Human Science*, in which he pioneered phenomenological methods of research in contrast to empirical and rational modes of research in psychology as a natural science. Along with his colleagues at Duquesne University, Giorgi was elaborating the program of Dilthey by focusing on the method issue with respect to the difference between psychology as a natural and as a human science. Method was still the priority, and thus, like Dilthey, Giorgi made no place for soul in his phenomenologically-based human science. Indeed, there is no mention of soul in his book at all.[4]

Second, as we have seen in Chapter 7, psychology is that strange discipline that offers its subject matter—soul—to a plurality of methods, including the empiricist methods of the natural sciences. In this respect, psychology as a science of soul seems to be a promiscuous discipline that methodically couples with numerous partners. In this regard, psychology is both a natural science, whose methods reveal and conceal something of soul, and a human science, whose methods also reveal and conceal something of soul. Psychology as a science of soul would be, therefore, a discipline in which method is secondary to subject matter. What method a psychologist might use would depend upon which aspect of soul he or she wanted to study.

What makes psychology a science, then, is not its adherence to method, which is what defines science in the modern sense. Rather, I would propose that psychology is a science in the older meaning of the term "science," which signifies simply "to know." Psychology, however, is unique as a way of knowing and being in the world because soul, which is the subject matter of psychology, is present in all that we do. Economics, for example, is a way of knowing and being in the world, but the economic attitude is not present, or desirable, in all our endeavors. Psychology, therefore, must be both pluralistic in its methods and interdisciplinary in its character. Psychology is wrongly conceived, or at least too narrowly conceived, as a stand-alone science. Psychology truly becomes a science when it gives itself away to other disciplines, when it holds on to soul by letting go of it.

Third, the distinction between the natural and the human sciences, which leaves soul in the lurch, also leaves the unconscious out of the picture in the human sciences. In Giorgi's book, for example, there is no mention of the depth tradition, especially Jung's work, apart from a few critical remarks about Freud that are basically aimed at rescuing consciousness from the unconscious of depth psychology. However, as we saw at the end of the last chapter, Paul Ricoeur has noted that philosophy cannot ignore a confrontation with the unconscious, and if philosophy cannot afford to do so, no psychology, whether as a natural or a human science, can afford to do so either.

Generally speaking, as I have shown elsewhere, phenomenology in philosophy and psychology has with few exceptions not come to terms with the unconscious.[5]

This brief historical account suggests that between Dilthey's natural and human sciences we need to make room for a science of soul. In addition, therefore, to *naturwissenschaften* and *geisteswissenschaften,* we need a *seelenwissenschaften* that does not define psychology in relation to method, but in relation to soul, which, as the subject matter of psychology, calls for an openness to a plurality of methods. And, among these methods, we need a hermeneutics of the depths, a complex hermeneutics, a hermeneutics that, keeping soul in mind, takes into account the unconscious dynamics in the "Hermes process."

At the beginning of this section, I asked what a hermeneutic method that keeps soul in mind would look like. The reply is that it would look like a method that belongs to a science of soul as opposed to psychology as either a natural or a human science. Alchemical hermeneutics is this method. Along with the process of transference dialogues, which belong to an imaginal approach to re-search and which systematically take into account the complex unconscious presence of the researcher to his or her work, the method of alchemical hermeneutics, as I will show in the next two chapters, makes a place for additional aspects of the unconscious in research.

An imaginal approach to re-search is one expression of a science of soul, and this way of conceiving a science of soul has been the *telos* of this book. This presence of the unconscious and the presence of systematic ways of dealing with it is what differentiates a science of soul from psychology as either a natural or a human science in its research and its therapeutic practices. Indeed, in the same way that the presence of the unconscious and systematic ways of dealing with it have differentiated analysis from psychotherapy, the presence of the unconscious and systematic ways of dealing with it differentiate research within an imaginal approach from empiricist, rationalist, and even hermeneutic approaches to research. Even when the tradition of hermeneutics does address the challenge of the unconscious, it does not offer a systematic way of exploring the presence and influence of the unconscious in research. In the next section, I want to give an extended example of this failure.

The Unconscious in Hermeneutics: A Case Study

The Unconscious of the Text

In his article, "A Critical Hermeneutics for Psychology: Beyond Positivism to an Exploration of the Textual Unconscious,"Robert Steele offers a masterful and persuasive reading of a text in psychology in order to show how "words are manipulated to reproduce a psychologist's vision of the world." To accomplish his task, Steele calls for a "prose poetics" for the hermeneutic process. "When poetics replaces positivism," he writes, "reading becomes radical." "Poetics brings language alive," he adds, because it "helps us hear the resonance in what we read by making us aware of the multiple meanings in words and by aiding us to see the features of a linguistic landscape that scientists have virtually ignored, especially in their own writings."[6]

A poetics of the re-search process, which I described in the Introduction to this book, rests upon this same premise of the non-univocal character of language. The multiple meanings of words, which require a poetic hermeneutics, always leave a gap between what is said and what is unsaid and between what is understood and what is not understood, and in this gap there resides the unfinished business in the soul of the work. To take this gap into account, Steele proposes a way of writing that is reflexive. He asserts, "Science will become truly reflexive, truly self-critical, when it allows the wisdom of a prose poetics … to alter its practice."[7]

While Steele does not directly illustrate his call for a mode of writing that is truly self-critical, he does illustrate his call indirectly by offering a poetics of the reading process of a text that is not self-critical. The text, by W. Mischel, is entitled "Continuity and Change in Personality," first published in *American Psychologist* in 1969 .

Steele prefaces his reading of Mischel's text by speaking about "the hermeneutic gaze," which, he says, "is a type of double vision." This double vision is a kind of reading that in addition to being able "to perform an average expectable reading" is also able to "read between the lines." To keep one eye, as it were, on line while keeping the other eye off line requires more than anything else that one "be aware of the forms of play in the text." After citing several examples of forms of play in texts, such as "the flexibility of meaning that words and phrases have," Steele points to "the fun a reader can have of discovering or making up something the author did not mean to be seen in his or her work."[8]

But what does it mean to have this kind of fun with a text or with one's work? What does it mean to "make up" what is not seen or was not meant to be seen in the text? I would argue here that what a reader might make up about a text, or a researcher about his or her work, is a complex process and not a completely or strictly rational one. A reader who plays with a text in this fashion, like a researcher who plays with his or her work, is reading into a text or a work by reading against it in terms of his or her complexes, and in this respect this complex form of play can distort the text or the work in terms of the reader's or researcher's complexes. But Steele, as we shall see, does not go in this direction. While he acknowledges the necessity "to examine ourselves as closely as we look at others,"[9] his critical reading of Mischel's text is not matched by a rigorous self-critical reading of himself as a critical, complex reader, who is obviously having some fun with his reading of Mischel's article.

In his critical reading of Mischel's article, Steele uses a mix of several forms of hermeneutic inquiry. Each of these forms—feminism, Marxism, phenomenology, psychoanalysis, structuralism, and deconstruction—plays with the text's possibilities. Each of these forms of critical inquiry is a way of uncovering what is "other" to the author's intentions in the text. They are ways of exposing an author's hidden meanings, or ways of deconstructing an author's unacknowledged biases or prejudices, or, in the language of this book, ways of uncovering an author's unconscious complexes. They are ways of getting at what Steele felicitously calls the "textual unconscious" of the work.

These six forms of critical inquiry cannot, however, simply be used as tools to be applied by a pristine reader. To read a text as a Marxist, one has to be informed by Marxism, and while a Marxist reading might reveal layers of meaning in the text that were unseen by the author, it also reveals who the reader is who uncovers these hidden meanings, and how he or she is reading the text. The reading, in other words, reflects the reader. Why one person reads a text from a Marxist perspective while another finds in it an unacknowledged feminist perspective is a complex problem.

Take for a moment the example of a dream that might be told by a patient to his or her analyst. A dream, by definition, is a text with multiple layers of meaning. If the analyst is a Jungian, he or she will be inclined to "read" the dream in a Jungian way. If the analyst is a Freudian, he or she will be inclined to "read" it in Freudian terms. Recall the discussion of Jung and Freud in Chapter 3. When Jung told Freud his dream of the house with many levels in which two skulls were in the basement, Jung said he felt not only dissatisfied with Freud's interpretation, but also forced by Freud to accede to that interpretation. Commenting on this, Jung wrote, "I saw from this that he was completely helpless in dealing with certain kinds of dreams and had to take refuge in his doctrine."[10]

The point of this example, as I said in Chapter 3, is not that Freud was wrong about the dream and Jung was right. The point is that the example illustrates the role of the complex in the work of understanding and interpretation. A Jungian or a Freudian can read a dream critically from his or her perspective and reveal what is hidden from the "author" of that text, i.e., the dreamer, but, unless the analyst who is reading the dream in either a Jungian or a Freudian way is aware of his or her perspective, the prejudice in the interpretation, its complex roots, remains hidden. In other words, the critical way of reading the dream as either a Jungian or a Freudian dream is not self-critical. Thus, the analyst may be as blind to his or her complex as the dreamer is to the meanings of the dream. The blind, then, are leading the blind in the dark-light of the soul.

This same point applies to Steele's critical hermeneutics. It needs to be balanced and checked by a self-critical re-gard, or second look, at itself, a look that acknowledges that the six forms of informed inquiry are also complex problems. An example of one of Steele's interpretations of the textual unconscious in Mischel's work will illustrate these remarks.

According to Steele, Mischel's text, "Continuity and Change in Personality," is an argument for making personality research more objective and reliable. In Steele's words, because "there is little continuity through the years or across situations in people's socio-emotional traits," which "is not, however, the case with cognitive styles that show considerable constancy through the years and consistency from situation to situation," Mischel was calling for a study of personality in terms of the "more scientifically viable study of the variety of ways in which people cognitively process their environments." What Steele's critical reading of Mischel's text uncovers, however, is an "elaborate sub-text in which one of the oldest personality stereotypes held by man is reproduced: women are dangerously inconsistent creatures, and men—when acting truly human—are cognitively consistent, rational, and predictable as machines." The point that Steele is making here is that "[w]hile Mischel is calling for more objectivity, his sub-text clearly shows that objectivity is simply a rationalization of the male point of view, a bias that is seen in Mischel's insistence on his authority, his taking away of other people's autonomy, and his animation of machines." Lest this point be missed, Steele adds, "In short, behind the author's positivist argument for cognitive continuity we will discover an emotionally disordered work held together by masculine dread."[11]

Steele begins uncovering the emotionally disordered subtext by showing how Mischel privileges himself as author by discrediting the subjects being studied. Steele notes that for Mischel the research on trait consistency in personality shows a "tension between what subjects do (that is, finding consistency in their behaviors) and what data sheets representing subjects show: no such consistency exists." Referring to the research subjects in Mischel's study, Steele adds, "Even though they claim a continuity in their lives, they are wrong because the scientific data says otherwise." Then, after discounting the subjects own experience of themselves, Mischel, according to Steele, makes the next move of privileging his position as the objective scientist who knows. Mischel, as quoted by Steele, says, "In my appraisal, the overall evidence ... shows the human mind to function like an extraordinarily effective reducing valve that creates and maintains the perception of continuity ... even in the face of changes."[12]

But, to make this claim, Mischel's own mind is clearly not functioning like a reducing valve. A strange contradiction, therefore, has emerged. A gap has emerged between the subjects, whose machine mind functions like a reducing valve, and the mind of Mischel, which functions like that of the scientist who knows. "He has reduced people to data on sheets," Steele claims, and "[h]e, like science, has failed to reflect upon himself and therefore has projected into the world the structures of his own subjectivity."[13]

While at the manifest level of his work, Mischel discovered that socio-emotional personality traits lack consistency, what Steele has revealed is that at the level of the latent text "Mischel has used his psychological science to affirm man's truth: Only thought-cognition-reason—the tools of science man—have continuity over time."[14] In other words, the personality of men is consistent only when they function cognitively and act reasonably. Then, they are as consistent and predictable as machines.

Steele has shown that a critical hermeneutics is valuable in opening up the textual unconscious in a work by uncovering how a researcher's own unconscious subjectivity is projected into the work. His critical hermeneutic reading of Mischel's work has shown that research is indeed a complex process, and in this regard his critical hermeneutics lends support to the notion of the wounded researcher. But Steele seems less critical with regard to his own work of uncovering the subtext in Mischel's work. He seems less critical about his own critical reading, about the textual unconscious in his own article, about the fact that he is a wounded reader. I want to illustrate this "failure" by following another thread in his otherwise excellent critical reading of Mischel's work.

Having uncovered the masculine bias as a hidden meaning in Mischel's work, Steele goes on to show that emotions and women also function as part of Mischel's disordered subtext. Returning to the trope of the mind as a reducing valve, Steele quotes Mischel as saying, "It is essential for the mind to be a reducing valve—if it were not it might literally blow itself!" Reflecting on this sentence, Steele points out that the simile of the mind functioning like a reducing valve has become a claim that the mind is a reducing valve. And it is essential that the mind be a reducing valve, otherwise it will "blow itself." Behind the claim, Steele identifies a threat. "Believe this metaphor is actual description or your mind will self-destruct." For Steele, Mischel "has been duped by the magic of his metaphor suddenly and miraculously becoming reality."[15] Recall the discussion in Chapter 7 regarding metaphor, method, and symptom. When the metaphors in our methods are forgotten, the method functions like a symptom. Steele, I would argue, correctly uncovers how the metaphor that mind is a reducing valve functions symptomatically as a projection of Mischel's masculine bias towards the cognitive side of personality and away from the emotional.

Continuing to unpack Mischel's metaphor that the mind is a reducing valve, Steele points out how the metaphor introduces emotion into the text. On the one hand, when the metaphor is forgotten, then the phrase "blow itself" might lead one to "see the brain, the materialist translation of mind, as 'blowing off steam' like valves do." The emotional impact here is an image that Steele notices in this extension from "blow itself" to "blowing off steam." In this extension, Steele says, "Mischel, then, would be referring to some sort of brain hemorrhage."[16]

But Steele is after bigger fish that lurk in the subterranean depths of Mischel's subtext. It is the latent sexual metaphors that attract, as it were, his attention. "A mind blowing itself," Steele says, "suggests the phrase 'blow my mind,' while the ejaculatory action of a valve gaining relief from pressure suggests the phrase 'blow job' with its orgasmic and penile connotations."[17]

I have taken some time with Steele's article in order to give a context for his own indirect questioning of himself at the close of his article. He wonders if his readers might be "startled by these revelations of the seething undercurrents of overwrought emotion in a seemingly rational text arguing the virtues of cognitive control" and think, "Steele's gone too far."[18] This is a key issue because it raises the question of whether Steele addresses his own reading of Mischel in a self-critical way. Does he have some doubt that he has gone too far? Is this a way in which his own complexes, disguised as a concern that his readers might have, slip into his work?

There are places in Steele's article where one has to wonder about the article's textual unconscious. For example, when he introduces the sentence we quoted above, in which Mischel says it is essential for the mind to be a reducing valve, Steele observes, "The climax in Mischel's use of the often repeated reducing valve trope is found nearly at the center of his article ...." And, a bit later, he says, with reference to this same sentence, "This single sentence will serve nicely to illustrate several keys deconstructionism uses to open texts that close too neatly on themselves." And once more with regard to the sentence in question, when he notes the punctuation mark at its end, he declares, "His [Mischel's] compositional composure can hardly be contained as he uses the most ejaculatory of all punctuation, the exclamation point, to emphasize his point."[19] The term "climax" itself leads the reader in a particular direction. Is Steele aware of his use of the term in the context of his critical reading of the sexual subtext in Mischel's work? And the same can be asked of his description of the exclamation point as the most ejaculatory form of punctuation. Is he being intentionally provocative, a good literary stylist? Or are we being led into the textual unconscious in Mischel's text through the textual unconscious in Steele's work? Also, when he says that Mischel's sentence illustrates several keys deconstuctionism uses to open a text that folds too neatly on itself, is he saying more than he realizes? Is he the one with the key to penetrate a text that is still virginal in its self-containment? Is Steele unconsciously projecting a masculine complex of domination over the feminine, just as he claims Mischel is doing in his disordered emotional subtext when he defends the cognitive bias of the male personality against feminine sexuality?

I do not raise these questions as a way of dismissing Steele's critical hermeneutic method. In fact, as I said above, I quite agree that it does open a way into the textual unconscious of a work. Indeed, I have used a similar procedure in a number of my own works. In "Psychology and the Attitude of Science," I offered a critical reading of a standard introductory textbook of psychology in order to show how its hidden anatomy structures its argument and organizes its knowledge.[20] The fourth chapter of *Psychological Life: From Science to Metaphor* did a similar thing with respect to showing how William Harvey's 17th-century text on the heart as a pump was encased within political, religious, and other cultural contexts of the age.[21] In addition, in *Technology as Symptom and Dream*, I presented a critical reading of Leon Battista Alberti's 15th-century text on linear perspective drawing to show how an artistic cultural-historical invention for reproducing three-dimensional space on a two-dimensional surface quickly became a cultural habit of mind with numerous unacknowledged assumptions hidden in the subtext of his work, assumptions that continue to function unconsciously in the modern spirit of our technological way of thinking and being that his text helped to create.[22] In each of these works, I uncovered the latent metaphors in the texts, which revealed the complex meanings hidden in each one. But, in a Orphic backward glance at these works, I have realized that my critical reading of those texts was not self-critical. The wounded researcher was not present in those works.

This is and has been my concern with Steele's work. It is an extensive example of how hermeneutics does take into account the unconscious in psychological work, but it does not make a place for Steele as a complex wounded researcher who has undertaken this hermeneutic exegesis of the textual unconscious. Indeed, while he wonders if his readers will think he has gone too far in his critical reading of Mischel's text, he does not share this wonder. He is sure he has offered an unbiased reading that opens the subtext in Mischel's work, and to make his point, he invites the readers of his article to read Mischel's article to check the validity of his reading of it. "Such a checking of interpretation against text by a critically sympathetic reader is at the heart of hermeneutical reflection,"[23] Steele says, and to some degree, he is right. But who is a critically sympathetic reader? Steele seems to assume that it would be a reader who sees what he sees in Mischel's text. What about someone who disagrees? Is that reader not a critical one?

Steele tips his hand about this issue when, referring to the comparison he invites between his reading and Mischel's text, he adds, "In making such a comparison the reader should be aware that her or his judgment may be warped by traditional misunderstandings and that such biases need to be analyzed as closely as the text itself." Exactly!—which is the term I use with exclamation point intentionally in mind. Steele adds that "this is self-criticism, the reflection by the reader on her or his resistances, and it is the complement to the reader's criticism of the text."[24] Again, exactly! But has Steele followed his own program? He implies that the reader who might disagree with him is someone who has not examined how her or his judgments might be warped by traditional misunderstandings. And what are these traditional misunderstandings? They are ones such as the male-centered bias that Steele has identified in Mischel's text and that have been unmasked by the six hermeneutic keys he has used to open that text. Presumably, then, the critically sympathetic reader who would see what Steele has seen in Mischel's text is the one who has opened that text with the keys of feminism, psychoanalysis, phenomenology, structuralism, deconstruction, and Marxism. The critically sympathetic reader, then, would be one who borrows these keys from Steele. But do not these keys also have to be examined? Are they not also biases that a reader brings to a text? And more to the point, are they biases that one can seemingly examine, or complexes that are more difficult to uncover?

Steele uses the term "resistance" to characterize six potential obstacles to engaging in the kind of critical reading he has proposed. Of the six that he discusses, four are cultural-historical resistances that a critical hermeneutic reader can, more or less, become conscious of, and Steele, therefore, rejects them. First, a reader might resist Steele's reading of Mischel because his critical hermeneutics is not empirical. Second, a reader might dismiss Steele's reading as a personal attack on Mischel. Third, he or she might resist because of an aversion in psychology to ideas that are new and go beyond its bias towards a scientific ideology. And, fourth, he or she might resist Steele's critical reading of Mischel because of American culture's xenophobia to ideas that are foreign imports and that go against the grain of a "progressive, all-American, problem-solving tradition of positivist psychology."[25]

The two other forms of resistance to critical hermeneutics cannot, however, be so easily dismissed, and, indeed, they lead back to the heart of the work being done in *The Wounded Researcher*. Is the exploration of the textual unconscious matched by an equally rigorous examination of the critical reader's unconscious? Steele, we have seen, says this is necessary. Critical hermeneutics has to be self-critical, and, as we saw, he attempts to move in this direction by inviting others to open the same text he has unlocked. But this process, while necessary and valid on its own terms, is not enough, and it is the other two forms of resistance that suggest as much.

To give voice to one of these two forms of resistance, Steele wonders, "If these deconstructionists can find this here, then what will they uncover in what I have written?" Fear of self-exposure is at the root of this resistance, and it points to the personal equation that shadows this work of critical reading. The work that one has written betrays who one is, and, once the text or the work is out there, it can be subjected to an analysis that is not unlike the situation that exists between a person and his or her analyst. In each situation, then, there is a fear of being exposed, of discovering a self-knowledge that one would rather not have of oneself. "Deconstruction, being reflexive, brings the fear of exposure to psychologists themselves for it calls us to examine ourselves as closely as we look at others."[26]

But this work of self-examination is hard work, and it does meet with resistance. As Freud has shown, where there is resistance, there is repression; and, where there is repression, there is the unconscious. Indeed, the stronger the resistance, the deeper the repression and the more ego-consciousness will defend itself against any increase in consciousness. This hard work cannot be sidestepped by denying the unconscious and its effects on all that we do. As necessary and valid as Steele's process of inviting a multitude of others to check his biases in his reading of a text is, it is not sufficient, because the work of becoming self-critical about one's biases is not the same thing as the work of overcoming one's resistance to self-knowledge by making one's unconscious more conscious. To say this in another way, the work of making one's assumptions or biases more conscious is not the same thing as the work of making one's unconscious complexes more conscious. Steele's procedure of inviting others to read the text he has read in order to make his critical hermeneutics self-critical needs to be supplemented by the self-critical process of transference dialogues, introduced in this work where one systematically encounters the complex character of one's work as well as the unconscious of the work itself, its unfinished business beyond the complex character of the researcher. I will return to this latter point at the end of this chapter in order to show another way in which critical hermeneutics does not engage the unconscious in a sufficiently radical way.

The other resistance to critical hermeneutics that challenges Steele's attempt to overcome bias by inviting others to read the text is the historically documented cases of intradisciplinary rivalry. Steele cites the well-known example of psychoanalysis, in which, rather than examining the merits of opposing theories, analysts attacked each other's neuroses. "All semblance of scientific decorum was often lost in personal attacks, backbiting, and gossip," Steele says, and as a result, "[t]he emotional gained ascendancy over the intellectual." While he admits that both need to have a place in any discourse—and how could he say otherwise, given his critical deconstruction of Mischel's article?—he adds, "… [W]e should be aware that the more we champion the rule of reason the more we ignore the emotional, thereby becoming prey to its unconscious expression."[27] What is of interest in these words is that Steele cites Jung's article "Analytical Psychology and Weltanschauung" in support of this point.[28]

This article appears in Volume 8 of Jung's *Collected Works*, the same volume in which his essays "A Review of the Complex Theory," "The Transcendent Function," and "On the Nature of the Psyche" appear. All of these have figured prominently in the development of an approach to research that, in keeping soul in mind, draws upon the process of transference dialogues in order to self-critically examine the role of unconscious complexes in one's work. Citing Jung here for support does not square with Steele's own process of self-criticism, in which he invites others to check the validity of his reading. He would need only to have read these other essays of Jung to see how insufficient his procedure is. "Complexes," Jung says, "are the real focus of psychic unrest, and its repercussions are so far-reaching that psychological investigators have no immediate hope of pursuing their work in peace."[29] At one point, Jung refers to the complexes as little devils, and it is because of these little devils that "[t]he present day shows with appalling clarity how little able people are to let the other man's argument count, although this capacity is the fundamental and indispensable condition for any human community."[30] But how does one let the other's argument count? Jung is very clear here. It is not enough simply to admit the validity of the other person. One also has to confront the "other" within oneself and acknowledge the validity of this other.

Self-criticism needs, therefore, more than the presence of other witnesses to how one reads a text. It needs the presence of that other within oneself, that complex other, the denial of which can only lead to discounting the other person's argument. "The capacity for inner dialogue is a touchstone for outer objectivity," Jung writes.[31] Indeed, there is no true outer objectivity apart from its connection to a deep subjectivity aware of its complexes. The crowd of witnesses called to check and validate one's critical reading of a text is in danger of becoming, without the presence of the complex other within, a mob. It is in danger of becoming a community of true believers, whether they are called Marxists, structuralists, phenomenologists, deconstructionists, feminists, psychoanalysts, or Jungians.

At the beginning of this case study, I asked whether critical hermeneutics does take the unconscious into account. The close reading of Steele's article presented above suggests a guarded affirmative reply. Clearly, he does acknowledge the role of unconscious dynamics in the making of a text, and thus critical hermeneutics would regard favorably the notion of the unconscious in the work of research. Steele's article shows quite convincingly that there is a textual unconscious in a text and in one's work. But my reply is guarded because, as I have tried to show, Steele does not apply to himself what he applies to the text of Mischel. His criticism of the text is not matched by a satisfactory self-criticism. His procedure of inviting others to bear witness to the validity of his reading does not confront the "other," the complex other, in himself. What I have tried to show is that his procedure for a self-critical analysis is insufficient and needs to be supplemented by the process of transference dialogues as presented in this work.

A CLOSING REFLECTION

Paul Ricoeur is perhaps the philosopher who has been the most rigorous in his consideration of the unconscious in hermeneutics. In *The Conflict of Interpretations,* he writes that Freud, along with Marx and Nietzsche, are "protagonists of suspicion who rip away masks and pose the novel problem of the lie of consciousness and consciousness as a lie."[32] Insofar as he gives himself over to this position, he has no recourse but to take the unconscious seriously. But the unconscious he takes seriously is limited to the unconscious of Freud, and herein lies a problem.

For Ricoeur, the problem that Freud poses to phenomenology in particular and to philosophy in general is the realist nature of the concepts in his metapsychology. The unconscious functions as a mechanism according to its own natural rhythms and laws, and for a consciousness that would enclose itself in its own self-certainty, this is a problem. The "mechanical" region of the unconscious cannot be penetrated by a consciousness that understands itself as being capable of knowing the genesis and meanings of its intentions. The dream is a good example, because it is a place where "two universes of discourse, the discourse of meaning and the discourse of force" collide. "To say," Ricoeur says, "that a dream is the *fulfillment* of a *repressed* wish is to put together two notions which belong to different orders: fulfillment (*Erfullung*), which belongs to the discourse of meaning (as attested by Husserl's use of the term) and repression (*Verdrangung*), which belongs to the discourse of force."[33] In this place where force and meaning collide, consciousness is operating in, we might say, dark-light. If consciousness is to be rescued in any form, then clearly it has to come to terms with Freud's realism and the order of force that he brings to the order of meaning. This is the goal that Ricoeur sets for himself and the program he carries out for "any form of thought which will allow itself to be dislodged from self-certainty."[34]

Ricoeur addresses this issue by emphasizing that for Freud the unconscious is known and is knowable only indirectly through the ideational representation of the instincts in consciousness. As Ricoeur says, "It is because Freud's analytical investigation forgoes any attempt to attain the being of instincts and remains within the limits of their conscious or unconscious representation that it does not get trapped in the realism of the unknowable." In other words, for Ricoeur the realism of the Freudian unconscious is saved for consciousness because it "can be defined *only* in terms of its relations with the Cs.-Pcs. system."[35]

Defined only within the circuit of this system and by its derivative representations, the reality of the unconscious is established within a hermeneutic exchange between a consciousness that is witnessed and the consciousness that does the witnessing. The unconscious is constituted in a partnership, we might say, and it is in the dialectical movement of this encounter that the ideational representation of the unconscious points back to its "origins." The marks around the term origins are essential here because they indicate that the origins of the unconscious are discovered only in the return through its derivatives. The origins of the unconscious do not in any meaningful sense pre-exist the work of return. On the contrary, they are established by this work of return, which takes place in a hermeneutic dialogical field. In other words, the origins to which one returns are and are not the same as the origins that induce the return through their derivative representations. Ricoeur says it this way: "But it is essential to the unconscious to be an object elaborated by someone other through a hermeneutics which its own consciousness cannot perform alone."[36]

For Ricoeur, then, the reality of the unconscious is an operational one. The reality of the unconscious is established via a hermeneutic methodological procedure, and it cannot be divorced from this procedure. It is "only for someone other that I *even* possess an unconscious." "*In the end*, of course, that makes no sense," he adds, "unless I can reaffirm the meanings which the other elaborates about and for me."[37] In short, as I once argued elsewhere, the unconscious is interpersonal and not intra-psychic, and as such it exists in the "between" of two people. We are each the unconscious of and for the other. The unconscious is a lateral and not a vertical depth.[38]

But when I made this argument more than twenty years ago, I had not yet encountered Jung in any significant way, and Jung does shift the argument. He shifted it for me, and he would have for Ricoeur as well. Summarizing Ricoeur's position, I want to indicate how Jung's understanding of the unconscious challenges Ricoeur's position in three ways.

First, the reality of the unconscious is established indirectly and is known only through its derivatives in consciousness. The key issue here is that the instinctual character of the Freudian unconscious is a piece of nature that is known through its ideational representations in consciousness. The naturalism and realism of the Freudian unconscious is, therefore, a relative one. In Ricoeur's language, "the 'reality' of the unconscious exists only as a reality which has been *diagnosed*."[39]

The implication, of course, is that consciousness has the privileged position over instinct in this tensile field of mind and nature. For Jung, however, soul is a third domain that holds the tension of these opposites together. As we saw in the first chapter, the psychoid nature of the archetype is the region where soul, before it "collapses" into either matter or mind, is neither one nor the other. The psychoid realm is the place where consciousness matters and matter is "conscious." While it is true that the archetype, even at the psychoid level, is known only through its representation in images (not unlike Freud's instincts that are known by their ideational representations), for Jung these image representations point to a reality that does exist in its own right. Although, therefore, the psychoid unconscious is unknowable in its own right, its existence for Jung cannot be dismissed or denied. What it does require, as we saw in the first chapter, is an attitude toward language that is always provisional. Every psychology, we said, has a complex about soul and something of soul is always left over in our psychologies as its unfinished business.

For Jung, then, the unconscious is a *sui generis* reality and not just the outcome of the conflict between instinct and culture. Jung's studies in alchemy and synchronicity bear witness to these depths of an

autonomous unconscious as the reality of soul. They bear witness to
the unconscious as more than a reality that is diagnosed. They bear
witness to the unconscious as the epiphany of an *other* world beside
matter and mind, an epiphany whose ontological surprise is an
epistemological shock.

But why an epistemological shock? It is because as a *sui generis*
reality the unconscious would have its own kind of consciousness. We
saw in Chapter 1 that Jung says as much about the psychoid archetype.
Its sparks of luminescence are flashes of consciousness, or what was
called in previous ages the *lumen naturae*, the light of nature. Thus,
the unconscious is not just in us. On the contrary, we are in the
unconscious of nature, and at the deepest levels of our consciousness
we retain these sparks of nature and remain perhaps in some dim way
aware of once, very long ago, having been a part of the world's dark-
light. In Chapter 1, I tried to give an example of this point with a
description of my experience of the Sea Lion Cave.

Such a view of the unconscious, however, would be for Ricoeur a
naïve realism, which he opposes. For Ricouer, "the unconscious must
be made relative" to consciousness lest we are tempted to "see in the
unconscious some fanciful reality with the extraordinary ability of
thinking in place of consciousness." "Against this naïve realism," he says,
"we must continually emphasize that the unconscious does not think."[40]

Jung's position, of course, does not discount the Freudian view. It
deepens it to that point where the unconscious as the struggle between
mind and nature becomes more than the repressed, where it becomes
collective, archetypal, and psychoid. But given Ricoeur's defense of
the Freudian unconscious, he cannot follow Jung into that region
where image is not just the ideational representation of the instinct
in consciousness, but co-equal with instinct on a continuum that
marks the range of soul. He cannot follow Jung into those depths where
the unconscious is the subject matter of a science of soul rather than
the subject matter of psychology as a natural science. "Psychoanalysis,"
Ricoeur says, "depends upon the same 'rationalistic approach' as the
natural sciences."[41]

For Ricoeur, "Freudian realism is a realism of the id in its ideational
representations and not a naïve realism of unconscious meaning." In
the final analysis, this is the view that Ricoeur is defending and the
way in which hermeneutics is able to make a place for the unconscious.

It is a defense, however, that defends itself against Jung's vastly different and expanded notion of the unconscious as a reality in its own right. For Ricoeur, Jung would be guilty of a naïve realism that "would end up by giving consciousness to the unconscious and would thus produce the monster of an idealism of unconscious consciousness."[42] And it is for this reason, for the fact that such a vision would produce a monster, that Ricoeur honestly confesses that he prefers Freud to Jung. "With Freud, I know where I am and where I am going; with Jung, everything (the psyche, the soul, the archetypes, the sacred) is in danger of becoming confused."[43]

Confused is the appropriate term here, because at the deepest level of Jung's extension of the unconscious into the psychoid realm lies the notion that consciousness is not limited to the human condition. It belongs to nature too, as quantum physics has suggested and as we saw in Chapter 1. The desire to know where one is and where one is going is the program of a consciousness that prizes consciousness as a human quality. It is the expression of the desire of consciousness for clarity, direction, and certainty, even to some relative degree when challenged, as Ricouer courageously allows, by the unconscious. It is, moreover, a desire that is as understandable as it is necessary and valid, but not at the expense of not allowing the challenge that Jung's notion of the unconscious presents to consciousness. In the end, hermeneutics has to widen its vision to make as much room for the Jungian unconscious as it has for the Freudian unconscious.

Second, the reality of the unconscious is established in a dialectical field between a witnessed and a witnessing consciousness. Referring to this dialectic in which one is asked to reaffirm the meanings that the other as witness to my unconscious has elaborated about and for me, Ricoeur says, "Yet that stage of the search for meaning in which I dispossess myself of my own consciousness for the benefit of another person is fundamental for the *constitution* of that psychic region that we call the unconscious."[44] In the field of praxis, what Ricoeur says is true. The unconscious is established between a witnessed and a witnessing consciousness. The full reality of the unconscious, however, cannot be limited to how it is made manifest in the field between the one who is witnessed and the one who does the witnessing, which is Ricoeur's way of defending the reality of the unconscious. "We define," he says, "both the validity and the limits of all assertions about the reality of the unconscious by referring it from the start, and on essential and non-accidental grounds, first to the hermeneutic method and then to a different hermeneutic witness-consciousness."[45] But Jung, as we saw above, would force us make a place in this field for the unconscious as an autonomous reality, as a third between the two. In such moments, the field is not composed of a witnessing and a witnessed consciousness. Rather, it is composed of two witnessing consciousnesses in the presence of the unconscious as a *sui generis* epiphany that belongs neither to the one nor the other. The philosopher Martin Heidegger alludes to this condition in his own way when he says, "When we are considering a man's thought, the greater the work accomplished, the richer the unthought-of element in that work."[46] In *The Wounded Researcher,* the un-thought in a work is what we have described as what waits as the weight of history in a work to think itself through us. In the hermeneutic field that establishes the presence of the unconscious, we are the ones whose task it is to set the stage, as it were, for this to happen.

Third, because for Ricoeur the reality of the unconscious is established by those hermeneutic methods that decode the traces of the unconscious through its representations, "[i]ts being is not absolute but only relative to hermeneutics as method and dialogue."[47] We have seen with the first two points, however, that Jung would challenge this notion of an unconscious that is not absolute. Thus, the question that we have been asking throughout this chapter regarding whether hermeneutics does make a place for the unconscious finally cannot be answered with a simple "yes" or "no." On the one hand, we would have to say that it does make a place for the unconscious. On the other, we would have to say that the place it makes is too narrow. The conclusion I would draw from this response is that we need a hermeneutic method that not only makes a place for the unconscious, but also is transformed by that gesture. We need a hermeneutic method that takes into account the full range and depth of the unconscious that Jung's work offers. Alchemical hermeneutics is such a method, and it is the subject of the next two chapters.

CHAPTER TEN

Alchemical Hermeneutics: Part One

Method, Method, what do you want from me?
You know that I have eaten of the fruit of the unconscious.[1]
—Jules Laforgue

INTRODUCTION

Throughout this book, I have emphasized that the processes of focusing on the vocational character of re-search, and using transference dialogues to differentiate the researcher's complex draw into a work from the unfinished business in the work, can be used with any method. However, as the imaginal approach to re-search with these processes has progressed, the specific method of alchemical hermeneutics has evolved. In this evolution, two points have become increasingly clear.

First, the alchemical hermeneutic method does not replace the more familiar methods of research. Alchemical hermeneutics is not a stand-alone method. It is a complementary method alongside more traditional ones. If we recall from the discussion of method in Chapter 7 that the word "method" signifies a path, then including the alchemical hermeneutic method alongside empirical, rational, and traditional hermeneutic methods is a way of widening the path into one's work to make room for those other aspects of how a researcher travels into his or her work. It is a means of making method more complete, more comprehensive in its service to soul, by making a place for those more subtle ways of knowing too often marginalized by

methods that do not take into account the unconscious presence of
the researcher to his or her work.

Second, in making a place for the unconscious presence of the
researcher in his or her work, the alchemical hermeneutic method
supplements the process of transference dialogues. Indeed, this method
has a natural affinity with that process because it makes a place for
other aspects of the researcher's unconscious in addition to his or her
complexes. Specifically, this method makes a place for feeling and
intuition as two of the four functions identified by Jung alongside
thinking (reflection) and sensation (observation and measurement).
It also makes a place for symptoms, dreams, and synchronicities. All
of these phenomena are doorways into one's work. Their inclusion
opens a space for a researcher to be more fully present to his or her
work as a complex embodied presence. In this approach, the claim of
empiricist and rationalist methods that psychology is a science is
expanded to the claim of alchemical hermeneutics that psychology is
a complex science of soul.

That a place needs to be made for dreams, feelings, intuitions,
symptoms, and synchronicities as expressions of a researcher's
unconscious participation in the work seems clear from the discussion
in the preceding chapters. Not only do empiricist and rationalist
methods ignore the unconscious in the research process, but the
unconscious is also only marginally present in hermeneutic methods
and restricted in that presence to Freud's view of the unconscious.
Jung's more comprehensive view of the unconscious has not been
systematically applied to hermeneutics. Having made a case in the
last three chapters for the necessity of a hermeneutics of deep
subjectivity, in this chapter I want to offer a description of the
experience of using this method through a description of some of its
characteristics. In the next chapter I will offer some examples of this
method's inclusion of dreams, feelings, intuitions, symptoms, and
synchronicities. Before I close this introduction, however, I want to
add a few words about the term *alchemical hermeneutics*. Why the
qualifier "alchemical" in the term?

The alchemical hermeneutic method is a way of making a place
for Jung's understanding of the unconscious. In Chapter 1 I described
how the psychoid nature of the archetype extended the unconscious
beyond its personal, cultural-historical, and collective-archetypal

levels. The psychoid archetype is a pivotal reality, the third between the two of matter and mind, or nature and spirit. Insofar as Jung's views about the unconscious were formed in part by his studies of alchemy, it makes sense to use the term alchemical to describe a hermeneutic method that applies his views of the unconscious to research. In fact, given that in her forthcoming book, *The Songlines of the Soul*, Veronica Goodchild shows that the notion of the psychoid archetype lies on a line of development that reaches back from Jung's studies of synchronicity to alchemy, the use of the term "alchemical" as a qualifier of the hermeneutic method not only makes sense, it also seems required.[2]

A second reason for using the term "alchemical" to qualify a hermeneutics of deep subjectivity lies in the descriptions of alchemy itself. Von Franz notes that alchemy offers "an astonishing amount of material from the unconscious, produced in a situation where the conscious mind did not follow a definite program." The alchemists, she says, "were studying the unknown phenomenon of matter ... but without any specific plan."[3] Her point is that alchemy offers immediate manifestations of the unconscious, a feature not to be seen elsewhere. Since we are looking for a hermeneutic procedure that keeps the unconscious of the researcher in mind, the term alchemical hermeneutics fits that intention.

Writing from a different tradition, that of phenomenology, Gaston Bachelard provides us with a third reason for qualifying our hermeneutic method as alchemical. He declares, ". . . [T]he psychology of the alchemist is that of reveries trying to constitute themselves in experiments on the exterior world."[4] The key point here is the alchemist's mood of reverie. Insofar as reverie is, as we saw in Chapter 5, a way of letting go of the work so that the unconscious of the work itself might speak, the adjective "alchemical" in front of hermeneutics again seems appropriate to signal a method that seeks to hold a place for the unconscious in research.

For a fourth reason to use the "alchemical" qualifier for a hermeneutics of the unconscious, I turn to the work of Stanton Marlan. In his excellent book *The Black Sun: The Alchemy and Art of Darkness*, Marlan writes: "In alchemy as in the literatures of deconstruction and analysis, the shorthand of erasure is richly expanded and amplified." What he means here is that the idea of erasure that belongs to the tradition of deconstruction "lends itself to comparison with certain operations of alchemy that have to do with the processes of mortification, calcination, and dissolution and entering into the blacker-than-black aspect of the nigredo, in which the self is ultimately reduced to no-self." The consequence of these alchemical operations is that "[s]uch a focus emphasizes the death aspect of the opus and the powerful reduction of narcissism."[5]

Throughout *The Wounded Researcher*, we have seen traces and signs of this alchemical attitude at work, and hence it makes sense that the method of research for an approach that requires the ego to let go of the work should be a hermeneutics that is alchemical. In the Introduction, I emphasized how, in the face of the greening of the world, words fail to hold onto that greening; in Chapter 1 we saw that each psychology, as a complex about soul, cannot hold onto soul through its language, which always reveals soul by concealing it. Chapter 2, on the mythic backdrop of Orpheus and Eurydice, introduced into the research process the issues of loss, mourning, and transformation, and in Chapter 3 I described a key aspect of an imaginal approach to re-search in terms of its attunement to the unfinished business that waits as the weight of history in the soul of the work. In Chapters 4 and 5, on the vocational aspect of research and the process of transference dialogues, I described how both of these processes call for the ego of the researcher to surrender into the work.

In each of these ways, I have been increasingly drawn towards the image of the Wounded Researcher as a kind of alchemist in relation to his or her work, or at least as one who belongs to that tradition. Like the alchemical process described above by Marlan, re-search with soul in mind is a process of making and unmaking, of constructing the work from the ego's point of view and having it deconstructed from the soul's point of view, of holding onto a work by letting go of it. "There is never simply an 'after' of analysis or deconstruction," Marlan says, "and expressing it conceptually recreates the illusion of a self-enclosed totality." In the same way, there is never simply an "after" of the work, a time when, after the work is finished, it is done. "No one," Marlan adds, "is ever fully analyzed; no deconstruction is ever complete; the unconscious or blackness is never totally eliminated."[6] *Mutatis mutandis*, the work that is finished is never done. Something of the soul of the work lies concealed and waits as the weight of its history in what has been revealed.

Having made something of a case for why a hermeneutic method that would make a place for the unconscious of the researcher in the work needs to be an alchemical hermeneutic method, I want to turn in the next section to a description of the experience of the practice of this method.

ALCHEMICAL HERMENEUTICS: A PHENOMENOLOGY OF THE PRACTICE OF THIS METHOD

As we have seen, the term *alchemical hermeneutics*, which was actually coined by Veronica Goodchild, not only connects this method to the philosophical tradition of hermeneutics, but also links it to an already established body of research, specifically Jung's psychology of the unconscious, which he deepened through his studies of alchemy. Alchemy, as we saw in the introduction to this chapter, offers an expression of the unconscious that is not mediated by any plans or projects of the conscious mind. In this respect, it is much like a dream, and it is worth remembering here that Jung was called into his research on alchemy through a dream in which he got stuck in the 17th century, the period in history when alchemy began to disappear in the West with the rise of modern science. Through his subsequent years of research into alchemical symbolism, Jung was reaching back and connecting with ancestors whose story was still unfinished, and in so doing he found the cultural, historical, and archetypal foundations of his own psychology. Indeed, alchemy was for him something of a bridge between the religious tradition of Gnosticism and his psychology of the unconscious. The name "alchemical hermeneutics," then, fits with that spirit of research that acknowledges that one is called by soul to follow a certain path of inquiry, which, when it is honored, holds together the tension between the personal interests, aims, intentions, and complexes of the researcher and the "others" in the work, the ancestors who carry the unfinished business of the soul in the work.

In this section, I want to provide a phenomenological description of the experience of practicing this method by describing some of its general characteristics. While not all of these characteristics are directly concerned with how this method makes a place in research for the researcher's dreams, symptoms, intuitions, feelings, and synchronicities, taken together they do indicate how this method impacts re-search that does keep soul in mind. Some of the features of this method have implications for writing, while others have implications for the ethical character of this approach to research and for the process of research.

A first characteristic of this method is that it is a *complex* method in the sense that it has grown out of the process of transference dialogues. As a complex method whose roots are in the process of those transference dialogues, alchemical hermeneutics fosters the continuation of the dialogues throughout the research process.

Second, alchemical hermeneutics is a *creative* method. The spirit of inquiry, therefore, is open-ended, giving the structure of one's research a degree of freedom to arise out of the ongoing relation between the researcher and the topic. A creative method is not rigidly wedded to an inflexible structure or to immutable procedures for the work. It is a method that is supple and subject to change as the research progresses. It is a method that encourages a way of inquiry that is first and foremost in tune with the spirit of the work as it unfolds. It is a method that remains open to the playful possibilities in the work, and one that invites, and even encourages, a researcher to get lost from time to time in his or her dreams, reveries, and fantasies of the work.

Third, alchemical hermeneutics is an *imaginative* method, in that it gives a place in research to "the primacy of the invisible." But what is this invisible? It is those imaginal landscapes of soul already described in Chapter 1. This invisible realm of soul does not imply the absence of the visual. On the contrary, it constitutes an ontological realm in its own right, which is neither the realm of the intellect nor of the senses, an invisible whose traces of the underworld and the otherworld of soul both haunt the visible world and break into it, an invisible, then, that lends to all sensible phenomena an *other*, suprasensible reality, just as the light, energy, and living spirit of Ellis Island haunted that place for the photographer Steven Wilkes, who, as we saw in Chapter 2, was called to be a witness for its presence. What would he have missed if he had been insensitive to that invisible presence that transformed, as he said, a one-hour assignment into a five-year odyssey? What would a researcher who would keep soul in mind miss if he or she were to approach his or her work without regard for the invisible, for how the subtle lines of synchronicity, for example, might be webbing those invisible connections of meaning between the matter of the work and its soul?

The invisible landscapes of the imaginal realm of soul are like that light that Wilkes described. It was not so much something to see as it was a way of seeing, a way of seeing into the depths of that landscape, into its invisible realms, into the energy and spirit of that place, as he says, which haunted and lingered in the forgotten and long-neglected physical structures. The phenomenologist Merleau-Ponty uses the same phenomenon of light when, in his final thoughts at the edges of phenomenology, he argues that the invisible is a level or system of levels, which, like light itself, is not what we see, but the means by which we see.[8] For Merleau-Ponty, the invisible is wound into the visible, just as the invisible lines of a magnetic field radiate a form and a pattern. The invisible vectors of soul shape the visible and material world in the same way. Archetypes are also magnetic or, if you wish, gravitational forces that in-form our experiences, and, like dreams, they are not what we see but are ways of seeing. What would a researcher who would keep soul in mind miss if he or she were to disregard the archetypal patterns of the work, those lines and vectors that deepen the work into its imaginal realms? What would he or she gain if he or she were to see the work through the dark-light of the dream?

Perception is not a photographic process. We perceive the world through the dark-light of the soul's complex and archetypal dreams, fantasies, memories, and imaginings. Alchemical hermeneutics as an imaginative method honors these ways of soul as alternative means of bringing the depth, presence, and shadows of the soul of the work into view. For surely a researcher does not just think about his or her work, he or she also dreams it. Or, to say this more precisely, while a researcher is thinking about the work, the work is dreaming itself through him or her.

I do not doubt that this characteristic of the alchemical hermeneutic method would be troublesome for much of psychology and rather out of bounds for much of psychological research. But that is so because the imaginal world of soul, as we have seen in this book, has all but lost its place in Western psychology. In her forthcoming book, however, Veronica Goodchild not only shows in detail the presence of this imaginal world in Jung's work, she also describes the venerable history of the invisible world of soul in the more esoteric traditions in the West and in many traditions of the East. Her book provides both a scholarly and experiential foundation for how this imaginal world has been and can be valued as a legitimate source of knowledge.[9]

A fourth feature of the alchemical hermeneutic method is its *aesthetic* character. This method encourages the gnosis of the heart mentioned in Chapter 4 and is open to those non-ordinary states of consciousness, such as reverie and active imagination, discussed in Chapter 5. The impact of this characteristic is felt especially in the area of writing from the place of soul, since this method is open to and even encourages non-discursive forms of writing. Writing down the soul in writing up one's work involves a style that is closer to poetry than to straightforward prose, and an engagement with the specifics of an embodied mode of writing, which arises out of actual experience as opposed to a mode of writing that is "about" experience. Examples of this kind of writing are the subject of Chapter 12. Here I will mention only two important texts that have explored these issues. One is *Jung as a Writer*, by Susan Rowland; the other is "Embodied Writing and Reflections of Embodiment," by Rosemary Anderson.[10]

A fifth aspect of the alchemical hermeneutic method is its *hieratic* character. "Hieratic" is a term used by Henri Corbin to describe *ta'wil*. As Corbin explains it, *ta'wil* is a symbolic mode of understanding, "the transmutation of everything visible into symbols." It is an "esoteric hermeneutics," which returns things to their origins in the spiritual world, a method that Corbin ties to what he calls a "prophetic psychology."[11] *Ta'wil* is a method that saves appearances (the exoteric) by returning them to their original form (the esoteric). The hieratic nature of the alchemical hermeneutic method is related to its imaginative aspect discussed above, especially insofar as Corbin cites active imagination as the organ of the hieratic process. What the hieratic understanding adds to the imaginative approach is the procedure of the return, the work of carrying a work back to its *other*, invisible, source. Indeed, we have already practiced this aspect of the alchemical hermeneutic method when in Chapter 2 we returned re-search with soul in mind to its archetypal roots in the Orpheus-Eurydice myth. This mythic archetypal presence is the other, invisible, dimension of re-search that would keep soul in mind.

To be sure, Corbin's notion of *ta'wil* is not specifically tied to a psychology of the archetypes, and work still needs to be done on the differences between his views and those of Jung. Nevertheless, Corbin had a strong influence on Jung's thought, and for our purposes it is sufficient to note the phenomenological similarity of the experience of thinking as return in Corbin and in Jung. Both of them, certainly, emphasize the importance of this return of the visible to its invisible source, but while Jung focuses on the psychological aspects of this movement of return, Corbin focuses on its spiritual aspects.

For Corbin, the other dimension of the work that *ta'wil* opens into is its "spiritual powers," which he illustrates by referring to such things as the "invisible aspect of a painting, the inaudible aspect of a symphony," those things that we do not see or hear but are the guides by which we see the painting and hear the music. These subtle virtualities, as he calls them, "are not simply the artist's message." On the contrary, they are what "has been transferred by him to this work and which he himself received from 'the Angel.'" To respond to the "'*Angel of a work* is to render oneself capable of the entire content of its *aura* of love.'"[12]

I grant that again this language might seem very foreign to our more traditional and familiar forms of research, but as before I would argue that if one is to make a place for the subtle imaginal reality of soul in research, then one has to enter into these unfamiliar realms. Certainly, one can appreciate the presence and power of the dialectic of love in research, which is perhaps the strongest motive force in continuing a work. And, certainly, Jung offers us numerous examples of how the "inner" voice of things, those "spiritual powers" of a thing that one does not hear, do draw one beyond the literal aspect of what shows itself to its "Angel." Jung's Ravenna vision, which he describes in his autobiography, is a good example of this process.

For a researcher who keeps soul in mind, *ta'wil* is a style or disposition that invites a researcher into a change of state, so that what is at first more hidden in reality becomes less hidden. We might say that in practicing *ta'wil* the topic is continuously drawing the researcher beyond his or her intentions more deeply and thoroughly into the source of the work, to its archetype, its angel, its imaginal history, its subtle essence, moving both researcher and work from the personal through the cultural-historical and collective-archetypal into the eco-cosmological and imaginal depths of the work. Or, we could say that through *ta'wil* the topic becomes a metaphor concealing a true event in the *mundus imaginalis*. I would suggest that Jung's seminal work, *Answer to Job*, is an excellent example of this process of hermeneutics as *ta'wil*. That book returns a piece of theological history to its hidden, invisible archetypal sources in the imaginal world of soul. It is a work that one could easily describe as a "spiritual exegesis" and a "prophetic psychology."[13]

Perhaps a holding image for this notion of *ta'wil* is the soul's lament over its condition of exile. "The Hymn of the Pearl," with its themes of the soul's captivity, exodus, initiation, and realization,[14] or the figure of Orpheus as the poet whose mythic presence accompanies the wounded researcher and whose music reconnects the soul to its original calling, are examples of this action of *ta'wil,* which, as we have seen throughout this book, situates all human acts of knowing within a sense of loss and a desire to return. Perhaps the path or method of re-search done with soul in mind is simply a recognition that all our acts of knowing are attempts at remembering what we once knew but have forgotten. Perhaps all our attempts at re-search are sacred acts whose deep motive is salvation or redemption. Maybe all our re-search re-enacts the Gnostic dream of the fall of soul into time and its desire to return home.

This little riff on *ta'wil* is not so far off the mark with regard to the issue of method in terms of its etymology as a path or a journey into one's work. Indeed, this notion of *ta'wil* seems essential if one is to capture the phenomenology of the experience of re-search as a searching again for what has already claimed one. Re-search that does keep soul in mind moves ahead by returning to what has already taken hold of a researcher as a vocation or a calling. In this return, one re-members the work, and in this process of re-membering, one is being re-membered, one is being changed and transformed in the work by the work.

Recall how Orpheus is re-membered by being dis-membered when he re-turns to Eurydice in the turn of his backward glance and how in this transformation the work of love between them is transformed. Recall also that in Chapter 3 I emphasized that an imaginal approach to research is a process in which a researcher has to "die" to the work so that the unfinished business in the soul of the work can speak. Well, *ta'wil* as a form of esoteric hermeneutics which returns a work to its source is also a process that returns the researcher who practices this form of hermeneutics to his or her source and in that process transforms him or her. "The *ta'wil* of texts," Corbin says, "presupposes the *ta'wil* of the soul: the soul cannot restore, return the text to its truth, unless it too returns to its truth."[15] Jung, we should remember, wrote *Answer to Job* after his heart attack, suggesting that his *ta'wil* of the Job text was related to a profound change of heart brought on by that event.

This truth of the soul to which it returns is, as this text has been arguing, the work of making the complex unconscious of the researcher more conscious in the work, a task that is undertaken in the transference dialogues. To the degree that this work is attempted, the text of the work is transformed from what the researcher would demand from the work to what the work itself desires. The work is freed into its truth to the degree that the researcher is able to let go of his or her complex relation to it. This letting go is that dying referred to above.

Following Corbin's description of *ta'wil* as a spiritual transformation, I would suggest that a sixth characteristic of the alchemical hermeneutic method is that it is a *spiritual* method in the sense that the researcher who practices this method undergoes a radical transformation as described above. It is a transformation in which a researcher is initiated into another way of knowing and being, as Jo Todd was, for example, in her work on the abortion issue. She was, as described in Chapter 6, freed from one state of being to another. She was, we might say, resurrected from the state of identifying with her pro-choice position while demonizing the pro-life position to a new gnosis, in which she could attend to the sources of each position in its respective hunger for the birth of the divine child.

In Corbin's work, it is clear that this spiritual aspect of *ta'wil* means, "your mode of understanding reveals your mode of being, and that the significance revealed in your manner of understanding is *dependent* on your mode of being."[16] As a spiritual method, then, alchemical hermeneutics affirms that a researcher knows his or her work as he or she lets himself or herself be known by the work. In the spiritual method, then, there is no separation between the work and the person doing the work, the person who, in working on the topic, is also being worked on, and even at times worked over, by the topic. The spiritual method of alchemical hermeneutics implies, therefore, that research as re-search can be profoundly therapeutic and that dissertation writing can become an aspect of the individuation process.

The question, "For whom is the work being done?"—which an imaginal approach to research keeps open—has its counterpart in the question, "Who is doing the work?" As a spiritual method, alchemical hermeneutics leads a complex researcher to an encounter with that one who, in service to that first question, is and has been doing the work. I suggested as much in the riff that I did in the Introduction on the painting that appears on the cover of this book. A researcher, in coming to be the work, catches up, as it were, with the one who has been doing the work.

This transformation of the researcher by the work, even to the point where he or she becomes the work, amounts to a profound ethical shift on the part of the researcher, who no longer simply projects his or her complexes onto the work. In Chapter 6, we saw how Erik Killinger, Kerry Ragain, Ellen Mcfarland, and Dennis Langhans were ethically transformed by their work. A seventh characteristic of the alchemical hermeneutic method, then, is that it is an *ethical* method. That is, this method has implications for the ethical character of an imaginal approach to research, which is the subject of Chapter 13.

As a method or journey of return, alchemical hermeneutics is also a method of *an-amnesis*, a method of un-forgetting, which is a way of putting into practice the devotion of the imaginal approach to the unfinished business in the soul of the work, its service to those ancestors for whom the work is being done. A fundamental characteristic of this eighth aspect of the alchemical hermeneutic method is the attitude of re-gard, in which the researcher is always taking a second look in order to attend to what has been and is forgotten and is asking to be remembered through the researcher doing the work. It is a re-gard for what has been marginalized or otherwise neglected. It is a healing act of un-forgetting, a method that recovers the myths that haunt our meanings, the dreams that haunt our reasons, the symptoms that haunt our symbols, the fantasies that haunt our facts, the fictions that haunt our ideas, and the images that dwell in events.

This feature of un-forgetting makes the method of alchemical hermeneutics particularly open to the place of dreams and symptoms in research. A dream can hold a gnosis of the work or point to a direction in the work that the conscious mind of the researcher does not yet know. And symptoms, by their very definition of being a tension between remembering something that is too vital to forget and forgetting it because it is too painful to remember, can often be a path into some forgotten but vital aspects of the work. In the next chapter I will give examples of dreams and symptoms in research.

As a work of un-forgetting, alchemical hermeneutics can also be described in a ninth way as a method of *re-creation* or reiteration of unfinished events. Research, then, is, as we have said all along, re-search, a creation that is a *creatio continua*, a way of working that, when it is finished, is not done, a way of working that is ceaselessly occurring. The alchemical hermeneutic characteristic of method as re-creation arises out of the reciprocity between the researcher and the ancestors whose unfinished stories are waiting to be told with our passion and sympathy. In this process of taking up the unfinished business in the soul of the work, the researcher, like the alchemist of old, might find himself or herself accompanied by a guide, with whom he or she may enter into dialogue for the purposes of the work. In the transference dialogues, the researcher might find what Jung has called the *spiritus rector* of the work, someone like the Old Woman in the Wheelchair, who guided Debbie Greenwood in her work, as I described in Chapter 6. Method as re-creation, then, is—or can be—a partnership between the researcher and these "others" who shepherd the work. In alchemy, this was called the *meditatio,* and it was used to define that moment "when a man has an inner dialogue with someone unseen."[17] Re-creation as a characteristic of the alchemical hermeneutic method can be, then, an ongoing act of meditation, which extends our sense of method beyond the notion of the application of procedures.

Since the gnosis of *ta'wil* takes place for Corbin in the *mundus imaginalis,* the world of the soul, the meeting ground of the encounter between the divine and the human imagination, the place where the archetypal intelligences enter human knowledge, and spirit and body become one in the third intermediate landscape of soul, alchemical hermeneutics can also be characterized and described in a tenth way as an *erotic* method. It is a method that follows a path of love, where love is the mode of knowledge whereby one being knows another. This erotic aspect of method allows the work to be that vessel in which the researcher and the ancestors in the work meet. Re-search with soul in mind is about erotic mutual seduction, a loving engagement with one's topic. In one of his descriptions of the attitude of the adept in alchemical work, Jung cites the phrase *amor perfectissimus* to express the devotion of the alchemist to his work.[18] This same attitude of devotion is present in this erotic tie between a researcher and his or her work. It is work whose method or path or way of going is not in the spirit of power but in the spirit of love, which Corbin notes is the only mode that allows illumination, unveiling, un-hiddenness, "the unveiling of what is hidden."[19]

Given these ten features of the alchemical hermeneutic method, I can best summarize the experience of using this method by referring to Corbin's way of differentiating three levels of the hermeneutic process.[20] In many ways, his distinction is like the arc of all the chapters on method, in which we have progressively made our way towards a hermeneutics of deep subjectivity. In these chapters, we have moved from an understanding of method as a way into one's work, a way in which one knows a work to the degree that one is separate and distant from it, to method as a matter of intimate engagement, in which one knows the work to the degree that one *is* the work.

The first level of the hermeneutic process is that of theoretical certainty. Corbin's example is the person who knows about fire because he or she has heard about it from someone else. The second level is the certainty of eyewitness testimony. Here the person knows because he or she has experienced it personally. The third level is a certainty that is gnostically lived and realized. Here the person becomes the fire or is consumed by it.

For Corbin, the transition from the first two levels to the third happens on the spiritual voyage. It is also the path of the researcher who enters the work via an alchemical hermeneutic method. Taking on a topic by which one is addressed (vocation), the researcher enters a ritual space (*mundus imaginalis*) in which—by the fires of love, and in the presence of a guide—he or she is both deepened by the work (transference levels), and worked over and transformed by the work, even becoming the work and living it in an embodied way.

The description given in this section of the experience of practicing the alchemical hermeneutic method argues that method in re-search that would keep soul in mind is much more than a set of external procedures that one adopts and applies to an area of investigation. The ten characteristics of the alchemical hermeneutic method strongly indicate that method is not only what a researcher does. Method is also who the researcher is in the work, who he or she is as he or she continuously opens a path into a work. Method is an attitude that pervades the whole process of research as a journey.

CONCLUSION

In the next, and final, chapter on method, I will supplement the description given in this chapter of the experience of utilizing the alchemical hermeneutic method with examples of how the alchemical hermeneutic method makes a place for dreams, feelings, intuitions, the body, and synchronicity in its praxis.

CHAPTER ELEVEN

Alchemical Hermeneutics: Part Two

ALCHEMICAL HERMENEUTICS AND DEEP SUBJECTIVITY: SOME EXAMPLES

In Chapter 5 I cited the example of George Callan's dissertation, in which her marginal notes during her three years of course work gradually became the theme of her study. The alchemical hermeneutic method attends to the margins of consciousness in research. It keeps open a space for the researcher's dreams, symptoms, synchronicities, feelings, and intuitions to come in from the margins throughout the research process.

Dreaming the Work

A good example of how dreams can play a part in research work is provided by one of my graduate students, Kiyanoosh Shamlu. In his dissertation, he is exploring what the work of the 12th-century Iranian thinker Sohrevardi might contribute to the theoretical foundations of Jung's psychology.[1]

Initially drawn into this work through his interests in the theme of the imaginal world as developed by Henri Corbin, whose work on Sohrevardi and other Islamic thinkers has had an important impact on Jung's work, Kiyanoosh was drawn deeper into this project when he discovered that Hillman considers Corbin to be, after Jung, the second father of archetypal psychology. At first, therefore, he was attracted to this work because of some parallels he found between

Sohrevardi's and Hillman's writings on the imaginal world. Over time, however, he realized he was drawn into this work with Sohrevardi because of his shared Iranian cultural background with him, and the parallels between Sohrevardi's project and the project he was imagining for his dissertation. Like Sohrevardi, who tried to bridge the gap between two cultures and two religions (pre-Islamic Zoroastrian thought and Islamic thought), Kiyanoosh is trying to show in his dissertation how an ancient Islamic tradition and the modern Western one of Jungian psychology converge and diverge in their understanding and treatment of imagination and its relation to the imaginal world.

Using language already developed in this work, it seems appropriate to say that Sohrevardi has become for Kiyanoosh the guide in the work, the one who has given him the work. But beyond this vocation, Kiyanoosh felt quite lost in the early stages of his research efforts. He was not sure what Sohrevardi was asking of him, and he was even more unsure about what possible contributions he could make. What aspects of Sohrevardi's work should be the focus of a dialogue with Jung's psychology? In short, he had a work, but not as yet a way into it. Reading, thinking about, and reflecting on the source material about Sohrevardi, Corbin, Jung, Hillman, and others, he was not able to form a question that would open a path into the work. But he was having a series of three recurring dreams.

In one dream, he is in a very dark forest, where he is running away from an old man who is chasing him. He would awaken from this dream in a state of panic, wondering who the old man was and what he wanted from him. In another dream, he finds himself on the top of a mountain with a book that has no writing in it. He turns page after page, but the book is always blank. In a third dream, he is riding in the sky on the back of an enormous bird while looking down on a green landscape that has no discernible figures or objects. Reading about the symbols in these dreams, he was unable to make sense of them or understand if and how they might be related to his work.

Continuing to read Sohrevardi, he came across the philosopher's visionary recitals, descriptions of the soul's spiritual journeys of descent from and return to the imaginal world. They stunned him. One story in the recitals involved an old man, another a cosmic mountain, and a third was about the journey of the birds. Stunned, indeed! Dreams and text had come together. Or perhaps a better way to say this is that he was led into this text of Sohrevardi's through his dreams. And through his dreams, a path (which, as we saw in Chapter 7, is the root meaning of "method") was opened to his work.

Through the path into his work opened up by these dreams, Kiyanoosh is now focusing on how Sohrevardi's work presents imagination as a spiritual power and how this aspect of imagination addresses some unfinished business in Jung's psychology. Sohrevardi's recitals depict imagination as a power that gives one access to the spiritual world of soul, that offers a spiritual metaphysics. Kiyanoosh hopes to show that there is in Jung's psychology an unacknowledged metaphysics, which is truncated by the use of the imagination exclusively as a psychological tool for increasing consciousness. In this view, the imaginal world is not so much an underworld as the epiphany of an *other* world, which, as we saw in Chapter 1, Jung himself was struggling to understand.

The three dreams of Kiyanoosh are quite vivid in the way they show how dreams can function as part of a comprehensive method or path into one's work. At the very least, they indicate that the dream might know more about the work than the conscious researcher does. The researcher has to make a place for dreams in how he or she goes about his or her research. The researcher has to make a place for the dream to "wound" him or her. Making such a place for dreams in research does not mean, as I have said throughout this work, that the dream becomes the content of the research, although the famous three dreams of Descartes did just that insofar as they became, by his own admission, the foundation of his philosophical thought, which, ironically enough, as I have described elsewhere, split the *Cogito* from the dream.[2] Making a place for dreams means that they are afforded an opportunity to function as a way into the work.

Debbie Greenwood offers another example of the role of dreams in research. In the first two months of her research work, she felt stuck most of the time, and in this place of being stuck she had the following dream:

I am in a darkened bedroom where a small television is playing. It is tucked in the corner of the room. I am very sick. I am indifferent to what is playing on the television but the sound and the flickering images fill my room. I begin to feel a constriction in my body, as if I am being starved of air. I push against it, but then I am liberated from the bodily sensation of being trapped and the panic that comes from losing one's breath. I feel a great sense of spaciousness, as I can move anywhere. I have lost the sense of my body as a box with a lid. I realize I have died. As I leave my body, I brush past an old woman in a wheelchair. She understands what is happening and says: "Another happy ending." I wander into the living room, where my parents are watching television. They sit in the darkened room transfixed by the images that move across the screen. I try to speak, but they can't seem to see or hear me. It seems that in my present state I cannot communicate with the living directly.[3]

There is much rich imagery in this dream, and many ways of commenting on it in relation to Greenwood's work (discussed in Chapter 6). But that is not my intention, because what matters with the dream in research is the ways in which the researcher understands the dream in relation to his or her work. In this case, Debbie acknowledges that she was liberated by this dream to begin her work. Something of her transfixed attitude "died," and a greater sense of spaciousness opened up for her work. In addition, the dream figure of the old woman in the wheelchair became something of a guide, appearing again in two subsequent transference dialogues. This dream figure opened for Debbie a path into her work and remained with her as a companion along the way.

Julie Sgarzi comments on the importance of dreams in relation to the issue of the unfinished business in her work. In her dissertation, "In the Labyrinth of Secret: A Meditation on the Nature of Secret,"[4] she asserts that dreams forced her to expand her study beyond the wounding nature of the secret to include its beneficial aspects. Commenting on this aspect of her dreams, she writes: "One dream enlarged the scope of inquiry of the work, insisting that the connection between secret and mystery had to be addressed." Another dream came at a time when she was feeling unsure of the work. "In the dream," she writes, "I was reading the oversized title of a newspaper that was upside down on a table in front of me. It read: 'Secret and Psyche: The Mystery Revealed.'" This dream "gave me the courage to continue with a topic that was elusive from the beginning." She adds, "I knew I was on the right track and my task was to continue to reveal some of the mystery."

In her beautifully crafted work, Julie explicitly acknowledges the value of the dream. "The dreams became," she observes, "a material part of the work itself and often kept the focus of the work well within the soul's realm."

Jung offers many examples of how his dreams opened a path into his work. In Chapter 3, for example, I discussed how one of Jung's dreams opened up for him the idea of the collective unconscious, and in his autobiography he recounts how, at a time when he was struggling with the issue of whether to pursue a career in science or the humanities, two dreams set him on the path to his decision.

In the first dream, he is in a dark wood that stretches along the Rhine. "I come to a little hill, a burial mound," he writes, "and I began to dig." He continues, "After a while I turned up, to my astonishment, some bones of prehistoric animals." This discovery "interested me enormously, and at that moment I knew: I must get to know nature, the world in which we live, and the things around us."

In the second dream, he is once again in a dark wood. "... [I]t was threaded with watercourses," he notes, "and in the darkest place I saw a circular pool, surrounded by dense undergrowth." In the pool he notices, half submerged in the water, "the strangest and most wonderful creature: a round animal, shimmering in opalescent hues, and consisting of innumerable little cells, or of organs shaped like tentacles." He recognizes immediately that this wonderful animal is "a giant radiolarian, measuring about three feet across." He is awestruck. "It seemed to me," he writes, "indescribably wonderful that this magnificent creature should be lying there undisturbed, in the hidden place, in the clear deep water." "It aroused in me," he confesses, "an intense desire for knowledge, so that I awoke with a beating heart."

Reading this description, one gets the feeling that that dream creature in that place was waiting for him, as if the dream knew what Jung himself did not yet know. Unable to make a conscious choice on his own about his studies, he was led on a path towards that choice by the two dreams. Commenting on the two dreams, Jung remarks, "These two dreams decided me overwhelmingly in favor of science, and removed all my doubts."[5]

Dreams have a place in a method that would keep soul in mind. The alchemical hermeneutic method trusts the wisdom of the dream in this way. It opens that path of dreaming the work, trusting that at times the dream knows the work in a way that the researcher does not yet know it. It is not that the dream is the work. Rather, it is a way of seeing the work, of coming to know it. And the alchemical hermeneutic method holds that dreaming is as legitimate a way of investigating one's work as thinking is. If we are such stuff as dreams are made on, then so too is our work.

To conclude these remarks on dreaming the work, I would remind the reader that this book itself owes something of its final beginning to the dream that I cited in Chapter 2. That dream has shaped this fifth beginning of the work after four previous false starts, and it is present throughout this work, in which I have struggled to integrate, within the context of research, the demands of the academy and the life of soul (which transcends the academic discourses of psychology). In that dream, a street poet is leading me out of the house of academia, where I see many colleagues in a large Victorian living room, all suited-and-tied for the occasion, to a threshold whose screen door opens onto a summer landscape filled with people living life. The contrast between these two worlds is quite pronounced and sharp, but the dream ends there on the threshold, as if to indicate the necessity of holding the tension between these two worlds. This dream has been present throughout this book. *The Wounded Researcher,* for better or for worse, has been written on the threshold between two worlds: that of scholarship in research and that of the poetics of a research process that keeps the life of soul in mind. And, indeed, as a book, it will be left there on that threshold.

Feeling into the Work

In the Introduction to this book, I emphasized that what one says and knows about his or her work always leaves something unsaid and unfinished in the work, and that in the gap between what one says and what remains unsaid, between the work that is finished and the work that is still not done, the feeling quality of mourning takes root. A poetics of the research process, I said, must attend to the feeling of mourning for what is left behind in this gap. What I was suggesting there—and what I have been arguing throughout this work, which would make a place for the deep subjectivity of the researcher—is that research as an act of coming to know one's work has, in the process, to give as much room to feeling as it does to thinking.

A number of my graduate students who have used the process of transference dialogues have commented to me that a particular virtue of these dialogues is that they open a place for a feeling relation to their work. In Chapter 6 I quoted Judith Orodenker, for example, who described her resistance to the dialogues in terms of "feelings of fear and sadness"; and, indeed, emotions of this kind, as well as anxiety, impatience, and awe, were often tied to the resistance encountered in this process. In each instance, what appeared to be happening was a kind of judgment or evaluation of the process from the ego's point of view, a feeling reaction to the invitation to let go of being in charge of the work, an affective response to surrendering to the depths of the unconscious in the work. The gap here is between the conscious and the unconscious, and the feeling quality of that gap is one of sorrow that a researcher might have about the difference between what he or she intuits and what he or she is able to say about the work, much like the difference between what I was able to grasp intuitively about the effulgent greening of that garden where this work began again and what I could say about it in calling that overflowing display "green."

This tension in the gap between thinking and feeling lies at the heart of a recently completed dissertation by Conrad Gratz, entitled "The Experience of Living with Enchantment."[6] Using the alchemical hermeneutic method, Gratz begins his work with a richly textured description of how he was initially drawn into the work. Before I quote a passage from him, I want to note that the process of attending to the vocational aspect of the work is, in addition to the process of transference dialogues, a way in which the feeling quality of the work becomes present. The alchemical hermeneutic method, as I have been saying throughout this chapter, extends this vocational process by making a place for the feelings of the researcher in the work.

> I grew up on the edge of a small town. When I was a child, I would sometimes go into the field behind my house during a dark, clear night. There I would gaze at the stars in wonder. Even then I knew that the stars were unimaginably far away. I would experience my own smallness in the presence of the immensity of the universe that was spread out in front of me. This experience would leave me with a feeling of being deeply held by God's overwhelming presence. This in turn led me to feel connected

to the world around me. I found a profound meaningfulness in
this connectedness to God and the universe. When I walked
away from the field and the stars, returning to the projects that
I occupied myself with, I wished I could take this immediate
sense of the presence of God with me. Even as this sense of
presence faded, the event and its memory left me with the
experience of having been changed.[7]

"Even as the sense of this experience has faded"! If we listen into
that statement, we hear one of the vocational seeds of his work, an
early experience of the world's enchantment, a feeling connection that
has lingered and has now flowered in this work, which has made its
claim upon him. We also hear a tone of lament, a feeling of mourning
for what has faded, a quality of feeling that permeates the work. In
fact, it is a tone that is present in the beginning, even before the work
begins. It is there in the poem that marks the dedication of the work,
that place where Gratz acknowledges those for whom the work has
been done.

It is difficult
to get the news from poems
yet men die miserably every day
for lack
of what is found there.[8]

"For lack of what is found there"! What is it that is not found in
the poem? It points to the asphodel, a mythical flower said to resemble
the narcissus and to cover the Elysian Fields. It is there in the poem
and not there, and in that gap between what the poet makes present
through what he says and what remains absent—the flower itself—
there is a sense of loss. That dying every day, just a little bit each day,
is for what has been lost and not found again. Is there a better way to
speak to the feeling tone of mourning in that pregnant gap between
what once was had and known and what has faded and asks to be re-
membered? Gratz's work is an imaginal exercise of re-search as a work
of mourning, return, recovery, and being re-membered. It is that
poetics of the re-search process called for in the Introduction to this
book, an elegiac poetics, a work that is both lament and praise, the
prerequisite for an imaginal approach that would transform a wound
into a work.

When we make a place in re-search that returns to the vocational claim that a work makes upon a researcher, as the one who searches again for what was once known but has faded, the question does indeed arise, as an issue of method, as to who is actually doing the work. Recall the riff on the cover of this book that I did in the Introduction. Well, the same riff can be done here. Who has written "The Experience of Living with Enchantment"? Was it that young boy staring up into the starry night sky so long ago? Or was it Conrad Gratz the man and graduate student, the one who did the library research, who read and digested the source material, and who wrote up the work?

The question is, of course, wrongly stated, since it is neither the one nor the other. The work was written between the two, and without that young boy, the work would never have been a calling. In the same way, without Conrad Gratz the man, the one who heeded the call into the work, the work would not have been started. I do not think it is off the mark to say that Conrad Gratz wrote up the work with the young boy who wanted it to be written down.

The example of Gratz indicates that feeling is a way of valuing the work, or, perhaps it is better to say, a response to how the work is valued by the researcher. It is important to note that feelings as a value judgment are not the same thing as emotions. Indeed, in the alchemical hermeneutic method, feeling refers to one of the four functions in Jung's typology alongside thinking, intuition, and sensing. Emotions, we could say, are *what* one has, or better, what has one; feelings, on the other hand, refer to *who* has the emotion. That is, feelings can be understood as differentiated emotion. Feeling is a function of consciousness; and in Jung's typology, feeling, along with thinking, is a rational function.

In *Psychological Types*, Jung describes feeling as "a process that takes place between the *ego* and a given content, a process moreover that imparts to the content a definite *value* in the sense of acceptance or rejection ["like" or "dislike"]."[9] In other words, with feelings, one is moved towards or away from something, such as a painting, for example, and this movement expresses the ego's evaluation of the thing. As a value, then, feelings can be a very subtle indication of a researcher's evaluation of his or her work, a deeper and different response from his or her critical thinking response.

How thinking and feeling, as the two rational functions, differ from each other is a subject I will discuss below. What is important now is the recognition that feeling as a way of knowing matters. Morris Berman has made this point quite forcefully. His work offers an excellent example from another discipline (history) that feelings belong in research. In his book, *Coming to Our Senses*, he writes: "... [W]e do not *have* methodologies of feeling, only ones of analyzing," and he calls for "a visceral approach to history," which would "create bodily and emotional echoes in the person who reads historical studies ...."[10]

Berman's work is excellent in diagnosing the effects of the absence of feeling methodologies in the discipline of history, but it does not develop such methodologies in any systematic fashion. In this respect, he leaves it as a work to be done. "We are," he notes, "in murky territory here," and to strengthen his point he adds, "in the same way that the physicists are." Extending his physics analogy, he points out, "[N]o physicist I know of has managed to construct a methodology that directly involves the experimenter in their [*sic*] own experiment." He concludes, "But that day may not be far off."[11]

With its processes of the vocational aspect of re-search and the transference dialogues, as well as with the development of the alchemical hermeneutic method, which makes a place for feelings in research, *The Wounded Researcher* brings that day one step closer. The place it makes for feeling, however, is more differentiated than that envisioned in Berman's call for methodologies of feeling, and this differentiation rests upon Jung's understanding of feeling as a conscious process and a rational function. Berman does not distinguish sufficiently between feeling as a rational evaluative process and emotion. His call, quoted above, for a visceral approach to history that would make a place for a methodology of feelings associates such methodologies with a researcher's bodily and emotional reactions.

This equation of feelings with emotions is also illustrated by a brief story that Berman tells about the poet Robert Bly. Berman once heard Bly say after reading one of his poems that he did not know what the last line meant, but he did know that it belonged there "because as he wrote it," Berman says, "he felt a twinge in his gut." Commenting on Bly's admission, Berman notes, "Of course, history is not poetry, and I very much doubt that 'gut-twingering' can serve as an adequate methodology for historians." He is right. It cannot serve as a methodology for feelings. "But to be honest," he adds, "I don't think it is a bad start."

For Berman, "gut-twingering" is not such a bad start because "[h]istory is *made* somatically; to be accurate it should be *written* somatically."[12] And herein lies the problem. Berman confuses bodily emotional responses with feelings, and although such bodily responses do have a place in relation to a methodology that makes a place for the symptomatic body in research (an idea I will consider in a later section), such bodily emotional responses are not feelings in Jung's sense of evaluative processes.

Jung's understanding of feelings as a rational function of evaluation raises the question of how feelings function as a method in research. Specifically, how does the feeling function operate in the alchemical hermeneutic method?

Jung notes that the process of feeling can "appear isolated, as it were, in the form of mood."[13] Mood, we might say, is a habitat of the feeling function. It is a temperament that marks a person's style of being across multiple situations. Mood is what lingers as a feeling quality over time, and in this respect it lends to feelings the dimension of time. Writing about feeling and time, Hillman says, "A prerequisite for feeling is therefore a structure of feeling memory ...," and he goes on to acknowledge the importance of childhood in the construction of such feeling memories as a foundation for the feeling function as a process of evaluation.[14] Hillman notes that for some writers the structure of feeling memories built upon the past means that there is a "preference of the feeling type for past time."[15] And Bachelard tells us that in reverie, which as we have seen throughout this work is the mood of research done with soul in mind, "we re-enter into contact with possibilities which destiny has not been able to make use of." For Bachelard, reverie is this great paradox: "... [I]n us, this dead past has a future, the future of its living images ...."[16]

Perhaps, then, the feeling function has a place particularly in an imaginal approach to re-search, in research that would attend to the unfinished business of the soul in the work, to a past that has faded, as Gratz says, or a past that has been forgotten, but still lingers as a mood between the researcher and the work. And perhaps here, the feeling function, in returning the researcher to the unfinished business that lingers in the work, finds its complement in the irrational function of intuition, which, as von Franz notes, "is a function by which we conceive possibilities."[17] In the next section I will discuss the place of intuition and how it operates in the alchemical hermeneutic method, but for the moment I will note only that the possibilities that von Franz mentions are in part the unfinished business that is the weight of history, that "dead past," that waits in the work to be re-membered.

What these remarks suggest is that the feeling function as a style or mood operates in the alchemical hermeneutic method as an image, as a personification of the one who feels in this or that way. This is the issue mentioned above about *who* is feeling, in contrast to *what* is the emotion. The personification of the feeling function as a way of differentiating it from emotions is a principal way of employing it in research. By asking this question about *who* is feeling the work, a researcher can uncover not only *who* is doing the work, but also what aspect of the work is being opened and what aspect of it is being hidden, since whoever that *who* is, he or she represents a perspective that values the work in a particular way. So, for example, Gratz is drawn into a work that recovers the wonder of the world as enchanted through the figure of the child who long ago was drawn to the majesty of the stars. Feeling as a rational function and conscious process can further the work of making the researcher's unconscious complex presence to the work more conscious. In short, attending to his or her feeling response to the work, a researcher can further discover *who* is doing the work and how the sources for the work are being evaluated.

A second way in which the feeling function operates in the alchemical hermeneutic method is as an index of evaluation, as a first-line response, as it were, to whether one's work does or does not make sense, not in a logical, but an aesthetic, way. The work does not feel right, or it does not have the right tone, or its rhythm feels awkward and forced and without a sense of flow, or its sense of proportion and balance feels out of joint. How the parts of the work fit together is not only a logical issue; it is also a feeling that one has about the work, and, indeed, this feeling evaluation often precedes the logical one. Because one feels the fit of the work to be ugly, as it were, one goes in search of a more fitting logic for it.

This kind of evaluation, as I said, has nothing to do with the logic of the work or with the facts. Rather, it concerns the aesthetic qualities of the work, the way, we could say, it sings. Hillman makes a similar point when he says of the feeling function, "To hit the mark truly does not mean always to tell the factual or logical truth."[18] The truth of one's research does, of course, rely upon the logic and the factual basis of one's arguments. But while that is the truth, it is not the whole truth of the work. Did not Einstein once say that the mathematical equations of physics were true because they were beautiful, and did not the poet Keats say the same thing when he said of truth that it is beauty? The thirst of mind for logic has its complement in the soul's search for beauty, and any method that relies solely on the logical mind leaves half of the human equation out of the picture.

Having offered two ways in which the feeling function operates in the alchemical hermeneutic method, we can still ask how a researcher applies the feeling function in a methodical way. This issue returns us to the question of how feeling as a rational function differs from thinking as a rational function. Concerning this difference, Jung asserts: "The intellect proves incapable of formulating the real nature of feeling in conceptual terms, since thinking belongs to a category incommensurable with feeling."[19] Hillman elaborates on this: "The developed feeling function is the reason of the heart which the reason of the mind does not quite understand."[20]

As rational functions, feeling and thinking belong to different domains. Thinking is a function of the rational mind, while feeling is a function of the feeling heart. We might say, then, that the feeling function is a cardiognosis, a way of knowing with and through the heart, and, in an essay entitled "On Being a Fool: In Defense of the Pathetic Heart," I proposed cardiognosis as a method. "It is a gnosis that begins in grief over loss," I noted, "in a sorrow that is attuned to absences that haunt presence …." If we take this path into our research, we are present as "witnesses for what has been forgotten, witnesses who, summoned by what has been left behind, engage in the work of an-amnesis, of un-forgetting … that starts with the gesture of the backward glance."[21] Cardiognosis as method, then, is about re-membering the ancestors who linger in the work, and in this respect the feeling function—as the method of the heart, as the path of the heart—is, as noted above, particularly suited to the imaginal approach to research insofar as one of its chief characteristics is this devotion to the unfinished business at the heart of the work.

As a matter of heart, one way to apply the feeling function in research is through the cultivation of sympathy as a method or path into the work. Corbin tells us that sympathy is "a condition and mode of perception" that belongs to the subtle heart.[22] Following Corbin, if the feeling function is the path of the heart in research, then sympathy belongs to a method that makes a place for feeling in research. Since the prefix "sym-" derives from the Greek word for "with" or "together," and the stem "path" is related to the Greek word *pathos*, which connotes feeling and suffering, the sym-pathetic researcher is one who becomes like the work by feeling with it and into it, and suffers in the sense of allowing the work to be what it wishes to be. Sym-pathy, then, as a method of understanding and engaging the work, is an act of surrendering oneself to what one wishes to know. It is a way in which the heart of the researcher and the heart of the work resonate *together* in sym-pathetic harmony.

Compassion also belongs to a method that makes room for the feeling function in research. Like sympathy, compassion is a virtue of the heart. The prefix "com-" derives from the Latin word for "with" or "together" so that in com-passion one feels and suffers with the other. Compassion, then, is a mode of understanding. In re-search with soul in mind, one is with the work, suffering it in the sense of bearing or carrying it along the way. As an important aspect of the alchemical hermeneutic method, compassion situates the researcher as a companion to the work, as a friend of the work. Since the stem "pan" in the word "companion" derives from the Latin word for bread, we should add that the methodical cultivation of compassion, as a way of applying the feeling function in research, indicates that a researcher does indeed feed the work with his or her own substance. The ink that flows on the page and the blood that flows in one's heart are in this sense com-panions in the process and along the path of research. And, as a researcher feeds the work in this way, he or she is also fed and nourished by the work. We should not forget or ignore, however, the darker side of the work as a companion. There are times when, instead of being nourished by the work, one is drained by it. Sometimes the work as companion can be a vampire that feeds off the researcher.

In her original and insightful development of the method of intuitive inquiry, Rosemarie Anderson makes a strong case for the place of compassion and sympathy in research methods. With regard to sympathy, she speaks about sympathetic resonance "as a validation procedure for the researcher's particular intuitive insights and syntheses."[23] For Anderson, the validity of one's research is tested by how it harmonizes with the experience of others. I am suggesting that sympathetic resonance as a measure of validity can occur because there has been a bond of sympathy between a researcher and the work. When there has been a deep and prolonged attunement between the heart of the researcher and the heart of the work, when a researcher has let himself or herself be drawn into the work through his or her own wounds, the truth of the work for others is, if not guaranteed, at least on the way to being established.

There are numerous similarities between Anderson's method of intuitive inquiry and the alchemical hermeneutic method, and indeed many similar descriptions of the process of research. But there is also a key difference, namely, the place of the unconscious in research and the presence of specific procedures that include the deep subjectivity of the researcher. Bearing this difference in mind, I would nevertheless encourage an ongoing dialogue between the two. The point of divergence as well as the points of convergence will enrich both methods.

Sympathy and compassion, as two ways of applying the feeling function in a method with heart, engender a radical shift in attitude, from one that understands knowledge as an exercise of power to one that understands it as an exercise of love. In this shift, method is not so much a procedure as a way of doing the work: doing it with love. Earlier in this book, I quoted Greg Mogenson to the effect that in order to learn something we must fall in love. Here I would add that love is the Great Teacher, something the poet Rilke reminds us of over and over again. We might ponder what is missed when we fail to include in our research methods the way that love e-ducates us, draws the researcher out of himself or herself into the work.

In the context of these remarks about sympathy and compassion, I want to return to the issue of the difference between thinking and feeling as rational functions. This difference might be summarized in this fashion: the distinction is between the "*who*" of the sympathetic and witnessing heart and the "*who*" of the critical mind. Both are needed in research methods, but we have tended, as we have seen throughout these chapters on method, to sacrifice the tender heart and its ways of knowing to the tough mind and *its* ways of knowing. Jung's typology reminds us not to forget that the feeling function is as legitimate a way of knowing as the thinking function.

As I come to the close of this section on the place of the feeling function in the alchemical hermeneutic method, I feel a gap between what I have been able to say and what still needs to be said. There is a piece of unfinished business regarding the feeling function in research: it has to do with Jung's typology. An approach to research that would make a place for the feeling function in research should ultimately develop a systematic approach to research in line with the four functions. Research that would keep soul in mind should ideally align methods of research with Jung's typology because a feeling type is not going to do research in the same way that a thinking type or a sensing type or an intuitive type would.

As far as I know, little work has been done in this area. William Braud notes that "Mitroff and Kilman adapted Jungian typology and applied their conceptualization to social science methodology to better understand possible congruencies between research interests and styles and personality." He also points out that "Stanley Krippner has applied the Mitroff and Kilman typology to the discipline of parapsychology." With regard to his own efforts in this direction, Braud calls for the construction of research teams assembled in relation to Jung's four types. While Braud acknowledges that other typologies could be used, he makes a specific case for Jung's system. "The Jungian typology comes to mind as especially relevant," he asserts, "because it is based, essentially, on differential epistemological sensitivities, and this is precisely what we are seeking in the design of an effective research team."[24] In other words, Braud is partial to Jung's system because it deals effectively with different ways of knowing, with different types of knowing. Jung's four functions are, in effect, four different epistemological strategies.

While Braud's suggestion of having research teams is a very sensible one, since no one individual can cover the entire type range and each has an inferior function, we should not ignore the value of making the researcher's complex unconscious expression of the inferior function more conscious through the process of transference dialogues presented in this book. In other words, extending the breadth of the research process by forming research teams cannot be used as a substitute for excavating the depths of the individual researcher. Ideally, these two movements, one horizontal and the other vertical, work together and complement each other. But however that might happen, we should note again that the unconscious cannot be ignored. True objectivity, we have seen, is achieved by taking into account deep subjectivity. The way down and in is the way out and into the world or a text or a work.

Hillman makes this point in his own way with respect to the feeling function: "It is crucial to the understanding of Jungian psychology that feeling be brought to bear upon it. We cannot read Jung by intellect alone. Conscious comprehension in Jungian psychology means as well feeling comprehension."[25] A team of four readers can help to make the unconscious complex of each reader more conscious. But, as I showed in "Complex Knowing: Toward a Psychological Hermeneutics," each reader of a text needs to do his or her complex work if that individual is to understand not only what the text says but also to whom it says it.[26]

The Place of Intuition in Research Method

In the last section, I noted that the application of Jungian typology to research methods is a piece of unfinished business in this work. However, without being conscious of any intention on my part to develop a method in relation to Jung's typology, my graduate students have done work with respect to the vocational character of research and the process of transference dialogues that shows that the feeling function and the function of intuition arise in the work itself. This situation, I would argue, is a good example of one of the core themes of this book. Beyond whatever outlines I have made of my plans and intentions for this book, the work itself has threaded its own course. Jung's typology has been a seed buried in the research processes of vocation and transference dialogues. Moreover, the function of intuition, like that of feeling, seems to be particularly suited to the imaginal approach to research, since, as Jung notes, intuition "is not concerned with the present but is rather a sixth sense for hidden possibilities."[27] The imaginal approach, with its devotion to the unfinished business in the soul of the work, is attuned to those hidden and not readily present possibilities that linger and wait as the weight of history in the work.

The seed, however, still needs to be harvested. The application of Jung's typology to research methodology remains as a work to be done. Such a work would not only enrich the imaginal approach to research by coupling research methods to the different epistemological styles of the four functions, it would also counterbalance the current approach to research, which emphasizes thinking and sensation and dismisses feeling and intuition as legitimate ways of knowing.

One of my students, Dennis Langhans, is a fine example of how the vocational character of research is, or at least can be, an expression of intuition. About his call to his dissertation, "An Odyssey of the Heart: A Return to the Place, Rhythm, and Time of the Imaginal Heart," he states that although he "had achieved a fair degree of success in the corporate world ... every time [he] achieved some exoteric success, [he] heard in [his] soul the refrain from the Peggy Lee song: 'Is That All There Is?'"[28] That call, he adds, "was a call from some *other* ... experienced only 'through a glass darkly.'" What he goes on to describe in some detail regarding the theme of the odyssey in his life and his work shows that he had an intuitive sense of the goal of the odyssey even before he was able to work out the path of the journey.

Langhans implies that the work is given before it is begun, and what is given of it is "arcane ... and elusive." In other words, the process is not very rational. While one might be more or less able to reconstruct the journey into a work after it is done, one cannot do so before one has completed the work. As I suggested in the Introduction, one knows how a book begins only when it has ended. Langhans had no path mapped in advance. On the contrary, he was drawn into the work before he had conceived its outlines, details, and clear form. As Langhans notes, what he set out to find found him.

Langhans' descriptions of the odyssey into his work fit quite nicely with Jung's descriptions of intuition. Intuition, he says, "is the function that mediates perceptions in an *unconscious way*." Unlike the feeling function, then, which is the evaluative dimension of consciousness and therefore a rational function (along with thinking), intuition (along with sensation) is an irrational function. Jung is quick to note that the term irrational does not connote "something *contrary* to reason, but something *beyond* reason, something, therefore, not grounded on reason." Hence, "[i]n intuition a content presents itself whole and complete, without our being able to explain or discover how this content came into existence."[29] Two questions naturally arise regarding intuition. The first: Can we trust such a seemingly subjective process? The second: How does one make systematic use of intuition as a method of research?

The answer to the first question has to be an unqualified "yes" for two reasons. First, we can trust intuition as part of our research method because, as we have emphasized throughout this work, the path to objectivity is through deep subjectivity. Second, we can trust it because it happens. It is a process that takes place more often than not in research, so how can we ignore it? It does not go away if we ignore it—it just gets covered over in the ways we logically construct and reconstruct the research process. Jung makes this point when speaking about his book *Psychological Types*. He notes that an author "likes to give you the finished product of his directed thinking and have you understand that so it was born in his mind, free of weakness." That is, writers are inclined to hide the fact that there is a darker side to the writing process, "a weaving about among mistakes, impure thinking." And in the context of this discussion I would add the surprises, detours, and new directions of intuitive thinking that emerge.[30]

Moreover, ignoring the place of intuition in the process can and does have detrimental effects, especially for researchers who are intuitive types and who process information in this fashion. Judith Orodenker is an example of this situation. Describing her resistance to the transference dialogues, she notes that they engendered in her "feelings of fear and sadness." Working with these feelings, however, she discovered *who* was evaluating the dialogues in these ways. It was, she says, the *one* who did not trust "my own intuition and inner guidance" about the work on "The Voice of the Goddess: The Reemergence of the Archetypal Divine Feminine."[31] And this one "was interfering with my ability to proceed with my work." Without identifying intuition with the feminine, I should note that this concern about trusting one's intuition is more often than not expressed by female graduate students, a fact that points to a cultural bias that identifies thinking and sensation with masculine modes of knowing over feeling and intuition, wihich are identified with feminine ways of knowing.

An approach to re-search that would keep soul in mind has to work against this bias, because each of the four functions is a legitimate style of the soul's way of engaging the world and a work. As Jung notes,

"For complete orientation all four functions should contribute equally
…." In the context of research, this would mean that "thinking should
facilitate cognition and judgment, feeling should tell us how and to
what extent a thing is important or unimportant for us, sensation
should convey concrete reality to us … and intuition should enable
us to divine the hidden possibilities in the background" of the work.[32]

    With regard to the second question, I believe there are several ways
to cultivate intuition as part of a research method. George Callan,
whose work I cited in Chapter 5, offers a good example of how to make
a place for intuition in the research process. It is worth quoting her
description again.

> It happened that in my first year of doctoral studies, while my
> conscious mind focused intently on the material delivered in
> the classroom, my right hand, having a mind of its own,
> strayed from its note-taking responsibilities. It idly scripted
> doodles in the margins of the page—spontaneous calligraphy,
> meaningless flourishes and scribbles. In the second year of my
> studies, these unbidden images became distinct, taking the
> form of sacred objects from my childhood memory: chalices,
> tabernacles, grottos, shrines, elaborate candlesticks. By the third
> year, the notes had been relegated to the margins and the pages
> were filled with iconic images: ornate boxes, baskets, bathtubs
> with wings, decorative envelopes, apothecary jars, teacups, circus
> tents, towers with whimsical spires, wardrobes on wheels, clocks
> in their casings, with little nooks and drawers and glass knobs.
> They all had something in common. They were vessels—
> containers. While the pure flow of the drawing soothed the
> intensity of academia's demand, I gave no particular value to
> these images. It had not yet entered my consciousness that I
> was being pursued. The messenger in the form of revelatory
> image had arrived from the margins, passing through the
> threshold of the right brain while the left brain still clung to
> the linear content at center stage.[33]

    Her language here is, I would suggest, descriptively evocative of
intuition. She speaks of her right hand as having a mind of its own
while her consciousness is otherwise engaged. In her right hand, there
is another kind of intelligence at work, but an intelligence that appears
when the directed thinking of her right hand strays from its
responsibilities and idly gives itself over to what presents itself at the

margins of her thought. This wandering right hand knows something that she does not know, and it takes her to the edges of her thinking. What else is intuition if it is not what happens at the margins of thought, if it is not a process that takes place at the border between conscious and unconscious thinking?

When I originally quoted the passage given above (in Chapter 5), it was within the context of the place of reverie in a re-search process that keeps soul in mind. Reveries happen, as Callan's description indicates. But they can also be a way of methodically making a place for that kind of thinking that happens at the edges of thought. In other words, the researcher can cultivate intuition as part of his or her methodology by developing ritual times and spaces for reverie. In such moments, a researcher might stray into activities that seem completely unrelated to the work. For example, a researcher might draw, or do dream work, or, thinking of the work, wait for his or her thoughts to express themselves in body gestures. In these ritual moments of reverie, a researcher is at play with the work.

Callan did in fact extend her right-hand reveries into a specific form of practice. Surprised by what the margins had given to her, she began to engage in a form of creative play. Her right-hand reveries at the margins of her thinking became a daily practice. "I began to nurture those whimsical images," she writes, "draw them on fine Italian paper, touch them with color, refine the details of their embellishments."[34] In these ritual moments, she was giving free reign to her imagination. She was encouraging a kind of unconscious, non-directed thinking that otherwise goes by the name of intuition.

Rosemarie Anderson's method of intuitive inquiry has developed the place of intuition in research into a fine art. In a particularly rich passage, she describes "trickstering" as an intuitive research skill. Trickstering creates "auspicious bewilderment" and, she rightly notes, "auspicious bewilderment may signal the beginning of renewed understanding." For the thinking function, intuition is bewildering. Intuition is a way of getting lost, a way of stepping off the path that thinking has made for the work. And the ritual practices of reverie, which can cultivate intuition, are ways of taking leave of the work for a time so that we might be surprised, as Callan was, by what seduces our intuition from the margins of the work. Anderson encourages such moments of bewilderment and suggests, "It is usually worthwhile even to exaggerate, dramatize, or extend the features of what bewilders, to look deeper." Such moments, she adds, counterbalance the tendency to think that we are completely in charge of the work. "If we go for long periods of time of not being surprised," she warns, "beware."[35] It is sound advice for an approach to research that, in keeping soul in mind, must linger in the margins of the work and cultivate intuition as a legitimate method of knowing.

The Body in the Work: Of Gestures and Symptoms

In this section, I want to discuss two issues regarding how the body is present in research methodology. The first concerns what phenomenology calls the *lived body*, which is the body one *is*, and not the body one *has*, the body as object. The second is the *symptomatic body*, which many of my students have encountered in their work.

With respect to the lived body, much has been written about the eclipse of the body in Western metaphysics and the necessity to restore our carnal ways of knowing the world. It is the foundational theme of phenomenology. In *Technology as Symptom and Dream*, I described the lived body as the gestural body and differentiated it from the body as object. In addition, I have also described the role and place of this lived, gestural body and its relation to the symptomatic body in the context of psychotherapy.[36] Although Anderson does not use the same language, the gestural body plays a prominent role in her work on research as well. For example, quite recently, she has developed a body intelligence scale, and her report of this work situates the body within a broad overview of the history of its return in various disciplines.[37] In addition, we have seen in the work of the historian Morris Berman a clarion call for a visceral method of reading history, which would give a prominent place to the way in which the historian interprets and understands the past through his or her emotional and bodily reactions. A recently completed doctoral dissertation by Ruth Meyer at Pacifica Graduate Institute offers a vivid example of this process. She writes:

> In 1984, in a dank corner of the Conciergerie Museum in Paris, France, a young student about to embark on a career as a history teacher stares at the rusty old blade of the guillotine and reads the last letter of Robespierre, architect of the Reign of Terror. She stares down at her hands in disbelief: inexplicably, blood is

dripping onto her hands. For years afterward, beheadings and guillotines haunt her dreams.[38]

My intention here, however, is not to retell the story of the body's eclipse and return. Rather, it is to focus on the body's indispensable place in the alchemical hermeneutic method. In an article entitled "Complex Knowing: Toward a Psychological Hermeneutics," which in many ways anticipated some key elements of this book, I cited a number of major authors who have called for a return to what we might term an "incarnate gnosis," and in that context I described an experiment in which I asked the readers of one of Freud's case histories to pay attention to their complex engagement with the text.[39] Two of these ways involved the body.

First, I asked each subject to pay attention to the places where they were stopped by the text. Such moments, I suggested, might be occasions when a reader is touched by the text at the level of a complex. In such moments of puzzlement—or what Anderson, in another context, calls bewilderment—we discover that "what perhaps initially announces itself as an intellectual difficulty might betray how our way into the text is through the text coming into us." To say this in another way, we discover that cognitive confusion often disguises affective ambivalence. These moments of being stopped by a text, these moments of puzzling over a passage, are a way in which the text is wounding the reader. Of course, such moments could also be occasions when a text is opening a fantasy and expanding the reader's imaginative grasp of the work, the experience that Bachelard, for example, describes when he says that sometimes when he is reading he leaves the page. The point is that this moment, when for whatever reason one's engagement with the text or the work is halted, needs to be acknowledged. The researcher with his or her work, like the reader with a text, has to wonder *who* is being arrested in these moments when the work or the text breaks down. He or she has to ask who or what is asking to break through in these moments of breakdown.

In these moments of being stopped in their reading, I asked the subjects "to wait for an image, a memory, or a felt bodily sense and then to work with it." But in the context of this experiment, I had not yet developed any systematic procedures for working with this material. Certainly, the transference dialogues based upon active imagination were not employed. Nevertheless, a seed was planted by this experiment, especially regarding the felt bodily sense of these moments of breakdown, and I noted the importance of "paying attention to the body as a way of recovering the body of psychological gnosis."[40]

The second way in which the body of the reader is present in the work is through the voice. I instructed the subjects in the experiment to read the text aloud. My intuition here was that in doing so the relation between the reader and the text would feel more like a conversation taking place in a present moment of time, thereby closing the gap somewhat between the author, who wrote the text in the past and is now absent, and the reader, who is present in the present. In addition, reading the text aloud would not only slow down the reader's thinking, it would most emphatically also bring thinking back down into the body. Reading aloud, one is not able to command the text from above, to take hold of it as a possession. Indeed, reading aloud imbricates reader and text. Reader and text overlap each other, and between them a con-spiracy emerges as the reader gives breath to the words through his or her voice, pauses for a moment, and on the in-breath drinks in the text that now in-spires him or her with its words. The reading itself becomes a living process, and something of the animal of mind is felt in the body, in the expansion and contraction of the chest, in the vibrations felt in the throat, and in the resonances experienced in the sinus cavities and in the ears. In this process of embodying one's reading, meaning is no longer a matter of a Cartesian mind making sense of a text. It is a matter of sense arising from sensing the text and being sensed by it.

Both of these ways of incorporating the body into the reading of a text are already active in the process of transference dialogues, insofar as that process systematically makes a ritual place for the work to slow down and break down, and insofar as that process is best served by having the researcher speak aloud the dialogues between himself or herself and the strangers in the work. And, since I have been insisting throughout this work that this ritual process can be applied to all methods, it certainly can be applied in the alchemical hermeneutic method as well. Apart from the systematic use of the process of transference dialogues, a researcher can also take note outside of that ritual space of those moments when the work stops. In such moments, he or she, like the readers of the text in the experiment, can attend to his or her complex presence to the work, to *who* is stuck in the work.

Getting in touch with that figure might help the researcher to discover those places where he or she is imposing an agenda upon the work, which the work itself resists. In addition, a researcher can on occasion read aloud the work as it is being done. Quite often, this latter action slows the work down and in that slowing down reveals new connections hitherto unnoticed between and among the themes of the work, as if these connections were only waiting to be noticed through the closer proximity of the researcher to the work that voicing the work brings. In the chapter "On Writing down the Soul," I will have more to say about giving voice and body to the work.

The two procedures described above for making a place for the body in the alchemical hermeneutic method are more or less intentional acts on the part of the researcher. Sometimes, however, the body of the researcher simply insists on its presence. I am speaking here of the symptomatic body, of the way in which a researcher suffers or bears the work in a bodily way, and in Chapter 6 I gave some examples from my graduate students of the presence of this symptomatic body in the context of the transference dialogues. Erik Killinger, for example, suffered several instances of the body's presence in his research. He had a choking incident that revealed several interrelated gastrointestinal ailments of which he was unaware and a bout of pleurisy. In his reflection on these episodes, he spoke of them as necessary Dionysian fragmentations, which had the effect of slowing down the work in order to digest it more completely.

Moreover, as I showed in that chapter, many of these examples arose in relation to the resistances that the students felt with respect to the transference dialogues. Debbie Greenwood, for example, stated that her resistance to the dialogues came to her in the form of an illness. She got pleurisy twice, became extremely depressed at times, and quite anxious on a few occasions. Reflecting on these expressions of the symptomatic body in her work, Greenwood, like Killinger, indicated that they functioned to slow her down so that she could more easily take in the material she was confronted with in the dialogues. What her example suggests is that the symptomatic body might often be a response to the ego's defense against letting go of the work. It might be a way in which the body expresses in symptomatic form what the complex of the researcher keeps hidden about the topic. Jo Todd's undigested affects about the abortion debate buried themselves so deeply within her body that she experienced physical symptoms. In her case, as we saw, the symptomatic body held the deeper wisdom of the work. It held the tension of the opposites between the pro-choice and pro-life positions, which her complex relation to her topic was not willing to accept. In symptomatic form, she had to suffer the work so that the work could find that place between the two polarized positions in the abortion debate. In this respect, I regard the symptomatic body as a tension between remembering something that is too vital to forget about the work, while forgetting it because it is too painful to acknowledge.

To conclude this section on the place of the body in the alchemical hermeneutic method, I want to give another example from one of my graduate students, Linda Lauver, who is working on a dissertation entitled "The Maya Tradition—A Living History: Re-membering What Wants to Be Remembered." In her introductory chapter, she describes a dream she had as she began to work on her dissertation. I need to report this dream because for Linda the dream is connected to the symptoms that followed several weeks later.

I am in a white Mayan dress and I go into the woods. When I come out I am sitting on a boulder and people are looking at me "aghast." I look down and see that my arms are cut and bloody. Red blood has covered my white dress. I do not remember what happened to me while in the woods. I then see a white dog standing nearby. He is a numinous guardian and was raised by Tibetan lamas.[41]

Reflecting on the dream, Linda says that it is a story of initiation. Coming as it did at the beginning of her work, the dream, she is suggesting, was a rite of passage into the work. "What I did not know at the time," she adds, "was what form it was going to take in my life."

The dream of initiation took on the form of the symptomatic body. "A few weeks later, I began to itch all over my body," she writes. "It started with hives," she adds, and then "[t]he hives turned into sores." Of these sores she writes: "When I scratched, they oozed a clear liquid and then became bloody." Unable to sleep because "the itching never stopped," she endured these symptoms for five months. "I knew," she writes, "I was in the midst of initiation."[42] After consulting numerous medical doctors and alternative healers, she finally discovered that she had psoriasis.

For Lauver, however, it was not enough to have a diagnosis. "I wondered," she said, "how this skin condition related to my Mayan dissertation topic." She knew that human sacrifice played a big part in Mayan life, and she was in the midst of reading one of the most important Mayan creation myths, the *Popul Vuh*. Working with this material in the transference dialogues, she became "even more convinced that my condition was directly related to my topic." As she continued to work with the symptoms in order to make the unconscious depths of her work more conscious, she discovered through her work with a Mayan astrologer that her date of birth in the Mayan calendar aligned her with the eagle, "the one who is a visionary and can see the larger picture." She also learned that the serpent, which is "more grounded because it lives close to the earth," is the symbol opposite the eagle in the Mayan system. Acknowledging that her "preference has always been to fly," she was reminded by her Mayan astrologer that "Kulkulkan, the Feathered Serpent, is a sacred deity of the Mayans." This deity, a combination of eagle and serpent, shed light upon her condition. With the aid of her Mayan astrologer, Linda began to understand "the challenges with [her] physical body as a Mayan initiation that is bringing more spirit energy into matter." Continuing to work with her symptoms at this symbolic level in order to gain a better understanding of the work she felt called to do, Linda sought the help of a yoga instructor, especially during the more severe outbreaks of the symptoms. About this part of the work Linda comments: "I believe I needed to become more grounded in order to bring the Mayan energies into my physical body."[43] In other words, Linda began to understand that if she was to listen to what the work wanted from her and how she was to be with it beyond her own assumptions and complexes, she would have to be initiated into the other wisdom in the work that her symptomatic body was experiencing.

I have taken some time with this example because it is a clear and dramatic instance of how the researcher's body is part of her or his method or way into the work. If Lauver was to understand the depths of her work about the Maya, she would have to suffer an initiation into the work at a level deeper than her thoughts or ideas about the work. While most instances of the role of the body in research might not be so clear, the fact remains that the body of the researcher in its gestural and symptomatic guises is present and has a place in research.

As with dreams, feelings, and intuitions, the symptomatic body is not
the data of research. On the contrary, it is path into the work, a way
of re-searching the work, another "tool," as it were, a tool especially
suited to uncovering the unconscious depths of the researcher and
exposing those layers of significance in the work that are otherwise
obscured from his or her view. A method that would keep soul in mind
has to be open to these possibilities if it is to include the researcher in
the research in a comprehensive way.

The Role of Synchronicity in Research

Synchronicity is one of the most significant contributions Jung
has made to our understanding of the ways of soul. Perhaps this is so
because, on the one hand, it gives us another way of understanding
connections between events beyond causality, and, on the other, it
assumes a meaningful connection between the physical and the
psychological worlds. As a principle, it describes "the simultaneous
occurrence of two meaningfully but not causally connected events."
Synchronicity is a "coincidence in time of two or more causally unrelated
events which have the same or similar meaning." More specifically,
synchronicity involves "the simultaneous occurrence of a certain
psychic state with one or more external events which appear as
meaningful parallels to the momentary subjective state." According
to Jung, synchronicity "consists of two factors: a) An unconscious image
comes into consciousness either directly (i.e., literally) or indirectly
(symbolized or suggested) in the form of a dream, idea, or premonition.
b) An objective situation coincides with this content."[44]

As with dreams, intuitions, feelings, and the body, re-search that
would keep soul in mind has to make a place for this possibility as well.
In doing so, it is important not to confuse synchronicity with
synchronism, which simply signifies the simultaneous occurrence of two
events. Synchronicity is not mere coincidence. In synchronicity, there
is a connection between psychic and material events, between the
unconscious and matter, that is not causal and that is experienced as
meaningful. In addition, there is an affective charge or component to
the experience. Von Franz captures something of the uniqueness of
synchronistic events when she says that "they are experienced as
miracles," and, indeed, what earlier ages called miracles might be

understood today as synchronicities. Be that as it may, the point to be made here is that the possibility of synchronicity requires, as von Franz notes, a religious sensibility, which has nothing to do with dogma, but is "the constant, careful attention toward unknown factors."[45]

Given this understanding of synchronicity, have there been instances of its occurrence in the work of my graduate students? I would argue in the affirmative in two cases. The first instance, which I mentioned in Chapter 6, comes from the work of Jo Todd. At the beginning of her work, she said that she found the material evoked in the transference dialogues to be "so hot" that she wondered if she could continue with the work. But she did go on, and as the work continued to heat up over a two-month period, she awoke one night to find herself in a life-threatening fire. Coincidence? A random event unrelated to her work? Perhaps! And yet, for Jo the experience felt quite connected to the work and to her emotional and psychological state. "Certainly over the next five years," she writes, "I sometimes felt as if I awoke to an unexpected fire in the work that threatened to devour me."

The second example, which I also mentioned in Chapter 6, is from Erik Killinger. In the course of his work, Erik had three laptop computer crashes, a car collision, in which he was blindsided by another driver, and a fall down a flight of stairs, which cracked two of his ribs. Again, we could ask if these events were only coincidences unrelated to his work—his work of exploring the unfamiliar landscape of the *intermundia*, that between-world for parish ministers who were making a transition out of that world. We could wonder, as Erik did, if the computer crashes, the car wreck, and the fall were accidental. And again we could say, perhaps! But as with the example of Jo Todd, one cannot simply take an outside view of these matters, and for Erik they carried not only a painful but also a powerful affective charge. In each of the three instances, Erik was caught in the grip of the idea that he was on the wrong track in his work. In addition, he had had the feeling that he was moving too fast with the work, making too many intuitive leaps, as he said, without working through the material experientially. He had been a minister who had found himself in that strange world between parish life and the outside world, and he knew in his bones, so to speak, the pain of that transition. Reflecting on these events, Erik discovered that he was not on the wrong track, but that he was neglecting his own experiences of having

been in that *intermundia* world, and that the work would not allow
that. These events, like the fire for Jo Todd, were, I would argue, ways
in which the unconscious of the researcher was in touch with the
matter of the work.

Although I could give examples from other sources, besides those
provided by my graduate students, I will leave the two I have provided
as an invitation to keep open to the possibility of synchronicity in research that keeps soul in mind. And I would end this section with the
question of whether it is possible to employ synchronicity in a more
intentional way in the alchemical hermeneutic method, as in fact one
of my graduate students attempted to do.

Debbie Greenwood developed a variety of strategies for working
with her resistances to her work. As I described in Chapter 6, sometimes
she would watch the library videos from her classes on research, while
at other times she would just get out of the house to get away from
the work. The latter strategy is quite understandable, and it can occasion
moments of reverie that allow one to let go of the work. But another
strategy that she followed is more extraordinary. In this move, she
would intentionally invite an occasion of synchronicity by forming
and putting out into the world a question such as, "What might I
want to consider in relation to my work today?" Framing the intention,
she would then look for the signs that might possibly speak to the
work. She would, as she said, "pull a rune or a tarot card or go to the
library for fun and to see what turned up." Whether such invitations
for synchronicity to play a role in one's research activity work or do
not work depends, of course, on the situation and the psychological
state of the researcher. Nevertheless, it is an intriguing idea, which
might occasion a moment when the unconscious of the researcher
opens to the matter of the work. In any case, as Woody Allen is reported
to have said about his twenty years in psychoanalysis (when asked if
psychoanalysis had helped, he replied that it had not hurt), this way
of inviting synchronicity into one's research method cannot hurt, and
indeed might help. After all, as peculiar as it might seem, the invitation
does at least shift one's attitude toward the work away from ordinary
routines that are sensible and predictable towards an expectation of
something extraordinary. And, as the Jungian analyst Albert
Kreinheder once noted, "Miracles never happen to sensible people,"
and synchronicities are occasional miracles.[46]

Conclusion

This chapter and the four chapters on method that have preceded it transform our usual ideas about method in three important ways. First, method as a path into one's work involves the deep subjectivity of the researcher. An approach to re-search that would keep soul in mind requires a method that not only includes the researcher in the process, but also takes into account the deep unconscious of the researcher. Chapters 7, 8, and 9 showed not only that empiricist and rationalist methods fail to do this, but also that when hermeneutics does make a place for the unconscious, it is, by and large, restricted to the Freudian view of the unconscious. For re-search that would keep soul in mind, we need a hermeneutics that takes into account Jung's expanded notion of the unconscious. Alchemical hermeneutics, described in Chapter 10 and illustrated in this chapter, is that method.

Second, method as a path into one's work is not only a set of procedures applied by a researcher to the work. It is also about who and how a researcher is in the work. Method is not just a "tool": it is a way of being in and with the work, a way of being on the journey into the work, a way of going to work on the work.

Alchemical hermeneutics focuses on this latter aspect of method. It is a method that arises from and extends the research process of transference dialogues. As we saw in Chapter 5, the transference dialogues make a place for the researcher's complex unconscious relation to his or her work. A researcher's complexes are the ways in which a researcher projects into the work what he or she wants and needs from the work. Complex desires are the hooks that draw a researcher into a work. These complex desires are the ways in which research is truly, deeply, and madly a vocational process in which the researcher does not so much choose a work as he or she is chosen by a work. What the alchemical hermeneutic method adds to this process is those other subtle ways in which the unconscious of the researcher and the unconscious of the work, its unfinished business, are gripped together in dialogue and, perhaps on occasion, in moments of synchronicity.

Alchemical hermeneutics, then, is a method that has evolved over time as a supplement to the process of those dialogues. I should note here that this evolution was in large measure the outcome of the work that many of my students did. Committed to an imaginal approach to research, they have explored and extended the limits and boundaries of the transference process. And in many ways, the development of a method that includes other unconscious factors, such as feelings, dreams, intuitions, symptoms, and synchronicities, was a natural elaboration of their openness to the unconscious in their research work. While the inclusion of feelings and intuition is, as suggested above, a piece of unfinished business in this imaginal approach to research (which would require a more detailed consideration of Jung's typology and its application to research styles), their inclusion alongside dreams, symptoms, and synchronicities re-vision method as an ongoing flow that complements method as a procedural grid.

Third, method as flow and as grid describes method as a rhythm between these two moments, and in this respect the alchemical hermeneutic method has evolved over time as a supplement to method in its procedural aspects. The alchemical hermeneutic method is not a stand-alone method. It is a method that can be used alongside all other methods as a way of including those aspects of a researcher's deep subjectivity that would otherwise be excluded.

The wounded researcher is someone who adopts the imaginal approach to research, submits to the processes of vocational and transference dynamics in his or her work, and makes use of the alchemical hermeneutic method as a supplement to traditional modes of research. Now that I have laid out the approach, the processes, and the method for re-search that would keep soul in mind, it is time to finish this work with a consideration of two of its implications. This is the work of the two chapters in Part IV.

In Chapter 12 I will take up the issue of how writing up one's research is changed by inclusion of the unconscious in research. The question here is how does one write down the soul in writing up one's work. In Chapter 13 I will consider how the inclusion of the unconscious establishes a ground for an ethical epistemology.

PART IV

Implications

CHAPTER TWELVE

Writing down the Soul

Anything derived merely from rationality risks being profoundly inauthentic unless it also bears witness to the destabilizing presence of the unconscious.[1]

—Susan Rowland

INTRODUCTION

Throughout this book I have attempted to make a case and a place for research that would keep soul in mind. Now, as I near the end of this project, I return to its beginnings, to the Introduction, where this task encountered its initial challenge. How does one find words to bridge the gap between soul and its epiphanies, like the greening of the world in all its luxuriant and extravagant excess, and the mind that would take hold of them, give them shape and form in a concept or a theory? Or, as the poet Brendan Kennelly asks, how does one use the language of the day to speak about the things of the night? As we saw in Chapter 1, his struggle with the spectral presence of the "Man Made of Rain" was how to square the language of explanation with the dream-energized language of being. Something is always left out, something is always missing, and what is missing haunts the concepts and ideas we bring to clothe these epiphanies. In her remarkable and insightful book *Jung as a Writer*, Susan Rowland makes the same point about Jung. She says of Jung's psychology, "It is an attempt to evoke in writing what cannot be entirely grasped: the fleeting momentary presence of something that forever mutates and reaches beyond the ego's inadequate understanding."[2] And perhaps more to the point, she says in the chapter on gender, "Jung's entire psychology is a negotiation with the specter of the unconscious as that which defies rational meaning."[3] How does psychology translate the wildness of soul without taming it or breaking its spirit? How does psychology in its research practices write up its encounters with soul in a way that also writes down the soul?

In the wake of these questions, the style of this chapter breaks with the style of the previous chapters. This stylistic difference seems less my choice and more the force of the book itself. This chapter wants a different kind of writing, a style that reaches back to the garden in Christchurch, New Zealand where this work began again, to the Introduction where a poetics of the research process was suggested. The style is closer to the punctuated visions of poetry, to those momentary flashes of light that each line of a poem provides, like fireflies in the night. In fact, the style is modeled on what the poet Wallace Stevens does in his poem, "Thirteen Ways of Looking at a Blackbird," in which each of the thirteen stanzas offers a vignette, none of which by itself encapsulates the truth, but all of which are true in the illuminated moment and in the context of their appearance. I am not saying that this chapter is a poem about writing down the soul, nor am I saying that writing that keeps soul in mind is poetry. It is not. I do not have the talent required to write poetry, nor is that what this chapter wants. Rather, I am talking about the format of the chapter, and so what is offered are four ways of looking at writing down the soul. Each offers a perspective on writing down the soul, just as each of the thirteen stanzas in Stevens's poem offers a perspective on the blackbird.

FOUR WAYS OF LOOKING AT WRITING DOWN THE SOUL

Writing as Creative Repetition

In Chapter 5, I spoke about the difference between outlines and threads, and I said that the thread of the work runs beneath the outlines and always seems to call one back to the beginning of the work. The return to the beginnings of the work is a piece of creative repetition, a repetition that is not in service to some compulsion to keep things as they are by restoring things to what they were. Orpheus, who with Eurydice has been the archetypal and mythic presence guiding this work, failed—as he had to—in this attempt. He had to lose what he would possess and "She," as Rilke calls her, had to return them to the underworld if each and both of them were to continue the work of love. So, this return for the sake of repeating is in service to love for the work rather than an attempt to master it, in service to the soul's desire to break whatever wish one might have to possess the work. Writing as creative repetition is a return to the beginnings of the work for the sake of returning to what the work wants when one has gotten too far ahead of it, a return to hear again that story, that phrase, that word, and to fall once more into the rhythm and cadence of those moments when the work took hold of one, moments that still echo and linger like a dream atmosphere, intangible, subtle, insubstantial, but nevertheless present. In creative repetition, one gives up for a moment being the author who is in charge of the work to become the one who is again in service to it. Creative repetition is like falling in love again with the work, coming under its spell, being claimed again by it. Creative repetition is a return to the romance of the beginning.

Indeed, I was stuck as I began trying to write this penultimate chapter. I was feeling the excitement of the ending and, drawn towards it, I was losing touch with the feel of the work, with its rhythm, and tempo, and pace. Another deadline was approaching, and I was overwhelmed by the enormity of the task that had already been accomplished and the work that still needed to be done. But the more I gave in to the excitement and the panic, the more the chapter refused to submit to my willfulness. And then I had a dream. In this dream,

I am lost in a wild landscape of some foreign country in the Southern hemisphere, and the man who is supposed to be my guide is quite indifferent to our situation, and in particular to the fact that our vehicles keep breaking down. We are wandering aimlessly and there is no sense of a clear path to any defined destination. But then a woman whom I know very well appears. She takes little notice of me, but I can see quite clearly she is preparing to return to the place where we started in order to get a car. I confess my worry that she will not be able to find her way back on roads that are unfamiliar and in the darkness of the night. But she is confident and unconcerned about my fears.

I knew from this dream that I had been abandoning the core theme of this book. Too willful, I was not paying attention to what the work wanted from me in these final stages. All along I had been advocating the necessity to make a place for the unconscious in the work, and now I was rushing headlong into the still unmapped territory of the work, oblivious of the call to follow the soul of the work back to its beginnings, to the place where we started the journey—in the garden in Christchurch, New Zealand, now imaged in the dream through the landscape of some foreign country in the Southern hemisphere. But now, how could I refuse to heed the dream, when I had been arguing for a place for the dream in a research method that keeps soul in mind? So, before writing the first word of this chapter, I attended to this dream by asking who wants this work to be finished. I did some drawings, and the chapter began to unfold.

Lest I am misunderstood here, I do not have at the moment a clear outline of where this chapter is going. The dream has not given me an intellectual clarity. On the contrary, the dream has brought fresh energy to the work. And indeed, writing down the soul works in this way. The dream of the work loosens things up, especially when the writing has become too far removed from the soul of the work. I should also point out that this first way of looking at writing down the soul, that is, asking repeatedly for a return to beginnings, is fraught with anxiety, because in this return, I, as writer/researcher, have to confront not only the possibility that the work will come undone, fall apart, but also the feeling of its incompleteness. Indeed, the closer one gets to the finish line, the greater the temptation not to want to let go of the work, to surrender the process again to something other than one's own intentions for the work. Too much has been invested, and, as in life, one does not want to give up so easily what one believes and imagines he or she has built. Thus, to heed the call of the work to return to its beginnings for the sake of writing down the soul of the work is always an "egocide," a term borrowed from David Rosen's excellent book, *Transforming Depression: Healing the Soul Through Creativity.*[4] Writing down the soul of the work is the "death" of the ego as author. Writing down the soul of the work is a way of letting go of the work.

Elegiac writing

Recall the two pears of the poet Wallace Stevens discussed in the Introduction in connection with the gap we encounter between what we are able to say and what slips away. In that gap, we discovered a sense of sadness, a feeling of mourning, not only for what slips the net of our intentions, but also for what has been lost, forgotten, left behind, abandoned, and yet haunts our efforts to know the world and ourselves and to say what we know. Here, then, is a second way of looking at writing down the soul. To write down the soul of the work is to write from that feeling place of mourning that knows about what is lost and left behind and still waits for our attention. It is to write from that place that acknowledges not only that the work is incomplete, but also that it will always be so. It is to bring to a work something of an elegiac quality, a quality to the words and the writing that values not only the difference between the said and the unsaid, but also the difference between oneself as the one who does the saying and writing and those for whom it is being done.

Jung's psychology has this elegiac tone, as Greg Mogenson notes. "Psychology, for Jung," he says, "was an elegiac discipline, an attempt, 'ever renewed, to give an answer to the question of the interplay between here and hereafter.'" If writing down the soul takes an elegiac form, it is because re-search that would keep soul in mind attends to the unfinished business that waits as the weight of history in the work. The gap between consciousness and the unconscious is inhabited by the ancestors, and in the quote above at the beginning of this chapter, it is they who destabilize the work and make it authentic. As one sits at his or her desk, it is the ancestors who have a stake in the work who gather, that audience whom Jung describes as the "Unanswered, Unresolved, and Unredeemed."[5] We work in the ambience of their dark-light, and the researcher who would write down the soul must lend an ear to that assembly, to those who dwell in the imaginal realm of the work, where they are neither alive nor dead. Thus, elegiac writing has a ritual dimension to it; as a daily practice, one sets a place for the ancestors who gather around the writing table to eavesdrop on what is being said. In these moments, if one listens closely, one might hear their encouragement or criticism. Elegiac writing takes seriously this ancestral audience for whom the work is being done.

In addition, in elegiac writing, when one is writing from the place of soul, even the living authors one cites and with whom one dialogues have entered into the imaginal landscape of the soul. They, too, gather around the writing table and offer their wisdom and wisecracks. It is a dialogue of the complex and creative imagination in which what is unanswered, unredeemed, and unresolved in each partner in the conversation is engaged. When one writes from the soul, the boundary between the dead and the living is dissolved, and the conversation is always taking place now, in the present moment. So, Jung is as much here as is Greg Mogenson and Susan Rowland, and if one were to be radically in touch with the soul of one's words, one would have to acknowledge that in this imaginal space, Jung has not said his words, but *is saying* them. Elegiac writing, then, challenges the way in which traditional psychological writing falls into the realism of time when it quotes those authors who have died. Traditional psychological writing gives them no presence in the dialogue, and in that kind of writing the dead are dead, and we are no longer connected in any living way to the questions and issues that they have left behind. We work those questions and issues, but without their consent or participation. Those questions and issues have now become our property, an intellectual inheritance that has lost its animating spirit and its power to claim us and to give us a work that is a vocation.

In elegiac writing, a researcher dwells among the ruins because he or she knows that it is in the ruins that the living spirit of the work waits to be remembered. Indeed, no one is ever really dead until there is no one left to remember him or her, and there is perhaps no better representation of this final loss than an unkempt grave in an abandoned, weed-choked cemetery, an image not too far off the mark for much of the dust-covered psychological research that lies entombed in the libraries of the world. Elegiac writing, however, resurrects the dead and transforms them, as well as our relationship to them. We become their companions, the ones who continue the work they have left behind for us to redeem. Thus, elegiac writing has not only something of the quality of a lament to it as a writing that is responsive to what is lost and forgotten, left behind, or abandoned, but also a quality of impregnation and, hence, of celebration. In elegiac writing, in writing that writes down the soul, something that was lost is found again, and this makes the writing a kind of ode to joy for what is to be born.

Cultivating a Metaphoric Sensibility

Here is another poem by Wallace Stevens. It is called "The Motive for Metaphor." I will quote it first, and then do a riff on it, presented in italic type for a reason that will be made clear later.

You like it under the trees in autumn,
Because everything is half dead.
The wind moves like a cripple among the leaves
And repeats words without meaning.

In the same way, you were happy in spring,
With the half colors of quarter-things,
The slightly brighter sky, the melting clouds,
The single bird, the obscure moon—

The obscure moon lighting an obscure world
Of things that would never be quite expressed,
Where you yourself were not quite yourself
And did not want nor have to be,

Desiring the exhilarations of changes:
The motive for metaphor, shrinking from
The weight of primary noon,
The ABC of being,

The ruddy temper, the hammer
Of red and blue, the hard sound—
Steel against intimation—the sharp flash,
The vital, arrogant, fatal, dominant X.[6]

If we read the poem slowly and aloud, we begin to wonder who is being addressed in the first line, and indeed in the first word of the poem. Who is this "You" who likes it under the trees in autumn? Is it not all of us? Does not the poet speak on behalf of us all, or perhaps it is better to say on behalf of that part of us that shares this delight in spring? Is it the soul of the world that he is evoking, and through these epiphanies addressing all of us in those moments when we are brought home to some elemental and archetypal dimension of soul? If that is the case, then the motive for metaphor lies in those moments when soul in its autumnal season is neither alive nor dead, and in its springtime when it is filled, not with things that are complete in themselves, but things that are just a part of what they will or can be, quarter-things in their half colors, not yet ripe in their blossom, but which in their incompleteness and ambiguity hint at and suggest something else that seems to hover over there, just a bit farther off, elusive, and not quite within our grasp to say it, because we ourselves are not quite ourselves and perhaps do not want to be, like those times when we are awakened from a dream that for a moment has freed us from being who we have to be; and it lies in those moments beneath a sky that is neither bright nor dark, but slightly brighter, a comparison to some other sky that is absent and yet somehow hauntingly present in this adjectival allusion, a sky that harbors clouds that melt, clouds that are polymorphously perverse, like the soul itself, shifting and changing form and shape, and a moon, too, that offers a dark-light that shines on an obscure world, a world whose obscurity loves the play of shadow and light and shrinks from a too-bright light, "the weight of primary noon," of high noon, when there are no shadows through which matters become ambiguous and shaded, the high noon of the gunfight where differences are either/or affairs, the moment where there are no shades of gray, the moment when things are black or white, the moment for the bloodied temper, for the hammer blow, for the harsh and definitive word, that "hard sound" that strikes like steel against what is only intimated, the force of the dominant X—and what does he mean here?: is it the X that marks the exact spot of the hammer blow, or the X in the mathematical equations of the language of a science that has learned to plot the elusive, or is it somehow perhaps an oblique reference to the chromosomal X, the single, solitary X, that slice of split-off feminine potential, which paired with Y gives us that masculine form of domination, the language of science so different from the voice of soul? Is this the motive for metaphor: this shrinking away from the hammer blow of language, so direct, so forceful, so dominant against the subtle, barely whispered, indirect language of soul, a way of speaking that forgets the other half, the feminine, that it has left behind?

Another poet, John Keats, says, "Call the world if you Please, 'the vale of Soul-making.'"[7] The poem by Stevens situates the moment of soul-making in those seasons of the soul, its autumn and its spring. But what are these seasons? I am not talking of them in any literal way. I am not referring to the seasons of autumn and spring as they are marked on a calendar. "While you and i have lips and voices which/ are for kissing and to sing with/who cares if some oneeyed son of a bitch/invents an instrument to measure Spring with?" asks e. e. cummings. He replies: "the thing perhaps is/to eat flowers and not to be afraid."[8] Autumn and spring, these seasons of the soul, are qualities, activities, styles of being in and knowing the world, rhythmic tides of the soul, ways of engaging it through allusion and indirection, through comparisons that hint at an absence that is nevertheless present in what presents itself, an inclination towards things that are thresholds and borders, pivotal moments when things are both coming into being and passing away, like the natural seasons themselves where autumn minds the gap between the summer of the soul's high noon and its winter sleep, and spring holds in its smells and in the quality of its light and temperature the faintest memory of winter and the slightest hint of summer.

We need a psychology of the borders, of transitions and gaps, and a psychological language capable of writing down these moments, a seasonal writing, if you will—a writing that pivots, like spring does between winter and summer, and like autumn does between summer and winter; a writing for the springtime of the soul in the work, and for its autumnal shadows; a writing that takes place between the seasons of darkness and light; a writing that casts a dark-light, that darkens what is too light in the work and would thus be taken too lightly, and that lightens darkness where without some light we would lose our way, be swallowed in the night of the work. This is the motive for metaphor: to speak seasonally and in a pivotal way that is neither too dark nor too light. And this is the way of metaphor when one wants to write down the soul of the work in writing up its results and ideas— a writing that approximates those things that could never quite be fully expressed; a writing that intentionally leaves matters in some obscurity; a writing that postpones the dominant and fatal X of a fixed meaning; a writing that is tentative in its response to what asks to be spoken in the work.

Such writing is also a writing that takes place under the spell of Orpheus, for as the poet Mallarme says, "Orpheus is the sunset and the sunrise: those moments when the sun just touches the principle of darkness."[9] In this book, I have been making the case for an Orphic foundation for re-search that would keep these seasonal moments of soul in mind, these moments of dark-light that I mentioned in an earlier chapter, which have shadowed this book during its fifteen-year unfolding. The Jungian analyst Stan Marlan makes a powerful case for this shading process in his book, *The Black Sun: The Alchemy and Art of Darkness*. In this rich, evocative, even provocative book, he darkens Jungian psychology's preference for excessive light, and in this process, as one reviewer says, "Marlan practices the art of refusal elegantly with one hand while offering the embrace of generous inclusion with the other."[10]

This art of refusal is also the art of metaphor, which eschews the fixed meaning, the literal interpretation, the developmental line, or the fantasy of progression out of ambiguity into certainty. This art of metaphor is one that does not forget that while we do our psychologies and write our theories in the light, when we are awake, we do so in memory of the dream, which, if forgotten, becomes a writing that hammers our words into that dominant and fatal X position and gives to them their harsh sound, their arrogance. The wounded researcher who would write down the soul of the work is a threshold figure, one who crafts words between worlds, one who is at home with the obscure light that words bring to things and ideas, one who is at ease with the ways in which soul shadows and shades and qualifies the too-bright light of reason and mind.

As an art of refusal, metaphor nurtures a paradox about meaning that is also at the heart of the art of alchemy. David Miller highlights this paradoxical aspect of alchemy, its heart of dark-light, when he notes that for the alchemists the philosopher's stone, the goal of the alchemical opus, is "a stone that is not a stone."[11] How obscure that phrase sounds! Something is what it is because it is not what it is. How obscure this alchemy of the philosopher's stone is! And how like this art of alchemy, in its obscurity, is the motive for metaphor! An obscure moon lights an obscure world; things are not quite what they seem; the half-color of quarter-things is never quite expressed. This similarity between alchemy and metaphor makes the metaphor of alchemy instructive for the alchemy of metaphor. And I would suggest that the alchemy of metaphor makes writing down the soul an alchemical art.

But what is an *alchemical* art of writing? To answer this question, let me begin with another poem.

> We put thirty spokes together and call it a wheel;
> But it is on the space where there is nothing that the
>   utility of the wheel depends
> We turn clay to make a vessel;
> But it is on the space where there is nothing that the
>   utility of the vessel depends.
> We pierce doors and windows to make a house;
> And it is on these spaces where there is nothing that the
>   utility of the house depends.

> Therefore just as we take advantage of what is, we
> should recognize the utility of what is not.[12]

Recognizing the utility of the "is not"—that is what metaphor does! Just as the space in the wheel or the clay vessel or the house where there is nothing, *no*-thing, *is* the wheel, the vessel, or the house, so the stone of alchemy is "a stone that is *not* a stone." It is in and through the emptiness of these spaces that the wheel, vessel, or house come into being. Indeed, the poem says that the usefulness of these things is given in and through this open space. What "is not" gives presence to what "is." What is absent makes manifest what is present.

Metaphor works in that same tension between what *is* and what *is not*, between absence and presence. In *Mirror and Metaphor: Images and Stories of Psychological Life*, I used an historical example from the life of Winston Churchill, who, in reference to Mussolini, used the phrase "that utensil." The metaphor is clear and provocative. In the pithiest fashion, Churchill, a master of metaphor, describes who Mussolini is and the relationship between him and Hitler. "Mussolini is to Hitler as a tool is to its user."[13]

The metaphor does not establish an identity between "Mussolini" and "utensil." Nor does it suggest that there is a likeness between the two. Or, to be more precise, here the likeness exists because there is a difference. Like the alchemical stone that is not a stone, Mussolini is a utensil that is not a utensil. In both instances, the "is" is undone by the "is not." The metaphor works, we might say, precisely because it fails. It fails to establish a literal identification, an exchange in which one reality, utensil, can substitute for another, Mussolini. Like the metaphor in alchemy of the stone that is not a stone, the alchemy of metaphor unsays what it says. Each metaphorical figure negates what it affirms, but the negation is not a negative quality. On the contrary, the negation opens the imagination because it liberates it beyond the fixed and literal categories of the mind. *To write with soul in mind is to practice this form of liberating negation.* It is to write in a way that stretches the imagination towards what is left unsaid. To write down the soul, one has to cultivate that attitude that knows that what one says is and is not the case. One has to cultivate that sensibility that knows that what one says is true because it is not true. One has to write in such a way that meaning is made and unmade.

One of the key operations in alchemy is the *solutio*. Edinger notes that this operation "is one of the major procedures in alchemy," and indeed he quotes one source to the effect that "*Solutio* is the root of alchemy." In addition, he says, "In many places the whole opus is summarized by the phrase 'Dissolve and coagulate.'"[14] The phrase implies, of course, that what is dissolved has already been coagulated and after being dissolved will coagulate again. If we read this procedure as a reflection of the alchemist's understanding of how the soul of mind works, then what the procedure is telling us is that consciousness moves between the tension of holding on to its meanings and letting go of them. The *solutio* dissolves what has been coagulated, which gets fixed again, only to be dissolved yet again. The "is/is not" tension of metaphor is this alchemical cycle of coagulation and dissolution. The alchemy of metaphor lies in this tension between the "is" that coagulates a meaning and the "is not" that dissolves it. For a researcher who would write down the soul in writing up the work, this rhythm is essential if he or she is to avoid the work's coagulating into a fixed ideology. To write down the soul of one's work is to be an alchemist of meaning. The researcher as alchemist is one who attends to what is not said in what one has said.[15]

Let me give another example of this metaphoric tension in which meaning is presented and dissolved: Magritte's painting of a pipe. Considered by itself, the image of the pipe is not so extraordinary. It becomes extraordinary only when one notices the caption: "*Ceci n'est pas une pipe*" ("This is not a pipe"). The painting with the caption is a piece of alchemy. The viewer who looks at it is invited into an alchemical moment. The image in the painting *is* of a pipe, but the words say that this *is not* a pipe. The tension of the "is/is not" assaults the viewer. No, that word—"assault"—is too harsh. Better, I think, to say that the tension plays with the viewer's head. It unsettles the categories of his or her mind. The painting with the caption dissolves one's fixed, coagulated views of what a painting is, what a pipe is, and what the relation is between image and thing. The image of the pipe alludes to what a pipe is, which remains elusive. The painting is a visual metaphor that plays with possibilities. That such fooling around can be upsetting is attested to by the following example from everyday life.

The example comes from an exhibition entitled "Contemporary Korean Painting: 'The Alchemy of Daily Life'" at the art gallery in

Christchurch, New Zealand. Having left the garden in Christchurch where this work began again, I was strolling through the art gallery, doing what I often do—watching people looking at paintings—when I spotted an old man with a younger woman standing in front of an installation that presented a kitchen scene made of noodles. Everything in the kitchen was made of noodles—the chairs, the table, the walls, and the utensils. The woman who was with the old man began to describe the display to him. It was clear, however, that the man was somewhat deaf, and so she had to repeat her description several times, and each time with increasing volume. Each time, the old man would say, "What?" and shake his head, and she would launch into another description. "It is a kitchen chair made of noodles," she would report, and he would respond, "What?" Or, "It is a table made of noodles," and he would say again, "What?" After about five minutes of this little drama of everyday life, which for me increasingly became part of the work itself, part of the alchemy of daily life, the woman gave up. Her descriptions always failed to get some acknowledgement from the man that he understood. Always he said, "What?" But finally, after some moments of silence, the old man looked at the woman, then at the objects in the kitchen made of noodles, shook his head, turned away, and as he left uttered two more words: "Why? Strange."

Why, indeed? And yes, how strange! Moreover, writing down the soul of one's work could elicit the same question, "Why?" It could also seem as strange as a kitchen made of noodles. But if our language is to suit its object, if writing up one's research is to make a place for writing down the soul of the work, then the question and the feeling of strangeness need to be tolerated. If I am too literal-minded, then I will be intolerant. Like the old man, I would have to wonder, "Why?" and following the track of that question, I would finally dismiss the work. Noodles used to make kitchen chairs cannot be eaten, and pipes in paintings cannot be smoked. Both are just plain and simple and straightforward facts—a fantasy that is at play in much of psychology. On the other hand, if I am delusional, then I might fall into the net of what the metaphor says: the painting of the pipe is the pipe itself, and the chair made of noodles might be an appetizer. *Between literal-mindedness and delusion, metaphor makes its stand. Between literal-mindedness and delusion, the soul makes its speech.* Where literal-mindedness sides with the "is not" of metaphor and delusion with the "is," a metaphoric sensibility holds the tension of these opposites. And within this tension, the "is" of metaphor becomes an affirmation without becoming a positivism, and the "is not" a negation without becoming a negativism. What the metaphoric "is" affirms is not an identity that is fixed and final, but rather, an identity that is also a difference. The alchemical stone, like the pipe and the noodle kitchen, are invitations to wonder, and that is a goal of re-search that would write down the soul of the work. It is a goal that says in effect that the work that is finished is not done, that there is more to do because there is more to wonder about in the work.

One of my graduate students, Julie Sgarzi, whose dissertation, "In the Labyrinth of the Secret: A Meditation on the Nature of Secret in Psyche," was cited in the last chapter, discovered that with respect to writing down the soul, "[l]anguage that expresses the understanding and perspectives of soul must be free to wander, free to dream within phrases and juxtapositions of words." She goes on to say, "I found words more significant …, that is, this writing demanded greater care in selecting words with some understanding and acknowledgement of their etymologies and histories. Words took on different connotations in some uses and the way dreams played with words opened new possibilities for inquiry and shifted old modes of understanding."[16]

With a metaphoric sensibility, one's work is placed on a threshold where the work is and is not what it seems to be. The alchemist's stone, the painter's pipe, and the artist's noodle kitchen are not facts. One cannot use the stone of the alchemists to drive a nail into that place marked with an X any more than one could snack on the noodle kitchen in the noodle kitchen, or smoke Magritte's pipe. But neither are they ideas of the mind. The pipe that is not a pipe hangs over there on the wall in a gallery, and the noodle kitchen puzzles an old man. The alchemy of metaphor dissolves these coagulated categories of fact and idea, and, in this dissolution, liberates the image.

A metaphoric sensibility, then, is an invitation to regard one's work through the image(s) that animate it. Between the facts and the ideas one has about one's work, the wounded researcher who keeps soul in mind is always asking after the image(s) at work in the work as well as the image(s) of the one doing the work. The image in the metaphor is the gold, so to speak, that the alchemy of metaphor distills from fixed facts and ideas. For example, a student who was doing a dissertation on Jefferson Davis, the man who was the President of the Confederacy during the American Civil War, had gathered many facts and ideas about his subject. But in a conversation with me on one occasion, he told me that what drew him into the work was the image of Davis as the "Lincoln of the South." Here was an image of the work in the work, and, as such, it was a reality that challenged and dissolved his fixed idea about his subject. And it mirrored who the researcher imagined himself to be: one who would rescue the tarnished image of Jefferson Davis as a traitor. This was the piece of unfinished business that drew this student into this work of rescue.

Adopting a metaphoric sensibility towards one's work allows the researcher to remain open, curious, and inclined towards the "not yet" of the work that is held as a possibility in the "is not" of metaphor. The "is not" of metaphor is always a mystery, and the mystery of metaphor invites the wounded researcher to keep the mystery in the work alive, primarily by avoiding any premature closure of meaning, by allowing the work to dissolve itself when it has become too fixed. When the researcher becomes too identified with what he or she thinks the work is all about, an impasse often occurs, followed by an effort to willfully forge ahead. In such moments, what lies unsaid in the work, what is present as an absence, calls for its place. The "is not" pole of metaphor stretches the work beyond itself, leads it out of itself, e-ducates it into a different meaning. Indeed, I would even dare to say here that the tension between the "is" and "is not" of metaphor is the tension between the ego's intentions for the work and the soul of the work. In the "is not" of one's metaphorical writing is the path to writing down the soul of the work.

Jung is a seasonal writer. He is a pivotal writer who turns psychology back to soul, who returns psychology to soul, and if one wants an example of what has been said above, then he or she could do no better than to read Jung, especially through Rowland's book, *Jung as a Writer*. In her insightful book, she shows how Jung's dialectical psychology, a psychology whose tension of opposites is rooted in the Hegelian-like dialectic of thesis and antithesis, positions Jung as both enemy and heir of the rational categories of the Enlightenment.

Rowland is especially good on this point in her chapter on gender, in which she shows how the anima "represents the founding presence of Jungian psychology (as mouthpiece of the unconscious) as a founding absence."[17] If that is the case, and it is the case that Rowland makes throughout her book with persuasive clarity, then the intention to write down what is present as an absence, to write down the soul of one's work, must undo any language that would regard itself as certain about its meanings and complete in its expression. It would require a language that is deliberately provisional, a way of writing that is constantly aware of its tentative, evasive character. Such is the language of metaphor, which makes present an absence to which it alludes but which remains elusive.

"Jung's unconscious as collective, the inheritance of all humanity," Rowland writes, "is the originating concept that by its very definition undoes, makes provisional, puts under erasure, all other Jungian concepts." I should note here that in these remarks Rowland is contrasting Jung's view of the unconscious with that of Freud. She notes, "Unlike Freudian psychoanalysis, the unconscious is not only that which is produced by the splitting of the subject, it is additionally the pre-existent given." It is this pre-existent reality of the unconscious, its *sui generis* character, which, as we saw in Chapter 10, poses for the philosopher Paul Ricoeur the most significant challenge to the language of philosophical speculation and the work of hermeneutic interpretation. Referring to the Jungian unconscious, Rowland says, "That which is most fundamental, the unconscious, is also the most undermining of any fixed conceptual scheme."[18] The unconscious as a reality on its own terms is the alchemical retort in which the idealized fiction of meaning as fixed, certain, and complete is always dissolved.

In reply to the question I asked earlier about what an alchemical art of writing is, I have used the examples of poetry, art, and alchemy to suggest that it is a way of writing that is evasive about meaning, that dissolves meaning, and that honors in its words the absence that always haunts what is present. It is a way of writing that is provisional about meaning; that is seasonal and pivotal (as I described these terms above); that lives on the edge, as it were, between the high noon of summer reason and its bright light and the deep sleep of winter night; that pivots between the desire to know something completely and say it fully and the desire to keep the creativity of the soul in mind. It is writing that arises within the gap between what is and what is not, writing that does not define what is not but alludes to it and keeps it elusive.

All of these qualities characterize the metaphoric sensibility, in which the appeal of metaphor is through an image that it evokes, which is neither an empirical fact nor a rational idea. To say that Jefferson Davis is the Lincoln of the South is not to proclaim a fact. Nor is it just a mental idea. The metaphor presents an image between fact and idea, which invites a way of seeing that opens a world of possibilities that might become a work. Hence, I would argue that the alchemical art of writing inclines one through an image towards a vision of something. The art of alchemical writing is not, therefore, about convincing the reader through facts and ideas about some truth, but rather, of persuading him or her to see, through an image, some issue in a particular way, to look at it from a specific perspective.

In this respect, psychological writing, writing that makes a place for the unconscious, writing that keeps soul in mind, is a rhetorical art. This description applies as well to scientific psychology, because the unconscious is also present there. Scientific writing, too, is a rhetorical exercise, and when it disguises this fact, it becomes an ideology and an exercise in the assertion of power. The presentation of Robert Steele's reading of Mischel's text in Chapter 9 is an example of this point.[19] Apart from any aesthetic or stylistic concerns, therefore, it seems crucial to develop a metaphoric sensibility about one's psychological work.

Rowland offers a good example of the rhetorical power of the metaphoric image. In the Introduction to her book, she presents two quotations from Jung regarding the collective unconscious. In the first one, Jung asks his readers to consider the unconscious "as a collective human being … having at his command a human experience of one or two million years, practically immortal." In the second, he proposes, "The collective unconscious … seems to be not a person, but something like an unceasing stream or perhaps an ocean of images and figures which drift into consciousness in our dreams or in our abnormal states of mind."[20] The first statement is a metaphorical one, and the second is a simile, a kind of half-hearted metaphor. Neither of them is a statement of fact, but both are more than an idea. In each, there is an image through which one "sees" the collective unconscious. The collective unconscious is a two-million-year-old human being, and it is not that. The collective unconscious is (like) an ocean of images, and is not that either. The two ways of looking at the collective unconscious are not unlike the poet Wallace Stevens's thirteen ways of looking at a blackbird, which, as I indicated earlier, eschew defining what a blackbird is for the sake of persuading one to regard a blackbird from different perspectives.

Do we know the blackbird any less than we would with its scientific definition? No! But we know it differently. Commenting on those two quotations, Rowland rightly notes, "Readers new to Jung could be forgiven for finding such—essentially playing with metaphors—unhelpful." And, for the moment, taking the part of those who would find it unhelpful, she poignantly asks, "[W]hy tell stories of the collective unconscious instead of offering a neat definition?"[21] Well, psychology needs to supplement its rational language, which is "the voice of an ego that rejects the functioning of the unconscious," with a language that welcomes the unconscious.[22] Psychological writing needs to attend as much to the aesthetic, literary quality of its language as it does to its rational, scientific quality, and the cultivation of a metaphoric sensibility, with its use of "fulsome and luscious metaphors," is a way to do that. This last quotation, by the way, is instructive because it was spoken by one Samuel Parker, who, in 1670, in defense of the language of science practiced by the members of The Royal Society, proposed to the English Parliament an act that would forbid the use of metaphors. About this episode, I wrote: "In an age when the science of psychology seeks to purify itself of the psychological, language seeks to purify itself of the metaphorical."[23]

So, does the research psychologist who would write down the soul become a poet, or an alchemist, or an artist? No! That has not been my intention. Rather, he or she deliberately adopts a poetic form of discourse, which means that he or she makes an intentional and conscious use of metaphorical language and deliberately cultivates a metaphorical sensibility. Such a sensibility pays attention to the cemetery of dead metaphors (which already haunt our words) and attempts to resurrect them, much as Rowland does with those places in Jung's writing where the unconscious metaphorical rhetoric hides personal and cultural shadows. Such a sensibility also attends to how, when, and where one's ideas need the flexibility of a good metaphor; to how, when, and where one is making an argument too literal and falling into the trap of taking what is said as the truth rather than as an approximation of it, a perspective on it, an allusion to it that remains elusive. The psychologist who would keep soul in mind in his or her work, and who would write down the soul of the work, does not have the luxury of the scientist or the philosopher, who can believe in the certainty of his or her observations and speculations. The psychologist who would keep soul in mind is closer to the poet, even though he or she is not a poet. He or she is perhaps a "failed poet." Like the poet, the psychologist as "failed poet" is a maker of truths that are true for the moment, but, as Rilke says of such a poet, for the moment that is enough.[24]

Writing with soul in mind is a way of writing that, without actually writing poetry, keeps the aesthetic quality of language alive, that quality, which alongside the rational quality of language, stirs the depths of soul before it touches the surface of mind and which, like the art of alchemy, keeps stirring the work so that what would become coagulated dissolves. Keeping this in mind, I would conclude with a delicious quote about writing from the Jungian analyst Lyn Cowan: "To use a friend's expression," she says, "writing protects from a hardening of the categories."[25]

Giving Voice and Body to the Work

To present this fourth way of looking at writing down the soul, I have to ask the reader to go back to the italicized portion at the beginning of the previous section and immediately after the poem, "The Motives for Metaphor," by Wallace Stevens and re-read it, first silently, as he or she probably did the first time, and then aloud. I am trying to draw attention here to the importance of rhythm in psychological writing. The sentences are deliberately long to allow the reader to experience how reading silently can obscure the rhythm of the passage, and without the rhythm one can easily get lost. Reading silently, one can lose touch with the meaning of the passage. Reading aloud, the meaning seems to be carried with the rhythm.

I am not saying here that psychological writing should be composed of long sentences. What I am saying is that psychological writing needs to attend to the rhythm of language if it is to write down the soul. Psychological writing at its best is perhaps closest to music. I know for myself that when I have a good writing day, when it truly feels that I am writing down the soul of the work, I feel the words, sentences, and at times an entire paragraph before I have a sense of the meaning. I feel the rhythm of the language, its tempo, pace, its beat, before I have a sense of the writing. In such moments, I try to keep up with the flow, and I am more often than not surprised that when the words are written down they make sense. The meaning is there, carried not by me, but by the rhythm of the words.

Rhythm, then, is a primary feature of writing that writes down the soul, and this rhythm of the soul in writing differs from the rhythm of mind. Gaston Bachelard hints at this difference when he says, "I am not the same man when I am reading a book of ideas ... as when I am reading a poet's book ...."[26] The difference I am pointing to is not, however, restricted to the issue of whether psychology is a science or philosophy compared to an art, like that of poetry. That argument misses the point because psychology has elements of all these disciplinary styles and, whether acknowledged or not, it imports the cadences of these rhythms into its speech. "Language is an intervention into psychology," as Rowland remarks, "not a neutral medium for it."[27] As an intervention, the language that one uses in psychology shapes the tone of that psychology, and for this reason one needs to be conscious of the voice he or she wants to make a place for in the work. What voice wants to be heard in one's work is a question that a researcher who would keep soul in mind needs to ask.

Historically, however, psychological writing has had philosophical and scientific cadences to it, and has too often lacked the cadence and rhythms of the poetic. Greg Mogenson makes this same point with respect to the status of hysteria in the vision of the early founders of depth psychology. "Coming from the fields of medicine and science, they developed a rather loveless language for the love with which they worked—words such as object-cathexis, transference neurosis, psychic energy, and projection." Warming to his point, he goes on to say that "analytic writing can suffer from a lack of liberal flourish, imaginative execution, and narrative richness." And, lest one has failed to get his point, he asks, "... [I]s the 'borderline' patient, so ubiquitous in the literature today, an artifact of the analysts' own dull prose—a jilted form of hysteria, a disintegrated form of the muse?"[28]

To feel the rhythm of one's work, the researcher who would keep soul in mind should periodically read his or her work aloud. My own practice with this book has been to do just that as I begin each morning of writing. Before I begin writing, I read aloud what I wrote the previous day. Apart from the virtue of slowing down the thinking process by allowing thought to sink into the body, reading one's work aloud often leads to a re-writing of the work. This happens because in reading aloud one hears the thoughts and is even addressed by them. In such moments of being addressed by the words one has written in silence, one begins to get a sense that this or that passage does not feel right. It might make logical sense. It might have meaning, but the feel of the passage is off. When this happens in my own morning ritual, I re-write because I trust the cadence of the work as much as I trust its logic to carry the meaning. Indeed, if truth be told, I have come to believe that in writing down the soul, meaning is a matter of rhythm. The soul of a work is carried by the rhythm of the words, in the way they hurry past each other or linger for a pause. My friend and colleague Joseph Coppin, with his co-author Elizabeth Nelson, speaks to this point of rhythm. In their fine book, *The Art of Inquiry*, they bring a depth perspective to the work of research. "Methods," they write, "must simply learn to move, even dance, if they are to follow the psyche."[29] Words, too, must learn to dance if they are to follow the soul of the work. Describing some of the dance steps, Coppin and Nelson are eloquent in their presentation of the dialectical rhythm of the soul. Careful to point out that dialectics is about a circumambulating exchange of ideas, a rhythm that flows between and among and around one's thoughts, a movement that keeps thinking from becoming too fixed and sclerotic, they arrive at the same conclusion that has animated this work from its beginnings long ago. Depth psychology, they say, "is a *psychology of the gap*."[30] It may, therefore, very well be the case that in reading one's work aloud, one hears from the gap what has been left unsaid in what one has thought and said. Perhaps, reading one's work aloud is similar to Orpheus's lyre-playing, singing descent into the underworld, where he learns what he does not yet know.

Perhaps the best test of whether or not a piece of psychological writing dances in step with the soul is how it feels when it is read aloud. Indeed, can it be read aloud, or does the work, like many psychological texts, not lend itself to the voice? Does it have a liberal flourish to it? Does it flow? Does it take you as the reader up in its tempo and move you, and, like a piece of music, lead you into its dance? Does it resonate with your body and not just make sense to your mind?

Of course, not all psychological writing has to be capable of being read aloud, and, indeed, writing that keeps soul in mind also has to be mindful of its words. Heart and head both have a place in psychological writing. I cannot, for example, sustain the rhetorical flourish of the italicized passage above, nor would I do that, even if I could. But there are moments when the soul of the work does take over from the author and ask to sing, and in those moments the rhythm of the work is different. Perhaps all psychology books should be read aloud to test if the soul is at all alive in the words, and those that fail the test should perhaps come with a warning not unlike the warning from the Surgeon General on cigarette packages: "Warning: Reading this book can be harmful for the health of the soul."

Giving voice to the work naturally drags the body into the work of writing. The researcher who would write down the soul of the work *thinks* while he or she is *sitting*, and the *cogito* of the writer is inseparable from the warm breeze that blows in from the open window and touches the skin. Reflecting on his own process of writing his major work, *The Phenomenology of Perception*, which is a sustained apology for the body, Merleau-Ponty makes the same point. "I am thinking of the Cartesian *cogito*, wanting to finish this work," he writes, "feeling the coolness of the paper under my hand, and perceiving the trees of the boulevard through the window."[31] A ghost does not write down the soul of the work. A being of flesh and blood does, and if the ancestors who gather around one's writing table and who carry the unfinished business of the soul of the work want our blood, then this is what writing down the soul of the work costs, and this is what we give.

James Hillman captures this cost of psychological writing in the opening remarks to his now classic work, *Re-visioning Psychology*. He tells us that while he was working on the initial draft of the chapters in that book, he had near his writing table a sentence from Ortega Y Gasset: "Why write, if this too easy activity of pushing a pen across paper is not given a certain bull-fighting risk and we do not approach dangerous, agile, and two-horned topics?"[32] Throughout his long career, Hillman has been such a bullfighter. He has approached two-horned topics that are agile and evasive, dangerous and unsettling. Such is the way of working with words in the arena of soul. One gets bloodied quite often, and there is no way around the fact that the ink on the page "is" the blood that flows through one's veins.[33] Writing down the soul is a bullfight, and if on occasion it produces bullshit, then so be it, because writing without soul in mind produces its own kind of shit. Better, I think, if one wants to write down the soul in writing up one's work, the shit that comes from below than the shit that comes from above. In any case, the researcher/writer who makes a place for soul in the work gets into a scrap where the soul of the work leaves its marks upon the flesh and takes its bloody, bodily toll.

Gloria Anzaldua makes this point in a vivid and provocative way:

> Writing is my whole life, it is my obsession. This vampire which is my talent does not suffer other suitors. Daily I court it, offer my neck to its teeth. This is the sacrifice that the act of creation requires, a blood sacrifice. For only through the body, through the pulling of flesh, can the human soul be transformed. And for images, words, stories to have this transformative power, they must arise from the human body—flesh and bone—and from the Earth's body—stone, sky, liquid, soil.[34]

Writing down the soul of the work requires one to open up the window of the mind. In giving voice and body to the work, one has to let the words breathe and be in touch with the world outside, with the Earth's body. One has to let the words of psychology echo the tumultuous cries of the arena where one takes on one's topic. One has to let the writing be animated, risky, even unreasonable at times, and perhaps even on occasion touched with a bit of rhetorical flourish that borders on excess and maybe even madness.[35]

TAKING LEAVE OF THIS CHAPTER

Speaking of Jung, Rowland writes, "The ability of anyone, including himself, to produce a comprehensive science of the psyche, even to describe psychic processes accurately in words, comes second to the innate property of the human mind to be mysterious." Given this inclination towards the creative character of the human mind, the question naturally arises concerning the ability of psychological language to keep soul in mind when writing down the soul. This has been the issue not only in this chapter but also throughout this book. If one starts from the place of being a wounded researcher who wants to take into account the destabilizing influence of the complex and creative unconscious in his or her work, then that researcher has to acknowledge that all psychological writing about soul succeeds because it fails. To quote again from Rowland, Jung's writing "is an attempt to evoke in writing what cannot be entirely grasped: the fleeting momentary presence of something that forever mutates and reaches beyond the ego's inadequate understanding."[36] Writing down the soul is as difficult as writing down the greening-green of the world.

CHAPTER THIRTEEN

——————————————

Towards an Ethical Epistemology

> ... [T]he old ethic ... an ethic of the conscious attitude ... is
> typified by the text from St. Augustine in which the saint thanks
> God that he is not responsible to him for his dreams.[1]
> —Erich Neumann

PRELUDE BEFORE THE INTRODUCTION

The sixth morning, as I sat at my desk trying to begin this chapter again, I was overwhelmed with anxiety. On this particular day, I had abandoned my usual routine of dedicating the day to the ancestors. In this ritual time and space, I asked only that I might be made capable to carry on the work that had been given to me and to understand how it might be in service to the unfinished business in their lives. But I was feeling pressured again about deadlines, more self-imposed than objective, as I had felt with the previous chapter and on many occasions throughout the writing of this book. I had already written two introductions, and while the second one felt better than the first—cleaner in its lines and clearer about what I wanted to say in this chapter—the anxiety was keeping me from continuing with that second effort. Who was this anxious one at the desk on that particular morning? Who was feeling the anxiety of self-imposed deadlines? If I was to be true to the vocation of this work, if I was to do this piece of research on re-search that would keep soul in mind, how could I avoid or dismiss these questions?

So I waited on this particular morning. I sank into the feeling, let myself be in it, and doing so, I realized that the anxiety I was feeling in relation to the pressure of a self-imposed deadline was the same feeling I had had in a dream the night before. In that dream, I was in a college setting, waiting to take an exam, and I realized that I did not have the right pencil and/or marker to fill in the blanks on the exam. I tried to get the attention of the proctor, a self-composed woman of middle-age, but she paid no attention to me. Then I saw that all the other people in the room had already started the exam, and I realized I was holding a practice copy of it and that I did not have the correct one. Now, I was feeling very anxious and I was acutely aware of time. Twenty minutes of a two-hour exam had already passed. Unable to attract the attention of the proctor again, I approached her at her desk. But now she was engaged with a younger woman, who was asking her help in locating a place to do her laundry. They were casual in their conversation, as if they were two women enjoying a chat, and they were completely indifferent to my attempts to get the proctor's attention.

I knew that the dream was related to the anxiety about time and deadlines that I was having about the book, but I was still unsure of what to do with it. I was sure, however, that I had to take notice of it. Jung asserts, "The images of the unconscious place a great responsibility upon a man" and "[i]nsight into them must be converted into an ethical obligation."[2] The old ethic described above in relation to St. Augustine does not hold here. If we are to take into account the unconscious in our lives and work, then we have a responsibility in relation to our dreams. This ethical obligation to allow the dream to transform who one is and how one goes about one's life is particularly relevant to the wounded researcher who would keep soul in mind and who would make a place for the dream in the alchemical hermeneutic method. Indeed, not to attend to the dream would be particularly unethical in this context.

Staying with the dream, I moved with it into my morning ritual space and later in the day worked on it in analysis. The subjective and objective levels of the dream became increasingly clear, and, as a result, I am writing this prelude before the introduction. Indeed, this prelude wants to be written, for as the dream images of the proctor and the woman who wants to wash her clothes (both of whom are indifferent to my anxious concerns about time and deadlines) indicate, the anima of the work will not be rushed by my anxious concerns. In the dream space, I do not have the right tools to write the exam, and in the space of my study, I do not have the right words to write this chapter. But hurrying on does not work either, in the dream or in the study, and it is the anima of the work who offers the solution. She will take no notice of the one who would force his will upon the situation and hurry it along. She will be indifferent to self-imposed deadlines and their generative anxieties. Like the washer-women in one of the plates from the alchemical text *Splendor Solis*,[3] she will attend to her cyclical practice of washing the clothes, of ridding them of their impurities, even as the work has to be cleansed of too much ego willfulness. The dream drags the work back into the underworld of the unconscious, where the anima of the work, in the guise of the proctor and the woman who wants to do her laundry, poses the Eurydician question, "*Who?*" In their indifference to my anxious concern about getting started— with the dream exam and with this chapter—they ask, in effect, who is this one who would impose his will upon the work? As I sat at my desk that morning with my anxiety over time and deadlines, the anima of the work did not know who I was and refused to give me the right tools with which to write the work.

In writing this prelude, I am making a place for the dream in the work, which is what an alchemical hermeneutic method does, as described in Chapter 11. But as I said in that chapter, the dream is not the content of the research any more than the dream reported here is the content of this chapter. The dream in research is a way of doing research, a path that can be followed, part of a method that would keep soul in mind, and, as a prelude to this chapter, the dream is a direct expression of the fact that this chapter is being written between me and the anima of the work, as in fact the book all along has been written and rewritten in this gap between what I want of the work and know about it and what the soul of the work wants and knows. In writing about re-search that would keep soul in mind, I certainly have to be the researcher who keeps soul in mind, the researcher who, in writing down the soul of this work in writing it up, writes within that space of collaboration, where I and the anima are in a con-spiracy. Out of this space, where the anima of the work and I breathe together, the chapter can now begin again.

INTRODUCTION

> ... [T]he old ethic is a partial ethic ... it fails to take into
> consideration or to evaluate the tendencies and effects of the
> unconscious. ... Within the life of the community, this takes
> the shape of the psychology of the scapegoat; in international
> relations it appears in the form of those epidemic outbreaks of
> atavistic mass reactions known as war.[4]

In the bodies of knowledge we create, our failure to take into
account the presence of the unconscious takes the shape of our
epistemologies, becoming one-sided, fixed truths and ideological
exercises of power. One has only to look at the multiple splitting that
has plagued the history and development of depth psychology to see
how differences with the other, without proper consideration of the
other in oneself, lead to animosity toward and the demonizing of the
other. Or, one has only to consider how the ethos of Western science,
despite its great achievements, has cast a huge shadow of destruction
over human life and the environment. We live today not only in the
shadow of the bomb, but also in the deepening darkness of
environmental collapse as the polar icecaps continue to melt, the seas
and oceans become increasingly polluted, and the buildup of carbon-
based greenhouse gases reaches ever higher levels. All the bodies of
knowledge we create, like the bodies of those who create them, cast
a shadow. To come to terms with the shadow side of our ways of
knowing and constructing the world, an ethical epistemology would
have to make a place for the unconscious in our ways of knowing
the world.

The Wounded Researcher does just that. An ethical epistemology is
one of the implications of the imaginal approach to research,
particularly its process of transference dialogues, in which the
researcher confronts the other in himself or herself and the others in
the work. Indeed, as I look back on the course of this book and recall
all its variations, I realize now that in one respect this book is and has
always been a book about the ethical responsibility we have to come
to terms as best we can with the shadow in our ways of knowing.

A Fable Inspired by a Poem

"Thirteen Ways of Looking at a Blackbird"

I

Among twenty snowy mountains,
The only moving thing
Was the eye of the blackbird.

II

I was of three minds,
Like a tree
In which there are three blackbirds.

III

The blackbird whirled in the autumn winds.
It was a small part of the pantomime.

IV

A man and a woman
Are one.
A man and a woman and a blackbird
Are one.

V

I do not know which to prefer,
The beauty of inflections
Or the beauty of innuendoes,
The blackbird whistling
Or just after.

VI

Icicles filled the long window
With barbaric glass.
The shadow of the blackbird
Crossed it, to and fro.
The mood
Traced in the shadow
An indecipherable cause.

VII

O thin men of Haddam,
Why do you imagine golden birds?
Do you not see how the blackbird

Walks around the feet
Of the women about you?

VIII
I know noble accents
And lucid inescapable rhythms;
But I know, too,
That the blackbird is involved
In what I know.

IX
When the blackbird flew out of sight,
It marked the edge
Of one of many circles.

X
At the sight of blackbirds
Flying in a green light,
Even the bawds of euphony
Would cry out sharply.

XI
He rode over Connecticut
In a glass coach.
Once, a fear pierced him,
In that he mistook
The shadow of his equipage
For blackbirds.

XII
The river is moving.
The blackbird must be flying.

XIII
It was evening all afternoon.
It was snowing
And it was going to snow.
The blackbird sat
In the cedar-limbs.[5]

For the fable inspired by this poem, imagine a convention of
ornithologists. Thirteen of them, each an expert on blackbirds, have
come together for the purpose of defining what a blackbird is, and
each has said his or her piece. After they have finished, there is the

silence before the storm. Then it hits, because each knows that what he or she has said is the truth. For one, the blackbird is the bird that sits in the cedar-limbs when it is snowing and it is going to snow. For another, the blackbird is the eye that is the only moving thing among twenty snowy mountains. And on it goes. But, they are all reasonable men and women, and, for the sake of civility, they agree to disagree. At least on the surface, then, there is tranquility, born of polite gestures, which masks, however, a darker feeling. For each departs the convention, honorarium in hand, still convinced that all the others are in error, if not fools. On the trip home, articles are planned in which each will show the fault that lies in the others, who border on becoming the enemy. That night, however, each has a dream, and it is the same dream for each of them. In this dream, an old man with white hair is standing in the hallway of the convention center, which they have just left. He is the janitor, the one charged with cleaning up the mess made by the experts. In his pocket he has a book by Carl Jung. The old man looks sad and is shaking his head. He pulls the book from his pocket and lets it open to a page, from which he reads the following passage:

> The present day shows with appalling clarity how little able people are to let the other man's argument count, although this capacity is a fundamental and indispensable condition for any human community. Everyone who proposes to come to terms with himself must reckon with this basic problem. For, to the degree that he does not admit the validity of the other person, he denies the 'other' within himself the right to exist—and vice versa. The capacity for inner dialogue is a touchstone for outer objectivity.[6]

Does he know what the passage means? He thinks he does, but he wonders about the experts. The fable ends here with this question. Upon awakening, will each of them remember the dream?

A Few Reflections

In various places throughout this text I have spoken about a metaphoric sensibility as a quality of consciousness necessary to keep soul in mind, and indeed in the last chapter I described how a metaphoric sensibility is one way of looking at writing down the soul. The fable inspired by Stevens's poem describes two moments that comprise this sensibility, each of which is essential to an ethical way of knowing.

The first moment is one that acknowledges that to appreciate oneself as an *other*, it is necessary to be in dialogue with an other. The other in this context reflects back to oneself that one is a perspective, a point of view. The other sees things differently, from another perspective, and with this recognition the other challenges who one is and how one imagines the world. With this challenge, then, one might become curious, and, becoming curious, might consider that dialogue with the other is necessary if one is to broaden one's consciousness. So, the ornithologist who knows that the blackbird that whirls in the autumn winds is a small part of the pantomime might find himself curious about and drawn to the woman who knows that a man and a woman and a blackbird are one. They may begin to talk, but if the conversation is to be truly transformative for each, if each is to see his or her view as a perspective among others, then each has to be able to listen. In other words, the dialogue that a metaphoric sensibility invites begins in the ear and not on the tongue. It is a sensibility that is steeped in the art of listening.

This capacity to listen is the second moment of a metaphoric sensibility. This capacity to listen is a disposition in which the words that the other speaks enter the ear and sink down to the heart before they rise to the brain. What I am suggesting here is that the capacity to listen is hard work because it is heart work. The capacity to listen requires a change of heart, and this change of heart involves an emotional aspect in one's confrontation with the other. The other whose different perspective challenges one's certitude by transforming it into a perspective presents an emotional challenge. As such, the other's perspective speaks to the other within oneself, and when that other within is unconscious, when it lives in one's life as a shadow, this emotional challenge is more often than not more than one wishes to hear.

In the Afterword to the updated version of her book *Invisible Guests*, Mary Watkins cites the work of Paulo Freire, the Brazilian-born educator, whose work consistently emphasizes the need for a pedagogy that liberates the individual from systems of oppression in which monologues of power only enforce obedient silence. Following on this point, I wrote in the Preface to her book the following:

> In Freire's work we learn that the ethics of dialogue requires more
> than the multiplication of voices in the conversation. Such
> multiplication results only in an overload of information. Beyond
> it, what is required is that the one who speaks recognizes and
> acknowledges the contexts, with their unarticulated assumptions
> and values, of his or her words and thoughts. The presence of
> the other is always an occasion for this act of critical self-regard.
> In Freire's terms, the other, whether it be a dream figure, or the
> homeless person on the street, or the caged animal is always the
> possibility of rupture, that moment of breakdown, when critical
> self-regard can become a breakthrough for the appeal of the other
> to be heard.[7]

Emotional deafness, however, is a real block to the development
of critical self-regard and to the cultivation of a metaphoric sensibility.
But without this cultivation, the dialogue with an other that is
necessary is not possible. A metaphoric sensibility may open one to
the necessity of dialogue with an other, but it is the inner work with
one's shadow other that makes the dialogue possible. This is why Jung
appears in the fable as the dream of the ornithologists. To the degree
that one does not admit the validity of the "other" within oneself, he
or she denies the other person the right to exist. This is the vice versa
of Jung's quote spelled out, and it is spelled out because it is essential
to understand the coupling between the other out there and the "other"
within. Just as this coupling is, as Jung notes, necessary for objectivity,
it is also necessary for any ethical epistemology.

RE-SEARCH AS AN ETHICAL RESPONSIBILITY

In traditional forms of research, we have, as we should have, an
ethical responsibility toward our subjects. This ethical obligation also
applies to the imaginal approach to research. The range of this
responsibility, however, is extended in re-search that would keep soul
in mind. It is extended vertically so that the researcher is ethically
obligated to consider the other(s) within himself or herself who
constitute his or her unconscious complex presence to the work. The
researcher is also ethically obligated to make a place for the strangers
in the work, those others who carry the unfinished business in the
soul of the work. The ancestors for whom the work is done, that great
extended family who line the corridors of history, as Jung speaks of

them, gather around the writing table, their questions waiting to be heard. We owe them our attention if we are to keep the soul of the work in mind. We have an ethical responsibility to lend them an ear. For re-search with soul in mind, the ethical responsibility we have towards our subjects extends to the ethical responsibility we have towards the work.

The transference dialogues, which are the core of the research process in an imaginal approach, are in service to this ethical command. Precisely because a researcher is a wounded researcher, he or she is obliged to commit himself or herself to the task of accepting responsibility for the shadow she or he casts upon the work, as well as to attend to the unfinished business in the soul of the work. In Chapter 6, I gave some examples from my graduate students who described the dialogues in this fashion. Recall how Kay Tomlinson, for example, described her deep feeling of responsibility to those others who appeared in the imaginal space of her dialogues. Unable to dismiss their presence as unreal, she felt as much of an obligation to attend to them, she said, as she did to the others in her "sticks and stones world." Jo Todd, Ellen MacFarland, and Kerry Ragain are some other examples from that chapter.

The point that I am making here is that once we admit the reality of the unconscious—and there is too much evidence to deny it—an ethical epistemology must take into account this deep subjectivity of the researcher. Jung makes this point quite forcefully:

> With the discovery of a possible unconscious psychic realm, man had the opportunity to embark upon a great adventure of the spirit, and one might have expected that a passionate interest would be turned in this direction. Not only was this not the case at all, but there arose on all sides an outcry against such an hypothesis. Nobody drew the conclusion that if the subject of knowledge, the psyche, were in fact a veiled form of existence not immediately accessible to consciousness, then all our knowledge must be incomplete, and moreover to a degree that we cannot determine. The validity of our conscious knowledge was questioned in an altogether different and more menacing way than it had ever been by the critical procedures of epistemology.[8]

It is not, however, difficult to understand the reason for this resistance. Without exception, every one of my graduate students felt some degree of anxiety over the transference dialogues. Indeed, one of my students, who has now entered Jungian analytic training, said to me that I should put a warning label on this work indicating that it can be dangerous to one's health. The process of transference dialogues can be a most dangerous one, and it serves no purpose to deny this fact. But weighed against the damage that the shadows in our epistemologies cause, the risk seems justified.

Regarding the anxiety that this process fosters, I want to point out that John Beebe views the experience of anxiety as "[a] proper starting point for the discovery of integrity." In his fine book *Integrity in Depth*, he says, "Only recently have I begun to realize that this experiencing and examining of anxiety is an ethical process in which, as the French philosopher Emmanuel Levinas says, 'one's infinite obligation to the other is expressed.'" Continuing along these lines, Beebe adds, "With the discovery of the scope of the shadow ... our questioning of ourselves has taken on a dimension of depth and urgency ...," so much so in fact that for Levinas "ethics as first philosophy" is now the way in which being justifies itself. In other words, with the discovery of the reality of the unconscious, ethics "has become the primary issue of philosophy."[9] If that is so, and I agree with Beebe that it is, then ethics has also become the primary issue at the root of our epistemologies, for the ways in which we construct the world are the ways in which we encounter and marginalize ourselves and others.

That Beebe finds support for his views about integrity in depth in Levinas is important, because in his major work, *Totality and Infinity*, Levinas brings the issue of our ethical obligation to the other right down to the face. "The epiphany of the face," he says, "is ethical."[10] The other, whether he or she or it be an imaginal presence or a presence in the world of sticks and stones, is an appeal, and in that naked appeal, the other calls me to be ethical. The other calls me to accept responsibility for the deep and hidden subjectivity that I am. The work as an *other* makes the same demand for a wounded researcher.

AMOR FATI

I am aware of how much has been written regarding ethics in relation to the unconscious. My purpose in this closing chapter was not, however, to write another text on this complex issue. It was and is more modest. It has been simply to show that an imaginal approach to research with its process of transference dialogues and the alchemical hermeneutic method has implications for an ethical epistemology. As I come to this closing, I realize that ethics in relation to the unconscious is, as the philosopher John Riker says, not about taking responsibility but about accepting responsibility. The latter in contrast to the former "means that one chooses to be responsible for who one is, knowing that in large part one has been fated to be this way."[11]

For re-search with soul in mind, to accept responsibility means that the researcher acknowledges the work that has been made, knowing fully that the work that has been made was not fully of his or her making. Facing the work, one accepts that one has been called into the work through one's complexes for the sake of becoming the agent of the work itself, accepting its imperfections and incompleteness, and, resting in that place, one knows that to the best of his or her abilities, one has been faithful to the dialogue with the others for whom the work has been done. The ethical question for the researcher who would keep soul in mind, the first ethical question, then, is whether he or she has been faithful to the call of the work, to what those others who carry the soul of the work have asked. Thus, *amor fati*! In the end, one has no other choice and no other obligation but to love the fate that one has been given. Thus, the work of thinking becomes a work of thanksgiving, and in this place of thanksgiving, what happens to the work not only no longer matters, but also is beyond one's concern. One has done what one has been asked to do, and there is nothing else to be done.

This book, which in one way began with the dream of the poet on the threshold between the world of academia and the street of life, ends with a ritual. As I prepared to write this closing passage, I knew that before I did so I had to enter that sacred space between me and the ancestors who have guided this work throughout its many beginnings. I owe them my thanks, and in preparing to close this book I asked them to gather with me around the table to witness this parting of the ways. Never before have I been so conscious of the ending of a book, and never before so moved by the realization of how deep my debt is to all those others for whom this work has been done.

Letting Go of the Work

Whoever you are: some evening take a step
out of your house, which you know so well.
Enormous space is near, your house lies where it begins,
whoever you are.
Your eyes find it hard to tear themselves
from the sloping threshold, but with your eyes,
slowly, slowly, lift one black tree
up, so it stands against the sky: skinny, alone.
With that you have made the world. The world is immense
and like a word that is still growing in the silence.
In the same moment that your will grasps it,
your eyes, feeling its subtlety, will leave it .... [1]

In light of this Epilogue, the Prologue may be read again. We fall into the soul of the work, and we find our way out—sometimes! Now, at least for the moment, the work is finished, but it is not done.

Appendix

September 13, 2006

Dear—,

I am writing to you to ask for your help with my book, *The Wounded Researcher,* which is scheduled to be published in the Fall of 2007. As you may recall, the imaginal approach to research is characterized by several innovations to a research process that would keep soul in mind. Your dissertation, which was directed either by Veronica Goodchild or me, has contributed to this work. Indeed, without the good work of your dissertations the imaginal approach is only a theory.

Below I have listed the key areas in which I am asking for your help. I know this will take some of your time, but you will be marking the trail you have taken for other students to follow. With your help I will be able to complete this project, which I have been working on these past 15 years.

I have listed the format for this request below.

For your efforts, I will send you a copy of the book when it is published, and, of course, I will cite your name in the text where I use your contributions.

I do hope you will be able to respond to my request and that in doing so you will find that it re-animates your work. From the response of students at Pacifica and of colleagues in other institutions and professional organizations, I believe that this work that we have been doing is important. It goes without saying that you have my sincere thanks for your help.

With my best wishes,

Robert

Format

Please reply to those items that figured in your study and please be as specific as you can in you replies.

I. Your Name

II. Title of your Dissertation and Date Completed

III. The Vocational Aspect

A. My Brief Description

From the soul's point of view, knowing something begins with being addressed. Depth psychology begins with the dream, and in general what it calls the unconscious is the "other" that challenges us and calls us into life, love, and work. Research with soul in mind is a complex vocation. The topic chooses you as much as, and perhaps even more than, you believe you choose it. What begins as an interest has its tangled roots in a complex, where some piece of unfinished business asks to be spoken. That unfinished business might be a wound in your own life, a generational legacy within the family complex, and/or a cultural-historical issue that claims you as its spokesperson.

B. Questions to You

1. What piece of unfinished business drew you into your work? A personal wound or trauma, a generational complex, a cultural-historical issue, and/or some combination of these?

2. Beyond your conscious interests, intentions, and plans about the work, how did you become aware of the unconscious vocational claim of the work? Was it through dreams, symptoms, the transference dialogues, conversations with someone such as your advisor or faculty person, or in some other way?

3. How did becoming more conscious of the vocational aspect of your work change the way you did the work? Was it helpful to make this discovery? Did it hinder your work, and if so how?

4. Attending to the complex vocational character of your work, did you feel that your work was in service to something or someone other than yourself? If so, could you describe that feeling?

5. Is there anything else that you would cite in regard to this vocational aspect of the work?

IV. The Transference Dialogues

A. My Brief Description

When one does research that keeps soul in mind, it is necessary to differentiate the researcher's complex unconscious presence to the work from the work itself. There is in this regard a transference relation between the researcher and his/her topic, and in the ritual space of the transference, the complex researcher is invited to differentiate what belongs to him/her in the work from what belongs to the "other" in the work, the stranger in the work by whom the researcher is addressed. In the ritual space of the transference, the researcher is addressed by the soul of the work, by the unfinished business at the heart of the work.

Over the years I have worked out four levels of this transference field in which the researcher who would keep soul in mind is questioned by the soul of the work. At each of these levels, the researcher begins with an invitation to be addressed. The purpose of these ritual dialogues is for the ego to let go of the work so that the soul of the work may speak. These four levels are as follows:

- **Personal**: Is there anyone from my family, my history, my biography who has something to say about this work?

- **Cultural-Historical**: Is there anyone from another gender, race, class, culture, and/or different historical time who has something to say about the work?

- **Collective-Archetypal**: Who are the guides of this work? For whom is this work being done?

- **Eco-Cosmological**: Is there anyone among the other creatures with whom I share this planet who has something to say about this work? Do the trees, animals, etc. have something to say?

Of course, these questions are only suggestions, and I have encouraged students to find their own ways into these dialogues, which are modeled on Jung's idea of active imagination. You might have used this procedure in your own way, and that is what I am asking you to describe.

B. Questions to You

1. Describe in general terms how you did these dialogues, how they changed your work, and how they changed you (if they did). At the end of the work how was the work different from what you initially imagined and how were you different?

2. In general terms, describe the value of these dialogues. Were some of the levels more valuable than others?

3. In general terms, describe the limits of these dialogues?

4. In specific terms, describe your resistances to these dialogues. What was the source of these resistances? How did you work with them?

5. In specific terms, describe how these dialogues helped you get in touch with your own unconscious complex presence to the work, with the personal, generational, and perhaps cultural-historical wounds that called you into the work and which, without these dialogues, might have been unconsciously informing and influencing your ideas and perceptions about your work.

6. In specific terms, describe how these dialogues helped you to get in touch with the soul of the work beyond your own personal complex relation to it, with the unfinished business of the work itself?

7. Is there one particularly specific and dramatic piece of dialogue that illustrates this process and shows its impact on the work?

8. Is there anything that you would add to these questions from your own experience of this process? Do you have any suggestions for refining this process?

V. Alchemical Hermeneutic Method

A. My Brief Description

Although the vocational aspect and the transference dialogues are applicable to all methods, over time a specific method in relation to an imaginal approach has arisen. It is a variation of hermeneutics called *alchemical hermeneutics*. Hermeneutics, in general, acknowledges the co-creation of meaning between a researcher and a text, who are related within a hermeneutic circle. Alchemical hermeneutics deepens that circle into a spiral and thus makes a place not only for the researcher's reasonable and more-or-less conscious assumptions about the work, but also for the researcher's dreams, symptoms, feelings, intuitions, and synchronicities in relation to the work. Like the alchemists of old were changed by their work, the researcher who uses this method knows the work not at a distance, but as one who has embodied the work. In alchemical hermeneutics, one becomes the work; one knows the work to the degree that one has let oneself become known by it.

B. Questions to You

1. How did dreams, symptoms, etc. fit into your study? Can you give a specific example?

2. How would you justify the inclusion of the non-rational elements in the research process?

3. How were you as the researcher changed by the inclusion of these elements?

VI. *Writing Down the Soul*

A. My Brief Description

Going into the depths of the work when one keeps soul in mind raises a challenge about how one then writes down the soul of the work in writing up one's work.

B. Questions to You

1. Did this imaginal approach to research change the way you felt you had to write down your work? Can you say how? Was there, for example, a felt need to be more expansive and perhaps passionate, and less controlled?

2. How would you describe your writing style within an imaginal approach that keeps soul in mind? What adjectives might best describe it? Can you give some examples? Was there, for example, a pull towards the way in which metaphor leaves things elusive rather than defined?

3. Did this challenge impact the way you think about the issue of language and the soul? If so, how?

Notes

PROLOGUE

1. Virgil, *The Aeneid*, Book 6, ll. 126-129, in *Ecologues, Georgics, Aeneid I-VI*, trans. H. R. Fairclough (Cambridge: Harvard University Press, 1916/1999), pp. 540-541.

INTRODUCTION: TOWARDS A POETICS OF THE RESEARCH PROCESS

1. Greg Mogenson, "The Afterlife of the Image," *Spring 71* (Fall 2004): 110, n. 31.
2. T. S. Eliot, "East Coker," *Four Quartets* (New York: Harcourt Brace, 1943/1971), p. 30, ll. 174-78.
3. *Ibid.*, ll. 186-187.
4. John Keats, "Ode to a Nightingale," in *John Keats: The Complete Poems*, ed. John Barnard (New York: Penguin, 1988), p. 347, ll. 59-60.
5. Wallace Stevens, quoted in Czeslaw Milosz, *A Book of Illuminous Things: An International Anthology of Poetry* (New York: Harcourt, 1996), pp. 64-65.
6. Robert Romanyshyn, "Dark Light," unpublished manuscript.
7. Robert Romanyshyn, *The Soul in Grief: Love, Death and Transformation* (Berkeley, CA: North Atlantic Books, 1999), pp. 54-56.
8. Romanyshyn, "Dark Light."
9. C. G. Jung, "The Transcendent Function," in *The Structure and Dynamics of the Psyche, The Collected Works of C. G. Jung*, vol. 8, trans. R. F. C. Hull (Princeton, NJ: Princeton University Press, 1916/1957).
10. Stevens, in Milosz, pp. 64-65.
11. Gaston Bachelard, *The Poetics of Reverie*, trans. Daniel Russell (New York: Orion Press, 1969), p. 65, his italics.
12. T. S. Eliot, "Little Gidding," *Four Quartets* (New York: Harcourt Brace, 1943/1971), p. 59, ll. 239-42.
13. Greg Mogenson, *Greeting the Angels: An Imaginal View of the Mourning Process* (Amityville, NY: Baywood Publishing Company, 1992), p. 18.
14. Peter Homans, *Symbolic Loss: The Ambiguity of Mourning and Memory at Century's End* (Charlottesville, VA: University of Virginia Press, 2000).
15. Martin Heidegger, quoted in Romanyshyn, "Yes, Indeed! Do Call the World

the Vale of Soul Making: Reveries toward an Archetypal Presence," in *Ways of the Heart: Essays toward an Imaginal Psychology* (Pittsburgh, PA: Trivium Publications, 2002), p. 63.

16. *Ibid.*

17. Eliot, "East Coker," p. 31, ll. 186-189.

CHAPTER 1: SOUL AND THE COMPLEX OF PSYCHOLOGY

1. James Hillman, "Anima Mundi: Return of the Soul to the World," in *The Thought of the Heart and the Soul of the World* (Dallas, TX: Spring, 1992), pp. 109-110.

2. Susan Rowland, *Jung as a Writer* (London and New York: Routledge, 2005), p. 70.

3. *Ibid.*, 94.

4. C. G. Jung, "On the Nature of Psyche," in *The Structure and Dynamics of the Psyche, The Collected Works of C. G. Jung*, vol. 8, trans. R. F. C. Hull (Princeton, NJ: Princeton University Press, 1947/1969), § 429.

5. *Ibid.*, § 421.

6. C. G. Jung, "Psychotherapy and a Philosophy of Life," in *The Practice of Psychotherapy: Essays on the Psychology of the Transference and Other Subjects, The Collected Works of C. G. Jung*, vol. 16, trans. R. F. C. Hull (Princeton, NJ: Princeton University Press, 1946/1966), § 181.

7. C. G. Jung, "Answer to Job," in *Psychology and Religion: West and East, The Collected Works of C. G. Jung*, vol. 11, trans. R. F. C. Hull (Princeton, NJ: Princeton University Press, 1952/1958).

8. Richard Noll, *The Aryan Christ: The Secret Life of Carl Jung* (New York: Random House, 1997).

9. Karen Armstrong, *The Battle for God* (New York: Ballantine Books, 2001).

10. Lionel Corbett, *The Religious Function of the Psyche* (New York and London: Routledge, 1996); and Edward Edinger, *New God Image: A Study of Jung's Key Letters Concerning The Evolution of the Western God Image* (Wilmette, IL: Chiron Publications, 1996).

11. Richard Tarnas, *Cosmos and Psyche: Intimations of a New World View* (New York: Viking, 2006).

12. James Hillman, *The Myth of Analysis: Three Essays in Archetypal Psychology* (New York: Harper Colophon, 1978) and Aniela Jaffé, *The Myth of Meaning in the Work of C. G. Jung*, trans. R. F. C. Hull (London and New York: G. P. Putnam's Sons, 1971).

13. Marie-Louise von Franz, *C. G. Jung: His Myth in Our Time* (New York: G. P. Putnam's Sons, 1975).

14. Robert Romanyshyn, *Psychological Life: From Science to Metaphor* (Austin: University of Texas Press, 1982). Reprinted as *Mirror and Metaphor: Images*

and Stories of Psychological Life (Pittsburgh, PA: Trivium Publications, 2001), pp. 4-5.

15. C. G. Jung, "Psychotherapy and a Philosophy of Life," *CW* 16 §190.

16. Romanyshyn, *Psychological Life: From Science to Metaphor.*

17. Jung, "On the Nature of Psyche," *CW* 8 § 421.

18. *Ibid.*, § 344.

19. *Ibid.*, § 369-70.

20. *Ibid.*, 425.

21. *Ibid.*, 426.

22. C. G. Jung, "The Transcendent Function," in *The Structure and Dynamics of the Psyche, The Collected Works of C. G. Jung*, vol. 8, trans. R. F. C. Hull (Princeton, NJ: Princeton University Press, 1916/1960).

23. Brendan Kennelly, *The Man Made of Rain* (Newcastle upon the Tyne: Bloodaxe Books Ltd., 1998), p. 7.

24. *Ibid.*, p. 8.

25. Jung, "On the Nature of Psyche," *CW* 8 § 400.

26. *Ibid.*, *CW* 8 § 356.

27. Kennelly, p. 9.

28. C. G. Jung, *Memories, Dreams, Reflections* (New York: Vintage Books, 1965), p. 4.

29. Robert Romanyshyn, "Anyway, Why Did it have to be the Poet? The Orphic Roots of Jung's Psychology," *Spring 71* (2004): 55.

30. Kennelly, p. 8.

31. Amit Goswami, *The Self-Aware Universe: How Consciousness Creates the Material World* (New York: Penguin Putnam, 1993), p. 43.

32. Jung, "On the Nature of Psyche," *CW* 8 § 440.

33. C. G. Jung, "Synchronicity: An Acausal Connecting Principle," in *The Structure and Dynamics of the Psyche, The Collected Works of C. G. Jung*, vol. 8, trans. R. F. C. Hull (Princeton, NJ: Princeton University Press, 1952/1981); Marie-Louise von Franz, *Psyche and Matter* (Boston: Shambala, 1992); *Atom and Archetype: The Pauli/Jung Letters (1932-1958)*, ed. C. A. Meier, trans. D. Roscoe (Princeton, NJ: Princeton University Press, 2001); F. Peat, *Synchronicity: The Bridge Between Matter and Mind* (New York: Bantam Books, 1987); Robert Aziz, *C. G. Jung's Psychology of Religion and Synchronicity* (Albany, NY: State University of New York Press, 1990); and Veronica Goodchild, "Songlines of the Soul," unpublished manuscript.

34. Norman Cohn, *Europe's Inner Demons* (New York: New American Library, 1975), p. 263.

35. *Ibid.*, p. 263.

36. Wolfgang Pauli, quoted in C. G. Jung, "On the Nature of Psyche," *CW* 8 § 440.

37. *Ibid.*, § 439, n.130.

38. *Ibid.*, § 440.

39. Henry Corbin, *Alone with the Alone: Creative Imagination in the Sūfism of Ibn 'Arabī*, trans. Ralph Manheim (Princeton, NJ: Princeton University Press, 1969).

40. For a detailed analysis of the issue of the psychoid archetype, see Veronica Goodchild, "Songlines of the Soul"; see also "Psychoid, Psychophysical, P-subtle! Alchemy a New Worldview," *Spring* 74 (2006): 63-89.

41. Jung, "On the Nature of the Psyche," *CW* 8 § 440.

42. *Ibid.*, § 439, n. 130.

43. *Ibid.*, § 439.

44. *Ibid.*

45. *Ibid.*, his italics.

46. *Ibid.*, § 388.

47. Stanton Marlan, *The Black Sun: The Alchemy and Art of Darkness* (College Station, Texas A&M University Press, 2005).

48. Rainer Maria Rilke, quoted in Romanyshyn, "The Orphan and The Angel: In Defense of Melancholy," in *Ways of the Heart: Essays toward an Imaginal Psychology* (Pittsburgh, PA: Trivium Publications, 2002), pp. 41-43.

49. Jung, "On the Nature of Psyche," *CW* 8 § 417.

50. *Ibid.*, § 416, n. 123.

51. Beverley Zabriskie, "Preface," *Atom and Archetype: The Pauli/Jung Letters* (Princeton, NJ: University of Princeton Press, 2001), p. xli.

52. Jung, "On the Nature of Psyche," *CW* 8 § 417.

53. *Ibid.*, § 440, his italics.

54. Goodchild, "Songlines of the Soul."

55. Marie-Louise von Franz, *Alchemy: An Introduction to the Symbolism and the Psychology* (Toronto, Canada: Inner City Books, 1980), pp. 37-38.

CHAPTER 2: RE-SEARCH: UNDER THE SPELL
OF ORPHEUS

1. James Hillman, *Re-visioning Psychology* (New York: Harpers Collins, 1975), p. 99.

2. Robert Romanyshyn, *Technology as Symptom and Dream* (London and New York: Routledge, 1989/2000).

3. Robert McGahey, *The Orphic Moment: Shaman to Poet-Thinker in Plato, Nietzsche, and Mallarme* (New York: State University of New York, 1994), pp. 4-5.

4. McGahey, p. 138.

5. Thomas Moore, "Foreword," *The Orphic Moment* (Albany: State University of New York Press, 1994), p. ix.

6. E. R. Dodds, *The Greeks and the Irrational* (Berkeley: University of California Press, 1951).

7. McGahey, p. 36.

8. W. K. C. Guthrie, *Orpheus and Greek Religion: A Study of the Orphic Movement* (London: Methuen, 1952), p. 27.

9. Robert Romanyshyn, "Anyway, Why Did it have to be the Poet: The Orphic Roots of Jung's Psychology," *Spring* 71 (2004): 55-87.

10. Guthrie, p. 29.

11. Christine Downing, "Looking Back at Orpheus," *Spring* 71 (2004): 1-35.

12. *Ibid.*, p. 12.

13. *Ibid.*, pp. 12-13, her italics.

14. Virgil, *Georgics*, in *Eclogues, Georgics, Aeneid, 1-6*, trans. H. R. Fairclough (Cambridge: Harvard University Press, 1916/1999), p. 255.

15. Downing, p. 19.

16. For the phrase "le regard d'Opree" see Maurice Blanchot, *L'Espace litteraire* (Paris: Gallimard, 1955); for the quote see Blanchot, *The Gaze of Orpheus*, trans. Lydia Davis (Barrytown, NY: Station Hill Press, 1981), p. 104.

17. Mark Greene, "Reimagining as a Method for the Elucidation of Myth: The Case of Orpheus and Eurydice Accompanied by a Screenplay Adaptation," Ph.D. dissertation, Pacifica Graduate Institute, 1999, pp. 86-87.

18. Rainer Maria Rilke, "Orpheus.Eurydice.Hermes," *The Selected Poetry of Rainer Maria Rilke*, ed./trans. Stephen Mitchell (New York: Vintage Books, 1989), pp. 49-53.

19. *Ibid.*, pp. 51-53, his italics.

20. Rainer Maria Rilke, *Sonnets to Orpheus*, trans. M. D. Herter Norton (New York: W.W. Norton & Company 1962), p. 67.

21. Robert Romanyshyn, "Phenomenology and Depth Psychology: Reverie and the Creative Imagination," Paper presented at The International Association of Jungian Studies, Greenwich, England, July 2006.

22. Greg Mogenson, *Greeting the Angels: An Imaginal View of the Mourning Process* (Amityville, NY: Baywood Publishing Company, 1992), p. 8.

23. *Ibid.*, p. 18.

24. Paul Ricoeur, *Freud and Philosophy: An Essay on Interpretation*, trans. Dennis Savage (New Haven, CT: Yale University Press, 1970).

25. C. G. Jung, *Memories, Dreams, Reflections* (New York: Vintage Books, 1965), p. 237.

26. Stephen Wilkes, *Ellis Island: Ghosts of Freedom* (New York: W. W. Norton & Co., 2006).

27. See www.repr.org/templates/story/story.php?storyid=6600709.

28. Robert Romanyshyn, *The Soul in Grief: Love, Death and Transformation* (Berkeley, CA: Frog Ltd., 1999).

29. Robert Romanyshyn, *Ways of the Heart: Essays toward an Imaginal Psychology* (Pittsburgh, PA: Trivium Publications, 2002), p. 59.

30. Debbie Greenwood, "Resting at the Crossroads: Working with Women's Narratives and Art-making," Ph.D. dissertation, Pacifica Graduate Institute,

2006. All quotations from my graduate students in this chapter and in subsequent chapters, unless otherwise noted, are in response to a letter sent by me to students who have used the imaginal approach to research and the process of transference dialogues. That letter is reprinted in the Appendix.

31. Mogenson, *Greeting the Angels*, p. xv.
32. Marie-Louise von Franz, *Alchemy: An Introduction to the Symbolism and the Psychology* (Toronto, Canada: Inner Books, 1980), p. 12.
33. Mogenson, *Greeting the Angels*, p. 18.
34. Rilke, "Sonnets to Orpheus," p. 67.
35. Mogenson, *Greeting the Angels*, p. xv.
36. Johanna Treichler, "Walk your own Walk," Ph.D. dissertation, Pacifica Graduate Institute, in progress.
37. Rainer Maria Rilke, *Duino Elegy*, trans. J. B. Leishman and Stephen Spender (New York: W. W. Norton & Co., 1939), p. 71.
38. Rilke, "Orpheus.Eurydice.Hermes," p. 53.
39. Mogenson, *Greeting the Angels*, pp. 120-121.

CHAPTER 3: AN IMAGINAL APPROACH TO RE-SEARCH

1. Greg Mogenson, *Greeting the Angels: An Imaginal View of the Mourning Process* (Amityville, NY: Baywood Publishing Co., 1992), p. xii.
2. Harold Bloom, "Preface," *Alone with the Alone: Creative Imagination in the Sufism of Ibn 'Arabi*, trans. Ralph Manheim (Princeton, NJ: Princeton University Press, 1958/1969), p. xvi.
3. For Jung, see again Chapter 1 for a discussion of the psychoid archetype, which is essential to his understanding of the imaginal world. For Hillman, see James Hillman, *Re-Visioning Psychology* (New York: Harper & Row, 1975), p. 68.
4. Mogenson, *Greeting the Angels*.
5. C. G. Jung, *Memories, Dreams, Reflections* (New York: Vintage, 1965), p. 237.
6. *Ibid.*, p. 191.
7. *Ibid.*, pp. 236-37.
8. Amedeo Giorgi, *Psychology as a Human Science: A Phenomenologically Based Approach* (New York: Harper & Row, 1970).
9. Maurice Merleau-Ponty, *The Phenomenology of Perception*, trans. Colin Smith (London: Routledge & Kegan Paul, 1962).
10. *Ibid.*, p. xx.
11. John Sallis, *Phenomenology and the Return to Beginnings* (Pittsburgh, PA: Duquesne University Press, 1973).
12. Merleau-Ponty, *Phenomenology of Perception*, p. xiv.
13. To appreciate this way of understanding phenomenology, see, for example, Erwin Strauss, *Phenomenological Psychology* (New York: Basic Books, 1966).
14. Sallis, p. 116.

15. J. H. van den Berg, "Phenomenology and Metabletics," *Humanitas* 8, no. 3 (Winter 1971): 286.
16. *Ibid.*
17. *Ibid.*
18. For a detailed consideration of the fate of Angels as illustrated in the history of painting between the late medieval world and the late Renaissance see my article, "On Angels and Other Anomalies of the Imaginal Life," *Temenos Academy Review*, Spring (2000), pp. 171-82. This article was reprinted in *Ways of the Heart: Essays toward an Imaginal Psychology* (Pittsburgh, PA: Trivium Publications, 2002), pp. 109-19.
19. Van den Berg, pp. 286-87.
20. *Ibid.*, p. 287.
21. Using Jung's psychology and van den Berg's phenomenology as two illustrations of an imaginal approach to research, shows a convergence between these two perspectives. But a reader might well point out what appears to be a contradiction between the two. Whereas van den Berg's metabletics strongly emphasizes the changing character of reality and humanity, Jung's psychology strongly emphasizes the archetypal background of continuity across history and cultures. How do we bring together for an imaginal approach the idea of metabletic discontinuity in van den Berg's work and the idea of archetypal continuity in Jung's? My reply is that both ideas are different ways of focusing on the unfinished business in the soul of the work, in the soul of the world. We are both continuous with that greater family that Jung speaks of and different from them, and it is in holding the tension of this paradox of continuity and difference that we avoid, on one hand, the errors of totally separating ourselves from the ancestors by insisting on the difference, and, on the other hand, of regarding them as only failed or incomplete expressions of what we have become by insisting on the continuity.
22. Jung, *Memories, Dreams, Reflections*, pp. 233-34.
23. *Ibid.*, pp. 158-59.
24. *Ibid.*, pp. 160-61.
25. Paul Jones, "City and Psyche: An Exploration into the Archetype of City," Ph.D. dissertation, Pacifica Graduate Institute, 2003.

CHAPTER 4: RE-SEARCH AS VOCATION

1. C. G. Jung, "On the Nature of Psyche," in *The Structure and Dynamics of the Psyche, The Collected Works of C. G. Jung*, vol. 8, trans. R. F. C. Hull (Princeton, NJ: Princeton University Press, 1947/1969), § 344, 421.
2. Amedeo Giorgi, *Psychology as a Human Science* (New York: Harper and Row, 1970).
3. Clark Moustakas, *Heuristic Research: Design, Methodology, and Applications* (London: Sage Publications, 1990).

4. Ruth Behar, *The Vulnerable Observer: Anthropology That Would Break Your Heart* (Boston: Beacon Press, 1996), p. 6.

5. George Devereux, *From Anxiety to Method in the Behavioral Sciences*, 1967, his italics, quoted in Behar, p. 6.

6. Behar, p. 6.

7. Devereux, quoted in Behar, p. 6.

8. Behar, p. 6.

9. *Ibid.*

10. In spite of Devereux's emphasis on countertransference, throughout this book I am using the term "transference" to cover the range of the researcher's complex presence to the work. An imaginal approach to research acknowledges two dynamics in this process. Thus, whether we refer to the researcher's complex presence to the work as transference or countertransference seems less the issue than noting that re-search with soul in mind is about attending to what the researcher wants from the work and brings to the work through his or her complex attachments to it, and also what the work wants from, brings to, and stirs up in the researcher. In any case, according to Winston Le Bare's introduction to Devereux's work, the theme of the unconscious that Devereux introduced into the research process was destined to be dismissed. Devereux's book, according to Le Bare, was so far ahead of its time that it was likely to be ignored. Perhaps, however, the time now is better suited to the theme.

11. Behar, p. 7.

12. Devereux, quoted in Behar, p. 1.

13. Behar, p. 8.

14. Kay Redfield Jamison, *An Unquiet Mind*, his italics, quoted in Behar, pp. 9-10.

15. Jamison, quoted in Behar, p. 11.

16. Behar, p. 3.

17. Sandra Harding, her italics, quoted in Behar, p. 29.

18. Friedrich Nietzsche, *Beyond Good and Evil*, trans. R. J. Hollingdale (Harmondsworth: Penguin, 1972), p. 19.

19. C. G. Jung, "A Review of the Complex Theory," in *The Structure and Dynamics of the Psyche, The Collected Works of C. G. Jung*, vol. 8, trans. R. F. C. Hull (Princeton, NJ: Princeton University Press, 1934/1960), § 213.

20. Robert Romanyshyn, *Psychological Life: From Science to Metaphor* (Austin: University of Texas Press, 1982), reprinted as *Mirror and Metaphor: Images and Stories of Psychological Life* (Pittsburgh, PA: Trivium Publications, 2001).

21. *Ibid.*

22. Robert Romanyshyn, *Technology as Symptom and Dream* (New York: Routledge, 1989/2000).

23. Robert Romanyshyn, *Ways of the Heart: Essays toward an Imaginal Psychology* (Pittsburgh, PA: Trivium Publications, 2002).

24. Henry Corbin, *Alone with the Alone: Creative Imagination in the Sūfism of Ibn 'Arabi*, with a new preface by Harold Bloom (Princeton, NJ: Princeton University Press, 1998), p. 164.

25. Robert Romanyshyn, *The Soul in Grief: Love, Death and Transformation* (Berkeley, CA: Frog Ltd., 1999).

26. Greg Mogenson, *Greeting the Angels: An Imaginal View of the Mourning Process* (Amityville, NY: Baywood Publishing Company, 1992).

27. T. S. Eliot, "Little Gidding," *Four Quartets* (New York: Harcourt Brace, 1943/ 1971), p. 58.

28. Robert Romanyshyn, "Dark Light," unpublished manuscript.

29. Martin Heidegger, *Poetry, Language, Thought*, trans. Albert Hofstadter (New York: Harper Row, 1975) and Peter Kingsley, *Reality* (Inverness, CA: The Golden Sufi Center, 2003).

30. Kerry Ragain, "Archetypal Threads in the Experience of Being Adopted," Ph.D. dissertation, Pacifica Graduate Institute, 2006.

CHAPTER 5: THE TRANSFERENCE FIELD BETWEEN THE RESEARCHER AND THE WORK

1. Gaston Bachelard, *The Poetics of Reverie*, trans. Danille Russell (Boston: Beacon Press, 1969), p. 58.

2. See Chapter 4, note 10 for my use of the term transference to cover the range of transference/countertransference.

3. C. G. Jung, *Memories, Dreams, Reflections* (New York: Vintage Books, 1965), p. 173.

4. August Cwik, "Active Imagination as Imaginal Play-Space," in *Liminality and Transitional Phenomena,* ed. Murray Stein and Nathan Schwartz-Salant (Wilmette, IL: Chiron, 1991), p. 101.

5. *Ibid.*

6. Jung, *Memories, Dreams, Reflections*, p. 174.

7. Robert Romanyshyn, *Ways of the Heart: Essays toward an Imaginal Psychology* (Pittsburgh, PA: Trivium Publications, 2002).

8. Bachelard, p. 73.

9. Joan Chodorow, ed., *Jung on Active Imagination* (Princeton, NJ: Princeton University Press, 1997), p. 2.

10. Bachelard, p. 17.

11. Marie-Louise von Franz, *Alchemy: An Introduction to the Symbolism and the Psychology* (Toronto: Inner City Books, 1980), p. 22.

12. Bachelard, p. 72.

13. George Callan, "Temenos: The Primordial Vessel and the Mysteries of 9/11," Ph.D. dissertation, Pacifica Graduate Institute, 2002.

14. George Callan, "Methodos: The Pursuit," unpublished manuscript, pp. 1-2.

15. *Ibid.*, p. 2.

16. Robert Romanyshyn, "The Wounded Researcher: Levels of Transference in the Research Process," *Harvest: International Journal for Jungian Studies* 52, no.1 (2006): 44.

17. Henry Corbin, *Spiritual Body and Celestial Earth*, trans. Nancy Pearson (Princeton, NJ: Princeton University Press, Bollingen Series XCI: 2, 1977), p. xviii.

18. Andrew Samuels, "Countertransference, The 'Mundus Imaginalis' and a Research Project," *Journal of Analytical Psychology*, (1985): 30, 58-59, his italics.

19. Romanyshyn, "The Wounded Researcher: Levels of Transference in the Research Process," p. 44.

20. *Ibid.*

21. C. G. Jung, "Two Kinds of Thinking," *Symbols of Transformation, The Collected Works of C. G. Jung*, vol. 5, trans. R. F. C. Hull (Princeton, NY: Princeton U Press, 1956), § 18.

22. John Keats, *The Complete Poems*, ed. John Barnard (New York: Penguin, 1973), p. 539.

23. Robert Romanyshyn, "Psychology is Useless: Or, It Should Be," in *Ways of the Heart: Essays toward an Imaginal Psychology* (Pittsburgh, PA: Trivium Publications, 2002), p. 121.

24. Greg Mogenson, *Greeting the Angels: An Imaginal View of the Mourning Process* (Amityville, NY: Baywood Publishing Company, 1992), 121, n. 11. His citation of Jung is *CW* 8 § 402.

25. Robert Romanyshyn, "On Angels and Other Anomalies of the Imaginal Life," in *Ways of the Heart: Essays toward an Imaginal Psychology* (Pittsburgh, PA: Trivium Publications, 2002), p. 118.

26. Karl Beckson and Arthur Ganz, *A Reader's Guide to Literary Terms* (New York: The Noonday Press, 1960), pp. 301-302.

27. Romanyshyn, "On Angels and Other Anomalies of the Imaginal Life," pp. 109-119.

28. T. S. Eliot, "East Coker," *Four Quartets* (New York: Harcourt, Brace and World, 1943/1971), p. 28.

29. Jo Todd, "Grieving with the Unborn," Ph.D. dissertation, Pacifica Graduate Institute, 2006.

30. Cwik, p. 103.

31. *Ibid.*, his italics.

32. *Ibid.*

33. C. G. Jung, "The Transcendent Function," in *The Structure and Dynamics of the Psyche, The Collected Works of C. G. Jung*, vol. 8, trans. R. F. C. Hull (Princeton, NJ: Princeton University Press, 1916/1960); Jung; "The Tavistock Lectures," in *The Symbolic Life, The Collected Works of C. G. Jung*, vol. 18, trans. R. F. C. Hull (Princeton, NJ: Princeton University Press 1936/1976).

34. Cwik.

35. *Ibid.*, p. 103.

36. *Ibid.*
37. Mary Watkins, *Invisible Guests* (Woodstock, CT: Spring Publications, 2000).
38. Robert Romanyshyn, "Preface," *Invisible Guests* (Woodstock, CT: Spring Publications, 2000), p. i.
39. Jung, "The Transcendent Function," *CW* 8 § 187.
40. *Ibid.*, 8 § 172.
41. *Ibid.*, § 176.
42. *Ibid.*
43. *Ibid.*, § 179.
44. Cwik, p. 104.
45. After I completed this chapter I began to see a connection between the ways in which I have described the transference dialogues and the Orphic myth that lies in the background of re-search that would keep soul in mind. Orpheus embodies the shamanic contradiction, which is that state of being in which one is both possessed by the gods and is most free. In the transference dialogues, this contradiction is also at work. In active imagination, the researcher, like the Orphic poet, is most bound and most free, dispossessed of himself or herself by the "others" in the work and in possession of himself or herself. In the transference dialogues, the ego of the researcher is addressed and dispossessed by the "others" in the work and consciously in relation to them.

CHAPTER 6: THE TRANSFERENCE FIELD: STUDENT EXAMPLES

1. Rainer Maria Rilke, quoted in Hans-Georg Gadamer, *Truth and Method* (New York: The Seabury Press, 1975), page before Contents.
2. Kerry Ragain, "Archetypal Threads in the Experience of Being Adopted," Ph.D. dissertation, Pacifica Graduate Institute, 2006.
3. Jo Todd, "Grieving with the Unborn," Ph.D. dissertation, Pacifica Graduate Institute, 2006.
4. Erik Killinger, "Between the Frying Pan and the Fire: The *Intermundia* of Clergy Transitioning out of parish Ministry," Ph.D. dissertation, Pacifica Graduate Institute, 2006.
5. Debbie Greenwood, "Resting at the Crossroads: Working with Women's Narratives and Art-Making," Ph.D. dissertation, Pacifica Graduate Institute, 2006.
6. Kay Tomlinson, "Conversations with the Ladies: Art-Making in Collaboration with Imaginal Figures," Ph.D. dissertation, Pacifica Graduate Institute, in progress.
7. Ellen Macfarland, "Discovering the Healing Power of Nature: A New Perspective for Healing the Wounds of Childhood Abuse," Ph.D. dissertation, Pacifica Graduate Institute, 2004.
8. Dennis Langhans, "An Odyssey of the Heart: A Return to the Place, Rhythm and Time of the Heart," Ph.D. dissertation, Pacifica Graduate Institute, 2002.

9.   Robert Romanyshyn, "Psychotherapy as Grief Work," in *Ways of the Heart: Essays toward an Imaginal Psychology* (Pittsburgh, PA: Trivium Publications, 2002), p. 57.

10. C. G. Jung, "The Development of Personality," in *The Development of Personality, The Collected Works of C. G. Jung*, vol. 17, trans. R. F. C. Hull (Princeton, NJ: Princeton University Press, 1934/ 1954).

11. Conrad Gratz, "The Experience of Living with Enchantment," Ph.D. dissertation, Pacifica Graduate Institute, 2007.

12. C. G. Jung, *Memories, Dreams, Reflections* (New York: Vintage Books, 1965), pp. 192-93.

13. Judith Orodenker, "The Voice of the Goddess: The Reemergence of the Archetypal Divine Feminine," Ph.D. dissertation, Pacifica Graduate Institute, in progress.

14. Robert Romanyshyn, *The Soul in Grief: Love, Death and Transformation* (Berkeley, CA: Frog Ltd., 1999), p. 110.

15. James Hillman, *The Dream and the Underworld* (New York: Harper & Row, 1979).

16. Kerry Ragain's use of projective identification as part of his method raises the issue of transference/countertransference to the work. See Chapter 4, note 10.

17. Robert Romanyshyn, "The Wounded Researcher: Levels of Transference in the Research Process," *Harvest: International Journal for Jungian Studies* 52, no.1 (2006): 43.

18. Robert Johnson, *Inner Work* (New York: HarperSanFrancisco, 1986), p. 137.

19. C. G. Jung, "The Transcendent Function," in *The Structure and Dynamics of the Psyche, The Collected Works of C. G. Jung*, vol. 8, trans. R. F. C. Hull (Princeton, NJ: Princeton University Press, 1916/1960), § 183.

20. Maurice Merleau-Ponty, "The Philosopher and His Shadow," *Signs* (1964): 161.

21. Virgil, *The Aeneid*, Book 6, ll. 126-129, in *Eclogues, Georgics, Aeneid I-VI*, trans. H. R. Fairclough (Cambridge: Harvard University Press, 1916/1999), pp. 540-541.

CHAPTER 7: RECOVERING THE SOUL OF METHOD

1.   Sonu Shamdasani, *Jung and the Making of Modern Psychology: The Dream of a Science* (New York: Cambridge University Press, 2003).

2.   William James. quoted in Shamdasani, p. 5.

3.   William James as quoted in Shamdasani, p. 5.

4.   Martin J. Packer and Richard B. Addison, *Entering the Circle* (Albany: State University of New York University, 1989), pp. 13-14, their italics.

5.   *Ibid.*, p. 17.

6.   Robert Romanyshyn, *Psychological Life: From Science to Metaphor* (Austin: University of Texas Press, 1982), reprinted as *Mirror and Metaphor: Images*

and Stories of Psychological Life (Pittsburgh, PA: Trivium Publications, 2001); *Technology as Symptom and Dream* (London and New York: Routledge, 1989/ 2000).

7. Packer and Addison, p. 17.
8. *Ibid.*, pp. 22-23.
9. *Ibid.*, p. 27.
10. *Ibid.*, p. 33.
11. *Ibid.*, p. 31.
12. Romanyshyn, *Psychological Life: From Science to Metaphor*, p. 176.
13. There is no getting around the fact that at some point in his investigation of dreams as brain function, the psychologist has to correlate the physiological measures with the experience of dreaming. At some point, he has to wake his dreaming subjects from sleep in order to establish the meanings of the electrical patterns he has recorded. Even empiricist methods lean upon hermeneutics. This is really the basis for the argument put forth by Packer and Addison regarding the need in psychology to replace empiricist and rationalist modes of inquiry with hermeneutic ones. But, as I said in the text, I do not accept this conclusion. While empiricist and rationalist procedures require acts of interpretation, they are not by this requirement hermeneutic methods. Empiricist and rationalist ways of talking in psychology have a distinct character as methods, a character different from that of the method in hermeneutic ways of talking in psychology, and it is better not to confuse them, since, as I try to show in this chapter, each of these methods is a way of revealing soul and concealing it. To use Heideggerean language here, the work of interpretation is an ontological structure of human being. There is no human act, then, that does not partake in this structure. Nevertheless, in empiricist and rationalist methods in psychology the work of interpretation becomes subsumed under the practice of the method, which progressively functions automatically, that is, apart from any connection with acts of evaluation or judgment. While Packer and Addison decry this development, I try to show how it opens a way of questioning method psychologically in terms of what it reveals and conceals of soul. For a detailed account of Heidegger's examination of interpretation as an ontological structure of human being, see *Being and Time,* trans. J. Macquarrie and E. Robinson (New York: Harper and Row, 1927/1962).
14. Richard Tarnas, *Cosmos and Psyche: Intimations of a New World View* (New York: Viking, 2006).
15. My very first publication, "Method and Meaning in Psychology: The Method Has Been the Message," *Journal of Phenomenological Psychology* 2 no. 1, (Fall 1971): 93-114, indicates not only how long this question of method has been with me, but also how one is continuously drawn deeper into those questions and issues that are part of the complex of one's vocation. A person begins his or her intellectual and creative life, and from that moment

forward he or she is in service to what has addressed him or her. We circle round and round as we are encircled by a vocation. To say this another way, just as Einstein said there are no straight lines in nature, there are no straight lines of progress in one's thinking from the point of view of soul. That fantasy belongs to the ego-mind. There is only a deepening spiral of engagement and understanding.

CHAPTER 8: HERMENEUTICS AND THE CIRCLE OF UNDERSTANDING

1. Richard E. Palmer, *Hermeneutics, Interpretation Theory in Shcleiermacher, Dilthey, Heidegger, and Gadamer* (Evanston, IL: Northwestern University Press, 1969), p. 13.
2. Martin Heidegger, quoted in Palmer, p. 13.
3. Robert Romanyshyn, "Complex Knowing: Toward a Psychological Hermeneutics," *The Humanistic Psychologist*, 19, no.1 (Spring 1991): 10-29.
4. Marie-Louise von Franz, *Alchemy: An Introduction to the Symbolism and the Psychology* (Toronto, Canada: Inner City Books, 1980).
5. Norman Cohn, *Europe's Inner Demons* (New York: New American Library, 1975), p. 263.
6. Sigmund Freud, *Beyond the Pleasure Principle, The Standard Edition of the Complete Psychological Works of Sigmund Freud*, trans. James Strachey, vol. XVIII (London: Hogarth Press, 1920/1955).
7. For a discussion of the metaphysics of presence, see David Michael Levin, *The Opening of Vision: Nihilism and the Postmodern Situation* (New York and London: Routledge, Chapman & Hall, 1988), pp. 241-49.
8. Paul Ricoeur, *Freud and Philosophy: An Essay on Interpretation,* trans. Dennis Savage (New Haven, CT: Yale University Press, 1970), p. 31.
9. Von Franz, *Alchemy*, pp. 44-48.
10. Rainer Maria Rilke, *Duino Elegies,* trans. J. B. Leishman and Stephen Spender (New York: W. W. Norton & Co., 1939), p. 75.
11. Brendan Kennelly, *The Man Made of Rain* (Newcastle upon the Tyne: Bloodaxe Books Ltd., 1998).
12. C. G. Jung, "Answer to Job," in *Psychology and Religion: West and East, The Collected Works of C. G. Jung*, Vol. 11, trans. R. F. C. Hull (Princeton, NJ: Princeton University Press, 1952).
13. Gaston Bachelard, *The Poetics of Reverie,* trans. Danille Russell (Boston: Beacon Press, 1969), p. 65, his italics.
14. Robert Romanyshyn, "Phenomenology and Depth Psychology: Reverie and the Creative Imagination," Paper presented at The International Association of Jungian Studies, Greenwich, England, July, 2006.
15. Robert Romanyshyn, "Psychotherapy as Grief Work: Ghosts and the Gestures of Compassion," in *Ways of the Heart: Essays toward an Imaginal Psychology*

(Pittsburgh, PA: Trivium Publications, 2002), 50-62. This article develops the notion of the transference field in relation to a phenomenology of the gestural body.

16. Edward F. Edinger, *Anatomy of the Psyche: Alchemical Symbolism in Psychotherapy* (La Salle, IL: Open Court 1984), p. 47.

17. Paul Ricoeur, "Consciousness and the Unconscious," trans. Willis Domingo, in *The Conflict of Interpretations*, ed. Don Ihde (Evanston, IL: Northwestern University Press, 1974), p. 99.

CHAPTER 9: TOWARDS A HERMENEUTICS OF DEEP SUBJECTIVITY

1. H. P. Rickman, "Introduction," *Pattern and Meaning in History: Thoughts on History and Society* (New York: Harper & Row, 1961), p. 22.

2. Wilhelm Dilthey, quoted in Richard E. Palmer, *Hermeneutics, Interpretation Theory in Shcleiermacher, Dilthey, Heidegger, and Gadamer* (Evanston, IL: Northwestern University Press, 1969), p. 105, n. 17.

3. Although the term *Seelenleben* translates as "the life of soul," Dilthey did not mean the discipline of psychology as the study of soul. In line with what his intention was, therefore, I have translated the phrase as it is usually translated, as "the life of mind or spirit."

4. Amedeo Giorgi, *Psychology as a Human Science* (New York, Harper and Row, 1970).

5. For a discussion of the importance of Merleau-Ponty's work in relation to this issue, see, for example, Robert Romanyshyn, "Phenomenology and Psychoanalysis: Contributions of Merleau-Ponty," *The Psychoanalytic Review* 64, no. 2 (Summer 1977): 211-23; Robert Romanyshyn, "Unconsciousness: Reflection and the Primacy of Perception," *Phenomenology: Dialogues and Bridges,* eds. Ronald Bruzina and Bruce Wilshire (Albany: State University of New York Press, 1982), pp. 145-63; Robert Romanyshyn, "Unconsciousness as a Lateral Depth: Perception and the Two Moments of Reflection," *Continental Philosophy in America*, eds. Hugh J. Silverman, John Sallis, and Thomas M. Seebohn (Pittsburgh, PA: Duquesne University Press, 1983), pp. 227-44.

6. Robert S. Steele, quoted in Martin J. Packer and Richard B. Addison, *Entering the Circle* (Albany: State of University of New York, 1989), p. 223.

7. *Ibid.*

8. *Ibid.*, p. 224.

9. *Ibid.*, p. 236.

10. C. G. Jung, *Memories, Dreams, Reflections* (New York: Vintage Books, 1965), pp. 160-61.

11. Steele, quoted in Packer and Addison, pp. 228-229.

12. *Ibid.*, pp. 229-30.

13. *Ibid.*

14. *Ibid.*, p. 235.
15. *Ibid.*, p. 231.
16. *Ibid.*, p. 232.
17. *Ibid.*
18. *Ibid.*, p. 235.
19. *Ibid.*, p. 231.
20. Ronald S. Valle and Mark King, eds., *Existential-Phenomenological Alternatives for Psychology* (New York: Oxford University Press, 1978), pp. 18-47.
21. Robert Romanyshyn, *Psychological Life: From Science to Metaphor* (Austin, TX: University of Texas Press, 1982), reprinted as *Mirror and Metaphor: Images and Stories of Psychological Life* (Pittsburgh, PA: Trivium Publications, 2001).
22. Robert Romanyshyn, *Technology as Symptom and Dream* (New York, London: Routledge, 1989/2002).
23. Steele, quoted in Packer and Addison, p. 235.
24. *Ibid.*, p. 235.
25. *Ibid.*, p. 237.
26. *Ibid.*, p. 236.
27. *Ibid.*
28. C. G. Jung, "Analytical Psychology and *Weltanschauung*," in *The Structure and Dynamics of the Psyche, The Collected Works of C. G. Jung*, vol. 8, trans. R. F. C. Hull (Princeton, NJ: Princeton University Press, 1931/1960).
29. C. G. Jung, "A Review of the Complex Theory," in *The Structure and Dynamics of the Psyche, The Collected Works of C. G. Jung*, vol. 8, trans. R. F. C. Hull (Princeton, NJ: Princeton University Press, 1948/1960), § 215.
30. C. G. Jung, "The Transcendent Function," in *The Structure and Dynamics of the Psyche, The Collected Works of C. G. Jung*, vol. 8, trans. R. F. C. Hull (Princeton, NJ: Princeton University Press, 1916/1960), § 187.
31. *Ibid.*
32. Paul Ricoeur, "Consciousness and the Unconscious," trans. Willis Domingo, in *The Conflict of Interpretations*, ed. Don Ihde (Evanston, IL: Northwestern University Press, 1974), p. 99.
33. Paul Ricoeur, *Freud and Philosophy: An Essay on Interpretation*, trans. by Dennis Savage (New Haven, CT: Yale University Press, 1970), p. 92, his italics.
34. Ricoeur, *Conflict of Interpretations*, p. 103.
35. *Ibid.*, p. 105, his italics.
36. *Ibid.*, p. 106.
37. *Ibid.*, p. 107, his italics.
38. See Note # 5.
39. Ricoeur, "Consciousness and the Unconscious," p. 105, his italics.
40. *Ibid.*, pp. 107-108.
41. *Ibid.*, p. 107.
42. *Ibid.*, p. 108.

43. Paul Ricoeur, "Art and Freudian Systematics," trans. Willis Domingo, in *The Conflict of Interpretations*, ed. Don Ihde (Evanston, IL: Northwestern University Press, 1974), p. 208.
44. Ricoeur, "Consciousness and the Unconscious," p. 107, his italics.
45. *Ibid.*
46. Quoted in Maurice Merleau-Ponty, "The Philosopher and His Shadow," in *Signs*, trans. Richard C. Mccleary (Evanston, IL: Northwestern University Press, 1964), p. 160.
47. *Ibid.*, p. 107.

CHAPTER 10: ALCHEMICAL HERMENEUTICS:
PART ONE

1. Jules Laforgue, quoted in Gaston Bachelard, *The Poetics of Reverie*, trans. Daniel Russell (Boston: Beacon Press, 1969), p. 1.
2. Veronica Goodchild, "Songlines of the Soul," unpublished manuscript.
3. Marie-Louise von Franz, *Alchemy: An Introduction to the Symbolism and the Psychology* (Toronto: Inner Books, 1980), pp. 22-21.
4. Gaston Bachelard, *The Poetics of Reverie*, trans. Daniel Russell (Boston: Beacon Press, 1969), p. 72.
5. Stanton Marlan, *The Black Sun: The Alchemy and Art of Darkness* (College Station, TX: A&M University Press, 2005), p. 188.
6. Marlan, p. 189.
7. Henry Corbin, *The Voyage and the Messenger* (Berkeley, CA: North Atlantic Books, 1998), p. xv.
8. Maurice Merleau-Ponty, *The Visible and the Invisible*, trans. Alphonso Lingis, (Evanston, IL: Northwestern University Press, 1968).
9. Goodchild, "Songlines of the Soul."
10. Susan Rowland, *Jung as a Writer* (New York and London: Routledge, 2005); Rosemarie Anderson, "Embodied Writing and Reflections of Embodiment," *The Journal of Transpersonal Psychology* 33 (2001): 83-98.
11. Henry Corbin, *Alone with the Alone: Creative Imagination in the Sūfism of Ibn 'Arabî*, trans. Ralph Manheim (Princeton, NJ: Princeton University Press, 1969), pp. 13, 78-79.
12. Etienne Souriau, "L'Ombre de Dieu," his intalics, quoted in Corbin, *Alone with the Alone*, p. 29.
13. C. G. Jung, "Answer to Job," in *Psychology and Religion: West and East, The Collected Works of C. G. Jung*, vol. 11, trans. R. F. C. Hull, (Princeton, NJ: Princeton University Press, 1952).
14. Robert Segal, *The Gnostic Jung* (Princeton, NJ: Princeton University Press 1992).
15. Henry Corbin, quoted by Stella Corbin, "Preface," *The Voyage and the Messenger: Iran and Philosophy* (Berkeley, CA: North Atlantic Books, 1998), p. xviii.

16. Henry Corbin, *The Voyage and the Messenger: Iran and Philosophy* (Berkeley, CA: North Atlantic Books, 1998), p. 25, his italics.

17. C. G. Jung, *Psychology and Alchemy,* in *The Collected Works of C. G. Jung,* vol. 12, trans. R. F. C. Hull (Princeton, NJ: Princeton University Press, 1958), § 390.

18. *Ibid.,* § 389.

19. Corbin, *Voyage and the Messenger,* p. xl.

20. *Ibid.,* p. 164.

CHAPTER 11: ALCHEMICAL HERMENEUTICS: PART TWO

1. Kiyanoosh Shamlu, "From Mundus Imaginalis To Nakoja-Abad: An Inquiry into Shihabuddin Yahya Sohrevardi's Imaginal World Of Soul Through the Visionary Recitals," Ph.D. dissertation, Pacifica Graduate Institute, in progress.

2. Robert Romanyshyn, *Psychological Life: From Science to Metaphor* (Austin: University of Texas Press, 1982), reprinted as *Mirror and Metaphor: Images and Stories of Psychological Life* (Pittsburgh, PA: Trivium Publications, 2001).

3. All quotations from my graduate students in this chapter and in subsequent chapters, unless otherwise noted, are in response to a letter sent by me to students who have used the imaginal approach to research and the process of transference dialogues. That letter is reprinted in the Appendix.

4. Julie Sgarzi, "In the Labyrinth of the Secret: A Meditation on the Nature of the Secret," Ph.D. dissertation, Pacifica Graduate Institute, 2002.

5. C. G. Jung, *Memories, Dreams, Reflections* (New York: Vintage Books, 1965), p. 85.

6. Conrad Gratz, "The Experience of Living with Enchantment," Ph.D. dissertation, Pacifica Graduate Institute, 2006. All citations are from this study.

7. Gratz, p. 1.

8. Willam Carlos Williams, "Asphodel, That Greeny Flower," quoted in Gratz.

9. C. G. Jung, *Psychological Types, The Collected Works of C. G. Jung,* vol. 6, trans. R. F. C. Hull (Princeton, NJ: Princeton University Press,1921/1971), § 724, his italics.

10. Morris Berman, *Coming to Our Senses* (New York: Bantam Books, 1990), pp. 131, 134, his italics.

11. *Ibid.,* p. 135.

12. *Ibid.,* p. 118, his italics.

13. Jung, *CW* 6 § 724.

14. Marie-Louise von Franz and James Hillman, *Lectures on Jung's Typology* (Woodstock, CT: Spring Publications, 1986), p. 109.

15. *Ibid.,* p. 109.

16. Gaston Bachelard, *The Poetics of Reverie,* trans. Daniel Russell (Boston: Beacon Press, 1969), p. 112.

17. Von Franz, *Lectures on Jung's Typology*, p. 37.
18. Hillman, *Lectures on Jung's Typology*, p. 111.
19. Jung, *CW* 6 § 728.
20. Hillman, *Lectures on Jung's Typology*, p. 110.
21. Robert Romanyshyn, *Ways of the Heart: Essays toward an Imaginal Psychology* (Pittsburgh, PA: Trivium Publications, 2002), p. 156.
22. Henry Corbin, quoted in Robert Romanyshyn, "On being a Fool: In Defense of the Pathetic Heart," *Ways of the Heart: Essays toward an Imaginal Psychology* (Pittsburgh, PA: Trivium Publications, 2002), p. 159.
23. Rosemarie Anderson, "Intuitive Inquiry: A Transpersonal Approach," in *Transpersonal Research Methods for the Social Sciences*, ed. William Braud and Rosemarie Anderson (Thousand Oaks, CA: Sage Publications, 1998), p. 73.
24. *Ibid.*, pp. 57, 234.
25. Hillman, *Lectures on Jung's Typology*, p. 101.
26. Robert Romanyshyn, "Complex Knowing: Toward a Psychological Hermeneutics," *The Humanistic Psychologist* 19, no.1 (Spring 1991): 10-29.
27. Jung, *CW* 6 § 983.
28. See note 3 above.
29. Jung, *CW* 6, § 770, 774, his italics.
30. C. G. Jung, *Analytical Psychology: Notes on a Seminar Given in 1925*, ed. William McGuire (Princeton, NJ: Princeton University Press, 1989), p. 32.
31. Judith Orodenker, "The Voice of the Goddess: The Reemergence of the Archetypal Divine Feminine," Ph.D. dissertation, Pacifica Graduate Institute, in progress.
32. Jung, *CW* 6 § 900.
33. George Callan, "Methodos: the Pursuit," unpublished manuscript, pp. 1-2.
34. *Ibid.*
35. Anderson, "Intuitive Inquiry," pp. 84-85. For a detailed description of Anderson's use of intuition in research the reader can consult her website at www.wellknowingconsulting.org/training/styles.html, where she distinguishes five styles of intuition.
36. Robert Romanyshyn, *Technology as Symptom and Dream* (London and New York: Routledge, 1989/2000); for the symptomatic body see, for example, "Psychotherapy as Grief Work: Ghosts and the Gestures of Compassion," in *Ways of the Heart* (Pittsburgh, PA: Trivium Publications, 2002), pp. 50-62.
37. Rosemarie Anderson, "Body Intelligence Scale: Defining and Measuring the Intelligence of the Body," in *The Humanistic Psychologist* 34-40 (2006): 357-67.
38. Ruth Meyer, "Clio's Circle: Entering the Imaginal World of Historians," Ph.D. dissertation, Pacifica Graduate Institute, 2007, p. ix.
39. Robert Romanyshyn, "Complex Knowing," pp. 10-29. In the References to this article see especially the work of Susan Bordo, Jane Gallop, Eugene Gendlin, Don Johnson, Stanley Kelerman, and David Michael Levin.

40. *Ibid.*, pp. 17-18.
41. Linda Lauver, "The Maya Tradition—A Living History: Re-membering what Wants to be Remembered," Ph.D. dissertation, Pacifica Graduate Institute, in progress, p. 4.
42. *Ibid.*
43. *Ibid.*, pp. 5-6.
44. C. G. Jung, "Synchronicity: An Acausal Connecting Principle," in *The Structure and Dynamics of the Psyche, The Collected Works of C. G. Jung*, vol. 8, trans. R. F. C. Hull (Princeton, NJ: Princeton University Press, 1952/ 1960), § 849-50, 858.
45. Marie-Louise von Franz, *Alchemy: An Introduction to the Symbolism and the Psychology* (Toronto: Inner City Books, 1980), pp. 78, 95.
46. Albert Kreinheder, "Alchemy and the Subtle Body," in *Psychological Perspectives* 6, no. 2 (1975): 135-36.

CHAPTER 12: WRITING DOWN THE SOUL

1. Susan Rowland, *Jung as a Writer* (New York: Routledge, 2005), p. 23.
2. *Ibid.*, p. 3.
3. *Ibid.*, p. 59.
4. David Rosen, *Transforming Depression: Healing the Soul Through Creativity* (York Beach, ME: Nicolas-Hays, 2002).
5. Greg Mogenson, "The Afterlife of the Image," *Spring* 71 (2004): 102.
6. Wallace Stevens, *Poems*, selected by Samuel French Morse (New York: Vintage Books, 1959), p. 109.
7. John Keats, *The Complete Poems*, ed. John Barnard (New York: Penguin, 1988), p. 549.
8. e. e. cummings, *100 Selected Poems* (New York: Grove Press, 1978), pp. 29-30.
9. Robert McGahey, *The Orphic Moment* (Albany: State University of New York Press, 1994), p. xxi.
10. Stanton Marlan, *The Black Sun: The Alchemy and Art of Darkness*, reviewed by Murray Stein, *Spring* 74, Spring, (2006): 323.
11. David L. Miller, "The 'Stone' which is not a Stone: C. G. Jung and the Post-Modern Meaning of 'Meaning,'" *Spring* 49 (1989): 110-22.
12. Lao Tse, *The Way and Its Power: A Study of the Tao Te Ching and its Place in Chinese Thought*, trans. and ed. Arthur Waley (Boston: Houghton Mifflin, 1934), p. 155.
13. Robert Romanyshyn, *Psychological Life: From Science to Metaphor* (Austin: University of Texas Press, 1982), reprinted as *Mirror and Metaphor: Images and Stories of Psychological Life* (Pittsburgh, PA: Trivium Publications, 2001), p. 176.
14. Edward F. Edinger, *Anatomy of the Psyche* (LaSalle, IL: Open Court, 1985), p. 47.

15. The alchemy of metaphor is similar in intention to Wolfgang Giegerich's ideas about the work of sublation in psychology but also differs in the execution of this intention. Giegerich's work about sublation, which is based in a Hegelian dialectic, is a style of discourse in service to the soul's logical life, whereas the alchemy of metaphor that I have worked at since 1982, which is rooted in Merleau-Pontys' phenomenology of embodied life, is a style of discourse in service to the poetic sensibility of soul. Each differs in the way it would write down the soul. Nevertheless, the points that I am making here about writing that does not fix the soul could be made through Giegerich's work. The "is not" functions as a negation in the soul's logical and metaphorical life. In a recent article, Giegerich notes, "You cannot say what you actually want to say. You can only negate the positive, that which is not meant." In addition, he says, "The negation of the positive equivalent is absolutely necessary." The "is not" must always haunt the "is." See Wolfgang Giegerich, "Once More 'The Stone Which Is Not A Stone: Further Reflections on 'Not,'" in *Disturbances in the Field: Essays in Honor of David L. Miller*, ed. Christine Downing (New Orleans, LA: Spring Journal Books, 2006), p. 129.
16. Julie Sgarzi, "In the Labyrinth of the Secret: A Meditation on the Nature of the Secret," Ph.D. dissertation, Pacifica Graduate Institute, 2002.
17. Rowland, p. 54, her italics. While it is not my intention in this book to follow Rowland in how she applies her insights about the anima to social issues of gender, I would strongly agree with her position. Rowland notes that in his descriptions of the anima in his autobiography, Jung portrays her as a nagging woman, and in doing so, she says, "What Jung never considers is the suspicious resemblance between controlling a gender other within and the conventions of masculine authority in exterior social relationships. Such an omission leaves his work open to the speculation that conventional social relationships are a spectre haunting Jungian psychology."
18. *Ibid.*
19. My concern over the years for this issue of scientific writing in psychology as a rhetorical art has expressed itself in terms of recovering the metaphoric character of psychological life. See, for example, *Psychological Life: From Science to Metaphor* (Austin: University of Texas Press, 1982), reprinted as *Mirror and Metaphor: Images and Stories of Psychological Life* (Pittsburgh, PA: Trivium Publications, 2001). In addition see, "Psychology and the Attitude of Science," in *Existential-Phenomenological Perspectives in Psychology*, eds. Ronald S. Valle and Steen Halling (New York: Plenum Press, 1989), pp. 17-39. In that article, I did an anatomy of an introductory textbook in psychology to show the underlying rhetorical aspect in the claim that psychology is a science.
20. Jung, quoted in Rowland, p. 1.
21. Jung, quoted in Rowland, p. 2.
22. Jung, quoted in Rowland, p. 9.
23. Romanyshyn, *Mirror and Metaphor*, p. 202. This book is an extended defense

of the metaphoric character of psychological life and it amplifies in some detail the remarks about metaphor made here.

24. Robert Romanyshyn, "For the Moment That's Enough: Reveries on Therapy and the Poetry of Language," in *Ways of the Heart: Essays toward an Imaginal Psychology* (Pittsburgh, PA: Trivium Publications, 2002), pp. 72-88.

25. Lyn Cowan, "On Writing," unpublished essay.

26. Gaston Bachelard, *The Poetics of Reverie*, trans. Daniel Russell (Boston: Beacon Press, 1969), p. 65.

27. Rowland, p. 79.

28. Greg Mogenson, *The Dove in the Consulting Room* (New York: Brunner-Routledge, 2003), p. 192.

29. Joseph Coppin and Elizabeth Nelson, *The Art of Inquiry* (Auburn, CA: Treehenge Press, 2004), p. 89.

30. *Ibid.*, p. 90, their italics.

31. Maurice Merleau-Ponty, *The Phenomenology of Perception*, trans. Colin Smith (London: Routledge & Kegan Paul, 1962), p. 369.

32. James Hillman, *Re-Visioning Psychology* (New York: Harper and Row, 1975), pp. ix-x.

33. Does the link between ink and blood hold with the computer? Of course, if one does not take the metaphor literally. Since, however, a metaphor also is about what is not the case, the ink-is-blood metaphor fails. The ink on the page is not the blood in one's veins. So what is the blood that flows in one's veins in relation to the act of writing? Is the blood that flows through one's veins the keystrokes made on a computer? Somehow the metaphor does not seem right to me and maybe there is something to learn here. Maybe the technology of the computer, for all its utility, distances the writer from the body too much and speeds up the process of writing. There is something about chewing on a pencil as one is chewing over a word or a phrase that just will not come. Soul moves slowly. Nevertheless, I have grown used to my computer and the task is to embody its use.

34. Gloria Anzalúda, "Tlilli, tlapalli: The Path of the Red and Black Ink," in *Borderlands/La Frontera* (San Francisco, CA: Aunt Lute Books, 1987), p. 97.

35. A more detailed exploration of the body in writing would require a thorough description of the lived body of phenomenology, which is beyond the intentions of this work. For a brief description of this body as the gestural body, see Robert Romanyshyn, *Technology as Symptom and Dream* (London and New York: Routledge, 1989/2002). Other references I would cite as useful sources include Jane Gallop, *Thinking through the Body* (New York: Columbia University Press, 1988) and Don Johnson, *Body* (Boston: Beacon, 1983). I would also highly recommend the work of Rosemarie Anderson; see especially "Embodied Riting and Reflections of Embodiment," in *The Journal of Transpersonal Psychology* 33, no. 2 (2001): 83-98.

36. Rowland, p. 3.

CHAPTER 13: TOWARDS AN ETHICAL EPISTEMOLOGY

1. Erich Neumann, *Depth Psychology and a New Ethic* (New York: Harper Torchbooks, 1973), p. 74.
2. C. G. Jung, *Memories, Dreams, Reflections* (New York: Vintage Books, 1965), p. 193.
3. Adam McLean, ed., *Splendor Solis*, trans. Joscelyn Godwin (Edinburgh: Magnum Opus Hermetic Sourceworks, 1981).
4. Neumann, p. 74.
5. Wallace Stevens, *Poems*, selected by Samuel French Morse (New York: Vintage Books, 1959), pp. 13-14.
6. C. G. Jung, "The Transcendent Function," in *The Structure and Dynamics of the Psyche, The Collected Works of C. G. Jung*, vol. 8, trans. R. F. C. Hull (Princeton, NJ: Princeton University Press, 1916/1960), § 187.
7. Robert Romanyshyn, "Preface," *Invisible Guests*, by Mary Watkins (Woodstock, CT: Spring Publications, 2000), p. ii.
8. C. G. Jung, "On the Nature of the Psyche," in *The Structure and Dynamics of the Psyche, The Collected Works of C. G. Jung*, vol. 8, trans. R. F. C. Hull (Princeton, NJ: Princeton University Press 1946/1960), § 358.
9. John Beebe, *Integrity in Depth* (New York: Fromm International Publishing, 1995), pp. 33-35.
10. Emmanuel Levinas, *Totality and Infinity*, trans. Alphonso Lingis (Pittsburgh, PA: Duquesne University Press, 1969), p. 199.
11. John Riker, *Ethics and the Discovery of the Unconscious* (Albany: State University of New York Press, 1997), p. 202.

EPILOGUE

1. Rainer Maria Rilke, "The Way In," *Selected Poems of Rainer Maria Rilke*, trans. Robert Bly (New York: Harper and Row, 1981), p. 71.

Index

SPRING JOURNAL BOOKS

The book publishing imprint of *Spring Journal*,
the oldest Jungian psychology journal in the world

STUDIES IN ARCHETYPAL PSYCHOLOGY SERIES
Series Editor: Greg Mogenson

Collected English Papers, Wolfgang Giegerich
  Vol. 1: *The Neurosis of Psychology: Primary Papers Towards a Critical Psychology*, ISBN 978-1-882670-42-6, 284 pp., $20.00
  Vol. 2: *Technology and the Soul: From the Nuclear Bomb to the World Wide Web*, ISBN 978-1-882670-43-4, 356 pp., $25.00
  Vol. 3: *Soul-Violence* ISBN 978-1-882670-44-2
  Vol. 4: *The Soul Always Thinks* ISBN 978-1-882670-45-0

Dialectics & Analytical Psychology: The El Capitan Canyon Seminar, Wolfgang Giegerich, David L. Miller, and Greg Mogenson, ISBN 978-1-882670-92-2, 136 pp., $20.00

Northern Gnosis: Thor, Baldr, and the Volsungs in the Thought of Freud and Jung, Greg Mogenson, ISBN 978-1-882670-90-6, 140 pp., $20.00

Raids on the Unthinkable: Freudian and Jungian Psychoanalyses, Paul Kugler, ISBN 978-1-882670-91-4, 160 pp., $20.00

The Essentials of Style: A Handbook for Seeing and Being Seen, Benjamin Sells, ISBN 978-1-882670-68-X, 141 pp., $21.95

The Wounded Researcher: A Depth Psychological Approach to Research, Robert Romanyshyn, ISBN 978-1-882670-47-7

The Sunken Quest, the Wasted Fisher, the Pregnant Fish: Postmodern Reflections on Depth Psychology, Ronald Schenk, ISBN 978-1-882670-48-5, $20.00

Fire in the Stone: The Alchemy of Desire, Stanton Marlan, ed., ISBN 978-1-882670-49-3, 206 pp., $22.95

Honoring David L. Miller

Disturbances in the Field: Essays in Honor of David L. Miller, Christine Downing, ed., ISBN 978-1-882670-37-X, 318 pp., $23.95

The David L. Miller Trilogy

Three Faces of God: Traces of the Trinity in Literature and Life, David L. Miller, ISBN 978-1-882670-94-9, 197 pp., $20.00

Christs: Meditations on Archetypal Images in Christian Theology, David L. Miller, ISBN 978-1-882670-93-0, 249 pp., $20.00

Hells and Holy Ghosts: A Theopoetics of Christian Belief, David L. Miller, ISBN 978-1-882670-99-3, 238 pp., $20.00

The Electra Series

Electra: Tracing a Feminine Myth through the Western Imagination, Nancy Cater, ISBN 978-1-882670-98-1, 137 pp., $20.00

Fathers' Daughters: Breaking the Ties That Bind, Maureen Murdock, ISBN 978-1-882670-31-0, 258 pp., $20.00

Daughters of Saturn: From Father's Daughter to Creative Woman, Patricia Reis, ISBN 978-1-882670-32-9, 361 pp., $23.95

Women's Mysteries: Twoard a Poetics of Gender, Christine Downing, ISBN 978-1-882670-99-XX, 237 pp., $20.00

Gods in Our Midst: Mythological Images of the Masculine—A Woman's View, Christine Downing, ISBN 978-1-882670-28-0, 152 pp., $20.00

Journey through Menopause: A Personal Rite of Passage, Christine Downing, ISBN 978-1-882670-33-7, 172 pp., $20.00

Portrait of the Blue Lady: The Character of Melancholy, Lyn Cowan, ISBN 978-1-882670-96-5, 314 pp., $23.95

MORE SPRING JOURNAL BOOKS

Field, Form, and Fate: Patterns in Mind, Nature, and Psyche, Michael Conforti, ISBN 978-1-882670-40-X, 181 pp., $20.00

Dark Voices: The Genesis of Roy Hart Theatre, Noah Pikes, ISBN 978-1-882670-19-1, 155 pp., $20.00

The World Turned Inside Out: Henry Corbin and Islamic Mysticism, Tom Cheetham, ISBN 978-1-882670-24-8, 210 pp., $20.00

Teachers of Myth: Interviews on Educational and Psychological Uses of Myth with Adolescents, Maren Tonder Hansen, ISBN 978-1-882670-89-2, 73 pp., $15.95

Following the Reindeer Woman: Path of Peace and Harmony, Linda Schierse Leonard, ISBN 978-1-882670-95-7, 229 pp., $20.00

An Oedipus—The Untold Story: A Ghostly Mythodrama in One Act, Armando Nascimento Rosa, ISBN 978-1-882670-38-8, 103 pp., $20.00

The Dreaming Way: Dreamwork and Art for Remembering and Recovery, Patricia Reis and Susan Snow, ISBN 978-1-882670-46-9, 174 pp. $24.95

Living with Jung: "Enterviews" with Jungian Analysts, Volume 1, Robert and Janis Henderson, ISBN 978-1-882670-35-3, 225 pp., $21.95.

Terraspychology: Re-engaging the Soul of Place, Craig Chalquist, ISBN978-1-882670-65-5, 162 pp., $21.95.

Psyche and the Sacred: Spirituality beyond Religion, Lionel Corbet, ISBN978-1-882670-34-5, 288 pp., $23.95.

Brothers and Sisters: Discovering the Psychology of Companionship, Lara Newton, ISBN 978-1-882670-70-1, 214 pp., $23.95.

Evocations of Absence: Multidisciplinary Perspectives on Void States, ed. by Paul W. Ashton, ISBN 978-1-882670-75-8, 214 pp.

HOW TO ORDER:

Mail: Spring Journal Books, 627 Ursulines Street # 7, New Orleans, Louisiana 70116, USA
Tel.: (504) 524-5117; **Website:** www.springjournalandbooks.com